Canadian Institute

Essays Received in Response to an Appeal by the Canadian Institute

On the Rectification of Parliament, together with the conditions on which the

council of the institute offers to award one thousand dollars for prize essays

Canadian Institute

Essays Received in Response to an Appeal by the Canadian Institute
On the Rectification of Parliament, together with the conditions on which the council of the institute offers to award one thousand dollars for prize essays

ISBN/EAN: 9783337154769

Printed in Europe, USA, Canada, Australia, Japan

Cover: Foto ©Suzi / pixelio.de

More available books at **www.hansebooks.com**

ESSAYS

RECEIVED IN RESPONSE TO AN APPEAL

BY

THE CANADIAN INSTITUTE

ON THE

Rectification of Parliament

TOGETHER WITH THE CONDITIONS ON WHICH THE COUNCIL OF THE
INSTITUTE OFFERS TO AWARD

ONE THOUSAND DOLLARS FOR PRIZE ESSAYS.

TORONTO :
THE COPP, CLARK COMPANY, LIMITED.
1893.

MEMORANDUM BY THE COUNCIL.

Early in the present year a letter was received from a member of the Society, Dr. Sandford Fleming, bringing to the attention of the Institute the importance of an enquiry into the possibility of rectifying our electoral and parliamentary system, with the view of averting many evils now attending it. He appealed to the Institute as a body which, while non-political in its corporate character, is representative through its members of all shades of opinion. The object expressed was to awaken an interest in a difficult problem, which vitally concerns the whole community, in the hope that some practical and beneficial solution may be obtained.

The Council has had the matter under serious consideration for some time ; meanwhile an old friend of the Institute, deeply impressed with its importance, and the great public need of a satisfactory solution, has placed at the disposal of the Council the sum of one thousand dollars to assist, as far as possible, in the attainment of the desired end.

The matter was formally brought before the Institute, at a largely attended meeting, on the 20th February last, when after the reading of Dr. Fleming's communication and the discussion on the "Note" attached, the following resolution passed with substantial unanimity :—

" That the generous offer of a friend (who does not wish his name to be known) to contribute the sum of $1,000 to aid in obtaining a satisfactory solution of the problem referred to in Dr. Sandford Fleming's paper, be accepted with the best thanks of the Institute, and that the Council be empowered to take the necessary steps to obtain essays or treatises, and award the premium to the best workable measure, which, if made law, would give the whole Canadian people equal representation in Parliament, and each elector due weight in the government through Parliament."

The Council thereupon appointed a special committee to carefully weigh the whole subject, and consider how best to deal with the matter and carry into effect the wishes of the meeting and the authority and trust conferred on it by the Institute.

After many meetings and conferences, the Council has adopted the recommendations of the special committee, and now appeals to every member of the Institute and to all thoughtful persons within the Dominion, for their assistance in obtaining a complete solution of the problem.

While the Institute addresses Canadians as being specially interested in the good government of their own land, the prize competition is extended to all persons of whatever country, on equal terms, as set forth in the conditions issued herewith.

ARTHUR HARVEY,
President.

ALAN MACDOUGALL,
Secretary.

Canadian Institute,
Toronto, April 4th, 1892.

CONDITIONS

On which The Canadian Institute offers to award prizes for essays on "ELECTORAL REPRESENTA-
TION AND THE RECTIFICATION OF PARLIAMENT."

The sum of one thousand dollars ($1,000) has been placed at the disposal of the Council of the Canadian Institute to be awarded in whole or in part by the Institute for the best workable measure (Bill or Act of Parliament) which, if made law, would give the whole Canadian people equal representation in Parliament and each elector due weight in the Government, through Parliament.

The Council of the Institute accordingly invites essays on Electoral Representation and the Rectification of Parliament, accompanied by a draft bill applicable to countries with a Parliamentary System similar in general features to that of Canada.

The essays will be received by the Council before the first day of July, 1893. As the Transactions of the Institute are printed in English, it is desirable the essays should be in that language. They are to be signed with a motto, and the name and address of the writer are to be enclosed in a sealed envelope, endorsed with that motto ; the whole under one cover, to be addressed

ELECTORAL REPRESENTATION.

TO THE SECRETARY,

CANADIAN INSTITUTE,

TORONTO, CANADA.

The sealed envelopes to remain unopened until final adjudication by the Council of the Institute.

The Council will, immediately after the 1st July, 1893, examine all the Essays received.

All treatises of merit, to which an apparently "workable measure" is appended (in which considerable latitude must necessarily be allowed), will then be referred to an independent tribunal for a report. It will be the aim of the Council to have this tribunal composed of men of the highest standing in their several spheres, comprising persons learned in political science, law and practical politics.

The Council proposes that one award be given of not less than five hundred dollars ($500), and others, proportionate to the merits of the works submitted.

If the essays and draft bills shall not be thought by the above tribunal of sufficient merit to entitle them to receive the principal or any premium, or if the Council on receiving the report shall be of that opinion, the Council reserves to itself the right not to award any premium.

The Canadian Institute reserves to itself the right to publish the successful essays and draft bills to which premiums may be awarded.

CANADIAN INSTITUTE,   ALAN MACDOUGALL.
Toronto, April 4th, 1892.   Secretary.

THE REAL MAJORITY.

AN ACT

PROVIDING FOR THE ELECTION OF THE MEMBERS OF THE HOUSE OF COMMONS BY MEANS OF PROPORTIONAL REPRESENTATION.

Whereas, the present method of electing members to the House of Commons fails in its purpose of securing the representation of the real majority, Therefore Her Majesty, by and with the advice and consent of the Senate and House of Commons of Canada, enacts as follows :

1. That for purposes of representation in the House of Commons the Province of Ontario shall be divided into four districts, as nearly equal in population as may be, each of which districts shall elect twenty-two members, as hereinafter provided : The Province of Quebec shall in like manner be divided into three districts, each of which shall elect twenty-one members ; the Province of Nova Scotia shall constitute one district, and shall have nineteen members ; the Province of New Brunswick shall constitute one district, and shall have thirteen members ; the Province of Manitoba shall constitute one district, and shall have six members ; the Province of Prince Edward Island shall constitute one district, and shall have five members ; the Province of British Columbia shall constitute one district, and shall have four members ; the Province of Alberta shall constitute one district, and shall have three members.

2. That the members of the House of Commons shall be voted for at large in their respective districts.

3. That any body of electors in any district which polled at the last preceding parliamentary election votes to the number of one half a quota, as hereinafter determined, or which shall be endorsed by a petition of voters amounting to one half such quota, may nominate any number of candidates not to exceed the number of seats to which such district is entitled in the House of Commons, and cause their names to be printed on the official ballot.

4. That every voter shall vote as a whole such ballot as he may choose, designating thereon the names of the candidates whom he most prefers.

5. The sum of all ballots cast in any district shall be divided by the number of seats to which such district is entitled, and the quotient to the nearest unit shall be known as the quota of representation.

6. That the sums of all the ballots cast by each party or political body nominating candidates shall be severally divided by the quota of representation, and the units of the quotients thus obtained will show the number of representatives to which each body of voters is entitled ; and if the sum of such quotients be less than the number of seats to be filled, the body of electors having the largest remainder after division of the sum of the votes cast by the quota of representation, as herein specified, shall be entitled to the first vacancy, and so on until all the vacancies are filled.

7. That the candidates of each body of electors nominating candidates and found entitled to representation under the foregoing rules shall receive certificates of election in the order of the votes received, the candidate receiving the highest number of votes the first certificate, and so on ; but in case of a tie with but one vacancy to be filled, the matter shall be determined by lot between the candidates so tied.

8. That if a member of the House of Commons shall die or resign, or his seat become vacant for any reason, the remainder of his term shall be served by the candidate of the party or political body to which he belongs who received the highest number of votes of those not receiving certificates and belonging to such party or political body.

BALLOT

CONSERVATIVE.	× LIBERAL.	REFORM.
John Smith.	J. L. Peters.	Joseph E. Upright.
J. L. Roberts.	× Judah P. Dicky.	Hamilton Steed.
F. C. Jones.	× A. C. Markin.	Richard Black.
R. L. George.	F. H. House.	John Wilson.
B. C. Blanks.	H. C. Jenney.	H. D. Hernderson.
Joseph Budd.	× Hugh Josephs.	
Horatio Todd.	John Jacobs.	
Simon Black.	× Farlin Quit.	
J. Hopkins.	× Moses Soloman.	
Geo. Sterne.	× Wm. Dixon	
G. C. Albright.	Thos. Brown.	
H. L. Wills.	Geo. Smith.	
Geo. L. Green.	× Hamilton Judd.	

The accompanying ballot shows a convenient form for carrying into effect the quota system. The voter marks a cross in the square opposite the name of the party he wishes, and if he has any preference among the candidates which are named on that ticket he puts a cross in the square opposite those names. Different voters will of course have different preferences, and hence the votes will vary. Take as an illustration the vote of New Brunswick which may be supposed to amount all told to 76,420 votes. Dividing this by the number of seats, thirteen, to which that province is entitled, it is found that the quota is 5,878. That is to say, if 76,420 votes are to have thirteen representatives 5,878 votes, or one thirteenth part of the whole vote, should have one representative.

Dividing the 34,202 votes of the conservatives by the quota, 5,878, gives five full quotas and a remainder of 4,812. By the same process the 30,043 liberal votes make five quotas and a remainder of 653 votes. The 12,175 reform votes make two quotas and leave a remainder of 419. As there is still one seat to be filled it is given to the party having the largest unfilled quota, which is the conservative party. This makes the delegation from the province six conservatives, five liberals, and two reformers. The six conservatives are taken from their list in the order of their votes as has already been explained. It is well for parties to nominate a full list of candidates, as it does not alter the effect of the party vote, and offers the voter greater choice.

THE RULE OF THE REAL MAJORITY.

In presenting to your learned body the accompanying draft of an act of parliament, it is unnecessary to supplement it with additional words other than the briefest explanation. Nor will it be necessary to review the present system and enumerate its deplorable results, further than to say that the very principle upon which it is based is wrong. Not only do evil results flow from the system, but it must from the very nature of things be so. By dividing the voters into separate districts from each of which a member is elected by a plurality or majority vote as the case may be, all the votes cast for unsuccessful candidates are unrepresented; for a voter cannot be said to be represented by a candidate against whom he voted. But this is not the end. Legislation is accomplished by the will of the majority of the members of the legislature; and as all the members together represent but a bare majority of the votes and sometimes less, it follows that the action of a majority of these representatives is really the will of a very small minority of the voters who participated in the election. Taking a majority of the members of any legislative body who received the smallest votes and it will be found that they seldom represent more than one-third of the total vote of the election, often only one-fourth, and sometimes not more than one-fifth. Examples of such results are so common, and have been presented by so many writers that it is superfluous to enumerate them here; suffice it to say that the mere mention of the false principle upon which the present system is based will bring to mind many examples.

It needs no elaboration of reasons and facts to prove that the principle of electing representatives from single districts by majority votes is wanting in all the elements which are conducive to good government. The sole reason for the existence of representative government rests upon the assumption that all men are equally entitled to life; which involves the right to their own persons and to the results of their own labor. As the individual is the unit of the social and political order, and as governments are instituted among men for the purpose of performing those things which from their very nature cannot be performed by the individual, involving as it does the taking of the wealth of the individual for the use of the community, it naturally follows that the right to vote follows the postulate that all men are entitled to life. Not only are they entitled to vote but to vote in such a manner as will give effect to that vote. Hence, not only should every act of the government be that of the representatives of the people but of the representatives of a majority of the people. As in a natural state of society where all the members of the community can meet in common the majority will determine the action of the body, so should the action of the representatives of the larger body, which is the result of a sort of political boiling down process, be the will of the majority of the whole people of the community.

The system which is destined to prove a solution of this problem seems to be some form of elections by quotas. Whether it shall be by the single transferable vote, as advocated by Thomas Hare, by the multi-vote list of Switzerland, the cumulative vote list, or some other form, it seems that all new systems must be based upon the quota principle. The form which is herewith presented for your consideration is a modification of the list quota system, having as merits the two points that it is certain and definite, whereas the Hare system is not, and that it is simple and easily understood by those who are unaccustomed to the study of these matters, while the Swiss system is complicated and apt to confuse the average voter.

In presenting a plan of action which must meet the approval of the mass of the people and which must be operated by the mass of the people, it is necessary that it shall be of such a nature as will first meet their approval, and, having been adopted, will be within their capabilities and understanding. Not only must a just principle be set forth, but it must be in such form as will be within the comprehension of those to whom it is addressed. And not only must it be within the comprehension of the ordinary voters but it must be of such a nature that designing politicians who profit by the present system cannot torture from it objections which will prejudice the minds of the people.

Take as an example the objection which has so long been urged against the Hare system, that it is uncertain. That if a quota of 1000 be necessary to a choice and 1000 electors mark A first choice and B second choice, while another 1000 electors mark A first choice and C second choice it will be a matter of chance whether B or C or either of them is elected. For, if in counting the ballots the 1000 necessary for the election of A should contain B as second choice, then the surplus votes of A, which under the rules of the system go to the second choice would be counted for C, though B had just as many votes as C. Now, while it may be said that this accident may not happen more than once in a hundred elections, it may happen in all of a hundred elections; the mere fact that it may happen at all is of sufficient importance to make its friends pause in their advocacy. That it might cause grave complications at some time is possible if not probable; that every political beneficiary of the present system would greedily seize upon and exploit it for all it was worth cannot be doubted. It is really an objection; it can easily be magnified into the greatest of objections.

On the other hand the Swiss, and other multi-vote systems are complex enough to cause the uninitiated voter to hesitate, and to enable the designing politician to confound him in the mazes of complicated detail which are bewildering to any but students. The Swiss system is preferable to the Hare system because there can never be any uncertainty as to the result of the counting. It is a question for the statesmen of each country to decide for themselves whether it is so complicated as to confuse the electorate. It has been the experience of the writer that this is an objection urged by the voters to whom it is presented, and with that objection in mind the Swiss system has been modified to the form presented herewith.

The province has been made the unit of representation where possible, for the reason that it is a natural political division with which the people are familiar. It is desirable that the unit of representation under any form of proportional representation shall be large enough to admit of representation to all reasonable minorities, and at the same time not so large that citizens cannot acquaint themselves with the affairs of the whole district. A district of from ten to twenty-five members is preferable, and for that reason the provinces of Ontario and Quebec have been divided.

The third provision of the act provides for the nomination of all the candidates whose supporters have any reason to hope for success. The money forfeiture which has heretofore been required is unjust because it handicaps the poor people. The circulation of a petition for signatures is a work so light that any body of citizens can easily do it. Indeed in some of the states of the United States where any body is allowed to present names no confusion has resulted.

The fourth section is apt to meet with most opposition in that it requires the voting of party tickets. This is an objection, but it is one which upon second thought is brushed aside. It is urged mostly by those who deprecate party government in any form. Now, there is nothing objectionable in party government of itself. It is as natural for men and women to associate together in parties as in churches or clubs, or any other organizations which they may see fit to effect. There has always been a progressive party and a conservative party. Men are so constituted that they fall naturally into one or the other of these parties. The parties do not always bear the same names but their principles are the same. It is just as impossible for a man to be a liberal and conservative at the same time as to be an optimist and pessimist, or a protestant and catholic at the same time. And besides this the principle of proportional representation applies only to the election of legislators, or to bodies in which a number of members of the same grade are elected at once. The choice of an executive officer must be based upon his personality. He is to carry into effect the laws which others have made. It matters not whether he be a conservative or liberal so far as his executive duties are concerned; if he be an honest man he will perform his duties the same whatever may be his political creed. But when it comes to the law makers or the creators, all depends upon their opinions regarding public policies. Conservatives will enact conservative measures, and liberal members will enact liberal measures whether they are wise or foolish, honest or dishonest. Hence it is that the voter may with perfect consistency vote for a conservative executive officer and the liberal legislative ticket. But he cannot consistently vote for a conservative and liberal legislator at the same time, because they propose opposing policies. He may vote for the conservative executive because that candidate is honest and upright while his opponent is not; and he may vote for the liberal ticket because he believes in liberal laws, and knows the members of the party will enact them regardless of their personal character. In a word executive officers should be chosen on account of their personality, legislative officers on account of their belief in the principles of government.

Besides choosing among the several tickets in the field the voter can also choose among the names of the ballot which he does vote. And when the case of presenting tickets is taken into account it must be seen that the probability is that a party representing the belief of every considerable number of citizens will be in the field. It is necessary that the voter shall designate his preference among the names on the ticket; for if the successful candidates were taken in the order in which they appear, the nominating parties would be tempted to place the corrupt and self-seeking at the top and the virtuous at the bottom. This designation of the names by the voter is a safeguard against corrupt primaries, and enables him to exercise a double choice in the selection of his representatives.

Sections five, six and seven designate the method of applying the rules. This is practically the same in all systems based upon the quota principle, but it is much simpler in the method here presented than in either the Hare system or the Swiss. The quota having been obtained the votes of the several parties are divided by it, which shows the number of representatives to which each is entitled. This having been determined the successful men are taken from the ticket in the order of precedence as expressed by their respective votes. If the party polls enough votes to fill but one quota and is therefore entitled to one representatative the candidate who has received the most votes on that ticket is declared elected. If the party has two seats the next highest candidate goes in.

Section eight contains a very simple method of filling vacancies. The new man will be one who was voted for at the same time as the men among whom he must serve, and he always stands ready to respond when the proper officials call upon him, without the delay and expense of holding a new election.

For this method of applying the quota principle of electing representatives these advantage are claimed:

It is much simpler than the Swiss, and more definite than the Hare methods. It secures to each party representation in proportion to the votes polled, and at the same time it is as easy of application as the method now in vogue. It secures to the new or minority parties their just proportion of political power without in any way detracting from the rights of the old parties. By its means independent political parties can put candidates in the field with the full assurance that they will receive representation if they constitute an integral part of the body politic. It secures a representative body in which a majority of the members will always represent a majority of the voters, thus making representative government what it has long claimed to be, a government of the people for the people and by the people. And yet it is all done with so slight a change in the present electoral system as to scarcely be perceptible to the average voter. It involves the overturning of no long established customs, or the wrenching of political ties. It is a simple and logical step in advance of the position now occupied by representative governments : and will pave the way, when the people have grown accustomed to this system, for a still more nearly perfect system when it is developed.

In considering what is the best form of government for any people full account must be taken of the general factors which are to enter into the calculation. A form of government which is ideal for one people may be the worst possible for another. So patent has this become that the great Spanish republican Castelar admits that the Spaniards of this generation do not appreciate a republican form of government, and hence such a form of government would to-day be worse for that country than a monarchy. When the people have accustomed themselves to a limited monarchy they will the better appreciate the advantages of pure democracy ; in a word the Spanish people must evolve into a republic. The same is true of Russia, of Turkey, or of any of the oriental countries. The best form of government for them is not that which the philosopher may evolve by a process of indisputable reasoning, but that which while attaining the ends of government most nearly conforms to the people's habits of thought. Thus with a system for choosing representatives for the Canadian Parliament. It is not a question of what is the ideal system for the ideal country ; but of what is practicable to-day, for an existing country. The method which is to be submitted to the Canadian People you have well termed a workable measure. It must embrace the elements of justice and equity and at the same time it must be so simple and comprehensible that the ordinary citizen can understand and operate it. It is submitted that the bill herewith meets these requirements.

It is of no use to talk to-day of government without parties. Any reform which has for its purpose the destruction of political parties will be foredoomed to defeat. Parties are a natural and logical result of human activities, and any reform which is to be effective must operate through them, not in spite of them. The evils of party government are not from the party feature any more than are the bursting of boilers from the depravity of steam. Party government as heretofore known, has been a blind, unreasoning force which people have been unable to control. Like the steam in boilers before the invention of the safety valve they have often gotten beyond control and worked mischief. But the difficulties of party government may be overcome as were those of steam pressure by supplying a vent or safety valve. If the people have it always within their power to nominate independent candidates and elect them, their will be such a restraint put upon the old parties and political organizations that they will always be subject to the will of the people, instead of above it as they too often are to-day. With ballots furnished by the state and candidates nominated freely by all parties and political organizations entitled to a place on the ballot, and representatives chosen from them in proportion to the votes polled, it is patent that the voice of the people can be heard at any and all times.

Whether or not it shall be deemed desirable at some future time to elaborate the quota system by introducing the features of the cumulative vote, or of the single transferable vote of Hare we cannot tell ; but it does appear that the quota system herein set forth is all the innovation which we are warranted to-day in submitting for popular approval and exercise. It embraces the maximum of benefit from proportional representation with the minimum of change from the present methods and customs. It brings the representative into direct contact with the voter, compelling the candidates to submit to the scrutiny of the whole electoral unit, thus making it the advantage of parties to nominate men who are deserving and worthy of the honor conferred upon them. By enlarging the electoral unit the possibilities of bribery, intimidation, and all the evils which now afflict us are minimized ; and at the same time the power of secret organizations which vote as a unit, thereby deciding the election, will be destroyed ; their votes will simply count as part of the total, and will be effective only as they swell the number which is divided by the quota. There will be no hopeless minorities and wasted majorities penned up in single districts ; every vote will bear directly upon the final result. Gerrymandering, that dragon which threatens representative government, will be utterly destroyed, and men instead of territory will be represented.

NULLA VESTIGIA RETRORSUM.

No essay or treatise accompanies this draft of a bill, which is thought to be a "workable measure."

The main ideas of the plan are :

1st—Plural voting, in which property and intelligence both receive due weight. At the same time no franchise is taken away, and, if desired, both sexes may have the privilege and duty of voting.

2nd—The rectification of parliament by providing under the name of "candidates at large" a safe constituency for men of eminence, instructed in politics, who have acquired a wide reputation, but whom local interests might defeat in territorial constituencies.

Existing legislation with respect to registration of voters, bribery, nomination, the ballot, &c., is not materially interfered with by this proposed act, for it is not desired to introduce any violent change. The principles of the measure might be extended by degrees, if found as beneficial as expected.

Compulsory voting is not alluded to. If desired, it might be introduced with respect to the "votes at large," and perhaps with advantage.

NULLA VESTIGIA RETRORSUM.

Toronto, June 30th, 1893.

DRAFT BILL TO AMEND ELECTORAL REPRESENTATION.

Her Majesty, by and with the advice and consent of the Senate and House of Commons of Canada, enacts as follows :

I.—Every British subject of the full age of 21 years, excepting inmates of prisons or of insane or inebriate asylums, shall have the right to vote at elections for member of the House of Commons, if he be

1. Owner of real estate or mortgages thereon, government or municipal bonds, shares or obligations of solvent chartered banks or joint stock companies, or cash on deposit in any bank or savings institution to the value of five hundred dollars.

2. Or occupant of a house or lodgings of which the rental is not less than five dollars per month.

(Provision for enrollment or registration of voters.)

(Provision for the right to vote of sons of farmers or others, living with parents and jointly interested in their pursuits.)

II.—Any such voter shall have one additional vote in respect of each of the following qualifications.

1. If he be thirty years of age and over, married or a widower, with legitimate issue.

2. If he have property of the descriptions mentioned in the next preceding section to the value of two thousand dollars.

3. If he holds a lawfully recognised degree from a university or school of practical science, or be a member of the professions of law, engineering or medicine, or have held within five years the rank of sergeant or commissioned officer in the militia or volunteers.

III.—The additional votes which may be claimed (and duly proved and registered or enrolled, *vide* provision following section I.) shall be called "votes at large."

IV.—Of the members each Province of the Dominion elects to represent it in Parliament, nine-tenths shall be elected by constituencies with limited boundaries, and similar population, and one-tenth by the province at large.

(Provision for redistribution of the constituencies in each Province.)

V.—The mode of electing members for the territorial constituencies shall not be affected by this act.

VI.—The members at large shall be nominated at general elections, in any constituency, under the same rules which apply to other candidates, except that

1. The returning officer shall publish, within three days of the nomination, a list of any candidates who are nominated and accept the nomination in his constituency, and shall forward the same to..............who shall forthwith publish in.............. the names of all candidates so nominated and intending to go to the poll.

2. At the election, the returning officer shall give separate ballot papers to each voter who has votes at large, one for each such vote, not exceeding three in all, and the said votes shall only be cast for candidates at large. They shall be deposited in a separate ballot box, and counted the day after the election.

3. Returns of the number of votes given for each candidate at large shall be sent to .... and these candidates, to the number required by section IV. of this act, who have received the greatest number of votes shall be declared elected.

VII.—Members at large shall have the same duties and privileges as those elected from territorial constituencies, but no such member on accepting office shall thereby vacate his seat. In case of the death or resignation of any member at large or of his vacating his seat for any cause, the next of the candidates at large, according to the number of votes received at the last general election, shall become a member in his place.

(Provision for keeping the list of votes cast for each candidate at large.)

The qualification of a candidate at large shall be

He must, within the five years preceding his nomination, have been

1. A member of the Parliament of the Dominion, or of a Provincial Legislature.

2. A Warden of a County, or a Mayor of a City.

3. A Professor in some University, or a Colonel in command of a Regiment of Militia or Volunteers.

(Provision for proving the same.)

NULLA VESTIGIA RETRORSUM.

"DIGNUS VINDICE NODUS."

Although England is acknowledged to be the Mother of Parliaments, the word itself is of French not of English origin, and its primary meaning may be said to be the same as that of our word "colloquy". There is some obscurity as to the date when the term Parliament was first applied to a deliberative assembly, it was however used in 1146 when Louis VII of France called a council to organize the second Crusade. During the following century the term came more into use and henceforth it has been retained, bearing generally the meaning which it now possesses. We do not find in English history any mention of a Parliament earlier than 1215 when the Magna Charta was granted by John the term *Parliamentum Runnemede* was used incidentally a few years later in the documents which narrate that event. In 1246 a national assembly was held in London, some historians speak of this meeting as the first Parliament, but the assembly generally accepted as the origin of the House of Commons met in 1265 when Henry III. was a captive in the hands of Simon de Montfort, after the battle of Lewes. On that occasion two Burgesses from each city and Borough in the kingdom and two Knights from each County were summoned to take their seats in the national Council. This was not however the first occasion on which Knights took part in the assemblies summoned by the King. There is a record which goes to show that in 1254 Royal writs were issued direct ing the election and attendance in parliament of two Knights from each shire (Stubbs, Vol. II. p. 232). All previous State councils since the conquest by William (1066) were composed of Noblemen and Ecclesiastics of Rank. The parliaments mentioned (1215 and 1265) and others in the 13th Century mark the first successful efforts to shake off the fetters of despotism and restore the liberties and rights enjoyed at an earlier period by the English people. The Great Charter forcibly obtained from King John, and fifty years later the assembly of the memorable Parliament of Earl Simon, the reputed father of the House of Commons, were two cardinal turning points in English history. From the 13th century to the 19th century, the constitution has been moulded by circumstances; it has step by step been adapted to the varying necessities which have arisen; and the many struggles during the six hundred intervening years, have given the British constitution the character it to-day possesses.

While the constitution of the Dominion of Canada so far as circumstances admit, is a reflex of that of the United Kingdom, it differs from its prototype in some important respects. The most conspicuous of these distinctions is in the second Chamber. In the British Parliament the House of Lords has a character of its own and cannot be reproduced in any part of the outer Empire; it is the product of innumerable influences traceable to the past which in no way have existed on this side of the Atlantic; it may indeed be held to be the lineal descendant of the General Councils of the Barons which assembled during the centuries of feudalism. Whatever the desire to transplant to Canada the institutions of the Mother Country the House of Lords is the one which defies successful imitation. We have however created a substitute in the Canadian Senate and as such, this second house has functions to perform of the first importance. If the Senate is not directly elected by the people it may indirectly be affiliated with the popular suffrage for its members are nominated by the executive Government known as the "Ministry" in whose hands the power and authority of the people is placed by their representatives in Parliament.

The following in brief form, presents the legal constitution of Canada, established by statutory enactments :—

1. The Executive Government is vested in the Queen of Great Britain and Ireland, represented in Canada by the Governor General.

2. The Executive Government is exercised by and with the advice of the "Queen's Privy Council."

3. The "Queen's Privy Council" is nominated by the Governor General.

4. The Parliament consists of the Queen, the Senate and the House of Commons.

5. The Privileges, Immunities and Powers of Parliament shall never exceed those of the House of Commons of the British Parliament, at the passing of the British North America Act 1867.

In Canada as in the United Kingdom are recognised certain political theories and principles which do not appear on the Statute Book. There has grown up a conventional form of Government which is not always in accord with the written law on which it is nominally based. This unwritten constitution has during a long series of years been passing through the phase of its development and one of the remarkable results which have followed, is, that the Commons, the lower House in name, has become the upper House in fact. The popular assembly is the actual ruling power in the State, and as the historian Freeman puts it in "The growth of the English Constitution," "we have cast aside the legal subtleties which grew up from the thirteenth century to the seventeenth, and have gone back to the plain common sense of the eleventh or tenth, and of times earlier still."*

As relates to Canada the chief features of our unwritten or conventional constitution may be briefly set forth.

1. The Crown, the visible symbol of power and authority is represented by the Queen, her heirs and successors.

2. The Queen's representative in the Dominion is the Governor General.

3. All Legislative power and executive authority is derived from the people.

4. The power and authority of the people is vested in Parliament, consisting of the Senate and House of Commons.

5. The power vested in Parliament, is transmitted to an executive committee or council of Crown Ministers, known as the "Ministry" to be exercised for the common welfare.

6. All executive functions of Government are reposed in the Ministry.

7. The Ministry consisting of members of the Senate and House of Commons is appointed by the Governor General, subject to the approval of Parliament. As a body it is responsible to Parliament and the members composing it can remain in office so long only as they possess the confidence of the House of Commons.

8. The Members of the Senate are nominated by the Governor General on the recommendation of the Ministry.

9. The Members of the House of Commons are chosen by the people.

10. There are at present 78 members of the Senate and 215 members of the House of Commons.

The above presents in outline the theory of our constitution as it is generally understood. The essential fundamental principle is that the people is the origin of power and authority and that all power and authority proceeds through representatives of the people, to Parliament, constituting that body supreme. That is the theory, and in it we have a vital feature of the political constitution which we are privileged to possess ; unhappily however we have never been able to carry the theory into practice with any measure of success.

It is assumed that the people is represented in Parliament and that the power and authority proceeding from the people is vested in the assembled representatives. Our electoral usages fail to attain this end ; in effect they disfranchise a large majority of the electors and the true principle upon which Parliament should be constituted is not acted upon. This departure from the spirit of the constitution by which so large a number entitled to be represented in the councils of the Dominion, are left without any voice in state affairs, exercises an undesirable influence and constitutes a grave political injustice to the great bulk of the community.

If we enquire into the primary cause of this extraordinary irregularity, in the writer's view it may be traced to an early date. Parliamentary Government came into being in feudal times and has been developed to a large extent out of feudal materials. If we bear in view that the principles of feudalism were diametrically opposed to every theory of popular government we obtain a clue to the recurrences of grave difficulties which have continually arisen. To this circumstance, that is to say to the interpenetration of conflicting and directly antagonistic elements, viz. freedom and feudalism, may be attributed many of the struggles recorded in the history of the past six eventful centuries. We may trace to the same seemingly far remote origin, some of the obstacles which are met at the present day in the working out of the Parliamentary system.

Feudalism prevailed in Europe from the 10th to the 17th centuries. This remarkable organization with its various ramifications, extended in all directions throughout the whole social and political fabric. It was first established we are told as a means of common protection and defence, but whatever its necessity or supposed advantage, it had

* Page 121.

the effect of permanently separating the community into distinct classes, the feudal Lords and their vassals; it crushed out every principle of popular freedom and ended in becoming an engine of oppression to the great mass of the people. Feudalism attained its highest development in France and at the time of the conquest in 1066, the French Feudalism was superimposed upon that of England which had its own characteristics. This superimposition of continental Feudalism completely changed the social and political condition of the English people and destroyed what rights they had possessed under the early Saxon Kings. Thus imposed on the nation it became an exceedingly difficult task for the people to free themselves from its grasp. "England owes her escape," says Macaulay, "to an event which historians have generally represented as disastrous. Her interest was so directly opposed to the interest of her rulers that she had no hope but in their errors and misfortunes. The talents and even the virtues of her six first French Kings were a curse to her. The follies and vices of the seventh were her salvation." But the great Charter won by the united efforts of the Barons was but the beginning of her release from tyrannical rule, the struggle was continued in after years with the Tudor and Stewart despotism. The strength of Feudalism roughly assailed in the 13th century did not finally yield its power until the middle of the 17th. In Scotland, it was not abolished by Statute until 1747.*

Feudalism as a national organization has long ceased to exist but having held sway for seven hundred years it is not surprising that the influences it created have never been wholly removed. The British Constitution has been cast in a feudal mould to impress upon it indelibly the form of its origin, and it is not difficult to trace remnants of this once powerful factor in our Parliamentary usages.

As an illustration of the influence of traditional usages, reference may be made to the practice which without sufficient cause has come to be regarded as almost an essential part of our unwritten constitution. The writer alludes to the organization known as the "parliamentary opposition." A standing opposition appears to have been inherited by transmission from the period when King and people were in continual conflict, when ruler and ruled were in a condition of chronic antagonism. The "Ministry" in its executive functions takes the place of the King or ruler, but in this relationship there is no ground of quarrel between the Ministry and the people. Indeed the Ministry is the constitutional servant of the people, being recognised as the executive committee of Parliament to carry out the people's will expressed by the assembled representatives. It is difficult in this stage of our history to find good reason for the existence of a permanent organization whose main object is to oppose every Ministerial effort and impugn every Ministerial act. Can wise legislation best be secured by continually impeding the constitutional means taken to effect that end? Is the business of Parliament best promoted by systematically interposing obstacles? Is it not a wasteful expenditure of time, energy and talent to appoint one set of men to carry out the wishes of Parliament and to organize an antagonistic set of men to thwart them in every possible manner, on every possible occasion?

Long anterior to feudalism we can discern a system of Government based on the true principles of popular institutions. Before the age when Frank and Engle migrated from their German forests to give in after years their distinctive names to the French and English peoples, the historian describes a state of political life of deep interest at the present moment to the Canadian observer. In the tribal gatherings of those Teutonic races with which so many of us can claim remote ancestry, we may trace the primordial germs of the true parliament of the people. Centuries before the term Parliament was given to national assemblies, before even Christianity had penetrated the forests of Schleswick the free tribal communities met regularly to consult on State affairs. According to their custom these people assembled to enact laws and impose taxes or their equivalent. Every freeman had the right to be present and take part in the proceedings.†

On such occasions they elected their chiefs and rulers, and precisely as modern Parliaments will displace a Ministry in which confidence is lost, they exercised the right of

---

* "The Norman and English races, each unfit to endure oppression, forgetting their animosities in a common interest, enforced by arms the concession of a great charter of liberties. Privileges wrested from one faithless monarch, are preserved with continual vigilance against the machinations of another; the rights of the people become more precise, and their spirit more magnanimous, during the long reign of Henry III. With greater ambition and greater abilities than his father, Edward I. attempts in vain to govern in an arbitrary manner, and has the mortification of seeing his prerogative fettered by still more important limitations. The great council of the nation is opened to the representatives of the commons. They proceed by slow and cautious steps to remonstrate against public grievances, to check the abuses of administration, and sometimes to chastise public delinquency in the officers of the crown. A number of remedial provisions are added to the statutes; every Englishman learns to remember that he is the citizen of a free state, and to claim the common law as his birthright, even though the violence of power should interrupt its enjoyment. It were a strange misrepresentation of history to assert that the constitution had attained anything like a perfect state in the fifteenth century &c." *Hallam's Middle Ages, Chap. VIII. p. 450.*

† "They had Kings elected out of particular families; and other chiefs, both for war and administration of justice, whom merit alone recommended to the public choice. But the power of each was greatly limited; and the decision of all leading questions though subject to the previous deliberation of the Chieftains, sprung from the free voice of a popular assembly." *Hallam's Middle Ages, Chap. II. p. 64.*

deposing their King or other ruler whenever it was held by them to be expedient. These gatherings were Parliaments of a rudimentary character; by means of them they governed themselves and carried out a political constitution which suited the simple condition of untutored Teutonic life.* It is not a little remarkable that fifteen or eighteen centuries later, after all the struggles and changes of intervening years, civilized communities should return to the first principles of Government put in practice by our ancient forefathers. This fact itself shows that the principles themselves are natural and rational, and that the races who adopted them were in their imperfect civilization imbued with sound common sense and possessed strong moral force.

At an earlier period in European history, in the last days of the Greeek civilization, the Government was conducted according to the popular will. The citizens of Athens came together in formal assembly at regular intervals, to consider those matters which concerned the State. On such occasions all had the right to be present, and were required to be present to take part in the proceedings.

It was the same principles which at a later day prevailed when Anglo and Saxons settled in Britain. Beginning with the 5th century, the German races chiefly Angles, Saxons and Jutes crossed the sea to take possession of the land now known as England. They carried with them the simple organization to which reference has been made. For five centuries of its existence Anglo-Saxon society adapted its political system to the expansion and growth which resulted from fresh migration from the continent and from Danish and Norseman invasions, and indeed to all the circumstances of its changing situation ; in the end to be overwhelmed by the Feudalism of the 11th century. At this period the constitution of the Anglo-Saxon recognised the freeman as the fully qualified political unit, as such he had a voice in the "folkmoot" or popular meeting of the shire ; he had the right of expression at the "Witan" or national assembly ; he was consulted in the making of the laws by which he was ruled and he took part in the selection of those who administered them.†

Thus we learn that the ancient Greeks, the ancient Germans and the ancient English —Christian and Pagan alike—recognised the fundamental principle that the people should be assenting parties to their laws and participants in their own government ; principles rudely set aside in the Mother land, when the popular assemblies of the early English were transformed into feudal courts.‡

The fact cannot be disputed that feudalism supplanted a system of Government founded on rational principles, which had prevailed during a period extending over great part of the first half of the Christian era. In the constitution of Canada we possess in theory popular Government, based on the same or analogous principles as those which have been described ; the writer has however remarked that the essential principles of popular government are not carried into practice in the Dominion, and thus Government by the people exists only in theory. If we refer to the published official returns of the last census (1891) and the last general election (1891) we shall find as follows :—

    (a) Population of the Dominion.........................4,833,239
    (b) Number of families................................ 914,504
    (c) Voters on the Electoral lists.....................1,132,201
    (d) Total votes polled 720,459
    §(e) Votes polled for all Government candidates............ 368,357
    §(f) Votes polled for all Opposition candidates............ 352,102
    (g) Members elected 215
    (h) Government supporters elected...................... 123
    (i) Opposition members elected 92
    (k) Members elected with majorities under 100 50

---

* "Montesquieu said very truly, that the germs of parliamentary constitutions are to be found in the forests of Germany. In the primitive forms described by Tacitus in which the Teutonic Kings cooperated with the local princes and other chiefs on the one side and the great community of freemen on the other, we recognise clearly the rude beginnings of the free representative government." *Bluntschli.—Theory of the State.* Page 41.

† "There was a time when every freeman of England, no less than every freeman of Uri, could claim a direct voice in the councils of his country. There was a time when every freeman of England could raise his voice or clash his weapon in the assembly which chose Bishops and Ealdormen and Kings, when he could boast that the laws which he obeyed were laws of his own framing, and that the men who bore rule over him were rulers of his own choosing." *Freeman's Growth of the English Constitution,* Chap. I. p. 52.

‡ "We have seen, through the twilight of our Anglo-Saxon records, a form of civil policy established by our ancestors, marked, like the kindred governments of the continent, with aboriginal Teutonic features ; barbarous indeed, and insufficient for the great ends of society, but capable and worthy of the improvement it has received, because actuated by a sound and vital spirit, the love of freedom and of justice. We have seen a foreign conqueror and his descendants trample most rudely upon the prostrate nation, and upon those who had been companions of their victory, introduce the servitudes of feudal law with more than their usual rigour." *Hallam's Middle Ages,* Chap. VIII. p. 450.

§ There were five Government and two Opposition members elected by acclamation ; in these cases the statistician states that he took the figure of the previous general election in order to admit of a complete comparison.

(*l*) Of which there were Government supporters 28
(*m*) " " Opposition members 22
(*n*) Average majorities of Government members elected 476
(*o*) Average majorities of Opposition members elected 230

These are the actual returns. The number of votes polled for the members elected, is not furnished, but the figures given (*e*), (*f*), (*n*) and (*o*) admit of this being calculated approximately as follows :—

(*p*) Votes polled for 123 Government candidates *elected* 231,238
(*q*) Votes polled for 92 Government candidates *defeated* 137,119

Total as above (*e*) 368,357

(*r*) Votes polled for 92 Opposition candidates *elected* 168,350
(*s*) Votes polled for 123 Opposition candidates *defeated* 183,752

Total as above (*f*) 352,102

Several striking deductions may be drawn from these statements. I shall refer to two only.

First. If we examine (*k*), (*l*) and (*m*) the exceeding instability of the political equilibrium will at once be apparent. Fifty members on both sides, nearly one fourth of the whole House were elected by majorities under 100. Of these fifty, twenty-eight were elected Government supporters, by less than 2800 votes. Obviously the reversal, by any means whatever, of so small a number as 2800 votes, distributed over twenty-eight constituencies would give the following result :—

Members elected to *support* the Government 95
Members elected to *oppose* the Government 120

A result which would defeat the Government by an adverse majority of 25 and produce an administrative revolution. It is a possible result, and the illustration brings out one of the glaring defects of our electoral system ; establishing that a possible change of 2800 votes out of 720,459 the total votes polled, might revolutionize the Government. What better proof could we have that our electoral system fails to give us a fair representation in Parliament of the solid sense of the people, when the oscillation of a few votes, perhaps of the least intelligent voters, might reverse the whole public policy of the Dominion ?

Second. The returns point to an extraordinary dualism in the House of Commons. We have in all 215 members artificially separated into two antagonistic classes or divisions. Class A. the most numerous consists of 123 members. Class B. of 92 member ; two perfectly distinct organizations continually at war in all public matters. Power and authority is thrown into the hands of one class A while the other B is excluded from all participation in the direction of public affairs.

The 123 members composing class A were elected by the votes of 231,238 electors, and it is these voters alone who have any effective representation in Parliament. There was a total of 720,459 votes cast. if we take into account those given to the 123 Government supporters, there remains 489,221 votes describable as wasted, for they were given to defeated candidates and to opposition members neither of whom have any participation or voice in the Government. Thus the representatives of less than one third of those electors who went to the polls and recorded their votes, assume all power, and retain the right to exercise it in the name of the whole people.

Again, if we consider the whole electoral body, an anomaly still more striking presents itself. There are in the electoral lists 1,132,201 voters, but the comparatively small number of 231,238 of this number absolutely control Parliament. That is to say the Dominion of Canada is governed, today, not by the whole people or by representatives of the whole people, according to the theory of our constitution, but by the representatives of only one-fifth of the electors. There remains therefore four-fifths of the whole electoral body without any share whatever direct or indirect in the administration of public affairs.

From these indisputable facts established by the latest statistical returns, we may ask if we have made any advance in the development of popular government since introduced in the early centuries of the Christian era by our Anglo-Saxon forefathers. Every sphere of practical economy is characterized by advancement and development, can no explanation be given for the anomalous condition in which we find ourselves in respect to electoral representation ?

The popular national assemblies in ancient times, to which reference has been made, whether the elected head was chief or king may be described as "direct democracies." Institutions which partake of this character are only possible in small states, such as were found among the ancient Greeks, Teutons and Anglo-Saxons, or in modern times, remain in the mountain Cantons of Switzerland. In extensive territories and populous communities a government, on the simple type of "direct democracy," cannot be brought into successful operation. The assembly of the whole electors in one body in a country like Canada is impracticable; and if practicable, the confusion and clamour which are the inevitable consequence of assembling great multitudes, would in no sense conduce to calm deliberation or further the ends of legislation and good government. To meet the difficulty the representative system has been devised, with the design of having the mass of the population represented by a limited number of carefully chosen deputies; and the number necessarily must be sufficiently limited to admit of full and fair debate on the part of the representatives when gathered together in a deliberative assembly. It is by no means an easy task to carry out this design as it should in practice be realized. We require new electoral machinery, to attain, unimbittered by strife and contest, the choice of representatives who may command general respect; men worthy to be entrusted with the confidence of the nation and authorized on behalf and in the names of the whole people to act and speak in their stead in Parliament.

It has been shewn by the returns of the last general election (and it may be affirmed that the results of all general elections present the same features) how far short we are of obtaining in Parliament even an approximately true representation of the whole people. However unsatisfactory these results, it by no means proves the representative system to be a failure. It establishes, however, beyond all doubt that the means taken to obtain an accurate and faithful representation of the people is much in fault. To find some better means is the primary purpose, as the writer understands it, of the Appeal which the Canadian Institute has submitted to the public. This Appeal therefore presents a problem of profound interest to the political student, and its solution even affects the political well-being of future generations. The object of its solution is not to destroy, or reform, or even amend our constitution, it is simply to carry out the fundamental principles on which it has been established. One of the first consequences of the proposition is to revivify the conceptions of our remote ancestors who recognised the importance of ruling wisely and being wisely ruled.

Self Government was an essential principle with the ancient Teutonic commonwealths in their tribal gatherings, the type and precursor of that which we desire our own national assembly to be. They sought in a rude fashion to carry out the assurance of liberty and justice held by them to be the primary principles of their constitution. Had not the system conceived and begun by them, been set aside by the intrusion of the feudal system, the ideal Parliament we are to-day seeking would have been long since evolved. In a cursory view we may feel astonished that the intellectual activity observable in the last two or three centuries has not succeeded in putting the plain rational principles of free Government into practice. On examination the reason becomes apparent; the tardy generation of English freedom has been owing to causes deeply imbedded in the political groundwork of the English nation. The popular Government introduced by the Saxons was not only completely suspended for centuries, but it was crushed out, leaving it the memory that it had existed. The feudal system rose and fell, but it remained a great political force for nearly seven hundred years and it did not pass away without leaving its lasting impression on every phase of society.[*] The innovations introduced in these evil times have one by one been removed, but it exacted a long period for even the theory of free institutions to find general recognition. From the first day of their partial re-introduction they have been forced so to speak into a foreign matrix by which they have been cramped and confined so that natural growth and expansion became impossible. In this fact we find an explanation why the process of the evolution of popular Government has been prevented. It is Freeman who points out that from the 13th century onward the development of popular Government has been chronologically inverted, that the English constitution has from that period of history made progress by a retrograde movement, by a falling back "from the cumbrous and oppressive devices of feudalism, to a sounder, freer, and simpler principles of the days of our earliest freedom."

---

[*] "Transported to England in the eleventh century by the Normans, and firmly rooted there till the middle of the seventeenth century, the influence of feudalism on the habits and customs of this country, and on its social order, was doubtedly extensive." *Feudalism by Ably, page 111.*

Every age has to provide against its own difficulties and the dangers which beset it. Possibly there were special reasons for the extension of feudal institutions at one period of history which are unappreciated in another. We are not called upon to enquire whether feudalism was a necessity or a supposed necessity in the ages when war and conquest were the chief pursuits of mankind. We have only to recognise that these institutions at one time universally prevailed, in order to account for the marvellous influence they have had in determining much of our present political condition. The habit of thought of earlier generations is still to some extent rooted in our national life, and hence it is that we have long tried with but partial success to engraft our modern requirements on the traditions of the past.

It has been remarked that it was owing to the superimposition at the conquest of continental feudalism without any formal change in the English laws and Kingship, which determined much of the later features of English history. The despotism imposed by William under legal forms crushed Saxon national life but it did not obliterate Saxon laws; so likewise in the 13th century, and in succeeding centuries, when the old national spirit was evoked, to regain some concessions of early freedom, the super-imposed feudalism remained, at least in form. The political fabric was never wholly demolished and rebuilt; the old walls were conserved and in some parts reconstructed and improved. Hence arises much of the divergence between the legal and the actual, between fiction and fact, in our modern constitution. Hence the peculiar features of the traditional forms which cling to and characterise our parliamentary system.

There is indeed a long chain of causes extending over centuries which has operated in producing the parliamentary system and the electoral form and practices, as we find them established. Not a few of them spring from the feudal age rather than from the age of freedom which preceded the reign of feudalism. If therefore we attempt to solve the problem set before us, we must reject all that is baneful inherited from feudal times, and seek to rectify our national assembly on the early Teutonic model, so that every member of the community, by right entitled as were Saxon freemen of old, may have a voice in his own government. If it be an understood principle of our constitution that power and authority proceed from the people, it should be our aim to see that that fundamental principle is something more than a delusive fiction. At present our representation system is so imperfectly developed that we have but a figment of popular government, and no true responsible government. The Ministry is practically responsible to only one section of the House of Commons, the representatives of a comparatively small portion of the whole electorate. The Ministry is not and cannot be responsible to the people or the representatives of the people in Parliament seeing that the people as a whole is without representation.

With these brief remarks bearing on the origin of Parliament, its slow and imperfect development, and its need of rectification the writer respectfully submits a draft of a measure embracing the principles by which as he believes, the Canadian electorate may be fairly represented in the popular assembly, and each individual voter may through Parliament have due weight in the government of the country.

The first section of the Bill is a humble and respectful recognition of the symbol of Power and authority, represented by the Sovereign who stands at the head of our constitution. We cannot ignore the force of association and the prevailing attachment to the Crown. The Canadian people cling with confidence to the Monarchical character of government which had its origin not so much in the feudal days as in the age anterior to feudalism. In theory and practice it has happily become blended with our representative democracy. Beyond this recognition of the Crown, the measure submitted is limited in its range to the election of Members of the House of Commons. There is no reference to the Second Chamber, the Senate, with respect to which it may be remarked that we have not, as in England a powerful aristocracy, as a rule carefully trained and educated with a view to the station they have in after life to fill and the duties to perform, not the least important of which is that attendant on a seat in the House of Lords. Nevertheless the Canadian Senate by judicious appointments may become, as at one time that of Rome, an assembly of statesmen who have previously held high office, or in some measure have proved themselves, by their experience, capacity and patriotism, worthy occupants of the exalted position.

The first section of the Bill provides for the appointment of electoral officers. The highest officer proposed is an Electoral Commissioner, who as a Minister or Deputy Minister of the Crown would be held responsible for the proper regulation of all matters in his department. The other officers acting under him, would assist in carrying into effect the provisions of the Bill, the Commissioner and his deputies being governed by the Orders in Council from time to time issued for their guidance.

Section II provides for the holding of elections at stated times. It is proposed to have one-fifth of the members elected regularly each year. The annual elections to be evenly distributed throughout the several Provinces so as to bring to Parliament yearly from all sections of the country new members fresh from the people. By this means the House of Commons would be regularly renewed and the entire Assembly re-elected every five years. This system of renewal would practically result in maintaining a continuous or permanent Parliament annually brought into direct touch with the people, avoiding those general elections which are so familiar to us, and which every few years strain the State to its centre. These periodical convulsions are struggles for political supremacy, their tendency is to inflame the passions and arouse feelings which render it impossible to obtain a calm judgment. In these times of great popular excitement, even individuals of intelligence and character proceed to lengths which in their sober moments they would utterly condemn. As a consequence to the proposed system of annually renewing the House of Commons there would be a corresponding change in the Ministry, a proportion of which would be understood to retire each year, to be replaced by others or to be re-appointed, as might be found expedient. In other words there would be an annual reconstruction of the administration, to bring every branch of the Government into harmony with Parliament, to which the regular restorations at yearly intervals would give a character of flexibility combined with continuity.

Sections III. and IV. The provisions of these sections are designed with the view of constituting the House of Commons an express image of the general spirit of the nation and giving to each electoral unit in the community its due share of political power, and no more.

Admitting the generally recognised truth that every member of the community is individually concerned in the good government of the country, it follows that if we can adequately reproduce in Parliament the true spirit and will of the people we shall obtain the essential elements necessary to the wise and harmonious administration of affairs.

The community is composed of many members differing in age, education, religion, sex, occupation, position and intelligence. The existing statutes relating to the franchise define the qualification of persons entitled to be placed on the list of voters. Those excluded are, women of all ages, Mongolians or Chinese, male persons under 21 years of age, criminals, certain Judges and certain Government Officers.

In England and elsewhere there has for some time been a movement for the enfranchisement of women and it must be confessed that it is difficult to give a reason, apart from special disqualification, why women should be debarred from taking part in a matter which concerns them equally with men. All will admit that there are many women in every community far better qualified by experience and intelligence to exercise the franchise than young men as they generally present themselves at 21 years of age. As the voter is the political unit, and the right of being well governed is the common heritage of both sexes, it is clear that no good reason can be found why women should be excluded wholly from representation. It is undeniable that woman's true sphere is in her household—she is associated generally with family life; the wife lives with her husband, the daughter with her father or elder brother, the widowed mother with her son. Moreover the family is the true unit of the state and the family life is or ought to be, an important factor in the development of a high moral public life. Why then should we not recognise the family as the political unit and bestow the voting power on the family, to be exercised through its head? In this way the just right of woman would be recognised and her influence felt, she would thus share with her husband, or senior male relative, the political dignity which full citizenship confers. A reasonable exception to the rule that families only should be allowed to vote, would be in the cases of unmarried or widowed householders of mature years. It does not appear to the writer that youths of twenty-one would consider their disqualification a great deprivation, if they regarded the matter in its true light. The privilege would in their case only be deferred and they would look forward to the day when they too would become heads of families, when their interest in the State and its affairs would be increased and when they would be better fitted by the wisdom which experience brings to exercise one of the privileges of the highest condition of manhood.

On whatever basis the franchise may be established, it would in no way affect the principles of the Bill. In any case the names of the qualified electors would be regularly enrolled on the voters' list for each Electoral District, and each elector would be entitled to a certificate setting forth the facts as in form E. The Bill provides that the certificate shall be required for the purposes of identification whenever the elector is called upon to vote.

It has been pointed out that a large percentage of the electors of Canada, are at this moment deprived of their rightful share in the Government of the country. I do not hesitate to say that this is a political condition deeply to be deplored. The men in power may be wise and capable, their public policy may be beneficial, the country may be advancing and commerce may be flourishing, but there can be no political peace so long at any considerable number of the people are without participation in public affairs. When no less than four-fifths of the whole electoral body are practically shut out from any direct or indirect share in their own Government, is it to be wondered at, that, leading men from all parts of the Dominion should have recently assembled in a great political convention at Ottawa, (June, 1893) planning, devising and urging means to overthrow those in power? To secure confidence and a general sympathetic interest throughout the community there must be a change in the Government, not merely a transference of power from one portion of the community to another. It cannot be in the public interest to perpetuate the system, and in order that there may be an entire change, the goodwill the support and the co-operation of the whole people must be sought and obtained. The people generally should be made to feel that each elector by the part he takes under the electoral law is fairly made an assenting party in all matters which concern the common weal. It is unwise and inexpedient to narrow down the governing power to a portion of the people. The Legislative Assembly, the supreme governing body, should not be permitted to stand on the narrow basis of one fifth of the population, it should be supported by the whole five-fifths. It is therefore expedient to widen representation and enlarge the base of responsibility by seeking the co-operation of all, and by acceding to as many individuals as possible, a share in the administration of public affairs. The meaning of this proposition is by no means that each individual elector should become a ruler, or attempt to rule. Government by the people does not mean government by each voter, manifestly an impossibility; it means government *by the collective will and spirit of the people* expressed by the people's deputies in a national assembly. The very least that should be done, perhaps the most which can be done, is to extend to each individual elector a voice through his deputy and give him the freest possible choice in the selection of that deputy.

Bearing on this point I will quote from a well known democratic writer (Stickney) with whose view to a large extent I agree. "If it were a possible thing to give to every individual a direct voice on measures other than in local affairs, it would not be desirable. I believe in the expediency of giving to the individual citizen the fullest part that he can possibly take, under any political system that can be devised, in the administration of public affairs. But the function of the individual citizen must be limited to his voice in the selection of men. As to measures other than local, the individual citizen never is and never can be, able to act wisely. I do not here draw any distinction between rich men and poor men, between learned and unlearned. I say that all individual citizens, rich and poor, learned and unlearned, alike, are incapable of forming a wise judgment on the great questions of State and national policy. The large public questions, if they are to be decided wisely, must be decided by men carefully selected, who can take time to learn the special facts of special cases, who can take part in the common deliberations of men who represent diverse interests, and who can, after such conference and deliberation take part in the forming and uttering of a calm common judgment. The judgment of single individuals however learned or skilled, on great public questions, has comparatively little value. That the individual citizen however intelligent he may be, however able he may be, shall be allowed to pass his individual judgment on great public questions to which he cannot give special study, on which he cannot deliberate with other men, is not in accordance with any sound theory of democratic government. Democratic government means, not that every citizen shall have a separate individual voice on every public measure in his own person, but that every citizen shall, in the person of his representative, have one voice in the people's meeting, by which all questions of general public policy are decided. On mere local questions he can have this voice in his own person. On questions other than local he must have this voice always in the person of his representative, in whose selection he has had, with all other citizens, his equal part. The actual decision of actual questions is, and necessarily must be, in the hands of representatives."

Representation is a comparatively modern device; it was unknown to the Saxon freeman of old, who claimed a direct voice in his tribal legislative assembly; it introduces a new principle and the only principle adaptable to the circumstances of populous states. In the Bill, it is proposed to carry the representative principle a little further than has been customary in electoral matters in order effectively to accomplish that which has hitherto been impracticable, viz. government by the great mass of the electors.

In an ordinary Electoral District there are let us say 5000 electors. The number is too large to allow each elector to meet for consultation in order to arrive at a common opinion as to the choice of a Member of Parliament. The Bill provides a means by which they can reach this end by a gradual process. The proposal is for groups of electors of similar views to nominate one of their number as a representative elector and in this each voter will have a perfectly free choice and he will only have to associate himself with a few others entertaining similar views. The number in each group in no way affects the principle, provided all groups have an equal number. Twenty-five is considered a convenient number for each group and this number would reduce the 5000 political units in the district to 200. Precisely as the design of Parliament itself is to bring the whole nation within a compass small enough to admit of orderly debate so likewise by means of the representative principle we propose to bring the whole electoral district for the purpose of consultation and concentration of action within the compass of a court consisting of 200 persons. The selection of 200 representative electors would involve time and attention mostly of a routine character. Electoral Agents would be appointed to assist, and supervise, the expense being borne by the public exchequer. The task no doubt would be attended with difficulty but the ultimate object, the formation of the people's national assembly, in accordance with the theory of our constitution, is a matter of paramount importance and no trouble, no reasonable expense should be held too great to secure its accomplishment.

On a day to be determined all the representative electors appointed would assemble in a general court, presided over by the Electoral Warden, for the express purpose of electing a Member for the House of Commons. Section IV. prescribes how the election is to be proceeded with. As any ten electors present may nominate a candidate, there would be perfect freedom of choice and any number of candidates from one to twenty may be nominated. If there be but one candidate nominated, after a sufficient lapse of time he would be declared elected. If there be several candidates the election would be decided by Ballot; dependent on circumstances there may be a series of ballots the number of candidates being reduced by the process of elimination until one candidate receives the requisite number of votes—viz., more than half the number of Representative electors. If no candidate receives the required number of votes, then as a last resort the choice to be determined by Lot in a fair and equitable manner as set forth in the Bill. This extension of the representative principle has incidental advantages. * As a rule the best men in the community, certainly not inferior men, would be chosen as representative electors and the latter would elect the members of the House of Commons. Thus our modern representative democracy would become exalted above a democracy which admits the ignorant and the corrupt equally with the better class of citizens. By the selection of the best men the representative electors might indeed be likened unto an aristocracy ; not that of the accident of *birth*, but an aristocracy of *worth*.

The remaining sections of the Bill deal with election returns, general provisions, and election expenses. With regard to the latter it is felt that in as much as the election of members to sit in Parliament is purely a public matter and it is in the highest degree important that Parliament should be formed constitutionally without being dependent on the private means of candidates or individuals ; it should be a fixed principle that all just and reasonable expenses in connection with elections should be paid out of the public exchequer. To carry out this principle not only should the electoral officers in each district be paid for their services, but the representatives electors should be paid an indemnity for their attendance at the Electoral Court. Stringent regulations and a strict audit would be enforced as in other departments of the Government.

I read on page 117 of the Appeal issued by the Canadian Institute : "The central idea of Parliament at the present day, is an assembly of individuals representing the whole nation. The functions of Parliament are to act on behalf of the nation as the supreme authority, and—representing the nation—it possesses every power and every right and every attribute which the nation possesses. The fundamental idea and guiding principle of Parliament is, that it embraces all the separate parts which compose the realm, that in fact it is the nation in essence."

Agreeably to this public appeal I have set myself to the task of devising "the means of forming an elective assembly which practically as well as theoretically will be the nation in essence." I have endeavoured with all the earnestness I can command to discover a method by which the whole people of Canada "may be brought to a central point, to a focus so to speak, in a deliberative assembly or Parliament."

The train of research I have been led into has revealed to me many curious recorded facts. For long centuries England our political mother land was held in the grasp of a confederation of feudal despots, and Englishmen were then in a very different social condition to what they, or we, now are. For a long period the mass of the English people were thrown into a state of vassalage. Now the subjects of Queen Victoria on both sides of

2

the Atlantic enjoy the rights and privileges of free citizens. In Canada we are farther advanced as a representative democracy than our fellow subjects in England, for the reason that we are farther removed in some respects from the associations and still surviving influences of feudalism, the signs and marks of which are borne in the political constitution of the mother country. In Canada we find ourselves in a different condition. The voice of history teaches us that we have more in common with the early ages of the English race than with the less ancient period of English feudalism and that the germs of our Canadian constitution must be sought for in the primeval institutions of the Teutons.

Satisfied on this point the Teutonic germ is the one which it has been my endeavour to unfold and develope, with what success I must leave others to determine.

It is not to be expected that a solution of the problem propounded by the Canadian Institute could fail to interfere with old electoral methods and as in every sphere of life there are some persons whose attachment to old usages is so great that submission to the most indefensible abuses would be preferable to any vital change whatever. Happily all men are not so constituted, if they were, all improvement all advance in human affairs would be at an end. There is moreover a growing disposition, especially among men of a scientific habit of mind, to penetrate beneath the surface of things, to discern first causes, to recognize the actual facts, in order that rational conclusions may be reached.

The cardinal idea in our constitution is that *the people rule* and it must be understood to mean that the rule is of the whole not of a part. It is well that it should be so—the broader the base of any structure the greater its stability. The people of Canada can rule in one way only, and that is through a national assembly where every Canadian shall be present in person or by proxy—where the consent of the assembled body shall be taken to be the consent of the whole people. Our constitution is essentially that of a representative democracy and our future must mainly rest on the fair and full representation of all Canadians in their own Parliament. This noble purpose cannot be achieved without change; it will exact a deviation from old-fashioned ways; it will invite opposition; it will involve much trouble and difficulty to overcome obstacles; but its achievement is an object of the most vital importance to us as a people and it would ill become the offspring of the great historic races, the heirs of a vitality born of a thousand struggles, to hesitate to enter on the final stage in the development of free institutions.

"DIGNUS VINDICE NODUS."

(Draft.)
AN ACT RESPECTING THE ELECTION OF MEMBERS OF THE HOUSE OF COMMONS OF CANADA.

Her Majesty by and with the advice and consent of the Senate and House of Commons of Canada enacts as follows:—

I.—(ELECTORAL OFFICERS).

1. The Governor General in Council shall appoint an Electoral Commissioner whose duty it shall be, under the authority conferred on him from time to time by Order in Council, to carry into effect the provisions of this Act.

2. The Governor General in Council shall, on the recommendation of the Electoral Commissioner appoint an Electoral Warden for each electoral District in the Dominion and shall authorize the appointment of a sufficient number of Electoral Officers and such assistants as may be necessary to carry out efficiently the provisions of this Act.

II.—(PERIODICAL ELECTIONS.)

3. The election of Members of the House of Commons shall take place in each Electoral District of the Dominion every fifth year and it shall be arranged as nearly as practicable so that one-fifth of the whole number of Members shall be elected annually. To effect this object the several electoral districts shall be arranged (as in the schedule hereto) under the five headings or Classes A, B, C, D, E, so that one-fifth (approximately) of all the electoral Districts in each Province shall be in each class and elections shall be held in the following order, viz:—

In Class A in the year 1900, 1905, 1910, 1915, &c.
     "   B   "   "   1901, 1906, 1911, 1916, &c.
     "   C   "   "   1902, 1907, 1912, 1917, &c.
     ".   D   "   "   1903, 1908, 1913, 1918, &c.
     "   E   "   "   1904, 1909, 1914, 1919, &c.

4. Two months before the date of an election the Electoral Commissioner shall issue a proclamation directing the Electoral Warden in respect thereto and reciting such portions of the Act bearing on the choice of representative electors as may be deemed necessary.

5. Immediately after the issue of the Proclamation the Electoral Warden shall take the oath of Office (in the form A.) and shall appoint a sufficient number of Electoral Agents as may be necessary to assist him in carrying out the provision of this Act and who before acting as Electoral Agents shall be duly commissioned and shall take the oath of Office (in the form B).

III.—(REPRESENTATIVE ELECTORS).

6. The election of members of the House of Commons shall be made by representative electors chosen by the electors as herein provided.

7. Any twenty-five electors whose names are on the voters list may nominate and appoint a representative elector in the manner following :—

(a). Each elector shall sign an elector's nomination paper (according to form C.) deputing one other elector, a discreet and competent person, to act as proxy. The several signatures shall be made in the presence of an Electoral Agent who shall receive from each signatory his voter's certificate and the Electoral Agent shall require each elector to make oath or affirmation according to form D.

(b). For the purpose set forth in the preceding clause the clerk of the Municipality when called upon shall furnish any elector whose name is on the voter's list, a voter's certificate according to form E.

(c) When an elector's nomination paper shall be duly signed as aforesaid and witnessed by an Electoral Agent, the latter shall present it along with the twenty-five voter's certificates to the Electoral Warden for the purpose of filing the same.

(d) Before filing an elector's nomination paper the Electoral Warden shall require the Electoral Officer to make oath in the form F. and shall satisfy himself by comparing the names of the signatories with voters' certificates and the voters list that they had not previously voted and are duly qualified to vote.

(e) On satisfying himself as to the validity of the elector's nomination paper, the Electoral Warden shall place the same on file and shall issue a certificate according to form G. declaring the representative elector duly chosen.

8. It shall be the duty of the Electoral Warden to provide the fullest opportunity to every voter in the Electoral District to take part in the choice of electoral representatives. He shall employ all right and proper means to promote a free choice on the part of those entitled to vote. He shall at all convenient times furnish needed information and he shall exhibit and publish a list of voters distinguishing from time to time those who have, from those who have not, chosen a representative.

9. The choice of representative electors in any Electoral District shall commence not less than six weeks before the date fixed for the election of a Member and shall be continued until one week before the same date, when the list of representative electors shall be closed.

10. As soon as the list of representative electors shall be closed the Electoral Warden shall publish the names of all who have been chosen in the order in which they have been placed on file and he shall notify by letter sent to the post office address of each representative elector chosen, at what time and place he shall be required to meet in general court to elect a Member for the House of Commons.

IV.—GENERAL COURT OF REPRESENTATIVE ELECTORS.

11. On the day named in the proclamation of the Electoral Commissioner the representative electors shall assemble in a general court to elect a member to represent the electoral District in Parliament. Before regularly assembling they shall each present to

the Electoral Warden his certificate of appointment to be "vised," and who before taking his seat in the general Court shall make the oath of qualification according to form H.

12. The representative electors being duly sworn the Electoral Warden shall call the Court to order and shall make such announcements as may be necessary, the nomination of candidates shall then be proceeded with.

(A.)—NOMINATION OF CANDIDATES.

13. Any ten representative electors may nominate a candidate by signing a nomination paper in the form I. stating therein the name, residence and description of the candidate sufficiently to identify him. No representative elector shall nominate more than one candidate.

14. The Electoral Warden shall file nomination papers complying with the preceding section in the order in which he may receive them. The receipt of nominations shall be in order up to five o'clock on the first day of the general Court after which the Electoral Warden shall cause to be published a certified list of the candidates nominated.

(B.)—ELECTION OF A MEMBER.

15. The election of a Member shall be proceeded with at ten o'clock on the morning of the second day of the general Court.

16. Should there be one nomination only, the candidate nominated shall be held to be the choice of the general Court and he shall be declared by the Electoral Warden, elected by acclamation.

17. In the event of there being several candidates, the election shall be accomplished by ballot or by a series of ballots as each case may require, reducing step by step the number of candidates by elimination in accordance with the degree of preference indicated by the votes. Should there be no marked preference for any one candidate made manifest by the weight of the votes given, the selection shall be made from the candidates receiving the largest number of votes and shall as hereinafter provided be determined by Lot.

18. Two of the Electoral Agents shall be appointed tellers to receive the votes and who shall be duly sworn according to form K.

19. The voting shall take place in the immediate presence of the Electoral Warden who shall mark off the name of the elector voting, on the list of qualified representative electors, as each vote is received.

20. The ballot of each voter shall be a small white card with the name of the candidate printed or written thereon, it shall be placed in a blank envelope by the voter before handing it at the proper time to the receiving teller. Cards and envelopes uniform in size for this and other similar purposes shall be supplied to those voting, during the general Court.

21. Should there be two candidates nominated, a ballot shall be taken as follows :—

(a). Each representative elector shall in turn present himself at the voting table and shall show his qualification certificate to the first teller who shall report to the Electoral Warden.

(b). All being found in order the elector shall pass the envelope containing his ballot to the 2nd teller to be stamped. The elector shall immediately thereafter place the same in the ballot urn.

(c). When all the representative electors present have voted, the Electoral Warden shall open the ballot urn, and with the assistance of the Tellers count the votes and announce the number given for each candidate.

(d). In the event of one of the candidates receiving votes numbering more than half the whole number of representative electors in the electoral district, he shall be declared by the Electoral Warden duly elected. Should neither of the candidates receive votes equal to half the total number of representative electors the selection shall be determined as hereinafter provided, by Lot.

22. Should three candidates be nominated a ballot shall be taken as in Section 21, and if one of the candidates receive votes numbering more than half the whole number of representative electors in the district he shall be held to be the successful candidate and shall be declared elected. In the event of no one candidate receiving more than half, the selection shall be determined by Lot as hereinafter provided.

23. Should four candidates be nominated, a ballot shall be taken as in section 21, and one of the candidates receives votes numbering more than half the number of representative electors in the district he shall be declared elected. If no one candidate receives more than half the total number, then the three candidates who have received the highest number of votes shall be eligible for a second ballot. The second ballot shall be effected as in section 22 and the election determined in the manner therein laid down.

24. Should five candidates be nominated or a larger number than five, a first ballot shall be taken as in section 21 and if one of the candidates receives votes numbering more than half the total number of representative electors in the electoral district he shall be declared elected, but if no one candidate receives more than half, the four candidates who have received the largest number of votes shall be eligible for a second ballot. In this case the second ballot shall be conducted as if there were four candidates (see section 23) and the election of a member determined accordingly as therein provided.

(C.)—Determination by Lot.

25. When in any case it becomes expedient to determine the election by Lot as in that alluded to in Section 22, the names of the candidates from whom a selection is to be made shall be inscribed on small white cards. The number of cards for each candidate shall correspond with the number of votes received by each, that is to say should the votes cast have been for Candidate A   78

" B 67
" C 55   Total votes 200,

then the name of A shall be inscribed on 78 cards

" B " " 67 "
" C " " 55 "

making in all 200 cards. Each card shall be put in a blank envelope sealed and placed in a ballot urn. In another ballot urn there shall be placed an equal number of blank envelopes containing in every instance except one, a blank card. In one envelope *only* shall be placed a card similar to the other cards but having inscribed thereon the words "This is the Member."

26. The two ballot urns shall each have been shaken so as sufficiently to mix the cards after which the drawing shall be proceeded with, the teller at each urn shall simultaneously and indiscriminately draw an envelope from each and after stamping and numbering both alike the two shall be placed together in a third envelope and handed to the Electoral Warden.

27. After all the envelopes are drawn and disposed of, the Electoral Warden shall proceed to open them one by one in their order. He shall make known the contents of each as he proceeds, replacing the whole in the original envelopes.

28. The candidate whose name shall be found associated with the card bearing the inscription "This is the Member" shall be declared by the Electoral Warden duly elected.

29. So soon as the member shall be declared elected, the Electoral Warden shall close the General Court and proceed to pay the representative electors their attendance fees and mileage allowances as provided in Section VI.

V.—Election Returns.

30. The Electoral Warden shall on the day after the closing of the General Court of representative electors, transmit to the Electoral Commissioner a return of the election in the form L, certifying who has been elected Member. He shall likewise forward to the Member elect a copy thereof.

31. The Electoral Warden shall accompany his return to the Electoral Commissioner with a report of the proceedings mentioning the several stages thereof and he shall make any observations he may think proper.

32. The Electoral Warden shall transmit to the Electoral Commission, the nomination papers of the representative electors, the nomination papers of the several candidates, copies of the voters list and roll of representative electors and all other lists and documents used or required at the election. The Electoral Commissioner shall retain in his possession all papers transmitted to him by the Electoral Warden for at least two years after the date of the election.

33. The Electoral Commissioner shall on receiving the return of any Member elected

to the House of Commons, enter such return in a book to be kept by him for such purpose, in the order in which the same is received by him, and thereupon give notice in the ordinary issue of the Canada Gazette of the name of the Member so elected.

VI.—ELECTION EXPENSES.

34. The Governor General in Council shall determine the salary of the Electoral Commissioner and his assistants, the fees and expenses to be paid the Electoral Warden, Electoral Officers, the mileage and other allowances to be paid Representative Electors attending the Electoral Courts and all other legitimate and proper expenses necessary to carry into effect this statute. And shall establish a regular tariff in respect thereto, which tariff may be amended from time to time as circumstances may require. All such salaries, fees, allowances and disbursements shall be paid as the Governor General may determine, by warrant directed to the Minister of Finance, out of the Consolidated Revenue Fund of Canada and shall be distributed as may be directed by the Electoral Commissioner, to the several officers and persons entitled to the same under the provisions of this Act, which distribution he. the Electoral Commissioner, shall report to the Governor General through the Secretary of State; and the Electoral Wardens shall certify the correctness of all accounts within their respective Electoral Districts.

VII.—GENERAL PROVISIONS.

(The general provisions with respect to issuing of proclamations, giving notices, administration of oaths, transmission of information, &c., may be similar to those in the present statute 49 Victoria Chap. 8).

(A.)—OATH OF OFFICE OF ELECTORAL WARDEN.

I, the undersigned A.B. Electoral Warden for the Electoral District of   .
solemnly swear (or affirm) that I am legally qualified according to law to act as Electoral Warden for the said Electoral District and that I will act faithfully in that capacity, without partiality, fear, favour or affection. So help me God.

Signature (A.B.)
Electoral Warden.

CERTIFICATE OF ELECTORAL WARDEN HAVING TAKEN OATH OF OFFICE.

I, the undersigned, hereby certify that on the   day of the month of   ,
18   (A.B.) the Electoral Warden for the Electoral District of   , took and subscribed before me, the oath (or affirmation) of Office in such case required of an Electoral Warden.

In testimony whereof, I have delivered to him this certificate.

Signature (C.D.)
Justice of the Peace.

(B.)

The Commission of an electoral officer the oath of Office and certificate of his having taken the oath of Office may be similar to those provided in the Dominion Election Act, in the case of an election clerk (see page 45.)

(C.)—NOMINATION OF A REPRESENTATIVE ELECTOR.

We the undersigned twenty-five electors of the Electoral District of
hereby nominate and appoint   as our representative elector and deputy to appear and act for us at any Electoral Court held in the Electoral District of   and in our behalf to elect a fit and proper person to represent the people of the said Electoral District in the Commons House of Parliament.

Witness our hands in the said Electoral District this   day   18

Signatures with the numbers of electors on the voters list.

Names.	Numbers on voters list.
1.	
2.	
3.	
4. &c. &c.	

x

(*D.*)—OATH OF QUALIFICATION OF ELECTOR.

1. I solemnly swear (or affirm) that I am the person named on the voters list for the Electoral District of that I am numbered on said list and that I deliver to the Electoral Officer my voter's certificate entitling me to the privilege of a voter.

2. That I am a British subject and have not before appointed any person to represent me as an elector.

3. That I have not received anything nor has anything been promised me directly or indirectly nor have I paid or promised anything to any person, unlawfully, in connection with this election. So help me God.

(*E.*)—VOTER'S CERTIFICATE

I hereby certify that is a duly qualified elector in the Electoral District of and that his number on the voters list is and that he is entitled to all the rights and privileges of an Elector for the said District.

(Sd) Clerk of the Municipality of Electoral District of

(*F.*)—OATH OF ELECTORAL OFFICER ON FILING NOMINATION PAPER.

I the undersigned Electoral Officer duly appointed for the Electoral District of do solemnly swear (or affirm) that the accompanying nomination paper appointing a representative elector for the said District was duly executed by all the twenty-five electors in my presence in the manner provided by law. So help me God.

Signature A.B.

Date. Electoral Officer.

(*G.*)—CERTIFICATE OF APPOINTMENT OF REPRESENTATIVE ELECTOR.

I hereby certify that has been duly nominated by twenty-five electors of the Electoral District of , a representative elector in their behalf and in their stead to elect a Member for the Common House of Commons and that I have placed the nomination on file and I hereby declare the said nominee duly appointed representative elector for this Electoral District.

Signature ————

Electoral Warden, Electoral District of

(*H.*)—OATH OF QUALIFICATION OF REPRESENTATIVE ELECTOR.

1. I solemnly swear (or affirm) that I am the person named in the nomination paper duly filed by the Electoral Warden of the Electoral District of and now shown to me.

2. That I am a British subject and am duly qualified to act as a representative elector for this district.

3. That I have not received anything nor has anything been promised me directly or indirectly, nor have I paid or promised anything to any person in connection with this election, unlawfully, and I will act faithfully as representative elector to the best of my ability. So help me God.

(*I.*)—NOMINATION OF CANDIDATE.

We the undersigned ten representatative electors hereby nominate a fit and proper person to represent the Electoral District of as a Member of the House of Commons of Canada. We have not nominated any other candidate at this election.

Witness our hands this day of

Signatures.		Signatures.
1.	6.	
2.	7.	
3.	8.	
4.	9.	
5.	10.	

(*K.*)—Oath of Tellers.

I, the undersigned   appointed Teller in this election of a Member to represent the Electoral District of   in the House of Commons, do solemnly swear (or affirm) that I will act faithfully in my capacity of Teller and do my duty according to law without partiality, fear, favour, or affection. So help me God.

(*L.*)—Return after an Election.

I hereby certify that the Member elected for the Electoral District of   by the General Court of Representative Electors on the   day of   18   is (name &c. as in the nomination paper).

                                         (Sd.) E. W.

Date.   Electoral Warden.

"NEW OCCASIONS TEACH NEW DUTIES."

It has been pointed out by one of the foremost Canadian investigators of parliamentary abuses and shortcomings that it is a "necessary result of our human nature that the end of government is primarily and essentially the welfare of the ruling class." The defects in our laws, the corruption in legislative circles and the turmoil of party politics are a necessary consequence of entrusting the government of the country to an absolute parliament, the members of which being human are more or less self seeking, and being selected with reference to their position upon a confused jumble of various public questions manipulated by scheming individuals and inseparably bound together, are not fitted to represent the people upon any one question taken by itself.

Is not this pooling of issues a legitimate outcome of the system of the entire abdication by the voter of the law making power in relation to many subjects in favor of one nominal representative? By far the better part of the community is practically almost defranchised through the platform system of polictics. For men of thought and sincere patriotism will naturally arrive at independent conclusions upon public topics. But if they support measures of which they approve they are forced by the system to support those also to which they are opposed; thus, to them, the value of the franchise is lessened or destroyed. But the thoughtless, the narrow minded, the corrupt elements and those who place party before country, who think more of triumph than of truth are not hampered, but have an undue influence in public affairs.

It may be contended that the party platform system while it may in individual cases bring to the support of certain principles those who otherwise would strongly oppose them, yet will, by a law of averages—by counteracting one error by another—by bringing one to support a certain proposal to which he is opposed in the stead of another who would really wish to support it, were he free to do so, and not led by the necessities of the system to oppose it because he considered it in bad company and the system obliged him to endorse the whole list or none—all conflicting elements being eliminated by cancellation—may in its results in the community as a whole truly voice the wishes of the whole people. Is there any certainty that thus trusting to chance will straighten out interminable tangles? As well might a seaman endeavour to disentangle his lines by running his free end haphazard through the interstices of the snarl. It is the reasoning of the gambler who stakes his fortune trusting to a change of luck.

In theory, a portion of the community unites upon a set of principles which it unanimously wishes to advance, and the triumph of the platform denotes the will of the people with respect to these principles. But, in practice, such is far from being the case.

Few men would approve of all the propositions of their party were the judgement untrammeled; but being part of the machine they must go with the other gearing. The majority of a party decide what the platform shall be. That majority in its turn may be a faction whose votes in caucus or convention are previously decided by the majority of that faction meeting among themselves. Similarly, the policy of this last faction may have been decided upon by the majority rule. This system of party within party is capable of expansion in theory until a minority of a very few individuals could impose a policy upon the public at large, having the political power rightfully belonging to a majority of the people. As a matter of fact, it is sufficiently developed to greatly impair the usefulness of parliament, to have an unwholesome influence upon the course of legislation and materially interfere with the welfare of the community.

Party government has been compared by its defenders to the balance-wheel system of a chronometer, the opposing tendencies counterbalancing each other in their excesses—in their variations from the proper mean. But if we consider a moment, the seeming analogy disappears. It is not the balance-wheel, going first to the one side, then to the other, which marks the time, but it is the steady advancement of the hands. With partyism it is the fanatical element, the opposing tendencies, first going one way, then another, which record the workings of the machine, leaving the sober judgement, the steady advancing sentiment of the people helpless and unused. Moreover, the waste of power in timepiece escapements is a defect such as is always sought to be avoided where economy of force is an important consideration. In horological science, the waste of power being so small in comparison with man's physical force, we tolerate the defect for the sake of its convenience, having arranged for a perfect resultant action. In politics we exhaust our strength in pulling in opposite directions and the resultant action is

25

necessarily erroneous, being secured by corruption or through incapacity, or a haphazard many-sided conflict of multitudinous interests.

Dr. Fleming has compared political parties to the crew of a row-boat determined to pull in opposite directions. "There would be much agitation of the water, but little or no satisfactory progress." Might I venture to add that this metaphorical row-boat is in dangerous waters, and the force of the crew's efforts being spent against itself the current is bearing the craft steadily towards the rapids. In the strife between the evil and the good, let the good that is in men have but fair play, and we need not fear for the ultimate triumph of Truth and Justice and the progress of the race. But if we continue to render our best propensities powerless, our noblest efforts inoperative, the forces of evil, engineered with better tact will continue to maintain their ascendency in politics and their interference with the welfare of the community.

Where the electorate is divided into two hostile parties and a summing up of the aggregate vote determines which shall govern the country, the best intentioned and most intelligent voters but nullify each other's votes. The majority of voters are fully resolved that they will never change their political faith. With many it is a boast that they vote as their father and grandfather voted. In all probability they will continue voting in the same way be it on the reform or conservative side, to the end.

If we were to despair of doing away with party politics, it would be a vast saving to the state and the individuals concerned if the votes of these self-proclaimed slaves of their present opinion or their grandfather's opinion, could be eliminated by cancellation, by a kind of clearing house operation without the useless requirement of going to the voting booth. Majorities only are counted in the end. The shifting vote governs. The "dyed in the wool" voters, reformers and conservatives would as much affect the result if they would arrange for their mutual disfranchisement. Those who hold the "balance of power" are not slow to make the best of their opportunities. Some will sell their support openly to the highest bidder, others for promise of office or political advancement. Or, it may be a particular church or a society or those of a particular profession or trade which desires government favor.

But great as are the evils of the party system, they are not the only cause of the decadence of popular government. The average legislator in his public conduct is influenced by self interest. Personal favors, direct or indirect, from those seeking to influence parliament, frequently a money bribe, have much to do with shaping legislation, having no connection with party politics. A lawyer or a doctor or a money lender is selected as a candidate, not owing to any special fitness for the position, but on account of his ability to secure votes. They have bills and other financial claims against a large number of voters who by concession or pressure are brought to political servitude. The ballot has perhaps lessened this evil, but has failed to effect a cure. When the candidate has become the representative he usually recoups himself in some way for the trouble and expense of the election struggle. Not that legislators necessarily accumulate riches, for politics is a costly game. When the corrupt representative does not fatten upon his ill-gotten gains, he is often losing his substance to the parasites which he carries.

As an instance of corrupt influence in a country of similar institutions and political morals to our own, the New York Central Railway runs a weekly dead-head train from New York to Albany and return during the legislative session, and gives passes generously for other trains. The fares, if collected, have been computed at four thousand dollars per week for the twenty-one weeks, a total of eighty-four thousand dollars per annum. The New York Central Railway is not a philanthropic enterprise. It expects value for its service.

That is but one act of a single corporation. Other interests adopt the same policy in this and other countries where parliament has the power of abusing its position. The Panama Canal Co. controlled by bribery so far as suited its purpose, both the French Assembly and the Congress of the United States.

The lobby is in every legislative hall. Money or its equivalent can secure almost any legislation, or prevent it, until some particular abuse becomes so glaring that the people are aroused and candidates are pledged to oppose it.

It has been advanced that the "representatives of the people in parliament should be left free to act according to the dictates of their own judgement, after full examination and full consideration of every subject."

But is it not "a necessary result of our human nature," that the removal of what restriction we now have upon the representative would open still wider the flood-gates of corruption by giving the dishonest legislator a greatly extended field of operations? Though it is not true that all men have their price, it is exemplified continually in the commercial and legislative world that a very large number of men have their price either in money or personal advancement. And since majorities rule and under the present system of delegating the legislative power to individuals, corruptionists can easily afford the price necessary to attain their ends. Capital and knavery combined will continue to unduly influence legislation until men are vastly more moral or until the power of betraying the public is taken from the hands of the politicians. So long as such glittering premiums upon dishonesty are displayed before the politician—so long as a man may attain riches without incurring legal penalties or forfeiting the respect of the community and has his sense of honor perverted by an unwholesome environment, he will not grow in moral character. Those who have observed the different aspect in which the dishonest politician is viewed from the petty thief can attest to the demoralizing influence of political corruption.

In trying to remedy political abuses, we must deprive not only partisanship of its power, but corruption of its opportunity.

The recognition of the people's right of sovereignty has come slowly but steadily as that right has become more and more manifest. First parliament had to struggle for its existence. Then the franchise was gradually extended as people became enlightened until now we have so nearly approached manhood suffrage that practically speaking the term "the people" is synonymous with "the electorate."

In the early part of the century Guizot in his college lectures defended a limited franchise, the confining of the voting power to "a fragment of society," "the most capable." Thirty years later he wrote, "If I should apply, at the present day, to these historical studies of 1820 all the lessons which political life has given me since that period, I should perhaps modify some of the ideas which I have expressed in reference to some of the conditions and forms of representative government. This system of government has no unique and solely good type, in conformity to which it must necessarily and universally be instituted. Providence, which allots to nations different origins and destinies, also opens to justice and liberty more than one way of entering into governments; and it would be foolishly to reduce their chances of success if we condemned them to appear always with the same lineaments, and to develop themselves by the same means. One thing only is important, and that is, that the essential principles of order and liberty should subsist beneath the different forms which the interference of the country in its own affairs may assume amongst different peoples and at different epochs."

A growing public intelligence assisted by the press has fitted progressive countries for self government. We have now accepted the principle of the sovereignty of the people. But the electoral machinery is not in harmony with the design, and the sovereignty is largely exercised by the mighty dollar, political cunning and blind chance.

In confining our efforts to voting for representatives we are nearly powerless as to measures. As this paper proposes a measure of practical direction of parliament, let us consider the exceptions to the rule when voters have been allowed to indicate their wishes independent of party politics. Perhaps we may learn something from the history of direct voting by the people. It is no experiment. It is an old institution. The germ of it, the right of petition, dates from the fourteenth century. That was the initiative without the referendum.

In Canada we have been voting upon matters of municipal legislation for years ; railway by-laws, waterworks, the control of the liquor traffic and various propositions involving the expenditure of corporate funds, and there are few who will say that the result has not been much more satisfactory than if those questions had been decided by the local parliament without this systematic consultation with the electorate. These questions were referred to the people for the same reason that the directing of parliament in all matters is here urged, to enable the people to separate measures from men, and from other measures, and to avoid corruption.

In the New England states direct legislation has been practised by the town meeting system ever since their settlement. In other parts of the Union laws concerning the liquor traffic, lotteries, tax rates, railroad regulations, public works of various kinds, the contraction of debts and many other matters must be submitted to a direct vote of the people. The practice has given unbounded satisfaction, and is now greatly on the increase.

It is in Switzerland, that most progressive country, that we find the principle receiving consistent treatment. In federal affairs and in nearly all the cantons the popular vote is either made obligatory or dependent upon the will of the people made known by petitions. After an experience of the system for over fifty years it is to-day more popular than ever. It has given them governmental control more or less absolute of all public monopolies, lowered taxes, withheld legislation sought by the privileged classes and removed the worst evils of party politics.

The successful working of the governing making power in municipal corporations, banks, insurance, railways and other commercial enterprises and the comparative absence of partisanship therein is due to their being more closely under the control of their constituents through annual elections and reviews of their legislative work—through being pledged to a certain policy and the views of the individuals being obtained by vote or conference upon all important questions.

In politics however, the legitimate directing power is silenced by an overwhelming mass platform planks. All the issues before the people are so crowded together in their submission for their approval or condemnation that all is confusion. The result is left to chance or is decided upon personal grounds or considerations foreign to the vital question to be decided. As well might a judge try all the prisoners in court in one trial and acquit all or punish all, as the weight of evidence against the various defendants is little or great in the aggregate—if the greater part are guilty, punishing all—if many are innocent, acquitting all. Or, if even a few are guilty of some atrocious crime, condemning the majority though admittedly innocent. Under any uncontrolled system of legislation we do with public questions as such a judge would do with those brought before him.

It has been assumed that the possession of a sound general judgement would result in the exercise of the best judgement of the people upon all questions. It is scarcely conceivable that a legislator could be found whose judgement upon a variety of questions would coincide with that of the majority of the people, or a legislature constituted which, even if the conflicting personal interest of the legislator did not intervene, would form a correct estimate of the popular will upon all questions.

The voters are forced by the incongruous mixing of measures and men to vote for a representative who, they know, will misrepresent them in many respects in order that they may be represented in the consideration of other questions. It has been claimed in the past that a legislator's judgement would be superior to that of the people, but that position has been abandoned in progressive countries.

To confound measures and men and seek for a plan of representation which will be even approximately representative of the nation without some provision for the nation making known its wishes upon each question at issue independently is to approach a problem impossible of solution upon the face of it. It would be the production of law and order by the methods of chaos. As well try to travel to a dozen destinations in as many different directions at the same time. With one representative upon several distinct issues the platform and partyism become a necessity.

The only practical plan of a truly representative parliament independent for a time of all control would be to have an entirely different set of representatives for every question to be decided. That would be a perfect scheme of representation were it not for the fallibility of the representative. To secure that true representation in parliament in a simpler and safer manner the scheme of a parliament at all times under the virtual direction of the people, the principle of which we have repeatedly tried and approved of, is herewith submitted for examination. To give "each elector due weight in the government through parliament and thereby to remove the gross political evils of this and other nominally democratic countries," I propose an adaptation of the optional form of the Initiative and Referendum, which has given such satisfaction in Switzerland, where it has long since passed the experimental stage. (Appendix). It is a reform rapidly gaining ground wherever brought prominently before the people, notably in the United States where it is fast coming into popular favor and most urgently needed.

It may be objected that giving the power of direct voting under certain circumstances would be giving the elector due weight in the government independent of rather than through parliament. It would do both. Parliament would be anxious to ascertain and give effect to the wishes of the electorate knowing that those wishes could be made effective without its concurrence. It is not proposed that the people shall vote direct, but that they may so vote in certain contingencies. The control would be mainly operative in its effect upon parliament. That body could not often oppose the apparent will of the people. Consequently, direct appeals to the electorate in opposition to parliamentary legislation would as the system made its influence felt upon politics, be few and generally unsuccessful. Parliament would anticipate the vote of the electorate.

It has been represented as lowering to the character of parliament to lessen its independence. Do we lose dignity in the faithful performance of a trust? Among the last public utterances of the late Phillips Brooks are these words : "Be master and servant. Obey and be obeyed ; and one afternoon's experience, if you can make it, will make you so in love with the life of service that you can never again during life give yourself up to the life that you led when you tried to be lord and master." Parliament should obey as well as command. It will not thereby forfeit our respect. Lord Lytton has said : "In proportion as the freedom of the representative is cramped and his responsibility im-

verished by the oxaction of exorbitant and vexatious pledges, the general character of
o representative class will be low and subservient, and the confidence it can command
ll be consequently small." That is the old aristocratic idea of government. Is there
t a better gospel coming to the front proclaiming the duty of those who are intrusted
th power by the people to sink selfish inclinations in the service of those who send them
represent them? Are the judges of our land "low and subservient," and do they fail
command confidence because, representing the public in its department of Justice, they
e pledged to a certain line of conduct by their oath of office, and are not free to deal
th criminals or litigants as they will, but must be guided by the law of the land?
oes the head of a municipal corporation lower his position who endeavors to ascertain
e wishes of the electorate and is guided thereby, though as a private citizen, he might
vor a different line of action? Is the president of a railway or other business objection-
ly low and subservient because he is guided in his conduct of the business by the wishes
the shareholders? When one performs a service voluntarily and receives recompense
r that service, where is the slavery? But if we admit the applicability of the term to
e one which is subordinate to the other, is it not better that the representative should
the slave of the people than that the people should be as they now are, the slaves of
e representative?

Is it not a virtue in a politician to make all possible effort to acquaint himself with
e wishes of his constituents and to be guided by their wishes? The object of the
nexed bill is to make that custom practically obligatory.

But we are told that voters are incompetent to legislate. If that were true we had
tter go back to a more select voter's list. One who is capable of analyzing character,
eighing motives and nicely balancing the interests which he entrusts to an independent
w maker is surely capable of forming as correct a judgement upon a simple proposition
vested of all personality. "Law cannot rise higher than its source." Nor can parlia-
ent be depended upon to rise higher than the electorate.

It has been assumed that public discussions on a large scale are necessary in order to
ach proper decisions, separating the wheat from the chaff by the agency of—wind. But
not the people meet repeatedly in sections at every elections? However, there is a
tter agency than wind in the winnowing of ideas. The press gives information and
ucation gives capacity of judgement. The average elector can gain more wisdom
diberating all alone for five minutes than in talking politics for five years. For in
ntroversy we strive to triumph, and grow more prejudiced, while in meditation we seek
e truth.

Every question is discussed by the public at large as thoroughly as in parliament,
d usually in advance of parliamentary treatment. Discussions in parliament are
dressed more to the country than to the legislators.

It is not designed to supplant parliament by Direct Legislation. That body would
ill retain its proper function of interpreting the people's will, arranging details, com-
omises and modifications and moulding legislative schemes into the most acceptable
rm. If they did not perform that duty then the people could assist. As an American
riter says, we would have "a fire extinguisher which will cost nothing if we do not use
; but which in some emergency may be worth millions." The actual work of legislation
ould remain with parliament. There would be no necessary delay in the legislative
ork. The people would only act in case of widespread dissatisfaction with any particular
rt of its work. Being subject to this ultimate control political sagacity would enable
rliamentary representatives to be the nation in essence as legislators no matter what
ey might be as individuals. And is not this the only important point? They would
in touch with the people and they must respect the touch.

Why should we make a distinction in favor of those questions hitherto submitted to
e people? Would not the same advantages arise from putting beyond the complicating
d corrupting influence of party politics the consideration of custom's tariff, of railroad
licies, of Civil Service Reform, and of the currency laws and of any and every question
general interest?

The people emancipated from party serfdom would be at liberty to change their
ews, and reasonable discussion would largely take the place of bitter controversy. The
ews of the people would be immediately reflected in the law-making chamber.

If we accept the modern idea of the sovereignty of the people, of parliament being
e people in essence, and not merely a condensation of a certain portion of the people
esumably more fitted to govern, it is difficult to imagine upon what grounds the principle
direct control by the nation over the law-making machinery can be logically assailed.

There are but two systems of government; by a majority of the people, accomplished
ther directly or by representatives giving effect to the will of the majority upon all

questions, which can only be attained by being under constant control of the people ; and by a part of the community, be it one or many, a king or a parliament, independent of the wishes and beyond the control of the people.

That a referendary control of legislation is feasible our own experience in submitting propositions to a popular vote, as well as similar instances in the United States and other countries, goes far to prove. That it is a satisfactory remedy for political evils nearly all Switzerland attests.

"If there be a political prophecy," says W. D. McCrackan in the *Arena* for May, "which it is safe to make at this time, it is that our representative system cannot remain in its present form for another decade, if the republic is to endure. . . . . . The institutions of the initiative and referendum, as practised in Switzerland, are the noblest political achievements of this waning century. They are capable of supplying our decaying democracy with the powers necessary for its redemption. . . . . . Making laws by means of all-powerful representatives will some day be looked upon as a method fully as crude and primitive as that of letter-writing by means of scribes on the street corners."

This proposition is designed to separate the issues before the people and to prevent the representative's betrayal of his trust. If it will do that, will it not solve the problem of our political decadence and rectify parliament?

A railroad company would not issue passes and grant other exceptional privileges to a sufficient number of voters to enable it to obtain coveted legislation, nor could it bribe the whole country.

It is incomparably more feasible to buy representatives every four or five years than the whole electorate annually. No individual or combinations of individuals could bribe the whole community. Therein consists the only hope of the salvation of popular government, assailed as it is by a more or less corrupt privileged class whose power over parliament is continually on the increase.

Under a controlled parliamentary system governments would not bargain for the support of purchasable members : they would not bribe constituencies to return their supporters by promised public works : nor would candidates bribe the voter, for the motive would be lacking. There would be no money or other personal gain in politics, as there would be no arbitrary power to barter for money or favor. And it is because there would be no money in politics and the privileged classes would be prevented from sapping the strength of the nation, that every proposition to remedy affairs is so bitterly opposed by those whose selfish interests would suffer. Let such self-seeking individuals remember that their descendants may not be politicians, and that they may be—tramps. Even they themselves may fall. The ups and downs of life are so frequent that the efforts of those who are up to make more hopeless the condition of those who are down may sometime be viewed from a different though still selfish standpoint.

Most schemes of minority representation are founded upon the assumption of the necessity of party government. Give to the people their rightful sovereignty which would enable every one to pass judgement upon all questions separately instead of in bulk, and the forces of partisanship will be scattered, and there will be no minorities, as we now understand the term, to represent, and no majorities to combat.

Though it might be desirable that some scheme should be adopted providing for giving due weight to the votes of every interest so far as practicable, representation of every interest would be secured by the knowledge that parliament was not supreme. It would be the tendency of the system to make every member of parliament the representative of every interest.

The savagery in the forest where man was free so far as governmental control was concerned, but living in discomfort and fear of his fellow man and of wild beasts :—the primitive monarchical systems which secured the welfare of the people or oppressed them as the ruler was wise and beneficent or ignorant and evil disposed—the feudal system with the masses in servitude—the uncontrolled representative government system with political power delegated absolutely for a stated period to a selected number of professional legislators—the complete sovereignty of the citizenship of the state through its practical retention of the law-making power—these mark the epochs of the political life of nations advancing from savagery to a complete civilization. That is government by regular evolution.

The old haphazard system of parliamentary representation, the best available perhaps in primitive times, is a monumental failure in our day. Our greater fitness for self government and our growing needs require that we seek something better.

"New occasions teach new duties : Time makes ancient good uncouth,
They must upward still and onward who would keep abreast of Truth."

To make the system complete, a like measure might be enacted by the Provincial Assemblies in harmony with this proposed Act, and providing for the optional submission of provincial and municipal measures to a popular vote.

"NEW OCCASIONS TEACH NEW DUTIES."

(Appendix).

BILL.

AN ACT TO PROVIDE FOR REFERENDARY VOTING.

(Applied to Canada, but applicable in principle to any country with a similar Parliamentary system.)

Her Majesty, by and with the advice and consent of the Senate and House of Commons of Canada, enacts as follows :—

1. It shall be lawful for fifteen per cent. of the whole number of electors of the Dominion of Canada, or twenty-five per cent. of the membership of Parliament, by petition, to obtain the submission to a popular vote of any measure for the repeal of an existing law or for the passage of a proposed law.

2. The text of proposed legislation may be deposited with the   *(Head of government department)*   together with its title. Copies shall be printed and sent to the clerks of municipalities and the titles only shall be used in petitioning and voting.

3. Such petitions shall be in similar wording to Form A., hereto appended, with a distinguishing heading as there designated.

4. Blank forms of petition shall be furnished by the government under regulations of the Governor General in Council at the computed cost of production.

5. It shall be the duty of the Government when the aggregate number of public petitioners for the submission of any measure shall exceed fifteen per cent. of the duly qualified voters of the Dominion ; or when the number of signatures on any petition of members of parliament shall exceed twenty-five per cent. of the whole number of representatives, to make provision for the submission of such measure to a popular vote at the next annual election provided for by this Act, providing there shall intervene a period of at least thirty days.

6. In the Provinces which shall concur by legislative enactment in the provisions of this Act the voter's list used for all Dominion purposes shall be prepared by a joint commission composed of an officer appointed by the Dominion government, an officer appointed by the Provincial government and a third appointed by the council of the municipality affected.

(1.) In case of dissatisfaction with the rulings of the Commission an appeal may be taken to the regular courts.

(2.) Such voter's list shall be used for Municipal, Provincial and Dominion purposes.

(3.) The voting upon any and every measure that may be submitted as well as the voting for members of Parliament so often as those elections shall occur, shall be at the same time and place as for municipal offices.

(4.) Voting shall be by ballot and one ballot shall serve for Municipal, Provincial and Dominion voting of every description.

7. In Provinces that shall not concur by legislative enactment in the provisions of this Act the voting shall be annually and at the same time as the municipal elections when there may be measures to be submitted.

8. Only titles of measures voted upon shall appear upon the ballot.

9. The majority of the aggregate vote shall decide all questions and upon the passage of a submitted measure and upon its approval by the Governor General shall be declared in force, and the government shall make proper provision for its enforcement.

10. All Acts or portions of Acts conflicting with this Act are hereby repealed.

Form A.

Public Petition for Referendary Vote.

(Or Petition of Member of Parliament for Referendary Vote.)

I hereby petition for the submission of   *(Title of Measure)* the text of which has been deposited with the   *(Head of Government Department.)*

(Signatures.)

SPERO MELIORA.

There is little doubt that the system of electing the members of Parliament, by the majority of the votes in each Constituency, is objectionable in the extreme. Though it is the general practice in countries with a representative form of government, the plan is attended with features totally incommensurate with a well ordered system of popular representation. The evils resulting from it have been repeatedly pointed out by political economists for many years past, of late, by Dr. Sandford Fleming, after whose able treatment of the subject it would be superfluous to repeat the objections against the system. All those men who have given the subject attention from an independent standpoint are practically unanimous in the opinion, that the injustice possible, and the abuses continually occurring are largely attributable to the fact that the system of election followed does not give the people equal representation in Parliament which aggravates and intensifies if not causes the strong party feeling which is so much deplored.

The desideratum is a plan which would " give the whole . . . . . . people equal representation in Parliament." How is this to be accomplished? It appears easier to denounce the evil than formulate a practicable remedy. Several plans have been proposed by which it was thought the problem could be surmounted, but all seem to contain provisions which largely counterbalance the advantages that would otherwise accrue from them. The plan known as the Hare system has met with the greatest favor containing more advantages than any other proposed, indeed with some modifications it has been the system of election in Denmark for many years, but it must be admitted that there are disadvantages which diminish its merits ; though it is greatly preferable to the present system.

As it is only by friendly criticism of the measures proposed, their weak points may be eliminated and a more perfect scheme evolved, I purpose to show in what respect they are faulty. The greatest objection to Mr. Hare's scheme and others founded upon it is the large proportion of votes counted for candidates who are only the second, third, fourth and even lower choice of the voters who in other words are represented eventually by persons inferior, in their estimation, to the candidates of their first choice.

An elector should be represented in Parliament by a candidate whom he considers the best for the position and in whom he has implicit confidence ; but as will be seen any vote cast for a candidate who does not secure the quota necessary for his return is applied to secure the return of another inferior in the opinion of the voter. In practice comparatively few of the candidates would poll sufficient first votes to equal the total voting power of a constituency. This is without the difficulty mentioned by Mrs. Fawcett, when a candidate A receives 2000 votes, the second name on half of them being B, the second on the other half of another candidate C, if all the ballots with B's name second were used for A's return as the ballot could only be used to elect one member, B would be left without a single vote, while A and C receiving the full quota of 1000 votes would be returned. Though B received the same number of second votes as C through the accident of the ballots with his name second being drawn out first and counted to A whose name was at the top of the ballot they were useless to B. How to prevent this occurrence is a yet unsolved problem.

Any scheme where the result would largely depend upon chance, as in those where the selection by lot is the ruling principle, however meritorious it might be would be likely to prove unsatisfactory. Many of the electors being uncertain as to whether they would really be represented at all would lose interest in the wh le subject. Another plan of proportional representation is to add up and divide by the unit of representation the total number of votes cast for the candidates of the different political parties allowing each party its proportionate number of members. The objection to this plan is that it would draw the line between the parties even more intensely than at present and recognize party distinctions which is one of the worst features of our political system.

It is now in order to formulate the writer's plan for the " Rectification of Parliament." Absolute perfection is perhaps unattainable but his endeavor will be to give a little assistance to the task of solving this difficult problem. A plan which in the writer's opinion would meet the requirements of the case is as follows :—beginning with the Registration of voters I would make personal application to the Registration Clerk necessary to the placing of an elector's name on the voters' list. This provision is rendered needful by the practice of Election Agents making applications wholesale without being particular, in many cases, whether the names are eligible or not. And in many cases the Registration Clerk is not over scrupulous if they are on his side of politics. Sometimes it is difficult for those legally qualified to get their names on the list if their views are known to be opposed to those of the Clerks, perhaps appointed by the government on account of their extreme partizanship. This is done by the Clerk omitting to enter their names on the Register, so when election day comes the voter finds he is not on the voters list, or, if he discovers it beforehand he has to attend the Court of Revision which he may be unable to do. Personal registration would prevent any dishonesty on the part of the Clerk. At the Office the applicant would be compelled to make an affidavit as to his qualifications when the Clerk would give him a certificate of registration similar to the following :—

No   Electoral Division of   Date
This is to certify that A. B. of   having complied with the statute governing the same, was this day placed on the list of Electors for the Electoral Division of
Signed.
Registration Clerk.

As it might be impossible or difficult for some to apply personally at the office, they could make their affidavit before a magistrate or J. P. who would send it by registered mail to the Registration Clerk together with stamps to pay postage. The Clerk would send the certificate by return mail to the appplicant. This would meet exceptional cases, but as the applicant would be at the expense of postage both ways and magistrates fee it would not become the practice. At the polling booth the voter before he received his ballot would have to produce his certificate which would prevent the personation often practised. The certificate would then be stamped on the back by the Deputy Returning Officer, stamp to bear date and class of eiection (this to prevent the certificate from being used again at the same election by another person) and then it would be returned to the voter.

The ballot before being handed to the voter would be stamped in the same manner so as to prevent the collusion sometimes practised ; for when the voter has been bribed, to ensure that he "stays bought," a counterfeit ballot, already marked, is given to the voter before he enters the booth ; this one is returned to the Returning Officer instead of the genuine ballot which is given to the briber as a proof of their mutual perfidy.

The appointing of the Returning Officers and Registration Clerks by a party government when strong partizans are always chosen has been the cause of much dishonesty and corruption, for these officials have opportunity to take an undue advantage of their position with little danger of detection. This consideration has led me to propose the formation of a " High Court of Election," such as appears in the second section of the accompanying act, the composition of which would command the respect of the whole Electorate.

No matter how Parliament might be divided the minority would have the same power in the Court as the majority while the three neutral members would ensure that no party could control it. This is no doubt an innovation and perhaps in the annexed " Act " in its crude state, but I am sure that the principle will commend itself to fair-minded people. If it does that, improvement can follow, it would at least remove the stigma of partizanism, whether merited or unmerited, from the Executive Government.

Another point where injustice is perpetrated is in cities, or manufacturing centres, where it is in the power of the employers to prevent their workmen from going to the polls or at least those whom they know to be of different politics. There are many ways this can be done without a positive command ; stress of work is the usual excuse and the employce dare not disobey as it would be met by instant dismissal. To obviate this in many European countries the elections are held on Sunday, but as this is liable to lead to desecration of the Sabbath I would have the day on which the General Election was to be held proclaimed a Public Holiday, or at least half the day on which all work in factories &c. would be suspended.

A plan for Electoral Representation to work satisfactorily must harmonize with the following propositions :—That the majority of Parliament represent the majority of the Electors. That the minority of the electors have a proportionate voice in Parliament. That every vote should have its due weight in securing this result. That the ordinary elector can easily comprehend and practise the system of voting. With these objects in view the writer proposes the plan of measuring the voting power of each member by the actual number of votes received thus securing the principle of a member representing the actual number of electors who vote for him. Of course the number of members would be increased by this plan, but an excessive number would be prevented by the provision that limits a seat in the House to those receiving a number equal to 20 per cent. or more, of the vote cast in their Electoral Division. If the number of members is an objection it could be met by reducing the number of Electoral Divisions, which in any event might prove beneficial, but I apprehend no difficulty on that account. Meritorious broad-minded candidates would offer themselves for the suffrages of the people and be elected where under the present system they would be *snowed under* by narrow-minded partizans with nothing to recommend them but slavish adherence to party. With reference to the relation of Parliament to the executive government it should be an understood principle for the Representative of the Sovereign to appoint as Prime Minister a member whom the House of Commons would by resolution designate as worthy of the position.

Further that the fact of a measure introduced or supported by the Government being defeated should not have to be followed by their resignation. Rather than face the prospect of defeat, the Government will often withhold beneficial legislation. On the other hand measures of very doubtful utility become law through their supporters not desiring to defeat them by voting against the Government and causing a new election or possibly a dead-lock which would render all practical legislation difficult if not impossible. To remedy this I would have a direct vote of want of confidence necessary to the resignation of a Government, a general election would not then be necessary, but the member in whom the House voted *confidence* would be intrusted with the administration.

It might be advisable, eventually, to extend the choice of the electors so as to allow them to give original votes for candidates in any part of the country, but perhaps for the present the act goes far enough in that direction. The Act will at least do away with *Gerrymandering* and the distrust often felt in the public mind, whenever a change is made by the administration in the boundaries, &c., and it would ensure each elector having his actual weight through his representative in the councils of the nation. In conclusion the writer ventures to hope that the general features of his plan will meet with the approval of those who wish for some improvement in the realm of politics. Imperfections there no doubt are, and to his ignorance of the legal form of legislative enactments must be attributed any errors in the accompanying draft, but in his humble opinion any difficulties that might be encountered in the working of his plan, could be easily surmounted.

SPERO MELIORA.

ELECTION ACT.

An Act for the better conduct of Elections and the choosing of Members of Parliament.

PREAMBLE.

Whereas it is expedient that provision should be made for the equitable representation of the people in Parliament and as such is not done under the Act at present in force :— Therefore Her Majesty by and with the consent of the Senate and House of Commons of Canada enacts as follows :—

INTERPRETATION.

1. This Act shall apply to all Elections held in the Dominion of Canada for the purpose of electing members to represent the people in the Dominion House of Commons; and this Act may be cited as the "Dominion Elections Act" and the following terms therein shall be held to have the meaning hereinafter assigned them unless such meaning be repugnant to the subject, or inconsistent with the context that is to say :—

(1). The term *Electoral District* means a district within certain defined bounds, the Electors of which return one or more members to Parliament. (2). The term *Elector* means a citizen entitled to vote. (3). The term *High Court of Election* means the Court where the result of the Election in each division is ascertained and the votes apportioned to the candidates entitled to them. (4). The term *Parliament* means the aggregation of members forming the Dominion House of Commons. (5). The term *Returning Officer* means the official appointed in each division to receive the nominations of Candidates, and the results of the polls from the Deputy Returning Officers. (6). The term *Deputy Returning Officer* means the official who presides over the poll at each polling place in the Division. (7). The term *Candidate* means a person who offers himself for election to Parliament. (8). The term *Member* means a person duly elected to Parliament. (9). The term *Section* means a section of this Act with a separate number, *sub-section* means a clause with a separate number or letter in smaller type.

THE HIGH COURT OF ELECTION.

2. The High Court of Election shall be charged with the supreme control and management of Elections to Parliament. (1.) The High Court of election shall be com

posed of seven members, as follows :—Four members of the House of Commons of Canada, one member of the Senate, and two judges of the Supreme Court of Canada. (2.) These shall be chosen in the following manner :—Two members of Parliament will be elected by a majority vote of the whole House of Commons, then two more will be elected by those who were in the minority at the previous division, alone. (3.) The four members so electd shall then choose a member of the Senate of Canada upon whom they can unanimously agree. (4.) The five members shall then choose two Judges of the Supreme Court who must also meet with the unanimous approval of the five members. (5.) The seven members so chosen shall constitute the High Court of Election of Canada.

3. Should any person chosen a member of the High Court of Election under the provisions of the preceding section after receiving a legal notification refuse to act in that capacity without giving a satisfactory reason for doing so, he shall be liable to a fine not exceeding   dollars and a substitute shall be elected in the manner provided under Sec. 2.

4. The members shall act for one year and be eligible to be again chosen.

5. After taking a prescribed oath the members when sitting in their official capacity shall have the full power of Judges on the bench as to the subpœnaing of witnesses, &c., on all matters within their jurisdiction.

DUTIES OF HIGH COURT OF ELECTION.

6. It shall be the duty of the High Court of Election to appoint the Returning Officer for each Electoral Division. (1). To keep records of all the candidates nominated previous to an election. (2). To finally apportion the ballots cast for the candidates and declare those elected together with the voting power of each member. (3). Finally adjudicate all appeals and disputed returns.

7. At least sixty days before the date fixed for an election the High Court of Election shall notify the Returning Officer in every electoral division of the date of the Election, which in a General Election shall be the same day in every Electoral Division, the said day to be a Public Holiday, by Proclamation of the Governor General. (1). On the receipt of the writ and notification, the Returning Officer shall appoint deputies to take the vote of the people, a Deputy for every polling place in the division. (2). It shall also be the duty of the Returning Officer to post up in a conspicuous place in the town or village where he will make his head-quarters during the Election (which shall be as centrally located in the Division as possible) a Public Notice giving the date of Election, and places where polls will be opened, also the dates and where nominations will be received, together with the Proclamation of Public Holiday. (3). The Returning Officer shall also send a copy of the Notice and Proclamation to each Deputy Returning Officer who shall post them up in a conspicuous part of the polling booth.

NOMINATION OF CANDIDATES.

8. Any citizen qualified to vote at an Election for members of Parliament, may be nominated as candidate for the said office in any Electoral Division in the Dominion. (1). The nomination must be in writing in the following form :—

Address and date

I hereby nominate (here put name address and occupation or profession of proposed candidate) as candidate for member of Parliament for the Electoral Division of and I consider the said (name) a fit and proper person for the position. (2). The nomination must be signed by, at least, five of the electors residing in the Electoral Division for which the candidate is nominated. (3). An acceptance of the nomination, signed by the candidate, must be endorsed thereon. (4). The nomination shall be deposited with the Returning Officer for the said Electoral Division not more than forty or less than thirty days before the date fixed for the Election. (5). There shall also be deposited with the nomination whatever sum in legal money of Canada, Parliament may by law direct, for which the Returning Officer shall give a legal receipt. (6). No candidate can offer himself for election in more than one division.

9. The Returning Officer shall immediately on receiving all the nominations for his division, send a certified copy of them, together with the deposits, to the secretary of the

High Court of Election and he, within ten days after the receipt thereof shall send a printed list with the names and addresses of all the candidates nominated in all the Electoral Divisions of Canada to every candidate, also Returning Officer, and Deputy Returning Officer in the Dominion, whose duty it shall be to post it up in a conspicuous position at each polling place. (1). Every candidate shall then make a sworn declaration before a Magistrate or Justice of the Peace, setting forth the candidate which may be any nominated in the Dominion of Canada to whom he wishes the votes cast for himself to be counted in the event of his failing to secure the number of votes necessary to his return, except the elector directs differently as provided by Sec. 10. (2). The candidate shall then send the declaration to the Returning Officer, who shall cause copies of it to be printed and sent to every Deputy Returning Officer in the division whose duty it shall be to post it up in a conspicuous place at every polling booth in the electoral division, at least six days before the election.

THE ELECTION OF CANDIDATES.

10. The ballots to be used at an election shall have the names of all the candidates legally nominated for the electoral division printed thereon, and opposite to each that of the alternative candidate mentioned in sec. 9, sub-sec. 1, as in the following form :—

Electoral Division of

INSTRUCTIONS TO VOTERS.

Names of Candidates.	Mark an X in this column, opposite the name of the candidate for whom you desire to vote.	The persons named below will receive the votes cast for the candidate opposite their respective names, should the said candidate not receive the number necessary to his return unless the voter otherwise directs, as hereinafter provided.
. . . .		
. . . .		
. . . .		
. . . .		
. . . .		If the alternative candidate opposite the name of the candidate voted for does not meet with the approval of the elector he can write the name and address of any candidate nominated in the Dominion, in the space below to whom his vote will be transferred.
		Name
		Address of candidate.

(1). At the polling booth each candidate can be represented by an agent or scrutineer appointed at least three days before the election under written authority of the candidate. (2). Such Agent or Scrutineer must be an elector in the Electoral Division. (3). The duties of the Agent or Scrutineer are, to exercise a general supervision over the election in the interest of his candidate so as to prevent any unfairness being practised. (4). Each Elector must present the certificate of Registration as provided in the Act for the Registration of voters, on the certificate being found satisfactory the Deputy Returning Officer shall stamp it on the back with a stamp bearing date and class of election, it shall then be returned to the elector. (5). The Deputy Returning Officer shall then, in the presence of the scrutineers, hand a blank ballot paper to the elector, after stamping it on the back as directed for the certificate in the preceding sub-section. (6). The elector shall then take the ballot to a part of the booth entirely secluded from observation, and after marking it shall fold it in such a manner as to leave the stamp exposed but prevent any person from seeing how it was marked without unfolding it. The Elector shall then hand the ballot to the Deputy Returning Officer who in the presence of the Elector and Scrutineers, shall without opening it, drop the ballot into the ballot-box which must be made of some incombustible material,

11. When the poll is closed the Deputy Returning Officer shall unlock the ballot-box and count the number of votes cast for each candidate. (1). After the ballots are counted they shall be placed in the ballot-box together with a declaration signed by the Deputy Returning Officer, and the Scrutineer of each candidate as to the number of votes cast for each. (2). The Deputy Returning Officer shall then give a similar statement to each Scrutineer. (3). The ballot-box shall then be securely locked and sealed. It shall then be the duty of the Deputy Returning Officer to take the ballot-box to the Returning Officer for the Electoral Division.

12. The Returning Officer on receiving all the ballot-boxes for the Electoral Division shall, in the presence of the scrutineers appointed under the provisions of (1), or of the candidates themselves, break the seals, unlock the ballot-boxes and proceed to count the ballots cast for each candidate. (1). When all are counted the Returning Officer shall write a statement of the result, said statement to contain the total number of votes cast for each candidate, together with the names of those to whom they were to be transferred as provided by sections 15, 16, and 17. (2). The form of statement shall be as follows :—

Electoral Division of   (Date)
Result of Election held on the   for the Election of members to the
Parliament of Canada.   I,   R. O. for the E. D. of   do
solemnly declare the following is a true statement of the votes cast on the above-mentioned date.

Names of Candidate	No. of votes cast for him.	The name or names of Candidates to whom they are to be counted if the original candidate does not receive 20 per cent. of the total votes cast in the E. D. either originally or by transference.	No. of votes to be counted to each.

and so on till all the result is given.

Signed   Returning Officer.
Names of witnesses, who are to be the candidates or their agents.

(3). This declaration must be made before a legally qualified magistrate or J. P. (4). This declaration must be deposited in the Office of the Clerk of the County Court for the Electoral Division, and a certified copy sent to the Secretary of the High Court of Election by the Returning Officer within three days thereafter.

13. Should there be any ballots marked in such a manner as to render the meaning of the voter doubtful or if the scrutineers cannot agree as to the candidate in whose favor it should be counted, the Returning Officer shall not count such ballots to any candidate, but shall make a note of the fact on the declaration mentioned in Sec. 12, Sub. Sec. (1.) and shall send all such ballots to the High Court of Election with such declaration.

14. The Secretary on receipt of the returns from every Electoral Division shall lay them before the High Court of Election who shall then proceed to ascertain the candidates elected together with the voting power of each : this will be accomplished in the following manner :—The Electoral Divisions will be taken in alphabetical order.   The name of the candidate or candidates who have received 20 per cent. or over, of the total vote polled in their respective Electoral Divisions, will be placed on a schedule as elected, together with the number of votes polled for each candidate so elected.

15. The candidates who may have failed to receive 20 per cent. of the total votes polled in their respective Electoral Divisions will then be considered in the same order of divisions. Any candidate who can make up with the assistance of the votes transferred to him from other candidates who failed to receive the required 20 per cent. or number of votes equalling 20 per cent. shall be placed on the schedule as elected, together with the number of votes, either original or transferred, cast for him.

16. Should two candidates who failed to receive the 20 per cent. quota be mutually mentioned as the alternative of each other on their respective ballots, the votes shall be counted to whichever candidate received the highest number of original votes.

17. If any candidate is unable to secure a number equal to 20 per cent. of the total vote cast in his Electoral Division, either by transference or otherwise, he shall be considered to have failed of Election, and the votes cast for him shall be counted to the candidate or candidates mentioned as alternative, and if the alternative is not elected they shall be counted to his alternative and so on till they are disposed of to a candidate elected.

18. The total number of votes standing to the credit of the members elected after the final apportionment, under the preceding section shall be their voting power in Parliament.

19. Each candidate elected shall be furnished by the High Court of Election with a certificate of such election and the number of votes received by him, which will be entered in the Journals of the House of Commons and be *prima facie* evidence of the member's voting power in Parliament.

20. All sums received under the provisions of Sec. 8, Sub-sec. (3), shall be returned to the candidates depositing them, unless any candidate failed to receive a number of votes equal to 10 per cent. of the total vote cast in his Electoral Division, in which case the amount deposited by him shall be forfeited to the Consolidated Revenue Fund.

21. In all divisions in the House of Commons each member shall vote the number of votes credited to him, and the side on any division which has the highest aggregate number of votes shall be considered a majority of the House.

22. The members shall be elected for two years.

23. Any vacancies through death shall not be filled unless the Electoral Division would be entirely unrepresented and the next General Elections are more than six months distant, and a session of Parliament is to be held between the election of a successor and the General Election, in which case a writ will be issued. (1). All bye-elections shall be held under the provisions of sec. 8, 10, 11, and 12, and thirty days after the issuance of the writ. (2). The Returning Officer shall send the declaration of result of election, direct to the Speaker of the House of Commons, and the candidate polling the highest vote shall take his seat in the House and vote according to the number of votes received by him.

24. All the expenses sustained by officials, candidates and members in complying with the provisions of this Act shall be reimbursed to them by the Government on the validity of the claim being proven.

25. The members of Parliament shall be paid whatever indemnity for their services Parliament may by law direct.

AMENDMENT TO SEC. 8.

Should only one nomination be received under the provisions of Sec. 8, the Returning Officer shall declare said candidate elected, and his vote in the House shall be half the total voting power of that Division.

SPERO MELIORA.

CANADIAN HOME RULE AND AMENDMENTS THERETO.

In suggesting a system of government that will give to the people of Canada equal representation and offer a feasible substitute for the present system of party government, it may be as well to consider the principles of the present system and glance at its origin and the results that have accrued to nations by which it has been adopted.

Party government seems to have arisen in England during the reign of William III., and in the time of Queen Anne it is found as a settled system of government in that country. England emerging from semi-despotism gladly turned to party government as a system promising a measure of freedom never before enjoyed, and a remedy for many evils she was then enduring. Other nations seem to have followed in the footsteps of England in this respect, until all the civilized countries of the world have framed their schemes of government more or less on the principles of "Party Rule;" but in these latter days the system has become corrupt—it has shackled the people it was intended to free, and is now the dangerous cause of an injurious effect. As a cure for the evils it was intended to remedy it has lost its efficacy, and as it has outlasted its day of usefulness it must at no distant day give place to new methods. England and Canada are not alone a prey to political corruption; both compare favorably with other nations in this respect. In France, Italy, Germany, and Russia, the exposures that from time to time take place, demonstrate but too clearly that party government has fostered in spite of the formidable power vested in the executive of those countries, a spirit of corruption that imperatively demands the sternest measures for its suppression and the protection of the people. If we turn to the great republic that borders our southern frontier we will perceive a similar condition of affairs. A recent writer on this subject says :—" By electing to office through the agency of party organizations, and subjecting to the domination of such organizations, and to the temptations to bribery and corruption, great numbers of politicians of pliable consciences and easy virtue and many of bad or doubtful character, the legislation of the country, all the departments of the national, state, and city governments, and nearly all branches of the public service have been more or less corrupted." In every direction, wherever we may turn, the pernicious influence of party government manifests itself. Speaking of our African colonies Lord Wolseley writing in March, 1886, says :— "The squabbles between party politicians in South Africa, who are more intent upon personal aggrandizement than the good of the people have hitherto prevented the adoption of any good scheme for the colonization of that vast country." Turning again to Canada we find that government by party is not and cannot be compatible with government for the people, and this fact has been forcibly demonstrated in the past, and is written on many pages of Canadian history. The principle upon which party government is organized is antagonistic to government by and for the people. The interests of party take precedence of the people's interests, and the identity of the nominally responsible minister is absorbed in the personality of the party leader. The party leader is maintained in office by the party combination, and the functions, authority and patronage of the office are applied to securing a party majority in the country or in parliament. Under no other system possible in Canada at the present day, could such transactions have taken place as those that have within the past two years occupied the attention of parliament and the several Royal Commissions; and the notorious expenditure of money for the unavowed purpose of influencing the return of members to the House of Commons, who in exchange for their seats were expected to give an undeviating support to the party interests, is not so much a circumstance to entail blame upon individuals as to call down unqualified condemnation on a system that renders such tactics available. In the different constituencies of Canada we have party organizations, clubs, and conventions, under party leaders subsidized directly or indirectly by the party government for party purposes, dividing the people politically and socially into hostile camps. We have an array of party managers, supporters, and hangers-on, to whom contracts must be given at extravagant rates, timber limits and crown lands sold at a nominal price, an army of incompetent persons on whom positions of emolument must be conferred in reward for party services ; and the same principles pervading as they do almost every branch of the public service, offer to our contemplation the lamentable spectacle of our public affairs year after year being carried on in a manner that would not be tolerated for a day, by any member of the administration in the conduct of his private business. The advocates of party government may contend that the abuses incidental to the system are not properly chargeable to the principles of the system ; but such contention is erroneous as the abuses are inherent in the system and generate and fester in it. Personal ambition and aggrandizement—the motives of the abuses—form the very life and essence of the system, and the most strenuous opposition that will ever be offered to the rectification of Parliament will emanate from those whose schemes of personal advancement and aggrandizement are most seriously menaced.

In order to devise a feasible scheme as a substitute for party government let it be considered what results it is intended to attain.

First.—The Franchise law must be amended so as to give to the whole people of Canada equal representation, so far as it is possible that such a result can be practically obtained.

Second. —The Election law must be entirely reconstructed so as to adapt its provisions to the amended franchise law, and to simplify the present elaborate procedure with a view to efficiency and economy.

Third.—Parliament must be so rectified as to place the members thereof in a position of complete independence and secure their permanent emancipation from party rule.

Fourth.—The official positions held by the ministers of the government must be bolished, and their functions transferred to a group of departments constituted in an unchangeable formation as corporate bodies.

In constructing a system that will secure to the people of Canada equal representation, it must be borne in mind that we are working on a line that has anarchy at the one extremity and despotism at the other, and that a strong administration effectively responsible to the people will only be attained by selecting a medium between the two extremes. Care must be taken on the one hand not to weaken and cripple the executive by unduly increasing the powers and functions of the deliberative body, and on the other hand the same caution must be exercised to avoid strengthening the administrative body by surrendering the rights of the people. In more than one instance nations on reaching the limits of endurance at the one extreme, have been driven to the other. The autocracy of Louis XVI. was followed by the revolution which represented anarchy in a brutal and unreasoning form. The anarchy of republican France gave place to the despotism of Bonaparte, to be succeeded at last by the constitutional government under a legitimate monarchy. In England during the latter days of the commonwealth under the parliamentary rule, the military anarchy that followed upon the death of Cromwell prepared the way for the reaction that led to the restoration of the House of Stuart, a despotism finally superseded by a constitutional government under William and Mary. The danger of autocracy with us has passed away and it is only the despotism of party government that we have to fear, while from many causes the danger from anarchy and socialism is vastly increased. The monarchies of Europe tardily acknowledged the principle that the king reigned but the administration governed—the principle to be recognized in the future is that the king may reign, but the people shall rule. Under such a principle the danger from anarchy and socialism is in no wise reduced, but may readily be vastly increased by a system embracing unlimited or universal suffrage ; and yet in constructing a system of representation applicable to the Dominion of Canada the principle of universal suffrage must be kept in view as no system intended to still further extend the already liberal provisions of the law can be framed without embracing that principle. The present franchise law extending as it does to those possessing a mere nominal property quali ication, to qualification by income, to fishermen, and to farmers' and owners' sons, so closely approaches the principle of universal suffrage, as to make it a difficult matter to suggest a more liberal measure without removing all limitations. And yet certain limitations are imperatively necessary, for without them the parliamentary representation would be largely controlled by the anarchist and socialist element and cease to represent the capital, the property, and the industry of the nation.

The scheme now submitted for consideration recognizes this position, and admits the principle of universal suffrage subject to certain disqualifications. The right to vote is limited to all British subjects, either by birth or naturalization who have been residents in Canada for one year—are of the age of 21 years, and can read and write in their native language. The exceptions consist of five classes, women under coverture, aliens, paupers, persons of unsound mind and persons twice convicted of felony.

In limiting the franchise to British subjects of full age the provisions of the present franchise law are followed, and as to the limitation to persons resident in the Dominion for a given period and possessed of some education, no reasonable objection can be urged, while much can be suggested in its favor. Some educational qualification must of necessity be required of an electoral body to whom is intrusted the important privilege of discriminating between a beneficial and an injurious policy. The right to so discriminate is based on the fact, that the general policy of the country is born of its internal necessities, its foreign relations and its financial, commercial, and geographical conditions, and no matter what political party may hold the reins of power, they are largely controlled by such general policy, and any essential deviation from that policy will ultimately involve the country in disaster. Hence, we find that no matter what peculiar lines of policy one party or the other may hold out to the people, those peculiar lines must be totally or partially abandoned, altered or varied if inconsistent with the policy of the nation, and the latter faithfully and intelligently pursued if a successful administration of public affairs is to be expected. The policy of the country (in contradistinction to party policy) is the policy of the people and should be initiated by the people who constitute the source from whence the legislative authority is derived, otherwise each elector would not have due weight in the government of the country. The policy of a party government is the policy of the leaders of the majority only, and may be initiated and carried into effect without the consent, approbation or knowledge of the people, unless indeed they have appealed to the electors on the policy previous to its adoption. If not it must be ratified or condemned by parliament at some subsequent time as circumstances and results may warrant, and if the policy should prove injurious to the interests of the country, no redress is within the power of the people except the removal of the party from office which has more than once been found an impracticable remedy when the government has been safely entrenched behind the votes of a partisan majority. But a policy conceived among the people, discussed on the public platform, debated in parliament, and finally repudiated or made law, as the case might be, would be dealt with in the interests of the people, and to serve the necessities of the country, without any regard to the special requirements of any party or faction. The limitation to persons resident in Canada for one year will practically exclude no one whose interests and sympathies are identical with those of our people, and will be found a necessary precaution—for situated as we are adjoining a colossal and populous foreign state - we would be open to the danger of having at the polls a class of voters—who, although resident beyond our frontiers—would yet claim the rights of electors as nominal British Subjects, but whose want of personal interest in our prosperity and knowledge of our affairs, would render them open to corrupt influence, and a dangerous element in the hands of ambitious or unscrupulous men. Aliens, paupers, and persons of unsound mind are exceptions recognized by the franchise law at the present time, and the same arguments that weighed with the legislature in framing that law must equally apply to the same exceptions now suggested. The admission of women to vote can hardly be discussed without entering on the question of " Womens' Rights ;" but their right to vote cannot be consistently ignored without departing from the principle of universal suffrage ; but the exception of women under coverture is undoubtedly advisable, because the interests of husband and wife being mutual a double vote would practically be conferred on one person.

The franchise law so amended would confer on the whole people of Canada the right to vote subject to the above exceptions which is the first step towards securing equal representation in parliament.

The election law must be amended with a view to relieve the procedure from the complicated machinery that at present exists, created partly for the purpose of preventing fraud at elections, and partly in order to secure some practical advantage to the party in power, and it should also be amended with a view to greater economy, which the abolition of property qualification would render both practicable and advisable. All matters connected with the representation of the people in parliament ought to be brought into closer relationship with the people and to a greater extent confided to their care and management ; therefore the scheme suggested imposes upon the municipal authorities of each electoral district a large share of the work at the electoral contests. The municipal authorities being directly elected by the local electors are in sympathy with them, and conversant with their local interests, and requirements, and would offer a better guarantee to the country that the electoral contests would be held in accordance with the true intent and spirit of the law, than would be the case, were the proceedings left to the manipulation of nominees of the government who would more likely look to the interests of the government than to securing a free and independent expression of public opinion.

In accordance with this idea it is suggested that the municipal council of every electoral district should cause the sworn assessors of each polling district to annually prepare a schedule of the names, ages, residence and nationality of every qualified voter in the polling district, a work that could be easily and effectually accomplished by such assessors at the time they assess the real and personal property in the district, as they are supposed to go, and generally do go, from house to house and farm to farm for such purpose. The Municipal Council would also be required to appoint a Recorder of Voters for each polling district to whom the schedule so prepared by the assessors would be delivered, and who would enter the same in a register to be provided for that purpose open for public inspection and subject to revision from time to time. The election of delegates to the Electoral Chamber would be conducted by the Recorder of Voters in each polling district, subject to the revision if necessary of the Municipal Council; and the Wardens of the Counties, and Mayors of the Towns and Cities, constituting electoral districts would be ex-officio returning officers at every parliamentary election. This method would reduce the expense of each election to the smallest amount consistent with the efficient performance of the work required, and as the cost would become a municipal, instead of a national charge, and the proceedings of the most simple form, the best results might be expected from an economical point of view. As the system of voting at present in operation would be found unsuitable in dealing with so numerous an electoral body as any scheme of universal suffrage would enfranchise, it is proposed, that the direct vote of the electors should be polled in a manner somewhat similar to that adopted at municipal elections, and confined to the election of local delegates to represent the several polling districts of the constituency, at the sessions of the Electoral Chamber. The limitation of the direct vote of the people to the election of their local delegates would be advisable for a further reason, that it would go far to prevent such a combination by party organizations as would materially influence the ultimate result of the election, and the delegates being presidents of the polling district, socially and politically known to the voters of the district, would be selected as presumably in sympathy with the policy and interests of the people.

No system whereby the whole people of Canada would have equal representation can be conceived, even theoretically, if it is defined to mean the representation of each and every individual elector and his private and peculiar opinions on each and every subject, nor can election by the majority be avoided until all persons can be brought to think alike, and no practicable system can be suggested to give both the majority and minority due weight in the government of the country; unless equal representation is defined to mean the represescentation of the social, commercial and political interests of the people, instead of the peculiar opinions of the individual voter. One voter at an election might give the preference to a particular candidate because he belonged to the same religious denomination, and two others vote for the successful candidate because he advocated the true interests of the country; yet the first voter would be in the minority because his preferential candidate had not been elected, but would be in the majority because his true interests would be represented. It seems clear that election by lot would fail to practically solve the problem, as the lot might fall, and frequently would fall to the candidate who represented the minority and then the majority would be disfranchised; but nevertheless it has been partially adopted in the present scheme in the event of a tie.

As an approximate solution of this problem, it is proposed that the local delegates at the meeting of the Electoral Chamber should nominate such candidates as they consider fit and proper persons to represent the constituency in the House of Commons, not exceeding one for each polling district, and the names of such candidates would be entered on the record of the proceedings. A ballot for the whole number of candidates would then be taken—and after the ballots for each have been counted, the name of the candidate having received the lowest number of votes would be struck from the list of names on the Record. A ballot would then be taken for second choice, and the ballots counted, and the name with the lowest number struck out as before—and so the balloting would continue until the requisite number of candidates alone remained on the Record who would be declared duly elected.

By this system—in theory—those whose names were struck from the record—not having obtained a unanimous vote—would have ceased to be candidates, while those that remained on the record would be unanimously elected as there would then be no candidate remaining in opposition to them. Practically, although the individual preferences of the delegates were not represented by the election of the successful candidate, yet the representation of the interests of the country—through the election of the successful candidates —would be secured. In the event of an equality of votes occurring between two candidates, the two delegates who had made the respective nominations would decide by lot which of the two names should be struck from the Record.

Parliament is supposed to be summoned for deliberation by the sovereign at any time or place their presence may be required. In early ages we find the kings of England commanding the lords spiritual and temporal to meet in council and at a subsequent period the loyal towns and cities of the realm were called upon to send burgesses to represent their several boroughs in parliament. The towns and cities had obtained many important privileges and immunities from successive sovereigns, who distrusting the loyalty and sincerity of the nobilty, sought to obtain through the burgesses and commons, the means of opposing the encroachments of the great factions, and to secure pecuniary support for the tottering throne; among other privileges granted to the towns and cities was immunity from taxation,—other than the farm-rent of the borough,—except by their own free consent. Hence the necessity for their representation in parliament; and the members of the community who were chosen to represent the borough, were selected for their ability to watch over and guard the interests of their special locality. The representatives of the people in parliament at the present day have a wider range of duties to perform, and national and foreign questions to decide; but it must not be forgotten that the obligation to watch over and guard the interests of their special localities binds them as strongly to-day as it did when first the burgesses of England gathered in the halls at Westminster, although local interests ought to give way to class interests, and class interests to national. To enable the representatives of the people to faithfully fulfil their obligations, and to deal with the interests of their respective localities, and the national, the foreign and the financial questions that affect the prosperity of the country, they must be placed in a position of absolute independence, free from any influence, interference or coercion that might tend to control their actions; and protected from all criticism and animadversion upon the course they might think proper to pursue. By so protecting the members of the House of Commons and rendering parliament no longer the arena of party strife, and the path to individual aggrandizement, a class of representatives would be attracted to the public service, patriots and statesmen in the best acceptation of the term, who having no views of personal ambition to serve would, for the love of country seek only the welfare and prosperity of the people. This result can be accomplished in no way except by the adoption by parliament of a system of secret voting, and therefore the scheme now suggested embraces the extension of the vote by ballot to the proceedings of the House of Commons.

The adoption by parliament of secret voting would doubtless meet with much opposition, but it would likewise meet with the approbation of the best and most honorable class of our politicians, because it would operate as a complete emancipation of the members of the House from subserviency to party rule, and it cannot be denied that members of the House have frequently found themselves much embarrassed by their obligation to support the party measures at the sacrifice of their personal opinions and the interests of their constituents. This was exemplified during the passage of the late Act to readjust the representation in the House of Commons, and the discussions on the tariff. All religious and temperance questions, are fruitful in examples of the equivocal position members are forced to assume, when the party policy clashes with their conscientious convictions, whereas if the votes of the House were taken by ballot instead of in the present form, those members would be at liberty to vote according to their own judgment untrammelled by any consideration as to the effect their vote might have on the party supremacy, for with secret voting party government would be at an end. Secret voting would also curtail the debates to no inconsiderable extent. At present the long and useless discussions that daily take place in parliament are largely attributable to the fact, that members feel themselves bound to find some apologetic or fictitious reason for supporting the party measures in opposition to the manifest wishes of those they profess to represent. By secret voting the will of the people would find expression in the House to an extent that could be obtained by no other means, and parliament would be placed in a position to deal with many vital questions in a manner unapproachable by the best form of party government. The question of reciprocal trade so essential to some of the provinces would be dealt with, the question of prohibition would be decided upon its merits. The labor question containing two antagonistic elements—Capital holding to its vested rights, and labor proclaiming in no uncertain tone its undisputable right to fair pay for hard work—all these questions, and others as important would call for settlement, but never can they be satisfactorily settled under a party government. But under such a representative government as the secret voting would create, screened by the ballot from intimidation, importunity and coercion, these questions and others as conflicting would be dealt with in such a manner as to cause many of the difficulties to disappear, and the complications incidental to the present situation would be so adjusted as to effect an equitable and feasible solution of these apparently insoluble problems. Is it not a lamentable sight to behold, almost one half the members of the House—some of the ablest men in Canada—occupying a position worse than useless, and a large proportion of the remainder degraded into human machinery for keeping a dozen or more men in office, bolstering up the policy and schemes of the office holders, while those in opposition waste their breath in ineffectual protestations? Such a sight would no longer dishearten the people, were secret voting adopted as the penal clauses embodied in the present scheme, would protect the members from the influence of corrupt men and the freedom and independence thus secured to the representatives, would fill the seats of the House with honest, able and disinterested politicians and enable them to work effectively and harmoniously in the interests of the country. That those results would naturally follow the adoption of the penal clauses is too obvious to admit of dispute, because so long as there remained one member of the House who adhered to the principle represented by those clauses, it would be a hazardous matter for any combination of members to attempt a violation or an evasion of the law. Such a clause may be ridiculed for making it penal to simply ask a member how he intended to vote, but such a question—simple though it might be—would pave the way for other questions, and as it is the object of the clause to prevent any attempt whatever being made—directly or indirectly—to tamper with the secrecy of the ballot, it is quite clear that the most effective way of accomplishing the end in view is the adoption of such a clause. Besides the penal clause is not intended in anywise to limit or restrict the free discussion of all questions and issues during the parliamentary debates. It is also considered advisable that the duration of each parliament should be limited to three years, as it is important that a frequent appeal to the people should be compulsory.

In the present government of Canada we have a certain number of ministers supposed to be the advisers of the crown—a harmless fiction as they generally act for the crown on their own responsibility. Actually they are the heads of the several departments of the public service, and holding as they generally do the same political opinions and having the same party interests, they endeavour to conduct the business of their respective departments in harmony with the views of the combined administration. Although they are responsible to parliament as a ministerial body, yet parliament has little or no control over them as far as relates to their official functions. The department is merely the bureau of the minister, and he is autocratic in the management of the business of the country so far as it concerns his particular department. The officials of the department are merely the servants of the minister; and the contracts, perquisites and emoluments in its gift, form the patronage of the minister and his party. The ministry as a body owe their position to the party they belong to, and the leaders of the party although they may not be either in the ministry or in parliament are practically supreme rulers of the country so long as their party has a majority in the House. The ministers are supposed to be responsible to parliament for their official acts, but in reality they are responsible to no one so long as their majority can be maintained. When that majority from any cause has been reduced to a minority the ministry is forced to resign their position, and another party government take control of the departments, with a different policy and different opinions and interests. Such changes of administration cannot fail to disturb the working of departments so constituted, and to operate injuriously on the business of the country.

By abolishing the system of party rule through the adoption of secret voting in the House of Commons, a government organised as at present would be ineffective, and as it would be impolitic to cripple the executive in order to extend the power of the people, a different system must be found adapted to the different formation of the representative body. By the scheme now proposed each department would be constituted a corporate body, under the presidency of a "Director General" who would be appointed by, and be directly responsible to parliament. He would have no seat in the House of Commons, but would be required to communicate with and report to parliament on all occasions when necessary. The departments so constituted would have an unchangeable formation and be invested with all the powers and functions of the present ministers of the crown in permanent tenure. The House of Commons would elect by ballot three of its members for each department, to be called Councillors of State who would hold office during the pleasure of parliament, and those members so elected would constitute the executive council. The functions of the Councillors of State would be to represent their respective departments in the House of Commons, and to exercise an advisory superintendence over the business management, but without any controlling power—to advise the Executive Council as to the policy adopted by parliament, and to communicate to parliament the acts, opinions, and policy of the Executive Council. To communicate to the respective departments the views and requirements of the executive and to perform the duties and services now performed by members of the Privy Council. The Director General and officials of each department as a corporate body would have control of the internal economy and business affairs of the department subject to the supervision of parliament. They would submit to parliament the necessary estimates, make returns of expenditure and receipts, and perform the same duties and services now performed by the minister of the crown and other officials in relation to the affairs of the department. One Councillor of State for each department would retire each parliamentary year, and it would be competent for parliament by vote to remove at any time councillors or officials from their position if it was considered advisable so to do, and elect or appoint others in their place

The members of the Senate would be elected for life by the House of Commons. They would have no original legislative jurisdiction and would have no control over the proceedings or acts of parliament. They would possess judicial powers so far as such powers are adapted to the conditions and circumstances of the country and the people. All subjects for parliamentary enquiry, and matters at present referable under Royal Commission, would be submitted to the Members of the Senate by virtue of their inquisitorial jurisdiction, and questions of foreign and international policy would when necessary be referred to them for deliberation and advice.

The Executive Council would combine the functions and powers of the present Cabinet and Privy Council and would consist of the three Councillors of State for each department, and three members to be appointed by the Governor General who would be called Secretaries of State, but who would have no seats in the House of Commons. The Governor General would be ex-officio president of the Council, and a vice president would be elected by parliament to hold office for three years. He would represent the Executive Council in parliament and preside over the deliberations of the Council in the absence of the Governor General. It may be urged that with an Executive Council so constituted, composed perhaps of members holding different opinions, representing different classes and advocating different lines of policy, a degree of friction and misunderstanding would inevitably arise in the administrative body, seriously embarrassing the affairs of the country. But among other examples that can be found we have that of the Irish Synod as organized since the disestablishment of the Church of Ireland, composed of both clergy and laity, where "it was resolved from the first to keep the administration of its affairs clear of all party, religious, social or political differences, and for all to labour for the common good on the acknowledged principle, that if a member was able to do good service no question was to be raised as to what part he had taken in the debates of the Synod or what politics he had professed outside the House." If Ireland could produce men capable of enunciating and carrying into effect such principles, it may be reasonably presumed that Canada could do likewise.

In the present limited space it is impossible to follow this scheme through all its ramifications and details. Much would perhaps have to be changed before anything approaching perfection was attained, but as its defects became apparent under the critical analysis of those versed in the political science, and the experience of parliament brought to bear upon its defects, a more perfect system would be obtained. But nevertheless the scheme as presented suggests a system based on universal suffrage—an electorate represented by a delegate body in close sympathy with the people exercising the electoral franchise free from bribery and corruption, for the purpose of creating a parliament composed of able, honest and representative men. It suggests a parliament emancipated from party rule, factional strife, intimidation and ministerial control, through the adoption of an effective system of secret voting. It suggests a senate invested with judicial, inquisitorial and advisory jurisdiction, whose dignity and independence is secured by membership for life. It places the departments of the public service beyond the influence of political changes and the executive in harmony with the representatives of the people, without in any way decreasing the powers and authority of the Crown. Any scheme, in any degree calculated to attain these results might well occupy the attention of Canadian politicians.

"CANADIAN HOME RULE AND AMENDMENTS THERETO."

ACT RELATING TO THE ELECTORAL FRANCHISE AND THE ADMINISTRATION OF THE GOVERNMENT OF THE DOMINION OF CANADA.

PART I.—QUALIFICATION OF VOTERS.

1. All British subjects either by birth or naturalization who have been residents in Canada for one year and are of the age of 21 years, and can read and write in their native language shall be entitled to vote—except—

(a). Women under coverture.
(b). Aliens.
(c). Paupers.
(d). Persons of unsound mind.
(e). Persons twice convicted of any indictable offence.

2. Municipal Councils shall appoint a Recorder of Voters in each Polling District.

3. The Municipal Assessors in each Polling District shall at the time of making the annual property assessment enter on the Roll the name, age, occupation, nationality, and place of residence, of those persons who are qualified to vote and deliver to the Recorder of Voters on or before the 1st day of January in each year a certified list of the same.

4. The Recorder of Voters shall register such list in a book to be kept for that purpose, such register to be open for public inspection at all convenient times.

5. The register of voters shall be open from the 2nd day of January until the 1st day of February in each year, for the purpose of revision.

6. No person shall vote unless their name shall have been registered in the register of voters.

PROCEDURE AT ELECTIONS.

7. All persons offering for election as delegates to the Electoral Chamber shall be nominated in writing to be filed with the Recorder of Voters of the Polling District six days before the election.

8. Three Delegates shall be elected for each Polling District.

9. A Poll to be held if demanded.

10. Voting for Delegates to be by Ballot.

11. The Recorder of Voters in each Polling District shall certify to the Electoral Returning Officer the election of the several Delegates.

12. Any candidate for election as delegate, or the agent of any such candidate, or any person on his or their behalf, who shall canvass, solicit, or require, any voter or elector for any vote influence or support in or for any matter or thing relating to such election, shall be liable on conviction to a penalty in the discretion of the Court, but nothing herein contained shall be construed to limit, or restrict, the open and free discussion by the electors of all matters appertaining to any election, or relating to any political question or issue.

13. In the event of death or disability of any Delegate a Municipal Councillor of the same Polling District shall be selected as a substitute.

THE ELECTORAL CHAMBER.

14. The Wardens of Counties, and Mayors of Towns, and Cities, constituting the electoral districts, shall be ex-officio Electoral Returning Officers at Parliamentary elections.

15. The Writ of Election to be sent to Returning Officer.

16. Returning Officer to notify the Delegates as to time and place of holding the sessions of the Electoral Chamber.

17. The Returning Officer shall preside at the sessions of the Electoral Chamber but shall not vote.

18. Each Delegate present may nominate one candidate, not to exceed one for each polling district.

19. The names of the candidates nominated shall be entered on the record of the proceedings in the order of their nomination.

20. The Record of the proceedings of the Electoral Chamber shall be kept by the Returning Officer.

21. A vote of the Delegates present shall be taken for first choice of candidate.

22. The vote of the Delegates shall be taken by Ballot.

23. The vote so taken shall be counted by the Returning Officer and four tellers, and entered on the record of the proceedings.

24. The name of the candidate having the lowest number of votes shall be struck from the record of the proceedings by the Returning Officer; and in the event of an equality of votes between the two candidates having the lowest number of votes, the name to be struck from the Record shall be decided by lot drawn by the Delegates who made the respective nominations.

25. The voting shall be continued and the names of the candidates having the lowest number of votes shall be struck from the record of the proceedings in manner aforesaid, until the names of no more than the requisite number of candidates remain on the record, then the Electoral Chamber shall be dissolved, and the successful candidates · declared elected to represent the Electoral District in the House of Commons.

26. The Returning Officer shall make the Return of the Writ of Election to the Clerk of the Executive Council.

27. During the sessions of the Electoral Chamber it shall be lawful for any Delegate to address the members thereof, setting forth the opinions, views, arguments, and principles,

relating to all political matters and things at issue before the public, provided that the proceedings thereof are not thereby unreasonably interrupted or delayed, but no Delegate shall either openly or secretly ask, canvass, or solicit, any other Delegate for any vote, influence, or support, for or on behalf of any candidate under a penalty at the discretion of the Court.

28. Whosoever enquires either directly or indirectly, of any person qualified to vote in any electoral district, or who by any means or device whatsoever, attempts to ascertain how or in what manner or for whom any such person shall have voted at any election, or how or in what manner or for whom such person shall intend to vote at any election, shall be liable on conviction to a penalty in the discretion of the Court.

29. Any Returning Officer, Recorder of Voters, or other official, appointed under the provisions of this Act, who in discharging the functions of his office shall do any act, matter, or thing, which he, or they ought not to do, or who shall neglect or refuse to do any act, matter, or thing, which he or they ought to do, shall be liable on conviction to a penalty in the discretion of the Court.

30. Violations of the provisions of this Act shall be tried by the Judge of the County Court in and for the County constituting the electoral district where the offence was committed, sitting as a criminal Court.

31. All expenses incurred in carrying into effect the provisions of the first part of this Act shall be borne and paid by the Municipality consituting the electoral district.

PART II.—REPRESENTATION IN THE HOUSE OF COMMONS.

32. No person directly or indirectly, alone, or with any other, by himself, or by the interposition of any trustee, or third party, holding or enjoying or executing any contract or agreement, expressed or implied, with or for the Government of Canada, or on behalf of the Crown, or with or for the Government of any foreign state, or holding any office, commission, or employment, permanent, or temporary in the service of the Government of Canada, or on behalf of any foreign state, or at the nomination of any of the officers of the Government of Canada, shall be eligible as a member of the House of Commons, or shall sit or vote therein, and the election of any such person shall be null and void. But this section shall not apply to any person by reason of his being an officer in the Imperial military service, or Canadian militia, or a shareholder in any incorparated Railway, Banking, or other company having contracts with the Governments aforesaid.

33. No member of a Provincial Legislature, or officer of a Provincial Government, shall be eligible as a member of the House of Commons, or shall sit or vote therein and the election of any such person shall be null and void.

34. Penalty for sitting and voting in the House of Commons if not eligible.

35. As to the resignation or death of members of the House of Commons.

36. All voting in the House of Commons to be by Ballot.

37. During the sessions of the House of Commons it shall be lawful for any member to address the members thereof regarding his opinions, views, arguments, and principles touching all or any political matter and thing, in question, or at issue, provided the proceedings of Parliament are not thereby unreasonably interrupted or delayed, but no member shall either openly or secretly canvass, or solicit any other member for any vote, influence, or support, for or on behalf of any motion, resolution, act, matter or thing, under a penalty on conviction at the discretion of the Court.

38. Any member of the House of Commons who directly or indirectly enquires of any other member or who by any means or device whatsoever attempts to ascertain how or in what manner any vote in Parliament has been given or how or in what manner any such member shall intend to vote, shall be liable on conviction to a penalty in the discretion of the Court.

39. Any member of the House of Commons violating any of the provisions of this Act, shall be forever disqualified from sitting and voting in Parliament, or from holding any office under the Government of Canada.

40. All expenses incurred in carrying into effect the provisions of the second part of this Act, and the indemnity to the members of the House of Commons shall be paid by the Department of Finance.

41. Each Parliament to continue for three years.

PART III.—GOVERNMENT OF CANADA.

42. On and after the passing of this Act the offices of Secretary of State, Registrar General of Canada and Deputy Registrar shall be abolished.

43. The House of Commons shall appoint a Director General of the Department of State, who shall hold office during the pleasure of Parliament.

44. On and after the passing of this Act the powers, duties and functions of the Secretary of State, Under Secretary of State, Registrar General of Canada, and Deputy Registrar General, shall be vested in the Department of State, and the Director General thereof, the several officials of the said Department, and their successors in office, shall be, and are hereby constituted a body corporate and shall be called the Department of State

45. On and after the passing of this Act the offices of Minister of Finance, Receiver General, Deputy Minister of Finance, and Deputy Receiver General, shall be abolished.

46. The House of Commons shall appoint by Ballot a Director General of the Department of Finance, who shall hold office during the pleasure of Parliament.

47. On and after the passing of this Act the powers, duties, and functions of the Minister of Finance, Deputy Minister of Finance, Receiver General, Deputy Receiver General, and Treasury Board, shall be vested in the Department of Finance, and the Director General thereof, the several officials of the said Department and their successors in office, shall be, and are hereby constituted a body corporate and shall be called the Department of Finance.

48. The Department of Finance shall have the supervision, control and direction, of all matters relating to the financial affairs, public accounts, revenue and expenditure of Canada, which are not or in so far as they are not by law assigned to any other Department and such other duties as shall or may be, from time to time, assigned to it by Parliament.

49. Offices of Minister of Agriculture, and Deputy Minister, abolished and duties and powers vested in Department of Agriculture and Commerce.

50. Director General to be appointed by Ballot.

51. Department of Agriculture and Commerce constituted a body corporate.

52. Offices of Minister of Marine and Fisheries, Deputy Minister of Marine, and Deputy Minister of Fisheries, abolished, and duties and powers, vested in Department of Marine and Fisheries.

53. Director General to be appointed by Ballot.

54. Department of Marine and Fisheries constituted a body corporate.

55. Offices of Minister of Customs, Commissioner, Assistant, and Controller, abolished, and duties, and powers vested in Department of Customs.

56. Department of Customs constituted a body corporate.

57. Offices of Minister of Inland Revenue, Deputy Minister, Commissioner, and Inspector, abolished, and duties, and powers vested in Department of Inland Revenue.

58. Director General to be appointed by Ballot.

59. Department of Inland Revenue constituted a body corporate.

60. Offices of Post Master General, Deputy Post Master General, and Chief Inspector, abolished, and duties and powers vested in Department of Postal Service.

61. Director General to be appointed by Ballot.

62. Department of Postal Service constituted a body corporate.

63. Offices of Minister of Public Works, Deputy Minister, Secretary, Chief Engineer, and Chief Architect, abolished, and duties and powers vested in Department of Public Works.

64. Director General to be appointed by Ballot.

65. Department of Public Works constituted a body corporate.

66. Offices of Minister of Railways, and Canals, Deputy Minister, Secretary, and Chief Engineer, abolished, and duties and powers vested in Department of Railways and Canals.

67. Director General to be appointed by Ballot.

68. Department of Railways and Canals constituted a body corporate.

69. Offices of Minister of Militia and Defence, abolished, and duties, and powers vested in Department of Public Defence.

70. Director General to be appointed by Ballot.

71. Department of Public Defence constituted a body corporate.

72. Offices of Minister of Justice, and Deputy Minister of Justice, abolished, and duties and powers vested in Department of Justice.

73. Director General to be appointed by Ballot.

74. Department of Justice constituted a body corporate.

75. Offices of Minister of Interior, Deputy Minister, and Superintendent of Indian Affairs, abolished, and duties, and powers vested in Department of Interior.

76. Director General to be appointed by Ballot.

77. Department of Interior constituted a body corporate.

78. The Director General of each Department shall annually transmit to Parliament within 15 days after the meeting thereof, a report of the proceedings, transactions, and affairs, of the Department during the year next preceding, and supply all such further and other information relating thereto, as may from time to time be required.

79. The House of Commons shall appoint by Ballot three members thereof to be the Parliamentary representatives of each Department and who shall be designated Councillors of State.

80. The duties and functions of the Councillors of State shall be,—

(a). To represent each of the several Departments in the House of Commons.

(b). To supervise the management, and general affairs of the several Departments, and to report thereon to the House of Commons in which all controlling power shall be vested.

(c). To represent the several Departments in the Executive Council, and to cause to be carried into effect through the medium of the Department, the orders and requirements of the Executive Council, and the House of Commons.

(d). To perform the duties and services now performed by members of the Privy Council and Cabinet, so far as they are not required to be otherwise performed, and to perform such other duties, and services, as shall, or may, be, from time to time assigned to them by Parliament.

(e). One Councillor of State for each Department shall retire from office each year in the order of their appointment, and another member of the House of Commons shall be appointed in the place and stead of the member so retiring.

81. The Executive Council shall consist of the three Councillors of State for each incorporated Department, three Secretaries of State to be nominated and appointed by the Governor General, and a Vice President of the Council to be appointed by the House of Commons by Ballot, and who shall hold office during the pleasure of Parliament.

82. The Governor General shall be *ex-officio* President of the Council.

83. The Secretaries of State shall not be members of the House of Commons, or of the Senate of Canada.

84. The Executive Council shall perform the same duties, and have the same powers, as are now vested in the Ministers of the Crown, Cabinet and Privy Council, in so far as such duties shall not be otherwise assigned and shall be in all matters and things directly responsible to Parliament.

85. One Councillor of State for each Department, two Secretaries of State, and the President, or Vice President of the Executive Council, shall form a quorum thereof.

86. All members of the Senate of Canada, holding such appointment at the time of the passing of this Act, shall continue to hold such appointment during life, subject to the same conditions that have heretofore governed such appointments, but all future appointments to the said Senate shall be made by the House of Commons by Ballot, and shall be subject to the like qualifications and conditions.

87. After the passing of this Act, no Bill or Act of the House of Commons shall be sent to the Senate after the same shall have been passed by the House of Commons, and the Senate shall have no power to alter, amend, or annul any Act, passed by the House of Commons.

88. The House of Commons may refer any Act, Bill, or Measure, to the Senate for consideration before such Act, Bill, or Measure, shall have been passed, and the Senate shall report thereon to the House of Commons.

89. The Senate of Canada shall have the power and authority to inquire into, and adjudicate, upon all matters and things now referable under Royal Commission, and shall report thereon to the House of Commons.

90. The Senate of Canada shall have the same powers and authority as are now vested in the Official Arbitrators, and all other powers and functions as are now vested in the Senate, except such as are otherwise assigned, and shall perform all such other duties and services not inconsistent with this Act, that Parliament may, from time to time require.

91. All Acts, Sections, and parts of Acts, inconsistent with this Act are hereby repealed.

"CANADIAN HOME RULE AND AMENDMENTS THERETO."

"PER ASPERAM AD ASTRA."

A consideration of the remedy for any disorder involves a consideration of the nature of the disorder. The character of the remedy is of necessity conditioned on and determined by the character of the disease. Any system therefore which may be submitted for the reform of the method of electoral representation must be determined in its form and nature by the nature of the necessity of which it is born. It is obvious therefore that this essay which forms a preface and exposition of a system for the rectification of representation and parliament must concern itself with an inquiry into the nature of the disorder it professes to rectify.

The questions which this essay professes to answer therefore may briefly be stated as follows—

(1). What are the functions of a complete representative system?
(2). In what particulars and to what degree does the existing system fall short of the purposes for which it was instituted?
(3). To what causes are the deficiencies of the present system due?
(4). By what means can these deficiencies be rectified?

As the system of electing representatives has its origin in the nature and necessities of representative government, it is evident that a clear understanding of the purpose and functions of such a system involves an understanding of the nature and theory of representative government itself. So soon as the people of a country acquire the right to govern themselves the question at once arises :—in what way should they do so? The first method that suggests itself and the one most consistent with the principle of popular government is that the people of the nation should meet together, deliberate on all measures affecting their common interest, and after a discussion in which each man has a voice arrive at a conclusion in which each man has a vote. Accordingly, to realize completely the theory of popular self-government, the electors would require to meet in national convocation, and debate and determine as a people all matters of public import.

It is evident that in a nation of any large proportions it would be impossible for the people to adopt this ideal system of self-government. It would be practically impossible for all the citizens to meet together in a mass, and even if such a possibility were admitted it would be equally impossible for them after having met to deliberate, debate, and arrive at a peaceful and harmonious conclusion on the innumerable matters of public interest.

If the people cannot meet in a mass to transact their common affairs they must evidently adopt some other means of self-government and this method must be that which is most closely consistent with the ideal but impossible system of self-government *en masse*. They cannot act in a body, therefore they must act through representatives. Representative government therefore has its origin in the theoretical impossibility of popular or democratic government. It is a compromise between the theory and practice of popular government. It is a concession of the ideal form to the real. It is not the best imaginable but it is the best possible system of popular self-government. The first essential representative government therefore is that it should be popular government—that it should realize as far as possible that ideal form in which the people manage the affairs of the people. It must be consistent with the logic of the democratic principle. If it cannot bring about an assembly of the people in person, it must bring them together in spirit. It must be the nation in miniature, a small typical representative nation. The Legislature, (which is the name by which the representatives are known collectively) must be the microcosm of the people. It should be the type of which the nation is the prototype. It should be the essence, the concentrated spirit, the miniature personality, the perfect mirror of the nation. There should be no party of any strength, no sentiment of any power, no principle of any vitality in the country which was not also present in parliament in a strength proportioned to its strength in the nation. It is obvious that in order for parliament to attain this ideal character—to be perfectly representative of the people—it is necessary for every member to be perfectly representative of his constituency, to embody in his parliamentary personality the salient characteristics of all his constituents, to be a type of the collective character of those he represents. It would be necessary that in him his constituents should be seen, through him they should speak, and that his political personality should consist of ingredients contributed by the units of which he is theoretically the aggregate, and these ingredients should be grouped in his nature in the same precise and perfect proportion that they exist in his constituency. He would be as it were the parliamentary

50

molecule, the elements and atoms of whose being are contributed by the political atmosphere that surrounds him; a composite whose content consists in due proportion of miniature constituents. This is the ideal representative and theoretically he bears the same relation to his constituency as the parliament bears to the nation. He is the microcosm of his constituency. The parliament is the microcosm of the nation. A legislature consisting of such representatives as this is the closest approximation to the idea of absolute popular government.

Unfortunately for the existence of such a system of representative government, human nature conflicts with the conditions essential to its existence and stability. Man is not a mechanism, and representatives must be men. There is mixed with the web and woof of human nature an element of individuality. The man is older than the representative and earlier in the field. His parliamentary character must be built upon the basis of his individuality, and must bo subject to the re-actions of his thought. The electors may impress their character upon the mind of their representative, but the mind precedes the impression, and colors it with its own character, holds it subject to its varying moods.

The factors of his own personality must enter into the counsels of the representative, and exercise if not a predominant at least a determinate influence on his actions. He can never be an absolute representation of the people who elect him, at the best he can approximate towards the ideal standard.

As a matter of fact representative government in the truest sense of the word does not and cannot exist. The representatives cannot exactly and in every particular resemble the electors whom they represent. They cannot exactly combine in their persons the innumerable, diverse, and often conflicting opinions, desires and characteristics of a large number of citizens. On several large issues there may perhaps be an unanimity of opinion among the constituents, and between them and their representative, but it will be very evident that this unanimity cannot continue on the many other minor questions which may arise in parliamentary debate, or enter the arena of public discussion after the elections are over. The existing system of government in Canada might be more properly described as responsible than representative. Responsible government has its origin in the impracticability of representative government, as representative government has its origin in the impracticability of popular government. Theoretically parliament should exactly and in every particular represent the people. Practically it cannot do this because it is composed of diverse individualities each possessed of a judgment, volition, conscience and character of his own. But the right of the people to govern themselves is still valid, and is not altered by the fact that it is impossible for them to do so as a people. If the parliament cannot be made representative it can be made responsible. If the representatives cannot be impressed with the collective personality of the electors so as to do precisely as the electors would have done on every occasion, they can at least be made responsible to the people for their acts and at certain fixed periods be called upon to justify and explain their parliamentary record, and stand or fall as the public may desire.

From this brief review of the theory and limitations of representative and responsible government we may be able to derive the purposes of the system of electoral representation which forms the connecting link between the parliament and the people. So soon as it becomes necessary for the people to govern by representatives the question arises,—In what way shall the representatives be chosen? The answer to this is—in such a way as will best conserve the purposes of representative government. The purposes of representative government I have indicated above and from a careful study of the purposes we may arrive at the conclusion that any system of electoral representation in order to be completely consistent with them must possess the following essentials—

(1). It must enable every elector to be represented in parliament.

(2). It must give every elector the right and opportunity to vote for whoever he wishes to represent him.

(3). It must enable electors scattered throughout the country to unite their votes for a common candidate.

(4). It must ensure the representation in parliament of all classes and shades of opinion in the country, whose supporters have attained the numerical strength necessary to entitle their candidate to a seat.

It may be safely said that no system of electoral representation has realized the purpose for which it exists if it lacks any of the above essentials. And it may also be said that the existing electoral system lacks not one but all of these essentials. It does not enable every elector to be represented in parliament. It does not give every elector the opportunity to vote for the man he desires to represent him. It does not enable electors scattered throughout the country to unite their votes for a common candidate, nor does it by any means ensure representation in parliament to all classes and shades of opinion in the community, even where these classes or opinions have attained to large proportions, and even a large degree of public favor.

The deficiencies of the present and existing system of electing representatives may be briefly enumerated as follows—

(1). By it a very large number of the people do not obtain representation in parliametn and it is possible that a majority of the people should not be represented.

(2). It involves the existence of constituencies, arbitrary electoral districts, for the candidates in which the electors are forced to vote, and outside of which they are not permitted to support any candidate by their votes; and by this system of arbitrary localization of votes it prevents citizens and parties of national strength by local weakness from combining their votes to elect a representative.

(3). By thus weakening the minor parties and interests of the state and preventing their representation in the legislature, it tends to unduly encourage party government and divide the people and the parliament into two parties, who monopolize the House and prevent that independence and originality of thought which are essential to the well-being and progress of the nation.

I shall now deal briefly with each of these defects of the existing system, and endeavor to ascertain their origin and their effect, and indicate in what manner they may be rectified.

Under the present system a very large number of the people have no representatives in parliament. It therefore fails to realize the basic principle of representative government, namely, that the people should govern the people. Under the present system part of the people govern all the people, and the minority have not even an opportunity of sayng in what way they should be governed. Parliament does not contain the repro sentatives of the people, but only the representatives of a part of the people. This great blunder is not due to any narrowness of the franchise, nor to any flaw in the principle of representative government. It has its origin simply in the radical errors in the electoral system by means of which representative government is at the present time so ineffectually striving to realize its ends. The two blunders to which we allude are, the selection of candidates by a majority vote, and the existence of constituencies. The country at present is divided into a number of constituencies. Each of these is entitled to a representative in parliament. Candidates are nominated and the one receiving a majority of votes is elected. It is evident that in every constituency there will be a large number of electors who have voted for the unsuccessful candidate, and as these have no second vote they will have no representative in the legislature. If all the minorities of the various constituencies are combined they will be found to constitute almost half of the population of the country. The fact that the combined minorities of any two constituencies might create a group of electors numerically as strong as that which elected a representative, is apparently lost sight of by the present system which also overlooks the fact that any one group (say 5000) of the electors are as much entitled to a vote as any other 5000, and that their right is not in the slightest degree depreciated by the imposition of arbitrary lines of constitutional demarkation, dividing the land into certain fixed divisions called constituencies. The elector derives his right to vote from the fact that he is a citizen of the nation, and not from the fact that he is an inhabitant of any constituency. He is entitled to vote in the nation and in any part of it, and for any citizen of it and to unite his vote not only with his neighbors but with his countrymen.

The system of representation by constituencies which in Canada is borrowed from England, doubtless had its genesis and sought its justification there in the existence of large landed interests. It was not so much the people as the land which was represented in parliament. It was considered that the interest of a citizen in the state was proportioned to the amount of land he owned, and that as an owner of part of the country he was entitled to have a voice in the legislature which made the laws of the country. It was probably this old English conception of representation that caused the latter to be based on localized constituencies in that country. The great reforms of recent years and the great extension of the franchise have long since destroyed the feeling that representation should be based on land, and it is now generally conceded that the true basis of represeutation is population. But though the old principle is gone, its fruits survive, and in constituencies there are still prevalent some relics of constitutional feudalism. The great blunder of the existing system of representation is its attempt to realize the principle of representation by population through the same worn-out and antiquated means which were established to realize the older and narrower principle of representation by land. As a consequence of this an inevitable conflict arises between the means and the end, and the end is only half effected. Constituencies should be abolished, and in their place there should be established electoral groups, by a division of the population. Every member should be required to get a certain fixed number of votes in order to be elected, and the number necessary for election might best be ascertained by a division of the total number of representatives (as fixed by the constitution) into the total number of electors, and it should not be necessary that these votes should come from any particular locality as at present.

It is evident, therefore, that in order to rectify the errors in the existing system which I have pointed out, the following changes are necessary :—

(1). Every elector should have an opportunity to vote for a successful candidate.

(2). Abolition of constituencies.

(3). Division of electors into electoral groups based on numbers, not land.

(4). Abolition of election by majority vote, and establishment of a quota of votes, which it will be necessary for the candidate to obtain in order to be elected, and which would be ascertained by dividing the total number of electors by total number of representatives.

(5). Abolition of localization of votes, and adoption of a system which would enable elector to vote for candidate in any part of country.

All the above principles are embodied and harmonized in the system annexed to this essay. This system enables each voter to continue voting until he has voted for a successful candidate ; it enables him to cast his vote for any candidate he desires in any part of the country ; it establishes a quota of votes, and it preserves the secrecy of the ballot.

1. Constituencies are abolished, and there is substituted for them electoral groups. The electors of the country are divided (on the basis of the voters' list) into a number of divisions or groups, each one of which will return a representative to parliament. In order to ensure the election of any candidate he must obtain a definite number of votes (to be ascertained by dividing the number of voters by number of representatives). Assuming the total number of electors in Canada to be 900,000, and the number of representatives 300, it will be necessary for a candidate to obtain 3,000 votes to be elected.

In dividing the country into electoral groups the question naturally arises—what should be the numerical strength of these groups? It is impossible that the number of voters in each group should be limited to the number essential to ensure election (3000), as where there were several candidates in the field it would be almost impossible for either to get all the votes in the group which he would in that case require to do in order to be elected. It is therefore necessary that the electoral group should contain a considerably larger number of votes than that necessary to ensure election. In fact the number should be sufficiently large as to make it almost certain that one candidate at least would obtain 3000 votes. I have therefore placed the number of electors in each electoral group at three times the number of votes necessary to ensure election. Thus the quota for election is 3000, the numerical strength of each electoral group is 9000.

It is evident that if the total vote in the country is 900,000 and the number of representatives 300, the quota of votes essential to election 3000, and the numerical strength of each electoral group three times that of the quota, or 9000, that the number of electoral groups in which election can be held at one time will be only one-third the total number or 100. An election will therefore be held in 100 electoral groups. In each of these one candidate will be returned. One-third of the votes in each group will be satisfied, and two-thirds will as yet have no representative. The total number of representatives returned will be 100, (each group must return one representative, see clause 15 of Draft Bill). The total number of votes cast will be 300,000. The total votes remaining unrepresented will be 600,000.

Just as the original electoral groups were formed on a basis of 900,000 electors, now a second series will be formed on the minority, unsatisfied votes, or 600,000 basis. These electors are re-grouped into new groups of 9,000 each, and the second series is thus formed, in which voting takes place on the day following the first election and in the same manner. In this way the election proceeds, the minority or unsatisfied voters in each case forming the basis of a new system of electoral groups. The first series of groups will evidently be local in their nature, the last series consisting of one group will be co-extensive with the nation. Every series of groups will be smaller in numbers and wider in area than that preceding it. Every elector will continue voting until he votes for a successful candidate —until he is represented in the legislature. (Exc. Clause 11, Draft Bill).

The question will at once occur to the critic of this system, " In what way can the unsatisfied votes be ascertained without violating the secrecy of the ballot ? How will it be possible to know who is entitled to vote in each succeeding series ? " This difficulty

The election cannot conveniently be held on one day because it would be impossible to ascertain the name of the successful candidate between each series in that case, and the votes in the second series cannot be identified until the name of the candidate elected is known.

I wish to call particular attention to the fact that there can be no great delay or confusion about this election. *The electoral groups will all be found and candidates nominated in each before the first day of election.* It will not be necessary to know the result of the vote in the first series before forming the second, or in the second before forming the subsequent ones; because when the total number of votes in each group is known and the quota is limited, the remainder is known. Only one-third can vote successfully in first election. Therefore two-thirds is the basis for the second. See Clause 14.

The one objection of weight which I can conceive as being urged against this system of electoral representation which I have here submitted is, that it will prolong the period of choice—that the election instead of being hurried through in one day, as at present, may occupy several days before it is completed. It is a very debatable question whether if this were so it would not be a merit. There is nothing meritorious in the present system of rushing through the election on one day. The elections are held only once in five years, and the selection of representatives who will for that period of time hold the destinies of the nation in their hand, is not a matter of so light and trivial a nature as to be hurried through in one day, but should rather be a careful, deliberate proceeding in which the merits of the various candidates and parties can be duly and carefully balanced. It will be understood, however, that the only obstacle in the way of holding the election on one day under the new system arises from the difficulty of ascertaining what electors are entitled to vote in the second series, until the result of the first election is known. This difficulty is not so formidable that it cannot be overcome, and I desire to say that if it be considered a merit in any electoral system that it should provide an expedient for the selection of all the representatives on one and the same day, that I do not consider it impossible that such an expedient should be attached to the system I have submitted as well as to any other. It is not impossible to conceive of some ingenious and novel method of voting, involving a multiplicity of ballots, or otherwise by means of which this purely technical objection to the new system could be overcome. There are, however, many advantages arising from the method I have submitted which might render it rather desirable than otherwise, particularly in view of the fact that each successive group of electoral districts is wider than the other, and all classes and shades of public opinion would find a representative in the house.

In an earlier portion of this thesis I enumerated the prime essentials of a complete system of electoral representation. It will be seen that each of these essentials is present in the system I have here submitted. It may be well perhaps, in conclusion, to enumerate these advantages, and point out by what features and methods of the new system each one is achieved.

(1). Every elector will have an opportunity to vote for whoever he pleases. Clause 13 of the annexed Bill does not conflict with this privilege, because though the elector may not find the representative he desires in the first group, he can by voting for some purely nominal candidate earn the opportunity to continue voting until he enters the group in which the representative he desires has been nominated and in which, on account of its breadth, he has enough supporters to elect him.

(2). All parties and classes or men having 3,000 supporters can obtain a place in the legislature. These supporters need not, as under present system, be all living together in the same constituency, but may be scattered in various parts of the country. Thus if the scientists of Canada desired to elect a scientist to the legislature, they could not do so at present because not 3,000 strong in any one constituency. They could do so under the new system if they numbered 3,000, though scattered in every part of the country, by nominating a man in the last electoral group, which is co-extensive with the nation, or if 9,000 strong they could nominate candidates in three electoral groups, each co-extensive with one-third of country.

(3). Every class and shade of political thought will be represented in parliament which will thus become as far as possible the exact mirror of the people.

(4). Any man whose ability has impressed itself on the minds of 3,000 of his fellow citizens in the country can, by their support, be elected to parliament, and thus a new and original and invaluable element of genius and independence will find its way into the legislature.

(5). Party power weakened by abolition of its fortresses the constituencies.

A BILL

To Reform the System of Electing Representatives to the Legislature of Canada.

(Assuming total number of voters to be 900,000).

Whereas it is desirable to rectify the existing system of electoral representation, it is hereby enacted that the present system of electing representatives from constituencies be forthwith repealed, and that :—

1. The membership of the legislature shall be limited to 300 members.

2. In order to entitle a citizen to a seat in the legislature it shall be necessary for him to obtain 3,000 votes. (A number ascertained by the division of the total number of electors, 900,000, by the total number of members, 300).

3. Elections shall be held every five years.

4. For the purposes of election the electors shall be divided into groups containing each 9,000 electors. The first series of these groups shall be based on the voters' lists, will be in number 100 ($\frac{900000}{9000}$), and each elector will be assigned his group.

5. On a day and time appointed an election will take place in each of these electoral groups, and the candidate securing the quota of 3,000 votes shall be declared elected.

6. Not more than 3,000 votes shall be cast for any one candidate.

7. The electors who have voted for unsuccessful candidates shall be entitled to vote again on the following day, in the second series of electoral groups.

8. On the day following the election on first series of groups an election shall take place in a second series, to be arranged as follows : The minority or unsuccessful voters in the first series (consisting of 600,000 electors, whose identity as unsuccessful voters will be ascertained by method in Clause 12 of this Bill) will be divided and re-grouped into a new series of electoral groups, each containing 9,000 voters. On the day following the elections in first series the election shall take place in the new second series.

9. The unsuccessful voters in second series will be entitled to vote on the next day in a third series of electoral groups, which third series will be formed by re-grouping the minority or unsuccessful voters of the second series into new electoral groups consisting each of 9,000 electors.

10. The above system of election and re-grouping of unsuccessful voters will continue until the electors are reduced to less than the number required for one constituency (9,000). The final electoral group, which will be co-extensive with the nation, will consist of the residue of voters, and if over 3,000, an election shall take place, and the candidate securing 3,000 votes be elected. In case any candidate should not secure this number, the candidates having least number of votes will be struck off and election continue until one obtains 3,000.

11. Every elector shall be entitled to vote until he has voted for a successful candidate—with the exception of electors contained in minority less than 3,000 in last group, mentioned in Clause 10.

12. The method of voting shall be as follows :—

(a) The elector on entering polling booth will be given a ballot containing the names of the candidates in that group. These names will be printed one under the other on the paper, which will be perforated between each name. The elector will tear off the name of the candidate for whom he desires to vote, and drop it in the ballot box, *and retain the residue of the ballot.*

(b) If the candidate for whom he has voted is not elected, he will return to the polling booth the next day and present his old ballot and receive a new one, containing the names of candidates in the second group. *The fact that he is entitled to vote a second time, and that he voted unsuccessfully the first time is proved by the presence on his old ballot paper of the name of the successful candidate. Had he voted for the successful candidate, this name would be torn off the ballot, and be in the ballot box.*

13. No elector can vote in any series of the election unless he has voted in those preceding it.

14. All the 300 electoral groups shall be clearly outlined and numbered, and candidates nominated in each before the first day of the election. There shall be posted in every

polling booth instructions to voters as to manner of voting, and also a list of the alternative groups in which the unsuccessful voters in each division shall cast their subsequent votes.

15. If no candidate should succeed in obtaining the necessary quota of votes (3,000) in any single electoral group, the names of the candidates lowest on the list shall be struck out, and voting proceed until one of the candidates obtains the necessary quota.

16. If two candidates in any one group obtain each the necessary quota of votes (3,000 each), the candidate who received the essential number first shall be declared elected in that group, and the other candidate shall be entitled to run in the next group, to which his supporters are attached.

(This provision is necessary because the second series is based on the calculation that only one candidate will be returned in each group of the first series).

17. As soon as 3,000 votes have been cast for a candidate he shall be declared elected (subject to Clause 16), and any electors entering polling booths for the purpose of voting for the said candidate after he has secured the necessary number of votes shall be permitted to retain their ballots and vote on the following day in second series on presenting the said ballots.

IN DEO SPERO.

If we wish to find the sources of political institutions in England, or wherever the English language is spoken, we must go back to the historian Tacitus, who in his work "de Moribus Germanorum," tells us in his succinct style that "on affairs of small moment the chiefs consult—on those of greater import—the whole community take counsel—yet with this—that what is referred to the decision of the people is first of all maturely discussed by the chiefs." In this habit of our Teutonic ancestors, one is warranted in seeing the commencement of parliamentary gatherings, and almost tempted to find in it the germ-idea of the more modern "Plebiscitum."

One thing is sure, that as quickly as man ceased to be only a hunter, and merely a pastoral being, society having meanwhile coalesced for the mutuality of protection, popular gatherings became the order of the day. Further on, we shall find the expressed will of the majorities in these gatherings, evolving itself into law, *i.e.*, the opinion of a majority plus something else, which is a power to impose it on a minority.

That antique people the Hebrews had their gatherings, *e.g.*, "Joshua gathered all the tribes of Israel to Shechem, and called for the elders of Israel, and for their heads, and for the judges, and their officers etc., thus summoning in primitive form, an assembly of the peoples, not on political grounds, but on state religion, to them an absorbing issue, and this meeting was no doubt what we moderns describe as "an open air meeting."

Deborah also we are told gave judgment sitting under a palm tree.

The Greeks attributed such importance to the fact, that affairs of state should be the affairs of all individuals, that on voting days at Athens, a rope stained crimson was dragged through the streets, and so stretched that careless non-voters away from the polls should be marked by it and stained physically and receive stains mentally, objects of conspicuity to more diligent citizens. Compulsory voting is not quite the new idea some of us have thought.

It seems a redundancy to quote authority as to the assembling of the old Romans for political purposes—the product of their gatherings we have still in the widespread civil law, an active ingredient in our common law, and almost the vitality of continental law in Europe.

Sir H. Maine, in his "Ancient Law," reminds us that social necessities and social opinion are always more or less in advance of law; that law itself is stable, while societies are progressive, and that the greater or the lesser the happiness of a people, depends on the promptitude with which the gulf is bridged over. So there was a crying need for these large gatherings of people, each one of old was ready to contribute his share of the melioration of wrong and the suggestion of improvements. The Anglo-Saxon tribal meetings of freeholders, (Folk-Moot) the nucleus of modern parliaments, goes back historically with no break to the very origin of the English nation, till it fades in the mist of pre-historic time.

The Witena-gemot or "wise men's meeting," was a conjunction of the important officials of the kingdom summoned by the king, and invited to meet him wherever he might be staying.

The meetings were open air ones, and all that chose attended, but there was the difference between them and ourslves, that with us, the unit of society is the individual—with them it was the family. It was the lot of each family, then to have and uphold rights, and a status *qua* family in society just as now we speak of individual rights. For state purposes, all but the chief of the family were nobodies, and he attended to represent officially, and by summons the members he controlled.

Kemble has with diligence collected the records of 151 meetings of the "witan" and it is not doubted that the church or temple of primitive society was the very spot where the people gathered and where justice was weighed out, as soon as open air meetings were inconvenient. The first recorded Witen was held near York in A.D. 627 and outside its walls. Runnymede, says Matthew of Westminster was in days of yore used as a place of gathering, to consult and hear speeches, as to the state's welfare and as all know the cowardly John was brought to his knees by the fierce barons camped at Runnymede. Going on much later we know, that in A.D. 1290, Edward I. held a parliament at Clipston-Park, and down to modern days, there was a very old oak in that park commonly known as the "parliamentary oak."

The old "shire moot" of Kent, always preeminently conservative among conservative Englishmen, did not speedily relinquish the remembrances of the ancient air meetings, if obliged to abandon as time rolled on their actual use. On Pennenden Heath, the county house is even now situated on the north side of the heath, and the sheriff to this day holds his county courts there each month, and there takes the poll for the parliamentary representatives, till its adjournment to Maidstone, and in these primitive gatherings mentioned above, the shire, the great franchises, and the manors were all represented.

Leaving for a moment this most interesting inquiry, may be pardon will be extended if we venture to hope that some day woman will be accorded her rights in politics. We do not suggest the abandonment of the home influence, but surely if women are subject as men to laws, they might have some voice in the election of law-makers. The monastic element of the middle ages, while it exalted knightly defence of women tinged with a sad colouring of grey, the notion of her intellectual power. It is suggestive to find in some old treatises, that women had no political rights, simply because of inability to keep a secret.

But Anne, Countess of Pembroke, was considered not too weak of mind to be sheriff of Westmoreland, and no sinecure, either, was the office—she exercised it in person and at the assizes of Appleby sat on the Bench with the Royal Justices. Lucy, Countess of Kent, was returning officer and signed the return of the member for York, in A.D. 1412; and in A.D. 1415, Margaret, the widow of Sir H. Vavaseur, also acted as returning officer, and signed the return—so Lady Copley, in A.D. 1553.

Judicial opinions came from the High Bench that a Feme Sole, owning a freehold had a right to vote for members of Parliament. See Catherine vs. Surrey. cited 7 Mod. 264.

Women when sole had a power to vote for members, Coates vs. Lisle 14 Jac. 1, but if married is the woman owner of freehold, then her husband is to vote for her, Holt v. Lisle, 4 Jac. I. We suppose this lady of that remote day, gave her spouse a bad quarter of an hour, if he disobeyed her wishes. At all events, the principle was in these early days established to which we are not yet educated, that fairness to women insists on yielding them votes, but to guard against marital and other influences it is suggested that spinsters and widows alone go to the polls. However, to resume where we left off first asking pardon for quoting the Sage of Chelsea on woman. "Her magnificent emotional power capsuled during past aeons and mercilessly chained to the hearth or cloister, and in our time parched in that Golgotha of thought the drawing room will yet roll over the world in fructifying waves causing upheavals and destructions." The American woman movement seems to be holding Carlyle's florid idea in the front.

Our sturdy ancestors always battled for their rights, and whether opposing the encroachments of royalty, or baronial tyranny, the same brave spirit was always there, and the outspoken word, to condemn what was un-English and therefore unfair; so it came about that even the haughty Tudors when wrong doing, were compelled to use some crutch of legality, in wandering into bye-ways, which conscience said, were the abodes of lawlessness. What was wrongly done, it was attempted to be shown was done in colour of right, and any plausible pretext was cleverly made use of in quoting or forging precedents. The law always was respected, if the worship of it was not heart-felt—it was assumed to be an impelling factor—especially as to kings. What was earnestly desired by Englishmen, was embodied in petitions to the crown, and the monarch was allowed the grace of consenting to it, which often occurred to be more formal than sincere, but the ancient houses of parliament, always had the faculty of persistence in just demands; terrorised for a while they soon recovered themselves and haughty kings with their notions of divine rights had in the end to yield. The king's most gracious majesty feared the chimes of liberty that rang in on England with the Magna Charta of the tyrant John; they had a warning note for the ears of rapacious autocrats.

There was always in England, both anterior to and after the Norman conquest, a continuation of national assemblies, from the remote year, when all England met in the open field, down to when, from change of the conditions of our insular life, the many were represented by the few—the gathering of the whole community had ceased, simply because all could not come; and as is said, "the democratic aspect took on the oligarchical hue." Zeal perhaps was less ardent, and the distances had increased; and remember it was no slight work in those days to travel over poor roads and into dangerous positions to be patriotic; it was a task of many days to leave the extreme north, south, or west of England and be present at the annual gathering; there were a great many "lions" in the way. It was evolved as a necessity that chiefs only should represent the community at large—as a rule, occasionally, some of these celebrities would get luke-warm. Summoned by royalty they ceased to come, and in time their names were omitted from the list. After, it was come about that they were conceived as having no right to attend at all, but be that as it may, one of the best historians makes out that, paradoxical in sound, yet true is it in fact that the House of Lords, not the House of Commons, is the true modern unbroken identity with the primitive democratic meeting of old England. The Lords were the oldest, and the Commons grew up side by side, till the youthful giant absorbed nearly all the vigour and outstripped in combative energy its older brother. Barons in the Lords, Knights of the Shires in the Commons, mere commoners though knights, yet assuming and keeping its leadership, the old and modern phrase of "the Commons of England in parliament assembled" was about to become a mighty power and watchword. The early legislator of England got to the Parliament in spite of lonely forests, wolves, Robin Hoods, and other dangers, and in the absence of railroad passes the *amor patriæ* was a sturdy factor to him. And he really did represent those who sent him; he was known as a familiar object to all, he knew all their desires and wants, and entered the hall with his lesson well learned, and when all was over, he knew right well an account of a stewardship would have to be given; so that, if disposed to be unveracious or unmanly, he was aware that his omissions were unconcealable; it was the time of residential representation in purity. A time was coming on when the Crown would wrest from the sturdy knights and yeomanry of England the nomination of Parliament-representatives; seats in its halls were to be exposed in the political shambles; sessions were to be prolonged year in and year out; a big chasm was opening out between the constituents and the elected one, and the primitive and honest idea of delegated agency was fading into mist. Crown officials wishing acts passed which should be grateful to their master were in time to manipulate a new political weapon, in the shape of members of the House who were not ashamed of the designation of "managers;" even as late as James II. Middleton and Sir Dudley North wore this sycophantic livery. In social matters of policy it was to be seen that the great pendulum swing was to go back far in one direction, then to rebound in another till what physicists know as the "mean-force" should come in; the effacement of the sturdy unit from Kent was to be, and the "dauntless Hampden" was to be crushed in the cogs of political and kingly machines—or if not meeting so dire a fate he was to be in future crushed into the great mass, a thing without shape, vigour, or conscience.

Guizot truly says, "Representation is a natural process, by which public reason which alone has a right to govern society, may be extracted from the *bosom* of its members. All institutions, all conditions of the representative system flow from and return to this point. Election publicity and responsibility are so many tests applied to individual reasons which assume themselves to be the interpreters of the community at large."

And Mirabeau, "A representative body is to the nation what a chart is for the physical configuration of the soil, in all its parts and as a whole the representative body should at all times give out a reduced picture of the people, their opinions—their wishes—their aspirations." So it did in the early times, like all else that is good and pure, it continues good and pure for a while, longer or shorter, as the elements of life act on it, then it shows a gray spot here and there, then a black one or more sporadically, ferment and putrescence come on apace, and drastic remedies are applied heroically with good or bad results, as time goes along, till Guizot's fundamental electoral axiom finds a haven where it can be said that, "Les electeurs fassent qu'ils veulent et sachent ce qu'ils font." This is the goal we are striving for.

It was not till the 23rd year of the first Edward that the lower House in England can be said as rightly constituted, and the name of "Parliament" was first applied to the assembly early in that year, and till the middle of the 17th century no law existed as to the life of a Parliament, except that the monarch dying, Parliament died also. The writ by which Henry III. summoned Knights of the Shire and Burgesses of the Town is dated January, A.D., 1265, and this is the earliest record of a gathering both of knights and burgesses; but there always had been in the Saxon churls seeds of a national organization, a craving for a niche in the national order; municipal life never died out, and the revered names of freeholders and freemen were cherished with a whole nation's pride.

If the Charter of John and its announcements are looked on with a proud backward glance by Englishmen, they are equally bound to remember when shouting, "St. George for merrie England," that the 49th year of Henry III's reign looked on the first Parliament where knights, citizens, and burgesses, together with the Lords, were welded into a legislative body, and it was not till the reign of Henry VI. that suffrage became tightened. An act passed in his reign limiting the right to vote to electors and that to freeholders of forty shillings, and at the same time the idea of "polling" the electors took rise, but there is evidence that the right to a "poll" was not firmly established till the days of James I.

Speaking generally, parliamentary government was inaugurated in the reign of Edward I., but that we now and of old had only the two chambers is the result of the gravitation of accidents. Edward sometimes conceived of more than three estates of the realm of England; dim signs were there of a coming "house of merchants," and a "house of lawyers," but it narrowed down to the three houses, lords, clergy and commoners; of the central one we have only historical recollections in our day, and the clergy faded away as a legislative faculty, simply through their obstinate refusal to act as a parliamentary constituent, and in the 41st year of the reign of George III. they were debarred from even a seat in the commons, though for one hundred years before any such cleric could be a candidate, and if elected, could represent any constituency in England ; and the sarcastic Horne Tooke accused George's ministry of passing this act simply because one clergyman had dared to oppose the ministry of that day.

Having glanced at the skeleton of our ancient parliament, let us endeavour to get correct views of what representation should be, remembering the quotations from Guizot and Mirabeau given before, not omitting to see the spots time has cast on its ancient purity and referring to the evils gigantic that have come of "government by party."

The idea at the base of representation being that all classes have a voice in what concerns all, that which is injurious to the state be removed by parliament, and what is of benefit should be constructed, that the wants of a society running in advance of law should be supplied by legislation potential with a sanction ; law then becomes what it should be, "the embodied conscience of a nation of persons."

The state, as was well said, is "not to be regarded as a kind of God," as some would have it, with the hackneyed cry of "vox populi vox Dei." Such never stay to ask themselves, What is the state ? Destroy the units of individuals composing it, and where is your state ? The government should exist for the state, but too often strangles it, e. g., the Bourbons with their "l'état c'est moi." As the monarchs thought, so did the French nobles, and the nation in its frenzy of wrath dyed crimson-red the execution-place of Paris with the wet gore of fair aristocrats, the French tiger bathed his jaws deep in the blood of his former oppressors. We in England took things more steadily and quietly ; where wrong was we generally righted it legally, and while tyrants oppressed us we firmly stood to our charters—our "Bills of Rights" and our "Remonstrances."

Still the public is a large animal with many wants, it is many-sided, sometimes hard to please, complaining, often growling. It is of the nature of freedom to get free expression of feeling, even if some of this is hysterical, or as is prettily said that under despotism :—

> On souffre beaucoup,
> Et l'on crie peu."

while in a free land,

> "On souffre peu et l'on crie beaucoup."

Feeling what is called the "people's pulse," is much oftener done than we think. Arnold satirized this where he says, "The middle class is strong enough to attract attention, but it is like the enormous creature of Plato, surrounded by obsequious people, trying to find out what its noises meant, and to make in their turn the noises which might please it." Statesmen's sails too often are stretched out for the popular wind, the successful one must be as the Romans said, "populi studiosus."

Some one had so little worshipful respect for this kind of thing that he was daring enough to reduce the theory of premiership to a very fine shade when saying, "The whole duty of a political chief is to look sharp for the way in which the political coach is going, and then run on in front and bark aloud."

There is a class in England, and particularly in the back parts of that land, in whom is and has come down a terse epigrammatic mode of expression and comparison, which, while smile-provoking, is also truth-containing. A Sussex farmer of this kind teased about his idea of politics replied : "To me politics are this :—I has a sow in my yard with 12 little uns, and they little uns can't all feed to once, bekase there ain't room enough, so I shuts six on em out of the yard whiles t'other six be sucking, and they six as be shut out they just do make a hem of a noise till they be let in, and then they be just as quiet as the rest."

The beginnings of all institutions, as Freeman says, are commonly honest, and it is only later on that men find out with ingenuity that they can be worked corruptly for their own ends. What, as he says, is known to but few, is that of old, all constituencies, great as well as small, sent two members to Parliament, that each might act as a check on his fellow and debar him from voting contrary to the wishes and interests of constituents common to both of them.

These were the halcyon days ; ignorant of the rotting influences of bribery and influence, of rottenness ulcerating electors, free to use the voting power and Esau-like selling their consciences for guineas, and of that other rottenness where monied magnates had so manipulated politics, as that the corruptible voter had no vote to sell, simply because as the fact was, the vote was not his individual property.

The political aspirant "repro luces in *rain* what he had gathered in *mist* from his audience." The hustings everywhere convinces us of this. Liberty, says Hobbs, "is power divided up into fragments," therefore, every one should be allowed to vote in order that he may get his individual fragment, that is his birthright. Political opposition too often produces what oculists call "myopsis," only (in this) it unfortunately is *moral* and not simply physical merely ; sometimes only one eye is in use, and that so placed at the back of the moral head that it can only look back at what is gone, and sigh like the Chinese politician for a faded away golden age.

The people to be represented often rise in disgust and pitch the antiquated theories and their expositors into the wide sea, and the new political doctrines having passed through the successive ages of ridicule and of argumentation, finally and quietly glide into the calm haven of adoption.

Rousseau bade all France look only backwards to a state of nature, and the leaves of the revolution came down in rains of blood. A slender atom of truth was with impudent mendaciousness forced on Frenchmen as the whole gospel of ethics, politics and religion, and it took the cannons of a rough Napoleon to blow off from Paris the misty cobwebs of a philosophy having one grain of truth to ten thousand of falsity.

No one can say that the people here, or in England, or in our neighbours the Republicans of America, have or enjoy the full benefits of a political representation in the places where laws are made by the element of force to be imposed on them. The vis-major may be an obedience-compelling factor, but the nativity of morals is in no mundane sphere. The "ought" is born celestially and is immutably truth, whether applied to politics or religion, and can no where on this earth be less or more than "ought" in its potentiality any more than can there be found a spot in the universes where two$_{+}$ two equals five. No political refinements, nor political torrents of eloquence, nor political brute-force can make any man say that men or women, now, here, there, or anywhere, are properly represented. The royal or republican mint yearly turns out a great deal of debased coin, stamped as it may be with all the majesty of imperialism or simplicity of republicanism.

It is the object of these theses (asked for) to point out defects and, what is a harder task, to suggest remedies ; and we say it in no way of fulsome admiration, that the originator of the idea which brings out these theses, deserves a perpetual niche in the memory of our countrymen. True it is, the whole vast army of officialism will be gathered against it, political drums and war-cries will fill the air, ridicule will add its mite, but the attention of the day may be caught, and if no more good is done than the presentation of a bare fact, that in this great colony we have men who have been induced to turn aside from the day's din to the examination of what concerns their country, native or adopted, a real good has come to us.

One of the greatest evils that eats into the inner heart's core of modern politics, is what we know as "government by party," or if you will "government by majorities" so called.

Originally good in idea, and necessary in the promotion of some great and important principle of state, it is like a heavy two-edged sword rusty with age, and properly to be hung up till wanted again for some great and new emergency, but unfortunately it is still yearly brandished, to cut and hack at the vitality of the state, on each and all and every occasion that the party holding it with a death grasp, chooses to cleave the air of politics. At the *now* we in Canada have little or nothing before us in the shape of cardinal points of statecraft, the foundations of a great Dominion were well and faithfully laid years ago ; what we need most is to get rid of the chains of party lines and party strife. These wise words of Hegel apply to our case : "The will of the many expels the now government and their opponents take office, but these in turn have to depart ; and thus this unrest and agitation like the sea, never ceases." There are no great principles to be fought for, calling up the necessity of a union of men to fight for the assertion of any truth, dear to man. Formerly party as party was excusable in the Government of England, and in some pages of our colonial history there were wrongs to be righted, there were principles to be adjusted, and frequently these had to be battled for by a small but brave band, uniform in honesty of purpose, and superior to the blandishments of office ; but their work was parallel to the cutting down of primeval forests by our pioneers, and the weapons of war by "party" should long ago have been quietly laid in the museum of political curiosities. -

The evils of competition, replacing, co-operation, have left the desk of 'he merchant, to find a haven in the bosom of parliaments, and it required no prophet, to see that the ferocious and tiger maxim of "*spolia opima ad debellatores et væ victis*" would follow

The elections, held on the lines of government by party, exhibit nature in curious phases. A philosophic writer long ago, called attention to this one naked fact, that men, who all along had been good friends the moment the fiery cross of politics was carried through the land, suddenly became hostile, so as to allow no obstacle in the way of scruple, to be a lion in the path, in fact it has solidified in the common phrase that "all and everything is fair in politics and war and in love." Arraying themselves in party ribbons and decorations, they proceed to demolish the enemy politically and sometimes physically, distinctively party terms are used—even flowers are made to yield their beauties to the strife—roses, lilies and primroses all have to go in the procession, and the victor's war cry, is heard by the sulking ear of the vanquished. Is not all this a remnant of savagery, when each stranger was accounted as a foe, and all not of the tribe had to be beaten into insensibility or death? Is the league of any political party, with its party emblems, in any way superior to the savage's totem? Distinction with this difference that the Indian and New Zealander, is a savage and a savage only, while the man of the eighteenth, and part of the nineteenth century, is supposed and arrogated to be civilised, and a civiliser of his savage brother. Hark back to the old election days, when the "blues and the yellows" were at it con amore for days, nay for weeks—when beer and blood flowed into the same gutter, when as once occurred, even ladies forgot their reserve and mingled in the din, when the rosy lips of a duchess were pouted to receive the embrace of a drunken butcher, merely to gain the low vote, and ask not where party strife begins and ends. Dickens has well satirised the "Eatanswill" elections and the fights of the rival editors of the political papers of the "blues" and the "buffs" in his Pickwick papers and well he might. Look at the vast sums spent in bribing electors, ruining their views of moral rights, and corrupting whole communities. The Reform Bill like a neat-handed Phyllis swept away many of these cob-webs, from the scene of politics, but the spiders have been spinning new ones in quiet darkness. We have strangled open bribery, by the tawny fingers of law, and have removed much of the evils of intimidation, and force, by the ballot but the monster of partyism, is as much a living factor as ever he was in the days of Pitt or Walpole, his power is little impaired yet lingers to be felt—"ex ungue leonem" is still true.

Cleisthenes, 509 years before Christ divided Greece into townships of one hundred each, and by bounds, and every one had to register his name and property, doing so he was a free man, and every one voted and was taxed at his own home. What a picture of Arcadian simplicity in antithesis to our gigantic system of wheels within wheels! As was well said, we are when getting pure copper, obliged to rid it of dross, so with political institutions, the whole series of civilisations is one effort prolonged through ages to get pure copper. It is so easy when figures count up, to make them suit our pre-conceived theories, and notions on political matters, and a leader has only to marshal them in a meretricious array, to make good the proposition, which falls like gentle dew on the ears of his adherents, and which they were quite willing to hug complacently even if no figures existed. "Great is Diana of the Ephesians!" is no new cry. To go roaming about the political world without a "label" pinned on one, is more atrocious than a dog without a muzzle, and any member of a party, original enough to think and act for himself, is doomed to political ostracism—a wounded beast stands a better chance for mercy at the horns of his fellows than an independent thinker or asserter of his thoughts in the arena of politics—traitor, renegade, Judas are colloquial terms in the air of politics.

The truth is that in politics a sentimental bigotry has become indurated generation after generation, so as to assume the features of heredity. It is no uncommon thing to be certain as to what ground a son of an aristocratic house will occupy on the political field, as the ancestors always were Whig or Tory, as the case may be, and a desertion from the beaten path would be regarded as a monstrosity. There is no honest looking at a subject with eyes blurred by the steam of the cauldron of politics. If it originates with friends, it is bolted, however unpalatable; it with opponents, every effort is put out for its strangulation; if every conscience whispers that it is "good for food and calculated to make one wise," the only possibility of its existence lies in the fact that an outside world may insist on the measure becoming law. Political foes are pelted with mud in the hopes that some of it will not wash off.

Monarchs in England did very long ago help to keep up the fires of political strife, but fancy it being done in 1780; when Keppel ran for the borough of Windsor against the candidate of royalty, poor old George III. canvassed in person against Keppel, and actually was seen going into a sick mercer's shop muttering in his jumbled up style of iterated dictation, "The Queen wants a gown—wants a gown. No Keppel! no Keppel!"

The purchase of a lady's silk gown was a very mild and innocent bribery in those days of corruption. We have put a stop to isolated bribing, but wholesale bribery is still in the air. It assumes now the expenditure of large monies where no pressing need is for public works, gigantic monopolies granted to favoured corporations (willing hands to sustain the party in power), the immoral poison of corruption percolates through these strata of public life.

Political creeds, as they affect both head and heart, are lugged with solemn gravity, and there is a species of eloquence redundant with catch-phrases lying like a fringe around the creeds—"the working man's friend," the "coming economist of public money," the "asserter of the equal rights of all," the champion of this or the other *ism*, etc., the "patriot," etc., and the more noise that ensues the better, while the best classes, the thinking, educated and pure minded keep aloof from the dirty sawdust of the political arena. Go back a little in our own House of Commons, and as was pointed out, look at the enormous waste of money and time over the Pacific Railroad inquiry, and contrast the expense with the net result.

Guizot tersely says "that the aim of representation is to oppose a barrier at once to tyranny and to confusion." How widely is the aim separated in real life from the results !

"Plurality (said Pascal) which does not reduce itself to unity is confusion ; unity which is not the result of plurality is tyranny."

Fabré (another French thinker) reminds us that "all political struggles have a root in the variance of two principles, a new, which seeks to shape itself beside an old one already there. . . There always has been a party which laid the greater stress on the old, and rejected the new with emphasis. When this tendency is dominant, conservatism is the watch-word, and a condition of seeming stagnation begins, but after reaching its culmination it has to give way to the steadily increasing pressure of the new, which now, frequently with violent commotions, declares a war on the old, in a more or less radical fashion, and every revolution is based on a violently repressed or badly directed *evolution.* So strong has "party" gone in France, that any party would welcome a foreign invasion which would overthrow their adversaries."

Speaking of the tyranny of politics, a late American writer characterises it very justly, as a survival of the savage or neo-savage community, *e.g.*, as is shown in the Russian *Mir* and in the Hindoo village community and also the Indian tribe, whoever submits not to what the rest dictate in custom, religion and ideas of morality becomes an outcast, is tabooed -- while the Hindoo who changes his theological theories, (his brethren remaining firm in Brahmanism or the profession of Mahomet) must go, if not, they will cut off both "his pipe and his water." Communism in land, coin, and property is an anachronism, but the imposition of communal shackles on thought, religious or political, is an outrage and more so if backed up by the terrorising influences of majorities. As Sir H. Maine truly said, the vast majority of mankind have stereotyped their institutions—a political party is tolerant of just so much and no more of truth than falls within its own political lines—any truth struggling into or within the lines of the opposing party is to be treated both with suspicion, scorn, and decapitation unless it is evident that the great creature, the public at large wills it, it is easy then to become proprietor and sole owner of it—the patent medicine.

There is no trace of "party government" in England till after the Revolution, before that the King's ministers were his personal friends. William III. first formed a ministry based on political bases ; he had essayed to rule by a ministry culled from the best men of all parties, but so deeply rooted was the poison of political hostility that his ministry was no exemplification of the "happy family ;" growling and scratching assailed his royal ears and he was forced to form a cabinet of a one-party *materiel*, who were ready to rely and hope for a majority of their own creed, on the floor of the houses. This inaugurated policy was completed by 1697—fond delusion—as we shall see that government by party by no means is in the correct sense a government by majority, but is really, when examined, perceived to be merely government by the *majority of a majority. i. e.,* by the majority of whichever party holds for the time in its powerful arm a majority in the House.

With all classes of politicians all is fair in party warfare. The Jesuitical principle of the "end justifying the means" has full swing, and as was said, truth, honour, and fair dealing are all alike sacrificed to the exigencies of either party ; and while parliament should exercise an influence over any ministry, (with the reins in hand of officialism) the ministry in one way or another by devious devices, is able to mould a parliament into plasticity, and "strong governments are by no means *ex necessitate* good governments." If this was true, then as an English writer says, Walpole's was the strongest England ever had, but strong though it was, its main strength developed from the use of a power of corrupting others, and being in itself corrupt to the very core. Twenty-one years it lived, but the whole series was barren of legislation. Pitt's lasted seventeen years, and his majority was so overwhelming, that as used to be said "all his opponents could be carried about in a hackney coach." Party government is an unknown factor in ecclesiastical, municipal, banking, railroad and other great corporations meeting together, and if indulged in would involve stockholders, churches, and finally the public at large in a beautiful series of ruins ; the proposer of its use would require at once the attention of an insanity-expert, and yet strangely we go on year in and year out, still pursuing the absurd practice, in the most solemn affairs which touch every man, and that too in the halls of an assembly awful in its dignity, and superior almost to the law of the land. So much for political heredity.

In days of yore, Ministers of the Crown were not members of Parliament, the leavening influence in the House was not composed of the king's ministers but of private members. Somers (as has been pointed out), long before he became a minister, drew up the " Bill of Rights." The "Triennial Bill " was the work of a private member, and it is to a committee of the House that we owe the complete " Habeas Corpus Act " and the " Great Remonstrance." In matter of stern fact the whole procedure of government by party is parallel to a good fox hunt, where the chief minister is master of the hounds, the hounds are his majority and the unfortunate fox is the public who is too often given but little chance for a fair run, but is cajoled by flattery and promises with a constitution healthy at first but now weighted down by luxurious excesses.

Jacobinism in France was a fearful example of how the brutality of majorities would prostitute acquired power, abstract ideals were made the engines that crushed the individuality out of Parisian life, even the natural freedom of men and women, nay of children, went down before it. The maxim that the minority must yield to the majority was borne out to its utmost tether, till it finally arrived at the absurdity of moulding a real concrete whole population into the solidarity of a bare uniformity of dress, diet, religion, and political thought.

The evil of it lay, as Professor Clifford has shown, in pushing the "equation " too far. When you do so it begins to talk nonsense, and the leaders of the then Parisian thought seized on certain *a priori* principles and theories, true in the abstract, but distinctly of one class only, disregarding all principles of the other class. Half-truths were made to do duty as if they were whole-truths, and the *only* truths, and the government became at once theological, ethical, philanthropical, and pedagogical, till the *reductio ad absurdum* was reached, and shirts were taken from the owners to clothe the community, and in one day 10,000 people lost their shoes, but the benign influence of a rule by majorities had to be their comforter. The theory of the " vox populi" being a " vox Dei" came on to be shivered to atoms. Some of the germs floated to England, and we here are slightly inoculated with the poison. A French writer of power in thought says of man, " he is too unlike the brute to be guided by an instinct equal to infallibility, and on the other hand, too like the brute to be non-dominated by passion." Therefore he is doubly exposed to error. There is in modern politics another feature which minimises with force the theory that all of the state is represented, namely, the " American caucus," in which the name or names are arrived at of those who are to represent *all*, and no matter how impure the modes by which the conclusion is arrived at, the party or parties chosen, and they only, are the ones to go to the polls. What a field of fraudulent tricks and contrivances of wire-pulling this spreads out ! The majority of a mere minority of the electors arrogate to themselves (the wire-pullers) to speak for a community at large, and the long-suffering public endures all. " *Qui vult decipi decipiatur*" is where the great public stand. In truth, the falsity of representation as it is, and particularly of representation by majorities as they now are, is a lie, and " no lie rots away till its work is done." When the due time comes, and it is coming apace, the people will get tired of the mendacious theory, and pitch it into the sea, but public opinion must be wakened up and things looked at as they are in their naked deformity, and what George Eliot called " the right of private haziness " must be subdued. A brutal majority may proclaim that white is black, but no numerical force or counting by heads can make it true. As things are to-day, the result of elections is to evolve a majority-party holding in itself the potentiality of evolving in the House a second being, powerful enough to carry things with a high hand, but perhaps destined to be swamped out of political existence by its rival ; it is a species of moral or immoral play at see-saw, with old boys at each end of a plank. Writers and painters of the Indian council at all events represent the chiefs of our red brothers as dignified in their eloquence ; ours cannot be accused of much that is peculiar to themselves beyond vituperation of rivals and anxiety to keep the spoils of office and add to them if allowed, and such will continue to be till the sentimental error of partyism is killed out. We are by law in our day restrained from fuddling the electoral brain with alcohol and poisoning all of conscience that was in the heart by golden guineas, but we can still speciously promise and not fulfil, and when asked for a " fish " give a "serpent" instead.

Even that small portion of the republic of letters "the press" is preeminently distinguished by an adulterous prostitution in politics; paid by one side or the other, it repeats with parrot like fidelity, the story it is taught and flings all that it can of mud in a shower of vituperation, over the opposition—bought in "market-overt" it is no longer the dispenser of truth, but an engine strangling truth, more fiercely than an Indian thug, and painting as may be ordered the country in black colours, or white, and its masters and owners as the very saviours of mankind—this poison flows freely through the electoral veins, and so strong is the sentiment of partyism in politics, that "my own party's paper" whether government or opposition is to "me" a sort of "Protestant Koran" and I become equally ready with any follower of Mahomet to apply the fire and sword to unbelievers in my "doxy." There is a strong element of pope lom-infallibility in the transactions of majorities; power by no means carries truth in its embrace, as a vital necessity, any more than do mere numbers. The majority tyranny however speciously gilt over, is in essence as much arbitrary as the *fiat* of a Russia's Czar for Siberia.

In fact so ingrained in the Anglo-Saxon breast is the furor of political strife, that it requires both time and education up to a higher stand to get rid of it, and any one seeking to restore the condition of primitive political purity, may look to many as a kind of political "Dodo." The incongruous elements which go to make up a parliament, develop too often in a turgid verbosity, and certain it is that the laws made during a session, are often so unworkable as to be repealed in the next one, or if left to linger, they are the files on which judicial teeth are broken amid laments as to their unmeaningness, or if a reasonable construction is applicable, the unfortunate suitor has felt keenly the process arrived at, both in heart and pocket.

Applied science will alone kill out the evils of unrepresentation, majority's brutality and crude legislation, developed in the steaming hot-beds of political strife. There is in all our race an aggressive quasi-belligerent force, which if not directed in the intellectual line, is likely to be formidable in the direction of sentiment. In so far from a majority being the duplication of what is good, and of "honest report and calculated to make one wise," it is a fact that the ruling minds are most often the minority of a minority. Power crushing is always the distinguishing mark of majorities, but infallibility is by no means a necessary ingredient with them. In fact it is beyond a doubt that as we are *now*, the great mass of the heavily taxed electors have no representation in parliament, and even the crowds surging at a polling place, are simply the specimen bricks of a party system, monotonous in its solidarity, and guiltless of free choice or intellectual criticism. So long as "our man" is in we are happy.

Party government will not be torn away for a good while from the jaws of politicians, it is too sweet a morsel, and has been well called a "Fetish" garlanded with dirty laurels, for many a long year. In our system the melancholy minority on the floor of the House, keep company with their miserable friends who are a minority outside the House.

Too much time is absorbed in the House by legislation emanating from Treasury benches, a legislation which is really not the faculty of any government of any shade, but is the right and business of Parliament, not of a government. Ministers should be confined to a bare recommendation of measures, and there should be as in France, a legislative committee to put such measures into shape, and have the House at large discuss them. This however, would probably save a great deal of money and time, consumed in scolding harangues, and quietly kill out a great deal of ministerial éclat which now attaches itself to measures of government, and therefore for a good while we are not likely to see this melioration carried out. It would tend to make ministers the servants, not the mastering manipulators of Parliament, and shear them of power and patronage, but the country would be the gainer. This also would be too radically good to be welcomed, it would *perforce*, batter itself against the granite walls of officialism, and the hoary traditions of centuries of parliaments, some worse, some better than ours. Now leaving this branch of the subject, let us look at some of the patriotic schemes of remedy suggested. Of course it is easier to see faults than to remedy a disease, especially when the latter is very chronic, and the patient advanced in years, but the subject is a vitally important one, and comes home to every man's door.

Lubbock says the Swiss have in conjunction with a wide suffrage what is known as the "Referendum," *i. e.*, bills passing the assembly are referred directly to the whole electorate, and are often rejected by large majorities.

THE SCRUTIN DE LISTE.

In this, each constituency returns several members, each elector has a number of votes equal to the number of representatives, but can't give more than one vote to any one candidate.

PROPORTIONAL REPRESENTATION.

The Limited Vote.—Here each elector has a number of votes somewhat less than the number of representatives.

The Free List.—Where the elector votes for a list.

The Cumulative Vote.—Where each elector has a number of votes, equal to the number of representatives, but can divide them up as he chooses.

The Single Transferable Vote.—Here the elector has only one operative vote, but is allowed to indicate to which candidate he desires it to be transferred if not required, by the one to whom he first devotes it.

The Single System works badly, as is the fact when an election is to be had the Conservatives put one name up and the Reform party another, and the elector is presented with a sort of " Hobson's choice," as the bringing in of a third candidate would in the colloquial phraseology of politicians " split up the party." The *clique* system flows in the bed of *single representation, i. e.,* any number, few or large, of electors may have some one favourite " fad " which they hoist up into conspicuity, and the glare and noise they surround it with too often darkens and hushes the interest of a public, on whom far more pressing matters should be imposed for consideration. The candidate is generally too cunning not to catch the breeze with sails spread and is wafted into the parliamentary haven —often a person known to fame only for his noisy insistence of a new doctrine, probably an attenuated part merely of a half-truth.

A majority of electors in each constituency is by no means the same as a majority of all the electors. Suppose, says Lubbock, a community of 60,000 electors is divided in three divisions each containing 20,000, and that there are as a fact 32,000 Liberals and 28,000 Conservatives, the division might be and likely would be as follows—

	1st Division.	2nd Division.	3rd Division.
Liberals,	15,000	9,000	8,000
Conservatives,	5,000	11,000	12,000
	20,000	20,000	20,000

And thus though in a minority, the Conservatives actually return two members out of three, and this is no hypothetical case.

THE SCRUTIN DE LISTE.

Assume a constituency returning 7 members. The two great parties may be very evenly balanced, but whichever had the majority, however small, would return the whole of the 7 representatives, *e.g.,* Liverpool we will say has 31,000 Conservative electors and 30,000 Liberals, under this system the 31,000 electors would have 7 members while the 30,000 would have none at all. Lubbock concludes and justly that the " *Scrutin de Liste*" gives unfair preponderance to a majority, while where parties are at all evenly balanced, the transfer of a few votes from one side to the other, may entirely alter the balance of power.

The Single Transferable Vote we have spoken of was adopted in Denmark in 1855, and still is there now in active operation.

In the system of Proportional Representation, it is suggested that each elector shall have one vote, but he may vote in the alternative for as many candidates as he chooses, by writing simply the figures 1, 2, 3, etc., opposite to their respective names. Therefore, if A's vote be not required for his candidate 1, he should be allowed to have its weight transferred to candidate 2, or in other words his A's action at the polls is not a mere cipher in the political field. All votes for candidate No. 1 above what is required to put him in, are transferred to candidate No. 2, etc. The ballot papers are then all mixed up and drawn out successively and stamped with numbers, so as no two shall bear the same number. The quotient obtained by dividing the whole number of good ballots papers tendered by the number of members to be elected+1 and increasing the quotient by 1, is the *quota*, and so denominated. Each candidate who has a number of *first* votes equal to or greater than the *quota*, shall be declared elected, and so many of the ballot papers containing these votes as equal the *quota* shall be set aside as of no further use. On all other ballot papers the name of the elected candidate shall be cancelled, with the effect of raising by so much in the order of precedence all votes given to other candidates after him. *Rule 4.* This process is to be repeated till no candidate has more than a *quota* of first votes or votes deemed first. *Rule 5.* Then the candidate or candidates with the fewest *first* votes or votes deemed *first,* shall be declared to be *not elected,* with the effect of raising by so much in the order of preference all votes given to candidates after him or them. Rule 4 shall again be applied if possible. Rule 6. When by successive applications of Rules 4 and 5 the number of candidates is reduced to the number of members remaining to be elected, the remaining candidates shall be declared elected.

THE CUMULATIVE VOTE.

Here each elector has as many votes as there are candidates, and he may cumulate them all on one candidate or divide them up among the candidates as he chooses.

THE FREE LIST OR TICKET SYSTEM.

By this the elector would vote for a list.

THE LIMITED VOTE.

In this the constituency returns three or four members, but the elector has a number of votes somewhat less than the number of members to be elected, the most common arrangement being for the constituency to return three members, each elector having two votes of which, however, he may only give one to any one candidate.

There is a work of an American called *Sterne* which lauds the work of the English Mr. Hare, at the same time suggesting some improvements on Hare's great work on Representative Government.

In this system of Sterne the ideas are nearly on a line with Mr. Hare's. Each voter may cast votes equal to the number of candidates for election, the voter may concentrate on one or divide them up as he pleases, *e. g.,* there being three candidates, each voter may concentrate on one or divide his vote among the three. A minority having one-third of the voters or more can therefore always, by concentrating all their votes on one candidate, secure his election. In the limited voting, *e. g.,* where three members can be by law returned the voter may only vote for two, therefore the minority can return one member.

Canton after Canton of the Swiss, and State upon State in America adopted this mode.

MR. HARE'S SCHEME

Is to substitute for the dominance of local majorities, a true representation of the people. He proposes to divide at each general election the number who vote by the number of members to be elected. The balloting paper to be printed thus :—

> Name of voter.
> Address.
> Vote No.
> Town or city of

The above elector hereby records his vote for the candidate named 1, in the list below or in the event provided for by this act for the other candidates successively in their numerical order.

1. A. B.   2. C. D.   3. E. F.   4. G. H., &c.   That is if A.B. gets too many votes, C.D. gets the unrequired balance, or if A.B. has too few, all of A.B.'s go to C.D.

Each voting paper after the candidate is declared elected, shall be endorsed with the candidate's name to whom it is appropriated so that election agents may consult them.

To sum up.

1. No vote to be counted for more than one candidate.

2. No candidate to have more votes recorded or counted in his favour than is the "Quota" in numbers.

3. Each voter to have the right of naming several candidates in his order of preference so that if his vote be not counted for the *first,* then it may be counted for the *second* or the *third,* &c.

It has also been suggested that in a constituency, *e.g.,* say Glasgow—any elector may vote for say Mr. Glandstone or Lord S., or Sir J. B. who never represented Glasgow and are not candidates for representing Glasgow at the now election. In other words any elector may vote for any name that impresses him whether the owner is a candidate at the said elector's voting-place or not. The design of course is a good one to bring on the floor of the House all available talent, but it is respectfully submitted that Canada is not yet a field for such an experiment.

"IN DEO SPERO."

June 26, 1893.

THE REPRESENTATION ACT.

Whereas, minorities in elections have not heretofore had proper representation in Parliaments, and it is desirable to remedy this evil.

Be it enacted, &c. :—

1. This Act shall be known as the "Representation Act," and in the interpretation thereof shall be construed by all courts as having for its object the representation of minorities in Parliaments.

2. All Acts heretofore passed inconsistent with this Act, shall with regard to all inconsistent provisions be repealed, but all previous acts not so inconsistent shall remain in force. This Act shall come into force within one year from the passing thereof.

3. No property qualification shall be required from any candidate, but each candidate for election in the Dominion or any Provincial Parliament, must be either a British-born or naturalized subject of the Crown.

4. No person shall in future be a candidate for a seat in the Dominion or any Provincial Parliament who is in the employment of the Crown, or receives pay therefrom, but the members composing the Dominion and several Provincial Governments, now holding offices are exempt from the provisions of this clause, but they must on a change of ministry seek re-election as is now the practice.

5. Immediately upon the coming into force of this Act and within three calendar months from such date, it shall be the duty of the clerk of the House of Commons in Ottawa and of the clerk of each one of the respective Provincial Parliaments, to ascertain the numbers of voters recording votes at the last general elections for the Dominion and of the last general election in each of the Provinces, and the clerks of said Provinces shall officially certify within the time aforesaid such number to the clerk of the House of Commons in Ottawa.

6. On receipt of such information the said clerk of the House of Commons at Ottawa shall thereupon having previously added to such number the number of thousand or   as the case may require from the statistics of population, which addition is to be considered as a fair allowance for an increase in population, proceed to divide the number of electors for the Dominion Parliament by the number of members allowed by the now laws to sit therefor dispensing with fractions and the result so obtained shall hereafter be known as the "Quota" for Dominion elections and he shall at the same time proceed to divide the number of voters who voted at the last election in each Province by the number of members entitled to sit by law in such and each Provincial Legislature or Parliament, adding and allowing as above for increase in each Province of population or if diminution is shown by Provincial statistics, then allowing for such diminution as the case may be, and it shall be the duty of the said clerk of the House of Commons and of the clerk of each Provincial Legislature to similarly obtain the said "Quota" at all times hereafter within one month before any Dominion or Provincial election shall be had.

7. Within two weeks from obtaining such "Quota" the clerk of the House of Commons at Ottawa shall publish officially in the *Dominion Gazette*, the "Quota" for Dominion elections and the "Quota" for each respective Provincial election, of which all officials are to take notice and govern themselves thereby, and such "Quota" shall be the number each candidate for election must obtain to obtain a seat in the said House of Commons or of any Provincial Legislature.

8. All persons who acted as returning officers, or shall hereafter act as such, are to give all the information in their power to enable the clerk of the House of Commons and the clerks of the respective Provincial Legislatures to carry out this Act, and any one so refusing shall be compellable by a writ of mandamus from any competent court to do so, which shall be issued on *primâ facie* proof of such refusal, and the penalty of disobedience shall be enforced by fine and imprisonment of not less than six months in a jail.

9. When an election for either the Dominion Parliament or any Provincial Parliament is ordered to be had, the sheriff of each county in the province in which a provincial election is to be had, shall, 21 days before, cause the same to be duly proclaimed officially in the official paper of the province, and the clerk of the House of Commons, at Ottawa, shall likewise 21 days before such election, if the same is a Dominion election, cause the same to be advertised in the *Dominion Gazette*, and all candidates shall be called on thereby to put themselves in nomination, and the time for such elections shall be so proclaimed.

10. Within 14 days from the insertion of such notices in the *Dominion Gazette*, or any Provincial Official Gazette or paper, all returning officers are to be nominated by the respective governments of the Dominion or Provinces, and such returning officers shall proclaim the fact of such their appointment and shall appoint the proper number of deputy returning officers as by law now provided.

11. Such proclamations by returning officers shall specify the names and other information requisite for the guidance of electors, as to the deputy returning officers who shall issue official notices as to the time, day and hour and place of election, and the respective polling places in districts where such deputy returning officers reside.

12. All candidates for any Dominion election or Provincial election eligible as such under this Act, shall within seven days from such advertisement by the aforesaid returning officers, lodge with such returning officers a statutory declaration showing their being so eligible, and also deposit in current money of the Dominion the sum of two hundred dollars, which shall be returned to the person so depositing the same, provided he is not elected, but if elected, the same shall be paid in at once after such member takes his seat to the Treasurer of the Dominion or Province as the case may be, and by him applied to the payment of Dominion or Provincial elections, and the names of candidates so proposing themselves shall be duly advertised by all deputy returning officers, and shall by them be signified to the electors in their divisions, and shall be printed on all the ballot papers and numbered numerically in order with the numbers 1, 2, 3, 4, 5, etc., as the case may be, as follows :—

Name of voter.
Address.
Vote No.
County or —.

1. Name of candidate preferred, John Smith.   x
2.   "   "   next   "   W. Jones.   x
3.   "   . " next   "   C. Thomas.   x
4.   "   "   next   "   R. Williams. x
5.   "   "   next   "   B. Thomas.   x

The ballot papers shall be marked by a cross put by the elector as now required by law opposite to the name of the party he votes for, and no elector shall have more than one vote at any Dominion or Provincial election, but shall vote where his name appears on the legal list of voters, and the capacity of any elector to vote where he has a property qualification therefor, is by this Act abolished, but it is the intention of this Act that each elector voting may vote for all the candidates whose names appear on the ballot paper, by putting a cross opposite to all or any of their names in the order of preference he shall choose to make, but no elector's vote so recorded shall count for more than one, but if the candidate numbered one in his preference of choice shall obtain more than the "Quota" required for election by law, then such excess shall be transferred to the candidate numbered two in the voter's order of preference, expressed by such voter as aforesaid, and the same shall continue to be done till all candidates eligible through obtaining the required "Quota" are disposed of.

13. All provisions of the election laws not inconsistent with this Act are to be considered as in full force.

14. All ballot papers and other papers now required by law to be printed for use at elections, shall be prepared by the proper officials as heretofore has been the custom, but shall be altered to suit the changes made under the provisions of clause 12 or any succeeding clauses of this Act.

15. All voting shall be begun and ended as heretofore, in one day.

16. When any election is completed the ballot boxes shall be returned by the deputy returning officers to the returning officers from whom their appointments were received, and such returning officers shall within seven days after receipt thereof, and due advertisement in the official paper of the province where such election is had, either for Dominion or Provincial elections, proceed in accordance with the provisions of clause 12 of this Act, in the presence of agents who may attend (for candidates) to make count of such votes, and such counting shall be made in the order of preference and strictly in accord with the above section 12, and he shall declare what candidate or candidates are elected, and if the election is a Provincial election he shall forthwith officially declare the same, and transmit the said declaration with the ballot papers to the clerk of the Legislature of the Province where the election is had, with his statutory declaration as to the same, and if the same be an election for the Dominion each returning officer in each province shall similarly transmit the like papers to the clerk of the House of Commons in Ottawa, where the same may be inspected by parties interested, and the result shall be duly proclaimed by each clerk of the several Legislatures of the Provinces and of the House of Commons, if the same is a Dominion election, in the proper official papers, and any official wilfully contravening the provisions of this Act, shall be liable to a fine of five hundred dollars, or in default of payment thereof to imprisonment for six months, and any official guilty

of bribery or corruption shall be sentenced to imprisonment for three years, and to be incapacitated from ever voting thereafter, or holding any office or emolument from the Crown.

17. The official declarations of the clerks of the Houses, Dominion or Provincial respectively, shall be made within ten days from the receipt of the aforesaid papers from the returning officers, and all election returns and ballot papers shall be retained in proper custody till after one month shall have expired from the meeting of the Dominion Parliament or Provincial Parliament for which they were used, when they shall be destroyed, unless required for judicial purposes.

18. The constituencies in the Dominion elections and Provincial elections shall be entitled for the present to send the same number and no more representatives to Parliament, as is now their right.

19. To prevent the evils of what is commonly known as the " Gerrymandering system " it is declared hereby that no alteration of territorial election fields shall take place oftener than once in ten years, and all constituencies now returning members for Dominion or Provincial Parliaments shall return the same number and from the same places, and such number shall represent the same territories for the space of ten years from the passing of this Act.

20. Residence in any constituency shall not be required of any candidate, and any one properly qualified may be a candidate for any Dominion or Provincial election, whether he resides within the territory where such election is to be had or not, and any one may as aforesaid be a candidate at any number of election places, but in such case he shall be obliged to make only one deposit of two hundred dollars as aforesaid provided, and no more, and in case of his return for more than one constituency, Dominion or Provincial, he shall at once elect where he chooses to sit, and when he signifies his election in the way hereinafter provided for, then the person or persons next after him of candidates in the constituency who are preferentially entitled to the number of votes immediately less in order than his, shall be declared elected, and the returning officers shall before any other candidates are disposed of, proceed to dispose of those who are candidates for more than one constituency, and finding any one by reason of preferential votes entitled to sit for more than one constituency, such person shall be notified by the returning officer of the fact, and it shall be his duty within 24 hours of the transmission of such message to choose which constituency he shall represent, and in default of his doing so his name shall be dropped as if he never had been a candidate at such election, and he shall signify his election to such returning officer by telegram, and in case by reason of such his neglect or refusal so to signify his election, his name is so dropped, the officials aforesaid shall proceed with the names of the other candidates in order of preference designated by the electors, and the votes recorded in constituencies other than the one he chooses to sit for, shall be distributed in the order of designated preference among the other candidates at each such constituency so that such votes shall not be nugatory, and the acceptance aforesaid by telegram and notification from the said officials to the candidate shall be legal and final though transmitted by telegram.

21. The elections to be held next after the passing of this Act, whether Dominion or Provincial, shall not be held sooner than three months after the date of the proclamation directing the same to be held so as to allow full time for the proper carrying out of the provisions thereof, and the working out of the same by the officials for the purpose appointed, but this clause is not to be imperative as to subsequent elections after said first election.

MEMORANDUM.

I have ventured to put my ideas into the above form.

The bill can be altered *mutatis mutandis* to suit any country where the style &c. of officials in parliament are different from ours.

I have spent a great deal of time in considering what is to be done with the surplus or unused votes in any constituency after the return of a candidate is arrived at, there will likely be many such which as a fact are left in the "air" and utterly wasted. After considering it anxiously in every light I can arrive at no solution satisfactory to my mind, so that they shall be saved as *atoms* of representation, one cannot rightly take them from say constituency A and give them to constituency B because in doing so you are robbing the voter in A of what the law has given him as a right.

"In Deo Spero."

PACIFICO.

When the French Academicians were getting up their dictionary, they submitted to Cuvier their definition of a crab as "a red fish that walks backward," whereupon he remarked that their definition was correct, excepting that the crab was not red, was not a fish, and did not walk backward.

King Charles II. asked the members of the Royal Society how it was that when a fish was placed in a bucket of water, the weight of the bucket and its contents was not thereby increased. Several presented ingenious explanations, after which one of the members rose up and denied the fact, when the king rejoined: "Odds; fish! but you're right."

Those who write so fluently and frequently about "the people's rule," "the government is what the people make it," "the power of the ballot," which "drops as snow upon the sod," etc., are as wide of the mark as the savans above mentioned, in that they have not themselves ascertained the facts, but merely accept and reiterate current dogmas. They expatiate at length on "Democracy" which has no existence outside of Switzerland, and there only partially. W. D. Stead, in the *Review of Reviews* says that "Demos will regard millionaires as the cottager regards his bees." But his and others' "Demos" is as much a myth as the pagan Bacchus or Venus. De Tocqueville about half a century ago wrote a large volume entitled "Democracy in America"—thing that never existed on this continent; neither does "Representative government" really exist, excepting very partially in the elections of members of British school boards and, lately, in three Cantons of Switzerland.

It is primarily important to the consideration of any of the fundamental political questions now taken up by thinking persons to ascertain what is and what is not representation; how much influence voters, as such, really exert in the making of laws, or in any legislative act; and how far they might do in practice, through a better mechanism, they are now said to do in theory. The answers to these questions lie at the very foundation of all intelligent effort to improve industrial and moral conditions by legislative or politica processes.

CHAPTER I.

A PRIORI NEGATIVE DEMONSTRATION.

It can be demonstrated, irrespective of any experience, that under representation (so-called) by districts, minorities, from one-third down (the proportion growing less as the number of parties increases), can return a majority of the members in elective bodies. Suppose three constituencies of 3,000 voters each elect for each constituency a member of a so-called "representative" body. Let each "representative" be designed by capitals and each thousand voters by "lower case" letters; then

Constituencies.	Representatives.
a a b	A
a a b	A
b b b	B

Here two constituencies with 2,000 "a" voters each, and 1,000 "b" voters each, return an "A" member each. The third constituency, consisting entirely of "b" voters, returns one "B" member. But the "b" voters in the three constituencies number 5,000, and get but one member, while the "a" voters, with 1,000 less voters, get two members.

Now let us try with seven constituencies, each having 7,000 voters:

a	a	a	a	b	b	b	A
a	a	a	a	b	b	b	A
a	a	a	a	b	b	b	A
a	a	a	a	b	b	b	A
b	b	b	b	b	b	b	B
b	b	b	b	b	b	b	B
b	b	b	b	b	b	b	B

Here we have 16,000 "a" voters electing 4 members, and 33,000 "b" voters electing but 3 members, so that less than a third of the voters elect a majority of the so-called "representatives."

But to attempt to represent all grades of opinion by means of two parties is as absurd as it would be to undertake to fit every one by two sizes and makes of coats, hats or shoes. In proportion as people think for themselves—differentiate—the need is felt for a third, a fourth or even a fifth party; and still the current varieties of opinion on subjects pertaining to legislative action would be inadequately voiced, especially as these differences would extend to the exponents as well as to the principles or platform of a party. But let us try a third party "c."

Constituencies.							Representatives.
b	b	c	c	a	a	a	A
b	b	c	c	a	a	a	A
b	b	c	c	a	a	a	A
b	b	c	c	a	a	a	A
c	c	c	b	b	b	b	B
c	c	c	b	b	b	b	B
c	c	c	b	b	b	b	B

Here we have 49,000 voters in 7 constituencies. The "a's" with but 12,000—less than a fourth of the whole—still return 4 of the 7 "representatives," while the "c's" with nearly 50 per cent. more votes (17,000) than the "a's," do not obtain one member, and the "b's," with 8,000 more votes than the "a's" get one representative less.

Were there four, five, or six parties, the minority of voters that might thus secure a majority of the elected body would necessarily become less and less. That is, the more intelligent voters become, the less representation—if they vote according to their convictions—do they obtain, while the least intelligent are the most represented.

It may be claimed that the cases presented are extreme, not occurring in actual life. But there are other factors, not yet considered, that would increase these disparities. One is that it is practically impossible for voters, in a mass, to control party management; and a very small minority of the party not only *can*, but *do*—not only *do*, but *must* control the nominations, so that the *alternation*—not *choice*—of the voter is, in most cases, to vote for one man that he does not like in preference to another that he dislikes. If his party wins, he is *mis*-represented; if the other party wins, he is *un* represented.

CHAPTER II.

A POSTERIORI DEMONSTRATION ; THE "MAJORITY RULE" MYTH.

I might fill volumes with most conclusive proof from the figures of electoral votes, that a minority of voters, or a small majority, elect all the legislators in nearly every case, waiving for the time the fact that even those voters who do elect only have a choice of evils as a rule. But a few recent examples may suffice to establish that which no one well informed on such subjects would undertake to controvert.

In Oakland, Cal., seven councilmen and seven school trustees are elected from as many wards, into which the city is divided, and four more of each are elected "at large"; that is, all the voters in that city vote for four candidates "at large" and one from their respective wards. At the election of March, 1893, 28,488 votes were cast for the four councilmen elected "at large" (*scrutin de liste*) but only 10,195, or nearly 36 per cent., were cast for the candidates elect; thus over 64 per cent.—nearly two-thirds— of the votes cast were ineffective. For the members of the board of education so chosen 26,588 votes were cast, of which but 10,739, or a little over 40 per cent., were cast for the candidates elected. The votes cast in the seven several wards for school trustees aggregated 7,127, of which 3,265 were effective for the elected members or nearly 46 per cent. The 7 candidates elected to the council by wards received 3,079 out of 8,141 votes cast, so that only 37.8 per cent. of these votes were, in the most latitudinarian sense, effective.

The successful candidate for the school board from the 6th ward received 297 out of the 803 votes cast, or nearly 36 per cent. The candidate elected from the 7th ward to that body received 724 out of the 1,114 voters, which is nearly two and a half times as many votes as the candidate elected from the 6th received, yet each has the same voting power on the board; that is, in our present system of political arithmetic 297 is equal to 724.

The elected candidate from the 6th ward received only four votes more than one who was defeated, so that a change in three votes out of 803 would have elected another man ; that is, three voters in that ward had power to determine who should "represent" 800 besides themselves ! In three wards (1st, 2nd and 4th) as many defeated candidates received more votes (329, 372, 292) than the candidate elected from the 6th.

Of the councilmen elected by wards, two received less than a third of the votes cast in each ward (30·9 and 33·15 per cent.); two more received but little over a third (34·4 and 36), and none of them received half.

Taking the average, six out of the 11 councilmen voting for a measure against five opposed would represent but 20 per cent. of the voters, and from the inequality of the votes in the several wards, might represent less. Yet this *minority* can enact ordinances binding upon the whole people of Oakland ! And this is called "government of the people, by the people, for the people " !

At the election of six assemblymen from as many districts in Alameda County, Cal., on Nov. 8th, 1892, 17,307 votes were cast, of which 8,078—46 per cent.—were effective in electing candidates. A change of from one to less than three per cent. of the voters in three of those districts, of less than a third of one per cent. in another, and of $5\frac{1}{4}$ and $7\frac{1}{2}$ per cent. in the other two would have elected an entirely different delegation to the assembly from that county. And it is much the same in most of the districts in California. That is, a few of the most worthless, the most vicious or the most weak-kneed voters can turn the scale, so that men of character, honesty and determination can, as a rule, neither be representatives or represented.

In the San Francisco municipal election of Nov. 8th, 1892, the average vote for 12 Supervisors, (who are elected "at" large, or *Scrutin de Liste*) was 51,131, and that for successful candidates was 19,085,—slightly over 37 per cent. The Democratic party, on a vote of 39 per cent. of the whole, secured $83\frac{1}{3}$ per cent.—10 out of 12—of the Board. A vote of seven-twelfths of that Board would not, then, average a representation of more than about $21\frac{1}{2}$ per cent. of the voters. The 12 members of the Board of Education, also elected at large, received nearly the same percentage of the total vote as the Supervisors.

By comparing these percentages with those of Oakland for similar bodies, and with those of Alameda county for the Assembly, it will be seen that election either at large or by districts is equally unrepresentative.

In 1890 the Congressmen elected from the State of California received 128,451 votes out of 252,012 cast, or 50·1 per cent. In 1892 they received 119,171 out of 240,210, or 49·6 per cent. The political elements at work in 1892 differed widely from those of 1890, by reason of the increase of votes for "outside" parties, yet the percentage of voters represented (in a degree) varied but little one from the other ; and until we have complete proportional representation, independent of parties, mere changes in party names, or the organization of new parties, will accomplish little.

It is similar in voluntary organizations. On March 29th, 1893, the Typographical Union of San Francisco elected three delegates to the International Convention of that body, each member voting for three of the 11 candidates. The votes numbered 1,758, which, divided by three, gives 653 voters. The successful candidates received 280, 224 and 228 votes respectively, being an average of 217. This shows an average of 38 per cent. of the voters represented. A change of one vote would have elected another candidate, who received 227, in place of that one who received 228.

In the whole State, on November 8th, 1892, 249,363 votes were cast for assemblymen from 80 single districts, of which 116,908 votes were cast for members elected, and 132,455 against them, so that only a small fraction over 17 per cent. of the voters elected every member of the Assembly, and nearly 53 per cent. were totally unrepresented even in form, while most of the 47 per cent. were not probably fully represented in fact. The vote of 41 out of the 80 members could not, therefore, be fairly considered as representing, on the average, over 24 per cent. of the voters ; yet that proportion has the power to enact laws, so far as that house is concerned. Where there are two houses, the other is elected in a similar manner, or it is appointed.

Fortunately, this House, at its ensuing session, by their votes on certain measures, positively proved the preceding position.

On February 23rd, 1893, an amendment to the State constitution, requiring that on request of ten per cent. of the voters of the State, any bill passed by the Legislature must be submitted to the voters at the polls for ratification or rejection, and that any bill proposed by that percentage should be similarly submitted, was rejected by 32 negative votes out of the 80 assemblymen, the constitution requiring a two-thirds majority for any amendment thereto. These 32 members received a total of 44,281 votes in their several constituencies or districts, being less than 18 per cent. of the 249,603 votes of the State received by all candidates for the Assembly. Thus *less than a fifth* of the voters of the State are empowered under this sham of representation –this "majority rule" myth – to determine that the other four-fifths shall have nothing to do with the laws except to vote for the class of men usually nominated by the machinery of new as well as of old parties.

But the positive, special and conclusive proof that a bare majority would represent on an average about 24 per cent. of the voters, is shown in regard to a proposed amendment to the constitution, giving the Legislature power to so amend the tax laws as to permit the voters of each county or incorporated city or town to decide by direct vote what classes of property should and what should not be taxed. There were 42 negative votes on this proposition, which 42 members received an aggregate of 60,803 votes, which is less than ∶4½ per cent. of the total vote for assemblymen in the State.

In the Assembly elected in November, 1890, 133,265 votes were cast for the successful candidates out of a total vote of 248,423 for assemblymen, which is 53 per cent. The Vagrant Bill was passed by 44 ayes to 26 noes; the ayes had received 70,277 votes at the polls—a little over 28 per cent. of the total vote; the 26 noes had received 47,294 votes; and 130,702 voters, being over half the voters in the State, had not even a negative voice as to that law.

The bill for an appropriation of $300,000 to the World's Fair received 44 ayes, those members representing or receiving the votes of 80,886—less than a third of the whole. The 24 members who wanted a less amount appropriated received 36,651 votes; and 130,-886 voters—52.7 per cent. of the whole—had no opportunity to be heard from.

When U. S. Senator Stanford was re-elected by that Legislature, he received in the Assembly 59 votes, these representing 97,939 voters at the polls, or less than two-fifths of the whole, though his majority only lacked one of being three-fourths of that "representative" body.

The whole course of legislation might thus be followed up in any session of almost any legislature in the world with similar results. And if these figures do not prove my position that legislatures do not represent the opinions of voters in the enactment of laws, &c., then no figures can prove anything, arithmetic is a delusion and all reasoning impossible. It is fully as reasonable to claim that the earth is flat, with the heavenly bodies revolving around it as to assert that by our electoral system even an approximation to true representation can be obtained. And the demonstration to the contrary is much more easily understood in the latter than in the former case. Were it not that the false view is so persistently taught in educational institutions of all grades and types, in periodicals of all sorts and sizes—in short, iterated and re-iterated on every possible occasion, the proposition that any country, outside of three Cantons in Switzerland, has a really representative government or that "the people make the government what it is," would be laughed to scorn as the gibberings of an idiot or the croaking of a parrot. Political *science* to-day is where physical science was in the fifteenth century; it hardly exists.

CHAPTER III.

DIRECT LEGISLATION.

This is accomplished negatively by the Referendum, positively by the Initiative. At first sight, these, with the power of recalling a member on demand of a majority of his local constituency might seem to be sufficient, and the workings of the Referendum and the Initiative in Switzerland, and of the former of these occasionally in the United States and British North America, have been such as to create a favorable impression. But direct legislation, compared with proportional representation is as pack mules to a railroad. By simplifying and improving our system of enacting and executing laws, their number and complexity could doubtless be much reduced. Yet with all that could be done in this line (and which *never will be done* under our present electoral system) the necessary collective business of any municipality, state, province or nation, to be provided for by general enactment, would be too great and diversified to be handled advantageously, or even possibly, by the whole mass of voters; nor could even any considerable fraction of these act intelligently, whatever their mental ability and moral endowments, on the hundreds and even thousands of propositions coming before them. It is not a question of the intelligence or morality of the voters, as compared with those acting as their agents in legislatures, etc. The point is that in any but a very small and sparse community, the business of society must be transacted through agencies and by division of labor; and the tendency of social and industrial advancement lies actually and necessarily in this direction. No longer does the farmer shear his sheep and his family turn the wool laboriously into cloth; but he sends the wool to market, and buys the materials for his clothing, if not the clothing itself. And so of every occupation. Whether the change is a benefit or otherwise, it had to come, and the old cannot be restored. Public business needs to keep pace with industrial changes. Progress in any direction necessitates differentiation. In the very lowest animals, the stomach is substantially the whole animal, and the functions of the various organs as they begin to develop are interchangeable. It is only as the species rises in the scale of being, that the several organs become more and more distinct. So as the body politic grows, its functions become more differentiated, so that the direct transaction of the business of the whole by the whole, becomes either impossible, or as costly as it would be for the pastoralist to weave the wool of his sheep into his garments, or the wheat grower of Manitoba to haul his grain to a sea or lake port by ox-teams. If it would be an advantage for men to lose the present differentiation of their organisms and become clams, it would be also of advantage for the people to legislate directly, rather than through freely chosen and really representative bodies. "Direct legislation" may be designated "clam reform."

Even in small voluntary organizations committees are elected or appointed to conduct the details of their business, as a matter of convenience, if not of necessity. In many such only a minority of members can be induced to attend meetings where a majority of those present have full power to act.

For instance : previous to a recent change, the attendance at the monthly meetings of the Typographical Union of San Francisco, numbering nearly 700 members, rarely exceeded 150 and often fell below 100 ; yet in voting for elective officers nearly the entire strength was called out. In the Mechanics' Institute of San Francisco, the vote in February, 1892, was some 1,400, and on February 28th, 1893, 905 ; but it is only of late, owing to the agitation connected with the proportional plan that the attendance at its quarterly meetings reached as high as 117 to 150, out of a membership of nearly 4,000. It is evident that nearly every one would rather vote for competent persons to conduct any sort of collective business than attend to the details themselves.

Many local trades unions and other organizations send delegations of their members to act for them in National, Dominion, State, or Provincial assemblages. On March 29th, 1893, the Typographical Union of San Francisco elected three delegates to the International Convention (as detailed in Chapter II.) by 38 per cent. of the vote. They had to be elected in some way from all the local unions, as it was impossible for every compositor in the United States and British America to visit Chicago, and if they had all gone there, such a large number could not deliberate or transact any business. It is true that the acts of the convention have to be ratified by the members of the Union at large ; but if that was all to be done, there need have been no convention at all, as any proposed measure could have been merely ratified or rejected without bringing several hundred persons hundreds or thousands of miles to a common centre. The purpose, however, of this convention, as of any similar body, legislature, or parliament, was to consult, deliberate and decide with a view to practical action ; hence the members of such bodies should, as nearly as possible, *represent* the general views of those who sent them, concentrating their efforts on devising such measures as would carry out these views, subserving the interests and securing the approval of their constituents. "Direct legislation" cannot meet these requirements ; proportional representation can.

I mention this because the Typographical Union has been cited to prove the sufficiency of "direct legislation" to solve the political problem, while the experience of that Union proves the contrary. And I may add that, as a member of that Union, I was not long since called upon to vote, at about twenty-four hours' notice, on some thirty different propositions, having no means of forming an intelligent opinion as to much over half of them.

Every one at all posted as to the exigencies of legislation, or other collective action, knows that where there is any opportunity (as there always would be under proportional representation) to select a few competent and reliable *men*, it is much easier to do so than to decide upon the merits of many *measures*. Even with our present *mis*-representative and *un*-representative processes this is shown by the popular vote. A striking instance of this occurred in the California election of Nov. 8th, 1892, when both men and measures were voted upon at the polls. Five "propositions" and four constitutional amendments were submitted for direct vote. While 249,363 voters in the whole State voted for assemblymen and over 268,000 for presidential electors, the vote *pro* and *con* on election of U. S. Senators by the people was 201,300, being but a little over 80 per cent. of the vote for assemblymen. The vote for and against a new ferry depot in San Francisco was 181,726, or nearly 73 per cent.; educational qualification for voters, 192,729, being 77·7 per cent.; on refunding the debt, 168,504. 67½ per cent.; constitutional amendment No. 10, 190,273—76·3 per cent.; constitutional amendment No. 7, 168,490—67½ per cent.; constitutional amendment No. 11, 132,199—a little over 53 per cent. of the vote for assemblymen and *not half* that for Presidential electors ; constitutional amendment 5, 156,994—63 per cent.; constitutional amendment 14, 156,693—less than 63 per cent.

These figures are the sums of the vote, *pro* and *con*.

It has been claimed that the working of Direct Legislation in Switzerland has been so satisfactory as to prove that no representative body is needed excepting to formulate measures for the approval of or rejection by the voters, and hence that with the "Obligatory" Referendum, (one providing that all measures must be referred to the body of voters) and the Initiative, the legislature would simply be "a body of powerless committeemen." Committeemen, whether in voluntary organizations or in legislatures, are, however, well known to be far from "powerless." Every one at all acquainted with legislative operations knows that a bill can very rarely be passed in a legislature when it has been handicapped by an adverse report of a committee. It is equally well known that very few legislators have the requisite knowledge to vote intelligently, upon half or quarter of the bills coming before them, and are virtually compelled as to all the others, to vote according to the committees' reports.

It is, then, a fundamental necessity for effective work not only that public and collective business should be transacted by agents, but that these agents should be chosen in such a manner as to secure the most capable persons, fairly and fully representing not merely a party, fraction of a party, clique or "ring," but the whole body of the constituents. That is, they should be actually, and not merely nominally, representatives. No merchant or manufacturer would be satisfied with an agent or clerk, especially at a place distant from his centre of business, when not allowed to use his best judgment in the selection of a person, merely because he could instruct such agent or clerk what to do, or over-rule his action.

Another serious objection to the efficiency of the Initiative is that to formulate any measure by that means, some person or persons must be selected or empowered to draft it by some irregular process, subject to no efficient checks. These persons would be no more "representative" of the community generally, or of any portion of it than the average legislator, but would probably be less so, being liable to be composed of the scum that usually rises to the top in times of excitement. What security would there be that the persons so selected would not be the worst enemies of the proposed measures, secretly paid by powerful classes opposed to it to introduce some provision fatal to its efficacy or con-stitutionality, which the mass of voters would fail to detect? Even if they did detect it, when too late, they could only vote it down, and that would be claimed as proof of their hostility to the principle of the measure. Even in our present legislatures, all measures are liable to be exposed to close criticism, while in a truly representative legislature, no bill could escape a close analysis both as to its principles and details. But a bill presented for direct vote of the people can only be voted on by ayes and noes, amendments and substitutes being out of the question.

And would it not be much easier by proportional representation, to secure a body of men that would be competent to act on all legislative business, rather than to spasmodi-cally and specially, by some uncertain and irregular process, to organize a special committee for each and every measure, for which there seemed to be a popular demand?

Legislation under the Initiative, would be even more a work of Sisyphus, than it is at present.

As to the experience of Switzerland, direct legislation would naturally work better in a small and nearly stationary population, where every man's record is known from childhood, and public opinion therefore a greater power, than in large cities, or in states or countries where the population is migratory and the people given to frequent changes of residence, or that the antecedents of individuals are, for ordinary purposes, untraceable. But even in Switzerland the Cantons of Ticino, Neuchatel and Geneva have found it altogether inadequate and have in succession adopted a form of proportional representation which admits of parties being represented measurably in proportion to the number of voters in each party. In the Canton of St. Gall, a similar plan was rejected at the polls on January 30th, 1893, by 21,982 against 19,826 : in Soleure, on January 15th, by 6,620 to 4,950 ; and in Bâle, on Nov. 23rd, 1890, by 4,217 to 2,755. In the Cantons of Zug, Lucerne, and Vaud, it will probably soon be adopted. These figures indicate a progressive and rapid increase of public sentiment in its favor, even in the three Cantons wherein it has been, for the time, defeated. In all these Cantons the Referendum and Initiative are in operation, and the action in each proves that they are inadequate.

The Imperative Mandate may be regarded as a species of direct legislation, consisting in the power of a majority of the voters in any elective body to recall a member with whose course they are dissatisfied. Whatever benefit could be accomplished thereby has been reached in Switzerland by the Referendum and Initiative, so that in that country it is no longer mentioned. As it can only be used by a majority in a district, it is incom-patible with a representation of the whole body of voters, and would make political agitation incessant and intrigues without end. I am not aware that it has ever been put in practice, and may be regarded as a political fossil.

Little, if anything can be accomplished on this continent by picking up Switerland's old clothes that are worn nearly threadbare or cast off altogether, when we can get something better than even its new apparel.

Finally, "Direct Legislation" in America (particularly on the Pacific Coast) would work on the plan of a Prohibitory liquor law passed by the Rhode Island Legislature some thirty years ago, in which the prohibitory clauses were clear and strong, but the penal clauses somehow "got left." One man remarked that everybody should be happy, in that the temperance men had secured the law, which was what *they* wanted, and the liquor sellers could continue their business unmolested, which was all *they* wanted. Even so, the people would get the shell by the permission to propose a law, but the financially strongest and the machine politicians would get the oyster by injecting what they pleased into the law before its submission, much the same as manufacturers of glass lamp chimneys are said to put materials in the glass to make the chimneys break quickly.

CHAPTER IV.

THE CUMULATIVE VOTE.

This process, as applied to the election of directors in corporations and trustees for Reclamation Districts, is thus defined in Art. XII., Sect. 12, of the Constitution of California :—

"In all elections for directors or managers of corporations, every stockholder shall have the right to vote, in person or by proxy, the number of shares of stock owned by him for as many persons as there are directors or managers to be elected, or to cumulate said shares, and give one candidate as many votes as the number of directors multiplied by the number of his shares of stock shall equal, or distribute them on the same principle, among as many candidates as he shall think fit," etc.

It is a movement *towards* the proportional representation of *parties* rather than of *people*, which can only be worked to advantage in small organizations where all can be present, or in districts returning three to five members, and then only imperfectly, whereas full proportional representation by the preferential process works with the greater accuracy as consituencies are enlarged. Sir Rowland Hill, the father of cheap postage, in 1840 drafted a form of organization for the municipality of Adelaide, South Australia (which colony was then new). and included therein a provision for cumulating the vote in the election of 20 town councillors, so that one-twentieth of the voters, by concentrating their twenty votes apiece on one man, could elect him. This was before the secret ballot was introduced, and hence it could be known when any candidate had been elected in time to avoid any waste of votes on him. It was used for three years, when the municipal organization was discontinued because of the expense to a scanty population.

The process was suggested in England in 1857, by James Garth Marshall. In 1868 it was advocated in the United States by U. S. Senator Buckalew. In 1870 it was used to elect members of school boards in Great Britain, and has been so used ever since. About that time it was introduced for the election of members of the House of Assembly in Illinois, in districts returning three members each. and is still so used, with the effect that the *absolute* waste of votes is much lessened ; but it perpetuates the evils of party rule in that nearly all votes are wasted that are not cast for one or the other of two leading parties, and hence the Illinois Assembly is but little if any more a reflex of public opinion than are other legislative bodies.

As applied to the election of more numerous bodies, it is liable to great inaccuracy and a large absolute waste of votes. In the Marylebone (London) election of November, 1870, for seven members of the school board, Miss Garrett received 47,858 votes out of 165,165 cast (each voter casting seven votes), of which total the successful candidates receiving in all 111,649 votes. The lowest of them received 8,355 votes, and the highest of the 15 unsuccessful ones 7,927, so that it appears Miss Garrett could have been elected on a much less number than she received, and had her supporters known their strength they could have elected several other candidates sharing her views. Besides this drawback, 53,516 votes—nearly a third of the whole—were entirely wasted for unsuccessful candidates. In the Board itself, Miss Garrett, representing over three times the vote of the highest elected candidate except herself, and nearly six times the lowest, had only the same voting power. This is, however, an extreme case. But at the best, it must require very much canvassing beforehand to enable this system to work out even an approach towards justice.

CHAPTER V.

THE FREE LIST OR TICKET.

This is said to have been first proposed by Mr. Gilpin of Philadelphia, in 1844, and has been advocated at different times in England. It is, however, principally interesting through its energetic advocacy in Belgium for many years, and in Switzerland since 1864, resulting in its adoption there in 1890-92 by three Cantons of Ticino, Neuchatel and Geneva, as previously stated in the chapter on direct legislation.

Under it the number of votes cast is divided by the number of candidates to be elected, and the quotient is 'the quota. Or the number of votes is divided by the number of candidates *plus* one, and one added to the quotient to form the quota, as is done in Ticino. Or it can be combined with the cumulative vote by a fractionizing process advocated by Messrs Seebohm and Parker Smith in England, and M. D'Hondt in Belgium, whereby a vote for one candidate counts as one, a vote for four as one-fourth, a vote for three as one-third, and so on. In the former processes, the voter, as in the cumulative vote, has as many votes as there are candidates to be elected from the district.

Stated generally, the principle is that the number of candidates elected from each list or ticket is proportioned to the aggregate vote cast for that ticket, and the fractions of quotas result in additional members either for the list in which there is the largest fraction, as in Neuchatel and Geneva, or for the list casting the largest vote in the district, as in Ticino. Three elections have now been held under it in that Canton, and one each in Neuchatel (May 1st, 1892) and Geneva (November 13th, 1892). The first in Ticino, was on March 10, 1892, in which the Conservative vote in its ten districts (each returning from five to 15 members) was 11,348, and the Liberal vote, 11,480; but the Conservatives returned 50 members, and the Liberals on a vote of 11,480 returned 45 members. (These figures represent the number of *voters*). In the election for five members of the " Council of State," on Feb. 19th, 1893, the Conservatives received 58,245 *votes* (each voter voting for five candidates) and the Liberals or Radicals 61,488, the former returning two and the latter three candidates. In each case the candidates taken on each list are those receiving the highest numbers, the voter signifying his preference for candidates at the same time as he votes for the list. In the election for the Grand Council (the cantonal legislative body), on March 5, 1893, the districts were reduced to eight instead of ten ; 172,390 Radical votes elected 53 members, and 143,089 Conservative votes elected 43 members. The following is a statement of the result in each district as tabulated by the Brussels *La Representation Proportionelle* :

DISTRICTS.	SUFFRAGES.		DEPUTIES.	
	Radical.	Conservative.	Radical.	Conservative.
I. Mendrisio	40,315	23,570	10	5
II. Lugano	19,706	11,597	7	4
III. Vezin-Tesserete	10,685	18,818	4	7
IV. Malcantone	11,349	9,532	5	4
V. Locarno	36,153	34,449	9	8
VI. Vallemagia ,	2,029	2,986	2	3
VII. Bellinzona	20,134	11,392	7	4
VIII. Tre Valli	31,989	30,745	9	8
	172,390	143,089	53	43

Under the usual system the Radicals would have secured 80 and the Conservatives 16 only. In September, 1890, there were armed conflicts in this Canton resulting in the death of one prominent politician, caused by a similar inequality the other way, under which the Radicals, with nearly half the vote, secured less than a third of the representatives. Nothing but the intervention of the Federal troops prevented a civil war. This led to the adoption of the improved system, with the result of removing that bitterness of feeling naturally resulting from the grossest injustice. *Proportional Representation is peace.*

In the Geneva election above mentioned, 13,349 persons voted in three districts for 100 members of the cantonal legislature. The wasted votes amounted to 3·9, 3·4 and 1·7 per cent. in the several districts, which were not equally apportioned, however, as 5,412 voters elected 40 deputies from Rive Gauche, 26 deputies were elected by the 2,972 voters of Rive Droite, and 34 by 4,965 voters of the City of Geneva. There were five parties represented substantially in proportion to the number of votes cast by each party.

One week earlier 53 per cent. of the votes of California were wasted.

In the Neuchatel election, three parties were represented, viz.: Radicals, Liberals, and Workingmen, besides local parties. The total of voters was 20,059, including 9,961 Radicals, who elected 57 members ; 5,786 Liberals, 29 members ; 2,906 Workingmen, 18 members ; and 1,106 " mixed " (local), 9 members. The strict proportion would have been 57, 33, 17 and 7. Under the old system, aside from coalitions, it would have been 65, 10, 30 and 9.

Professor Adrien Naville, of Neuchatel, in his Report as Secretary to the members of the Swiss P. R. Asssociation, remarks that before the election it was noticeable that, " notwithstanding the very active work of the electoral committees, the struggle was less bitter and less personal than at any preceding election, each party knowing that it would have its part ; " that is, secure its *pro rata* of representatives. He further states that more votes were cast than ever previously because all knew their votes would count ; that the counting of the ballots, etc., was rapid and easy. I repeat, *Proportional Representation is peace.*

Hon. Tom L. Johnson, in 1892, proposed a bill in Congress to enable members of the National House of Representatives to be elected in a similar manner, but rather more simply.

The imperfections in the List system are that without great complication, a voter cannot cast his ballot for candidates on two or more party tickets, and it requires as much elaborate party machinery to work it as the present system. It admits of much less absolute waste of votes than the present system, but still leaves the voter within party trammels, more or less, instead of leaving free play to his individuality in his selection of candidates without impairing the effectiveness of his vote.

M. D'Hondt, of Belgium, has devised an elaborate modification of this system, referred to at the beginning of this chapter, which would require three or four times the space of this pamphlet to explain, and much space is occupied in *La Représentation Proportionelle* in elaborate discussions on the details of the List plans, the complications of which would seriously obstruct its acceptance on this continent. Nor are the reasons which obtain for its acceptance in Belgium or Switzerland (where the people are in the practice of voting for a large number of candidates from one district, 32 from Brussels, for instance) operative in the U. S. or British North America, where single districts have always been largely predominant.

M. D'Hondt defines proportional representation as " the repartition of several seats between divers *parties* proportionally to their relative importance." But what is really required, and can be obtained by a much more simple process than the List system, is a repartition of seats not between *parties*, but between the *whole body of voters*, independently of party machinery or party leaders. This ideal accords with the spirit of a decision by the California Supreme Court, in October, 1892, that the clause in the so-called Australian ballot law permitting party headings on the ballot, so that a voter could vote for the entire party ticket by making one mark, was unconstitutional, because it was " an attempt to discriminate against classes of voters," and "its effects would be to subject such classes to partial disfranchisement, or the casting of such votes upon more burdensome conditions than others no better entitled, under the fundamental law, to the free and untrammeled exercise of the right of suffrage."

But this is done under our present system of so-called representation *by the mode of apportionment*, irrespective of and before the act of depositing the ballot. For it gives to voters acting with party organizations an advantage in securing an alleged representation over independent voters. And to the extent that the List systems do this, they retain the old leaven.

CHAPTER VI.

THE PREFERENTIAL PLAN.

This has been designated by Rev. Ernest Naville, of Geneva, to whom the success of the movement in Switzerland has been so largely due, as the ideal of proportional representation. It was introduced, in a very limited and imperfect way, into the election, by indirect vote, of the Denmark "Folkething" in 1855, by Prof. Andræ; and is still continued similarly in the election of a few members of the "Landsthing," or upper house, of that country; that is, a number of persons, designated "electors of the second degree," are elected by the ordinary mode, and these electors of the second degree elect the legislators by this preferential process.

It was independently discovered by the late Thomas Hare, barrister-at-law, London, and published in 1857. John Stuart Mill was among its earliest and most enthusiastic advocates, claiming that "it lifts the cloud that hangs over our civilization." It has since then been much simplified by Sir John Lubbock and others, and can now be claimed as at once the simplest (aside from the Gove system) and the most effective of any plan yet proposed, in that it upholds and expresses the individuality of the voter to the largest possible extent.

The quota is ascertained, as in one form of the "Free List," by dividing the number of votes cast by the number of candidates to be elected; but its paramount feature is that the wasted votes are reduced to a minimum. Each voter numbers the candidates on the ballot (all the candidates should be on one ballot) *in the order of his choice*, placing the figure "1" opposite the name of the candidate whom he most desires to see elected, "2" opposite the name of the candidate next "preferred" (hence "preferential") by him, "3" against his next choice, and so on. The ballots are then arranged according to the first choice (figure 1) and counted, so many for each candidate, after which the surplus ballots, over the quota, that any candidate may have received, are transferred to the second choice on each ballot, if that candidate has received no quota; but if, or when, such candidate of the second choice has received a quota, the ballot is transferred to the third choice candidate, and so on, until all the surplus ballots have thus been disposed of. These transferred ballots count the same as if they had been originally cast as first-choice for that candidate, and as soon as any candidate's quota is thus made up by transferred votes, that candidate's ballots forming the quota are withdrawn and packed up in any convenient manner, and the candidate declared elected.

After the surplus votes are thus disposed of, if there are still candidates remaining to be elected, the ballots of the candidate having the least number of first-choice votes, are transferred in the same manner as surplus ballots, to the second, third, fourth, or fifth choice, etc., as the case may be; and whenever by these transferred ballots any candidate reaches his quota, his ballots are withdrawn in the same manner as in the case of surplus ballots. This process—termed "elimination"—is continued until the number of candidates remaining is no greater than the number to be elected. The process is thus specified in the amendment to Section 2 of Article IX. of the Constitution of the Mechanics' Institute of this city, passed in September, 1892, and under which seven trustees of that institution were elected on February 28, 1893:

The voting shall be by the process known as the preferential method of proportional representation, as follows:

1. Each voter shall have one vote, but may vote in the alternative for as many candidates as he pleases, by writing the figures 1, 2, 3, etc., opposite the names of those candidates in the order of his preference.

2. The ballot papers having been all mixed, shall be drawn out in succession and stamped with numbers, so that no two shall bear the same number.

3. The number obtained by dividing the whole number of good ballot papers tendered at the election by the number of trustees to be elected shall be called the quota. If such number has a fraction, such fractional part shall be deducted.

4. Every candidate who has a number of first votes equal to, or greater than, the quota, shall be declared to be elected, and so many of the ballot papers containing those votes as shall be equal in number to the quota shall be set aside as the quota of that candidate, in a sealed envelope, and sealed and signed by the judges of election. On all other ballot papers, the name of such elected candidate shall be cancelled, with the effect of raising by so much in the order of preference, all votes given to other candidates after him. This process shall be repeated until no candidate has more than a quota of first votes, or votes deemed first.

5. Then the candidate or candidates having the fewest first votes, or votes deemed first, shall be declared not to be elected, with the effect of raising so much in the order of preference all votes given to candidates after him or them, and Rule 4 shall be again applied, if possible.

6. When by successive application of Rules 4 and 5, the number of candidates is reduced to the number of trustees remaining to be elected, the remaining candidates shall be declared elected.

On February 28th 905 votes were cast, the quota being 129. Two candidates received 187 and 178 votes respectively as first choice, but the distribution of their surplus did not raise any other candidate to the quota. By the "elimination" process two more gained full quotas ; one was elected on 123 votes, one on 128, and a third on 122. This shortage resulted from 15 votes being ineffective, eight of them having but one candidate marked. The counting was completed in four hours, but could probably have been done in half the time, had it not been considered desirable to so arrange the details as to secure publicity and exactness. Out of five judges and tally clerks only had any previous experience of the process ; yet none of them had the slightest difficulty in connection therewith.

The only objections made to it worth considering are these :—

1. Complexity. This is mainly apparent. It is much more simple in its working than in its description ; and its working should be exemplified, wherever possible, by "trial ballots." Any one who has assisted at one or two of these made under competent direction, can himself become an instructor. And any one in the least degree conversant with the elaborate and (to most persons) unintelligible organizations of political parties would know, if he understood the Hare system also, that it is simplicity itself.

2. It has been objected, in the case of the Mechanics' Institute election, that two candidates not elected, were on more ballots, *including sixth and seventh choice*, than others who were elected. To give this objection full force, I subjoin results of a count, giving the number of marks received by each candidate on all the voting papers, the names of the elected candidates being italicized :

Candidates.	1	2	3	4	5	6	7	Totals.
Ayers	186	63	74	66	82	195	87	753
Doolan	68	104	157	49	29	26	26	459
Dow	68	103	112	62	48	44	53	490
Dunn	33	45	82	67	186	65	40	518
Ewing	62	46	60	77	44	35	37	361
Formhals	47	172	76	63	32	38	31	459
Giesting	16	34	52	183	150	67	54	556
Lewis	59	74	68	80	70	70	32	453
Malm	180	71	55	56	39	53	83	537
McNicol	43	51	50	67	84	153	226	674
Mosebach	6	7	9	6	12	18	27	85
Symmes	79	50	31	36	34	64	81	375
Wilkie	42	61	58	46	53	31	85	376

To make the subject clearer, I will exemplify :

Ayers received 186 votes as first choice, 63 second, 74 third, etc. But of these no more than 129 (one-seventh of the 905 votes cast, dropping the fraction) were counted for him, the remainder having been distributed among the candidates marked 2, 3, etc., on them. Ewing received 62 first-choice votes and 46 second-choice. Doolan's total vote of all grades reached 459. And so on.

The following shows the *sum* of the 1st and 2nd choice votes cast for each candidate, including such as were on the 16 ineffective ballots :

Elected candidates—Ayers, 250 ; Doolan, 172 ; Dow, 171 ; Formhals, 226 ; Lewis, 132 : Malm, 251 ; Symmes, 129.

Candidates not elected—Dunn, 81 ; Ewing, 118 ; Giesting, 20 ; McNicol, 98 ; Mosebach, 13 ; Wilkie, 105.

That is, all the members who were elected received each a greater number of first and second-choice votes than any of those not elected, while the aggregate of the 1st and 2nd choice votes cast for the elected candidates exceeded those cast for the others by nearly three to one. The lowest elected candidate thus received more votes than the highest not elected. That is, all who received the highest 1st and 2nd choice votes—all that the voting members wanted *most*—were elected. What more could be reasonably asked ?

As further illustrating the perfect fairness and palpable advantages of the process, it may be stated that there were two distinct sets of candidates, one consisting of Messrs. Ayers, Doolan, Dunn, Formhals, Giesting, Malm and McNicol ; the other of Messrs. Dow, Ewing, Lewis, Mosebach and Wilkie. Symmes ran alone, entirely unsupported by any organization or body ; yet he was elected—a result that would have been entirely impossible under the usual plan. He has proved, from what I learn, to be remarkably capable and efficient ; and it is just such men that are certain to be brought to the front by proportional representation, and as certain to be kept in the rear by the usual method. For the first lot there was a total of 3,956 marks on all the ballots, of which 1,131 were first and second choice ; and four of them were elected. For the second list there were 1,756 marks on all the ballots, of which 538 were first and second choice, and two of them were elected, the due *proportion* being substantially retained even as to classes of votes that are not necessarily criterions of estimation.

I borrow from Miss Spence the following illustration of the purpose of marking different numbers opposite the names of several candidates when the vote is counted for only one : If any person wants a book out of a circulating library where but one book can be taken out at a time by one person, and sends a messenger, he—not knowing whether the book he wants most is out or not, writes a list of several books *in the order of his choice*, and if No. 1 is not in, he gets No. 2 on his list, if that is in ; if it is not, he is given No. 3, and so on ; he does not grumble because he does not get every book on the list. If a voter knew the exact state of the polls when he deposited his ballot, on the proportional system, he would simply mark *one* name ; but the ballot being secret and the situation as to the vote not being known until after the close of the polls, the *preferential* process of numbering the candidates' names in the order of his choice enables him to act with exactly the same effect as if he knew when depositing his ballot just how many votes each candidate had received.

The objectors under this head seem to have expected that a fraction over half the voters should, under proportional representation, have elected all the candidates, and that a system is not fair under which one voter cannot aid in electing several candidates, while it is quite fair when 53 per cent. of the voters in California, and similarly elsewhere, have not the ability to elect even one candidate. No just system can satisfy those who "want the earth."

3. *Chance.* This has been a never-failing objection, and a thousand refutations would not silence it. The "chance" of picking up a few drunken, corrupt or weak-kneed voters may, under our present system, decide the fate of nations or even civilizations ; but that counts for nothing with such objectors. Sir John Lubbock, on Feb. 3, 1885, wrote Professor Stokes, Secretary of the Royal Society and Professor of Mathematics in the University of Cambridge, asking him as follows :

"According to our calculation, supposing a constituency of 25,000 electors returning three members, and that a candidate receives 10,000 votes, of which one-half are marked for a candidate ' B,' and one-half for ' C,' and suppose that 4,000 have to be distributed, the element of chance would generally affect the result by less than 20. Your authority on such a question would, of course, be accepted as conclusive. Will you therefore allow me to ask you whether this is so, and also to state the odds would be against the result being affected by chance to the extent of 100."

To which the professor replied on February 5th, as follows :

"I have carefully calculated the chances and quite verify your result. I find that the average difference from two thousand in the votes assigned to ' B ' and ' C ' would be as nearly as may be sixteen, and that the odds against the difference being as great as one hundred would be, in round numbers, *44,000 to one.*"

As the ballots cast at the Mechanics' Institute were available, it was determined to test the "chance" objection somewhat *a posteriori*, which was done on June 5th, after every ballot had been previously marked with initials showing for what candidate it had been counted at the election in the following manner :

The ballots, including the 15 ineffective ones, were arranged according to the first choice. Next the ballots of Ayers and Malm were *each* arranged in two piles, one consisting of the ballots that had been set aside for the quotas of each, and the others of those that had been distributed, in the order of the voter's choice in each case, as not being needed to elect Ayers and Malm. Then came this important proceeding : All the 58 ballots with Ayers' name as first choice that had been transferred to other candidates at the election were now put in as part of his quota, and 58 other ballots that at the election were treated as part of his quota were transferred to other candidates in the order of the voter's choice. Mr. Malm's ballots were treated in like manner. Thus no ballots treated as surplus at the election were so treated at this count, thus making *the greatest possible difference in the order of the count.* Yet the same candidates were "eliminated" as at the election, and, as well as recollected, in the same order. It is certain that Ewing was the last "eliminated" and Lewis the last elected. There were, however, slight differences as to the number of votes on which each candidate was elected at the election of February 28th, and the figures that he would have been elected on had last Sunday's count been an election. They are as follows, the first figures denoting the number of votes on which each was elected, and the second the number that fell to each at the close of the last count :

Doolan, 128—124 ; Dow, 126—129 ; Lewis, 123—118 ; Symmes, 128—129. No candidate obtained a quota by *surplus* transferred votes, and but two candidates received any surplus votes. Moreover, at each succeeding election, as the strength of each candidate becomes better known, the surplus votes will become fewer.

The ineffective votes, which numbered 15 at the election, became 17 at this count, of which 9 voted for one candidate only, 2 for two, 1 for three, 1 for four, and 4 for seven. To test the "chance" objection in another manner, Mr. George Cumming, a Trustee of the Institute, counted the second choice votes on *all* the ballots cast for the candidates who received surplus votes, and then calculating by the proportion between the candidate's quota and his surplus, the number of the second-choice votes being treated as a third term, how many of these surplus votes belong equitably to each of the other candidates. The result corresponds substantially to the actual distribution.

THE GOVE PLAN.

The Gove System is similar to the Hare System in principle, and is also similar to two advocated by Archibald E. Dobbs, barrister-at-law, of London, as far back as 1879. It is embodied in a bill advocated by John M. Berry, of Worcester, Mass., offered to the Massachusetts Legislature in 1891, and given at length in the "Appeal to the Canadian Institute on the Rectification of Parliament," by Sandford Fleming, C.M.G., LL.D., pp. 143-149.

The quota is ascertained as before, but the voter marks *one name* only. Each candidate publishes, not less than three weeks before the election, a written statement containing the names of one or more others of said candidates "with whom he believes himself to be in accord upon the most important public questions, and to one or more of whom he wishes to transfer any ineffective votes cast for himself." "The Secretary of the Commonwealth" (Mass). is then to publish a list showing the names of the candidates and also the names of those candidates to whom each candidate wishes to transfer his ineffective votes, so that the voter may know in advance to whom such votes *may* be transferred. Every ineffective vote of a candidate (surplus or eliminated, as in the Hare plan) is to be transferred to the eligible candidate named on the first candidate's list for whom the largest number of votes were originally cast, but who has not a quota, until all are transferred as far as possible. Then the forty candidates having the highest number of votes (forty is the number of the Massachusetts State Senators to whose election the bill is made applicable) shall be declared elected.

The objections to this bill as compared with the Hare plan are as follows:—

1. A popular candidate would, in many places, be pestered with solicitations to place on his list persons whom he would not voluntarily select. Where an object was to be gained, intimidation and other undue influences would be brought to bear.

2. While the voter might desire his vote, if ineffective as cast, to be transferred to a candidate belonging to a different party, the candidate himself might feel obliged to name on his list only candidates of the same party. This might lead to great waste of votes, as in the List system. The voter himself is altogether free from such influences in a secret ballot, and it is his right to determine to whom his vote should be transferred.

The Gove system, however, might be of advantage in countries, such as the Province of Quebec, and perhaps Ontario, very sparsely settled in some parts, as the local returning officers could themselves count and report the votes, without the risk involved in transmitting the ballots themselves to be counted at some central point. The process would thus be simplified and expedited as compared with the Hare plan, which is the most accurate and would be best adapted for municipalities and thickly populated States or Provinces.

With the elevation in the moral tone of candidates and of voters that any plan of proportional representation would certainly bring about, it might prove entirely safe to assign the distribution of surplus or eliminated votes to the candidates themselves. But, by reason of the demoralizing effects of existing political systems, that is a question for the future. As to the present, any considerable loss of votes under the Hare system is simply impossible, while under the present one so large a loss is absolutely certain that a mere majority of a legislature, so far as the electoral process itself is concerned, never can represent, even approximately, a majority of the voters.

CHAPTER VII.

GENERAL CONSIDERATIONS.

grow into harmonization or relapse into veneered barbarism, combining and intensifying the vices of both the savage and civilized states, (such being the drift to-day) is mainly to be determined by action or inaction on this question of representation. This cancer of false and corrupt politics must be extirpated, and the body politic reconstructed on hygienic principles, or that cancer will permeate (as it is now doing) every form of industrial, social and individual life, to the extinction of all love of the good, the beautiful and the true. Of what use is it to prove a paradise possible without showing how to find the *key?* Purify politics by making representation accessible to all ; do justice politically to all, and the tendency will be upwards and onwards—a real, and not merely material advancement. As evil now permeates, so would good "leaven the whole lump." *Let one Province, one State,* even *one* municipality lead the way, by introducing full proportional representation, and the whole civilized world must eventually follow. Inspiration and aspiration will impart that superiority to evil it always secures in a fair field, and proportional represent a tion will *make the field a fair one.* Then,

> " Ever the right comes uppermost
> And ever is justice done,"

will become more than a poet's ideal.

> New occasions teach new duties ; Time makes ancient good uncouth ;
> They must upward still, and onward, who would keep abreast of truth ;
> Lo, before us gleam our camp-fires, we ourselves must Pilgrims be,
> Launch our Mayflower, and steer boldly through the desperate winter sea.
> Nor attempt the Future's portal with the Past's blood-rusted key.
> —J. R. LOWELL.

The false belief that the *people* rule, " the *people* make the laws," and that " to make governments better we need only to make the people better," are the most efficient paralyzers that could be devised to arrest any form of advancement through political action. The removal of that false belllief would invigorate a public opinion, now paralyzed, so that it would become a force so powerful that its insistance on being embodied in the processes of election would have to be heeded.

But if men of thought and conscience fail to realize how deep this political cancer reaches, their slumbers may be rudely broken. Better is chaos than systematized corruption; better is the insane than the satanic; better that the corpse of a rotten civilization should, preparatory to interment, taint the air, so that out of its putrefaction shall, in after ages, come new life, than that it should remain a walking pestilence—a living death.

Must our civilization thus perish? By no means. A few in earnest can arouse a demand for the right to *complete* representation of all voters. Already their voices echo and re-echo, each helping the other, from Canada in the far north to the lands of the Southern Cross, from the mountains of Switzerland to the plains of Illinois ; from the metropolis of the British empire to the marvellously beautiful and varied Pacific slope of America—from all these and more men and women will gather in the populous city on the shores of Lake Michigan, to inaugurate a vaster enterprise than was ever dreamed of by the founders of the World's Fair—a world's convention of workers for political equity.

The evolution of science by investigation, the evolution of industry by invention, the evolution of the social order by co-operation—all these demand as a concomitant, without which they may—yes. *must*—become curses, that political evolution which is in harmony with science, with industry, with social progress, and above all, with *justice.*

The old Roman said "*Fiat justitia, ruat cœlum* " – let justice be done, though the heavens fall. Rather I would say, Let justice be done *lest* the heavens fall. This political justice would bring not fallen heavens, but a risen, redeemed earth, seen by the prophet— " a new heavens and a new earth wherein dwelleth righteousness."

PACIFICO.

APPENDIX.

"DRAFT BILLS" FOR "THE BEST WORKABLE MEASURES."

An Act to amend the Dominion Elections Act, 37 V, c. 9, s. 135.

SECTION 1.—Hereafter the House of Commons shall be elected by the process known as the preferential method of proportional representation, also known as the transferable vote, as follows :—

SEC. 2.—Excepting as hereinafter provided for districting the Provinces of Ontario and Quebec, members of the House of Commons shall be elected by each Province without regard to districts for the number of members to which they shall be entitled by law, But each voter's vote shall count for one candidate only in the manner following :—

SEC. 3.—The voter shall place opposite the name of such candidate as he may prefer above all others the figure " 1 ; " and opposite the name of the candidate next preferred by him, as being his second choice the figure " 2 ; " for his third choice the figure " 3 " in like manner ; for his fourth choice, the figure " 4 ; " for his fifth choice the figure " 5 " and for his sixth choice, the figure " 6." But he can mark any number of candidates not exceeding six with figures from one to six.

SEC. 4.—The ballot boxes, after being duly sealed, as provided for in Sec. 58 of the aforesaid Dominion Elections Act, shall be forwarded to an official to be known as the Central Returning Officer, at the seat of government for each Province (excepting as hereinafter provided for the Provinces of Ontario and Quebec), where they shall be counted, in the presence of the candidates or their agents, by said Central Returning Officer and his deputies, in the manner following :

SEC. 5.—The ballot papers, having been fully shuffled and mixed, shall be drawn out in succession and stamped with numbers in the order of their being so drawn out, so that no two shall bear the same number, and the whole number as stamped shall correspond with the actual number of such ballot papers.

SEC. 6.—The whole number obtained by dividing the whole number of ballot papers by the number of members of the House of Commons to be elected from that Province, or from any district in the Provinces of Ontario and Quebec, shall be called the quota. But when such quotient has a fraction, that fraction shall be dropped to form such quota.

SEC. 7.—The ballot papers shall then be placed on files, or otherwise be conveniently segregated, according to the first choice votes on each ballot paper ; and, after that is done and the votes on such first choice for each candidate are duly recorded by the Central Returning Officer, if any candidate is found to have a surplus of first choice votes above the aforesaid quota, a number of ballot papers equal to that quota shall be taken from the file or pile of ballots of such candidate and set aside as his quota, placed in an envelope, or other suitable package and sealed and signed by the Central Returning Officer and his deputies or clerks. If more than one candidate has a surplus over the quota, the first candidate's ballots taken shall be that having the highest surplus, and so on in succession to the candidate having the least surplus, which shall be taken last.

SEC. 8.—All other ballot papers having the name of such candidate or candidates as first choice, shall be distributed in the same order, by cancelling with pencil the name of the first choice candidate and counting such ballots for the candidate numbered " 2 " for second choice ; and if that candidate shall have previously received a quota, the ballot shall be counted for the third choice ; and so on to the number of six, if so many are marked by figures as provided by Section 3 of this Act, the effect contemplated being to raise by so much in the order of preference all votes given to other candidates after the first choice. If all of the candidates marked on such ballot shall have been elected before such ballot has been reached, it shall be set aside, in an envelope or other suitable method, as an ineffective vote, with all similar ineffective ballots.

SEC. 9.—Whenever by the distribution of such ballot papers as are specified in the preceding Section, added to the ballots cast for any candidate as first choice, a quota shall be reached, such quota of ballots shall be sealed, certified to and set aside as provided in Sec. 7, the same as if such candidate had received a quota by first-choice votes. The process described in this and the preceding Section shall be repeated until no candidate has more than a quota of first-choice votes, or votes deemed first.

SEC. 10.—In case the requisite number of candidtes be not elected by the distribution of surplus votes as hereinbefore set forth, then the candidate having the fewest number of first votes, or votes deemed first, shall be declared not capable of being elected, with the effect of raising so much in the order of preference, all votes given to the candidate, or candidates after him, which ballots shall be counted for such candidates in the same order and manner as specified in Section 8 ; that is to say, the same as if they were surplus votes. Then the ballots of the candidate having next fewest votes as first choice shall be disposed of in like manner, and so on until there are no more candidates' ballots remaining than the number of candidates remaining to be elected. And whenever, by the distribution and transfer of such insufficient votes, any candidate shall receive a quota, the package of such ballot papers thus apportioned to him shall be sealed and set aside in the same manner, and with the same effect as provided in Section 9.

SEC. 11.—When, by the distribution of surplus votes as provided in Section 9 and of insufficient votes (" elimination ") as provided in Section 10, the number of candidates remaining is reduced to the number of members of the House of Commons remaining to be elected, the remaining candidates shall be declared elected.

SEC. 12.—In disposing of ballot papers not filled up according to rule, the primary purpose shall be to carry into effect, in counting the vote, the intention of the voter.

When it can be ascertained for what candidate the voter desired to vote, the ballot shall be counted accordingly, even if irregular in form.

Sec. 13.—For the purpose of avoiding the insertion of an inconvenient number of names on the ballot papers in the Provinces of Ontario and Quebec, the same shall be divided into electoral districts not exceeding six in each of said Provinces by a Commission of three members for each Province, to be appointed by the Governor General of the Dominion. Provided that no city, present electoral district or county shall be so divided into more than one district; provided also that the districts or counties contained in the Island of Montreal and such other islands adjacent, as may be comprised in the districts or counties of that island, shall not be divided, but shall constitute one entire district, or a part of one district. The commissioners shall also designate suitable places in each district in which all the ballots for such district shall be counted with a view to declare the return of candidates in substantially the same manner as at present, with such differences only as the proportional preferential system may necessitate. The number of candidates to be returned by each of said districts shall be made to conform, as nearly as possible, to the population of each district as determined by the last preceding census, and it shall be the duty of the said commissioners to make a re-apportionment as soon as possible after the result of each succeeding census shall be officially declared.

Sec. 14.— All the provisions of the sections 1 to 12 inclusive shall apply to the Provinces of Ontario and Quebec, excepting as to their division in districts, and the same shall apply to those districts, after they are formed, in the same manner as if they were separate provinces, excepting as to such general superintendence and revision as the parliament of each province may provide for at the capital of each province for the verification of returns.

Sec. 15.—Whenever one or more vacancies occur between elections, the ballots which have been counted for the vacant members shall be re-distributed among such of the previously unsuccessful candidates may be still eligible and willing to accept, as provided in sections 8, 9 and 10, and the candidate (or candidates, if there shall be more than one vacancy) highest on the list after such distribution shall be declared elected.

In view of the great extent, sparse population and other features of the Province of Quebec, or a large portion thereof, the Gove system may be more available, though less theoretically exact. Its workings are clearly defined in a bill prepared for the Massachusetts Legislature and given at length in pages 147-9 of "An Appeal to the Canadian Institute." For the words "Secretary of the Commonwealth" might be substituted the words "Secretary and Registrar," the word "Assemblymen" for "Senator" and "Province" for "Commonwealth."

The reduction of the number of Legislators would be very desirable, and forty would be sufficient for any Province or State.

I subjoin a copy (slightly modified) of the essential portions of this bill with some modifications.

Section 1.—In order to provide for a representation of the citizens of this Province founded upon the principle of equality ; any resident of this Province, eligible by law to the office of Assemblyman, may be nominated as a candidate to said office by any person.

No such nomination shall be valid unless the following conditions are compled with :—

(1). The nomination shall be in writing, signed by the person making it, and shall contain the name and place of residence of the candidate.

(2). An acceptance of the nomination, signed by the candidate, shall be endorsed thereon.

(3) It shall be deposited in the office of the Secretary and Registrar of the Province not more than three months nor less than five weeks before the day of election.

(4) There shall be deposited with such nomination the sum of ten dollars, or such other sum not exceeding fifty dollars, as the Legislature may hereafter direct.

Sec. 2.—Not less than four weeks before the day of election, the Secretary and Registrar shall furnish to each candidate and to every voter who shall request it, a printed list containing the names of all the candidates in alphabetical order, with the place of residence of each, and the name of the person by whom each was nominated.

Sec. 3.—At any time after his nomination and not less than three weeks before the day of election, any of said candidates may furnish to the Secretary and Registrar a statement in writing, signed by himself and acknowledged before any authorized notary, or other official authorized to take acknowledgement of deeds, which statement shall contain the names of one or more others of said candidates with whom he believes himself to be in accord on the most important public questions, and to one or more of which he wishes to transfer any ineffective votes cast for himself.

SEC. 4.—The Secretary and Registrar shall prepare a new list of candidates similar to that named in Section two of this article, but containing also against the name of each candidate the names in alphabetical order of all candidates named in the list, if any, furnished by that candidate, as provided in Section three ; and he shall, not less than two weeks before the day of election, furnish to the . . . . a sufficient number of copies of said new list. Every such . . . . shall, immediately upon the receipt thereof, post conspicuously, and open to the inspection of the public, one copy of said list at each and every place in his . . . . where votes are to be received at said election, and shall also furnish one copy to every legal voter resident in said . . . . . . who shall demand the same, to the extent of his supply over and above two copies reserved for file in his office.

SEC. 5.—Every legal voter, wherever resident, shall be entitled to cast his vote for Assemblyman in favor of any candidate whose name appears in the aforesaid list of candidates ; but no person shall vote for more than one candidate, nor for any person whose name does not appear upon the aforesaid list of candidates. But wherever a candidate duly nominated is omitted from the list published by the Secretary and Registrar, votes may be cast for him with the same effect as if his name appeared on said list. If the Secretary and Registrar shall knowingly omit such name from the list when the same is entitled legally to be there, he shall . . . .

SEC. 6.—The returns of votes having been transmitted to the Secretary and Registrar, as provided by law, he shall make a list of all candidates voted for, with the vote received by each candidate in each precinct or voting place, and his total vote, and said list shall be transmitted, published and distributed in the same manner provided in Section 4 concerning the list therein named ; and after the Secretary and Registrar shall have ascertained he shall make a list of the successful candidates, with the computation by which, as hereafter provided, their election has been ascertained, and shall forthwith furnish a copy of the same to each candidate and to every voter, especially publishers of newspapers or other periodicals, who shall request it.

SEC. 7.—Ineffective votes shall be transferred according to the request of the candidate for whom they were originally cast, to a person named in the list furnished by said candidate, as provided by Section 3. The . . candidates then having the highest number of votes shall then be declared elected, and the Secretary and Registrar shall issue certificates of election to them. In case two or more candidates have the same number of votes, the candidates residing at the greatest distance from the legislative capital of the Province shall be preferred.

SEC. 8.—The following shall be deemed ineffective votes, and shall be transferred in the order named :—

(1). Any vote cast for a candidate in excess of one-fortieth of the entire vote cast, beginning with the candidate receiving the largest vote, and proceeding to the one next highest, and so on. In the case of two or more receiving the same vote, the transfer shall be from each alternately in alphabetical order.

(2). Votes cast for candidates who have died or become ineligible in the same order.

(3). Original votes cast for candidates who fail of election, beginning with the candidate receiving the smallest total vote, and proceeding to the next lowest, and so on ; in case of two or more receiving the same vote, the transfer to be made from each alternately in alphabetical order. No voters shall be transferred from any candidate who has not furnished the statement named in Section 3.

SEC. 9.—Every ineffective vote of a candidate shall be transferred to the candidate named in his said list living and eligible at the time of counting the vote for whom the largest number of votes were originally cast and whose vote, by transfer or otherwise, does not equal one-fortieth of the vote cast, until all are transferred as far as possible.

Section 10 provides for return of money to candidates for whom a thousand or more votes were cast.

SEC. 11.—In case a vacancy shall occur in the Assembly after the declaration of election provided in Section 7, the votes cast for the member whose seat shall have become vacant, together with any ineffective votes assigned to him, shall be re-distributed in the same manner as if he had died or become ineligible before the canvassing of the votes ; and the candidate not before elected, who, after returning to him any votes originally cast for him, shall then appear to have the largest number of votes shall be declared elected.

[I prefer the phraseology of Section 15, Dominion Elections Act, to this].

Section 12.—Provides for the correction of errors by the Supreme Judicial Court, etc.

Section 13.—Provides for the election of representatives of the lower House by means of districts.

I have retained that part of the bill providing for the division of votes by *forty*, believing that the best interests of the community would be consulted by limiting the Provinces of Ontario and Quebec to that number, so as to enable their Legislatures to be really *deliberative* bodies. As I presume the number could be reduced by the Acts of the respective Legislatures, the proposition may not be out of place. Its bearing on the subject of proportional representation is that by the reduction in number there need be no division of those Provinces into electoral districts, such division invariably necessitating more or less inequality in legislative power of voters, and leading to endless and useless controversy. If, however, the present or similar numbers of representatives were to be retained concurrently with the enactment of proportional preferential representation, they could be divided into districts substantially as provided in the proposed Act to amend the Dominion Elections Act, Section 14, in this Appendix.

For the application of the Gove system to the Province of Ontario, the same bill would be adapted with the following changes :—

For "Secretary and Registrar" substitute "Secretary."

Fill up the first blank in Section four with the words "to the clerk of every city, town, village and township ;" the second blank with the word "clerk ;" the third blank with the words "city, town, village or township ;" the fourth blank the same.

PRINCE EDWARD ISLAND.

An Act to provide for the election of members of the Legislative Council and the Legislative Assembly.

SECTION 1.—Hereafter, the members of the Legislative Council and of the Legislative Assembly shall be elected by the process known as the preferential method of proportional representation, and also known as the transferable vote, in the manner following :

SEC. 2.—There shall be no division into districts, but the representation shall be quotas, each quota consisting of the quotient obtained by dividing the whole number of votes received at any election for each House by the number of candidates to be elected from the whole Province for each House, and dropping the fraction, if any, in such quotient, and any candidate receiving that number of votes shall be declared elected.

SEC. 3.—The voter shall place opposite the name of such candidate as he may prefer above all others the figure " 1," and opposite the name of the candidate next preferred by him, as being his second choice, the figure " 2," and opposite the name of his third choice, the figure " 3," and so on ; but any mark beyond " 6 " will not be noticed.

SEC. 4.—The boxes or other packages containing the ballots, having been duly sealed, as provided by law, shall be sent to the office of the Provincial Secretary and Treasurer, to be there counted by him in the presence of the candidates, or their agents, in the manner following :—

SEC. 5.—The ballot papers, having been fully shuffled and mixed, shall be drawn out in succession and stamped with numbers in the order of their being so drawn out, so that no two shall bear the same number, and the whole number so stamped shall correspond with the number of such ballot papers.

SEC. 6.—The ballot papers shall then be placed on files, or otherwise conveniently assorted, according to the first-choice votes on each ballot paper ; and after that is done, and the votes on such first choice duly recorded by the Provincial Secretary and Treasurer (the ballot papers being thus gone through for each House separately, if both are voted for on the same ballot by each voter), if any candidate is found to have a surplus of first-choice votes above the aforesaid quota, a number of ballot papers equal to that quota shall be set aside as his quota, placed in an envelope or other suitable package, and sealed and signed by the Provincial Secretary. If more than one candidate has a surplus over the quota, the ballots of that candidate shall first be taken having the highest surplus, and so on in succession to the candidate having the least surplus, which shall be taken last.

SEC. 7.—All other ballot papers having the name of such candidate or candidates, as first choice shall be distributed in a similar order, by cancelling with pencil the name of such candidate of first choice and counting the ballot for the candidate numbered " 2 " for second choice ; and if that candidate shall have previously received a quota, the ballot shall be counted for the candidate marked " 3," and so on to the number of six, if so many are marked by figures as provided for in section three of this Act, the effect contemplated being to raise by so much in the order of preference all votes given to other candidates after the first choice. If all the candidates marked on such ballot shall have been elected before such ballot has been reached in the order of counting, then it shall be set aside as an ineffective vote.

Sec. 8.—Whenever, by the distribution of such ballot papers as are specified in the preceding section, added to the ballots cast for any candidate as first choice, a quota shall be reached, the ballots constituting that quota shall be set aside as provided in section six for a like number of first-choice votes. The process specified in this and the preceding section shall be repeated until no candidate has more than a quota of first-choice votes, or votes counted for him as hereinbefore provided.

Sec. 9.—In case the required number of candidates be not elected by the distribution of surplus votes as hereinbefore provided, then the candidate having the fewest number of first votes, or votes deemed first, shall be declared not capable of being elected, with the effect of raising so much in the order of preference all votes given to the candidate or candidates after him, which ballots shall be counted for such candidates in the order and manner specified in Section 7 of this Act; that is to say, the same as if they were surplus votes. Then the ballot of the candidate having the next fewest votes as first choice shall be disposed of like manner, and so until there are no more candidates' ballots remaining than the number of candidates remaining to.be elected. And whenever, by the distribution and transfer of such insufficient ballots or votes, any candidate shall receive a quota, the package of such ballot papers shall be set aside in the same manner as provided in Section eight. And the process as defined in this Section shall be known as "elimination."

Sec. 10. When by the distribution of surplus votes, as provided in Sec. 8, and of insufficient votes, as provided in Sec. 9, the number of candidates remaining is reduced to the number of members remaining to be elected, the remaining candidates shall be declared elected.

Sec. 11. In the disposal of ballot papers not filled up according to rule, the primary purpose in counting and assigning such votes to the several candidates, shall be to carry into effect the intention of the voter,.so far as that can be ascertained.

Sec. 12.—(Same as Section 15, Dominion Elections Act).

These provisions can be readily adapted to the several Provinces of Nova Scotia, New Brunswick, British Columbia, Manitoba and the North-West Territory. It would facilitate operations if the membership was reduced to from ten to twenty members for each Province.

MUNICIPAL ELECTIONS.

Aside from the cities, as to which I am not informed in detail, the municipal organization of the Province of Ontario would need but slight modification to adapt it to the proportional and preferential system as hereinbefore defined for Prince Edward Island. The affairs of the townships and villages being administered by a reeve and four councillors and the election taking place entirely (as I presume) in one room, no transportation of ballots, etc., would be required and the votes could be counted then and there.

The towns are governed by a mayor and three councillors for each ward, if less than five, or two for each ward, if more than five wards. These would present but little more difficulty.

It might be a good measure to provide for the election of reeves and mayors in common with councillors, assigning the office of reeve or of mayor to the candidate for councillor receiving the highest number of first choice votes.

It appears to me that "the best workable measure" could be introduced more easily and work more smoothly in the municipalities than in the Legislatures, and that the practical experience to be reached through the municipalities (where the working would be as simple and clear as in the Mechanics' Institute of San Francisco) would be an excellent preparative for its introduction into legislatures.

It would work very smoothly from the outset in the smaller Provinces, especially in British Columbia, where the Victoria *Single Tax* has already commenced its advocacy.

PACIFICO.

SOUTHERN CROSS.

CHAPTER I.

After centuries of parliamentary government, carried on with, on the whole, fair success in the United Kingdom, and imitated in its main features in its offshoots all over the world, whether these have been separated like the United States of America, or remain still an integral part of the Empire, it is noteworthy that in the oldest and most populous of the British colonies, a demand should arise for the rectification of Parliament. This premises that in the opinion of thinking people, under present conditions, Parliament is not rightly organized or equitably worked ; that it does not give efficient representation to the people, or provide an efficient spur or check to the executive. Many writers and thinkers have pointed out the injustice and the dangers of the system of majority representation under which parliaments are chosen ; grave physicians and pretentious quacks have diagnosed the disease and prescribed remedies, and the latter generally with the larger following.

Party politics, local politics, and personal politics obscure the great national issues, and account for most of the blunders, administrative and financial, into which the self-governing colonies have fallen, and indeed these have been hurtful to the mother-country also, and it is only by resolutely casting these aside and considering what is best for the community as a whole, and by calling on men to co-operate rather than to fight for mastery and spoils, that we can hope to rectify parliament and to purify politics.

It has been well said, that under party politics when thoroughly organized, there is a conspiracy of half the cleverest men in the country to keep the other half out of public affairs ; and that whereas the right function of the opposition is to see that the ministry does the nation's work properly, the usual practice of the opposition is to try to prevent the ministry from doing it at all.

Local politics lead to the varying policy of submission and of obstruction, in order to force local demands on the public treasury for the constituency which the members represent, and these are as narrowing to genuine public spirit as they are costly to the community. Personal politics, which are powerful in Canada and in Australia, allow a strong leader to exploit the country for his own aggrandisement, and for the reward of the followers who follow him blindly, and turn as he turns.

We must therefore enquire how we may change or modify our representation so as to make it more truly represent the people, and to make parliament more amenable to the best public opinion, and helpful rather than hampering to any honest executive.

And in these directions, we shall do no good by harking back to old limitations of the suffrage, and allowing property and intelligence, besides their enormous material and mental advantages, additional weight at the polls. Conservatives are apt to say that the demoralising of politics is due to manhood suffrage, and to paid representatives, but look back a century or more in England, and ask if pocket boroughs and exclusive patronage in Church and State, lavished on political supporters ;—bribery and treating unblushingly practised even by such a man as Wilberforce, were not more demoralising and costly than what we see in England now-a-days. We could not if we would, resume the government of caste and privilege, and we should gain nothing and lose much by the change.

No despotism, however benevolent and intelligent—no oligarchy, however vigorous and high-minded—no bureaucracy, however vigilant and efficient, can do for the people what they are competent to do for themselves,—and it is from Democracy itself that the purification of our democratic institutions must come. Every community contains within itself the saving salt that is needed ; all that is wanted is the machinery which will give the better elements adequate expression, and full liberty of speech and action. "Democracy, according to its definition," says John Stuart Mill, "means the government of the whole people by the whole people equally represented, and not by a mere majority of the people exclusively represented," and this spurious democracy brings discredit on the grandest and the most progressive political truth in the world.

It may indeed seem to many well meaning and theoretical people that it would be advisable for rich, talented, educated and virtuous men to have more weight in the State than the poor and the stupid, the ignorant and the vicious. Property, they say, needs protection ; talent, education and virtue should be encouraged ; the world would be better governed if they had the larger share in the political representation.

But the State, in a pure democracy, draws no nice and invidious distinctions between man and man. She disclaims the right of favouring either property or education, talent or virtue. She considers that all alike have an interest in the protection of good government, and that all who form the community of full age and untainted by crime, have a right to a share in the representation. She allows education to exert its legitimate power through the press, talent in every department of business, property in its material and social advantages, and virtue to influence the public conscience and to moralise public opinion, but she regards all men as politically equal, and rightly so, if the equality is as real in operation as it is in theory.

If the equality is actual in the representation of the citizens, truth and virtue being stronger than error and vice, and wisdom being greater than folly, where a fair field is offered, the higher qualities subdue the lower, and penetrate all through society, making themselves felt in every department of the state, and especially in the political. But if the representation, from defective machinery or other cause, is not really equal, but partial and unjust, the whole balance is overthrown, and neither education nor talent, nor virtue, can work through public opinion to have their beneficial influence on public matters, while wealth is too often a demoralizing agent.

We know that in despotisms and oligarchies, where the majority are unrepresented and the few extinguish the many, independence of thought is crushed down—talent is bribed to do service to the tyranny, education is confined to a privileged class and denied to the people, property is sometimes pillaged and sometimes pampered, even virtue is degraded by lowering its field, and calling slavish subservience to the ruling powers by the sacred names of patience and loyalty ; while religion is too often made the handmaid of oppression—taxes fall heavily on the poor for the benefit of the rich and powerful, and the only check proceeds from the fear of rebellion.

When on the contrary, the majority extinguishes the minority, the evil effects are not so apparent. The body oppressed is smaller, generally wealthier, with many social advantages to draw off public attention from the political injustice from which they suffer ; but there is the same want of sympathy between class and class. Moral courage is rare, talent takes too low ground, genius is overlooked, education is general but superficial, the press and the pulpit are timid in denouncing popular crimes, or exposing popular errors. An average standard of virtue is all that is aimed at, and when no higher standard is set up, there is great fear of falling below it, and the most sweet voices of these poor average men are solicited by political adventurers and noisy demagogues, in order that they may win place and power.

The minority can exercise no physical force out of doors to compel attention to their grievances, but wealth, in such a one-sided democracy as grows up under mere majority representation in separated districts, can do as much mischief in underhand ways as it did in the old highhanded days of pocket boroughs in England. Therefore, it is incumbent on all democracies to look well that their representative systems really secure the political equality they profess to give, for until this is done, *democracy has had no fair trial.* '

I call Canada and Australia democracies, because though still attached to England, and loyal subjects of Queen Victoria, for all practical purposes, our weal and our woe are in our own hands. The Home Government allowed us to frame our own constitutions, and we did so on the broadest democratic principles, intending to give equality to all citizens, but as the system of representing minorities in equal proportion with majorities was then unknown, we did not embody that principle in our electoral law.

"One man, one vote" is not democratic enough. "One vote, one value" is the real key-stone of democracy. Political equality I understand as a very different thing from the popular acceptation of the term. It does not mean that if a man holds opinions that are popular in the district in which he lives, they will be of use to him in obtaining a representative, while another man who has different opinions, living next door, shall never be able to have his views represented. Equality means that every man's vote shall have its weight, whatever majority or minority he may belong to, and wherever he may happen to live. It is by the enfranchisement of minorities that we can arrive at the real state of public opinion, and this is of quite as much value to the majority itself as to the segments greater or smaller, into which the dissentients are divided. Equal or proportional representation—what I call "Effective voting," secures to a real majority its ascendancy, whereas by the great waste of votes at every election, the so-called majority representative has only what the Americans call a "plurality" or more than any other candidate, but not a majority of the votes polled ; not a majority, which is the ostensible principle on which the system is based.

Equal representation would prevent this anomaly. It would give power to the real majority, control to the minority, and a just representation to all. It would do more than this by its indirect effects; it would educate the voter, raise the tone of canvass, call out better men for public work, would cut off bribery and corrupt influence at its root, and would substitute for party, local, and personal politics, real national issues.

Hitherto, whatever may have been the growth and development of representative institutions, we see that however the constituency may be formed, for one member, for two, or for many members, whatever the electoral franchise may be—whether restricted or widened as far as manhood suffrage—the old idea of majority representation prevents any true presentment of the opinions of all sections of the people. That the majority must rule and the minority submit was the law which military conquerors imposed upon the vanquished; the bitter necessity of yielding to the strongest battalions, the most fortunate position and the most skilful tactics. It is an inheritance from the old militant spirit which had been introduced into politics, and that spirit acting in this arena drills its recruits, chooses its ground and outwits its opponents by all means in its power for victory for one side, and defeat or discouragement for the other.

The awakened spirit of man, however, which is protesting against the cruel and costly arbitrament of war in national disputes and differences, and which protests against the cut-throat competition of trade, as not only crushing out the weaker, but calling out the evil passions of jealousy and hatred all round, is also beginning to see in the old methods of obtaining political representation the same fatal flaw. It is in the substitution of the co-operative for the competitive spirit in politics that not only would Parliament be rectified, but politics would be moralised, and the war-spirit would be weakened in all other directions.

Under proportional representation, every man's vote counts for one man of whom he approves, but it does not neutralise the vote of any other man as much entitled to representation as himself. This would foster a spirit of friendly co-operation for the great end of securing an equitable representation, and good government founded thereupon, instead of the present neck-and-neck scramble for recognition or extinction between two parties, where one vote for Smith is lost to Brown, and a few wavering or corruptible votes may turn the scale in a hundred separated districts.

Under local majority representation, the evil is intensified by closer and closer organization of two main parties—call them Liberals and Conservatives in England—Republicans and Democrats in America—Catholics and Radicals in France, or Capital and Labour in Australia. Sleepless organization continues the campaign both outside and inside the walls of parliament, and instead of the true democratic ideal of making all votes effective, time, talents, and money are expended in order to make all votes ineffective except those polled by our own party candidate.

In the United States, where the electors are more numerous than elsewhere, politics have become a great business, needing capital to run them, and professionals to expend the money. Party caucuses and conventions prepare the ticket, draw out the programme, calculated to win most support—perhaps extreme on the party lines, but trimming and hedging on many important subjects, lest by sincerity or originality votes might be lost, or even risked, so that the party does not even bring out its own best man, while there is nothing it dreads so much as a good man on the other side. The ticket-preparers try to win votes from outsiders by promise or compromise, or better still, encourage them to run hopeless candidates so as to divide the forces against them, while they strictly limit the choice of their own party to the safe man fixed on by the caucus.

And this is not a mere accident or excrescence on a system otherwise just. It inheres in party government, and in majority representation essentially. Thus the more equally electorates are divided into uninominal districts, the more men have the right to vote, the more come to the poll, the more certain it is that all minorities will be extinguished in detail, and the more successful are party tactics such as I have described.

The more equal, too, are the conditions of a country, the less likelihood there is that minorites will find expression. In England, which has long had a restricted suffrage, and irregularly constituted electorates, and where there are agricultural, manufacturing interests paramount in various parts of the country, there has been in the past such a representation of different classes and opinions, that the idea found favour that the general average gives a fair representation of the whole people. We see however, that with the extension of the suffrage, labour, which was inarticulate in the past, is finding a voice for itself, and no longer depends on the utterances of kindly men of a different class. This voice will become stronger in the United Kingdom as time rolls on.

In such communities as we have in Canada and Australia, which are practically democracies, with no hereditary aristocracy, few merchant princes or financial millionaires, where the preponderating mass of voters are workingmen and small farmers, with much the same instincts and traditions, much the same education, and reading the same newspapers, it is quite possible that opinions commanding two-fifths of the voters might not obtain a majority in any constituency. The uninominal districts, marked out and gerrymandered in the interests of party in the United States, are the most successful fields for the extinction of all originality and independence, and for the destruction of true public spirit that could be devised by man. The law preventing a man from offering himself for any district in which he does not reside, is most mischievous, because if he is thrown out in his own electorate, he cannot try another. There is no such restriction in England or in Australia ; a man may offer himself for any locality. There is no positive restriction in Canada, but custom is nearly as strong as law, and the parochial spirit is encouraged thereby.

As a specimen of how this restriction works, Mr. Charles A. Sumner after having served a term in Congress with credit for his residential district of California, on seeking re-election, was opposed by his party convention—the Democratic—because he had advocated a genuine postal telegraph, and also the reduction of freights and fares on the subsidised railroads. This offended the telegraph and railroad monopolists, who are in point of fact, the same people, the wealthy corporations which are a standing menace to liberty. Their power is enormous, and rendered Mr. Sumner not "a safe man" for the Democratic ticket. There were thousands in San Francisco, and tens of thousands in California who would have voted for Mr. Sumner expressly on account of these views, but not a safe majority in any district. And he could not go elsewhere. The residential clause sits lightly on carpet-baggers who have nothing to leave, and on millionaires, who may have a house in several states, but it keeps out the best men for the service of the community. The railroad and telegraph men spent hundreds of thousands of dollars to oppose Sumner's bill and fifty thousand to oppose his nomination for a second term.

It requires not only capital, but astuteness and unscrupulousness to fight the political campaign. The capital is furnished by the corporations and the protected industries whose interests may be affected by legislation, also by black-mail from people who are in offices which they want to keep, or who are out of offices which they desire to get ; and probably also from the rank and file of the party. These last furnish the blind followers, whose loyalty makes the astuteness and unscrupulousness of the wire-pullers so successful.

Why should we say that there are only two parties worthy of consideration in a free country ? Majority representation takes no account of any others. There must indeed be always two main parties, the party of order and the party of progress. Woe to the land where crystallised order obstructs progress ; and woe to the country where progress tramples over order ! But allied to each of these, are various sections who see differently how progress is to be made, and how order is to be maintained. Sir John Lubbock says indeed that while there are innumerable ways of moving on, there is only one mode of standing still, and that the injustice of majority representation presses far harder on the Liberal than on the Conservative, but I think there is loss to both parties of the finest elements they contain in our clumsy electoral machinery.

While life becomes daily more complex, and political, moral and social questions are felt to be inextricably interwoven together ; while philosophy takes wider and deeper views, and history is being rewritten in every succeeding generation, and neither courts nor camps nor parliaments are held as including the whole life and development of a people, why should the representative machinery be constructed on a merely dual basis, and the most civilized and most enlightened nations in the world parcel out their territory into convenient lists for a duel à l'outrance ? England followed the bad example of America, and cut up her historic counties and her great cities into uninominal districts. It must have saddened the last years of the life of Thomas Hare, whose grand idea of equitable representation had been given to the world for thirty years, to see districts returning several members thus sub-divided, instead of being grouped together and obtaining, by means of the single transferable vote, the real clear voice of Liverpool and Manchester, of Glasgow and Birmingham. A catch or a snatch majority in nine separated districts, is a very different thing from the collective voice of Liverpool. If each elector of Liverpool voted for one man, giving contingent votes in case his first choice could not use his vote, or did not need it, according to Mr. Hare's plan, we might not only see the Liberals and the Conservatives represented according to their strength, but might have independent representatives of some side issues from which often a nation draws its most valuable elements.

All the loopholes are now closed through young men with little money but with brains and enterprise, used to enter parliament in old days ; and though such loopholes were not always justifiable on principle, we ought not to make it impossible for such men to get into parliament now.

England is only in the honeymoon of uninominal electorates and many voters, and already we see one bad thing copied from America, the raising of an election fund of £100,000, for the protection of the interests of the brewers and publicans, and this worked with such success that in almost every instance where the trade and temperance came to a close contest, the drink carried the day. In the United States, where the business has been elaborated for generations, election funds are raised as *sine qua non*. General Weaver, the defeated Populist candidate for the Presidency, asserts that it costs a million dollars to place a presidential candidate in the field, and a hundred thousand to launch and elect a man to the senate of the United States;—all the unsuccessful parties simply waste their money, while the funds of the successful are used, if not in bribery and corruption, to narrow the platform of the candidate, and thus rather to obfuscate than to enlighten the intelligence of the voters.

What greater check to patriotism and public spirit could be devised than a machinery which not incidentally but necessarily, makes the best efforts of large intelligent and conscientious minorities vanity, and worse than vanity—vexation of spirit through the absolute reversal of their wishes and aims? There are Conservatives in Scotland and Republicans in Mississippi who have voted at every election for forty years, with no more chance of getting in a representative than if they lived in Greenland. The only thing that can be said for the present system is that it represents localities, but in point of fact, all those who did not vote for the successful man, are *unrepresented*, and often these are the more numerous;—plurality is not majority;--while those who voted because he was the only man brought forward by the party, while neither liking nor trusting him, are *misrepresented*.

By a simple alteration in the method of taking votes, and by the enlargement of constituencies so as to allow of quota representation for six, seven, or better still, for ten men districts, dividing the number of votes polled by the number of representatives required, and making that number sufficient for his return, each elector in the country may aid in the return of one man of whom he approves, and this result is made absolutely secure by means of the single transferable vote. The state would gain by the raised character of the legislature and of the executive; the candidates would gain by their emancipation from party trammels and parish politics; and above all the elector would gain his full rights as a citizen of a free country.

In a free country, what we call the government is at once the master and the servant of the people. As our master, it must be obeyed. All the laws of the land, while they are its laws, must be respected, even if we do not think them just or wise, and though we may do our utmost to get them changed. But as our servant, the executive chosen by the representatives whom we have sent to Parliament, government ought to be watched and checked. Eternal vigilance is the price of liberty, and the unchecked power of any majority or plurality, making laws in its own interests, and filling public posts with its adherents, is as destructive to true liberty in our spurious democracies as unchecked power on the hands of an autocrat. In politics, in sociology, in finance, a numerous following is no guarantee for wise or equitable legislation or administration.

Jeremy Bentham made a great stride in politics and morals, when he advocated the greatest happiness of the greatest number, for, before his time the few were considered and the many ignored. But we have gone beyond that. The modern spirit feels that the greatest happiness even of the greatest number, ought not to be sought at the cost of the happiness of the smallest number. Each individual has the right to life, liberty, and the pursuit of happiness, and at our peril is it disregarded or denied.

It is more than a century since Condorcet, who believed in human perfectibility, and who kept that faith under the very shadow of the guillotine, showed the clumsiness and injustice of our present methods of representation. He said it was in the power of science to devise a method of taking and valuing votes mathematically accurate. But much that was excellent and practicable in the discoveries and suggestions of the early leaders of the great French Revolution, was discounted by their disastrous defeat, and by the blunders and crimes of those who rose on their ruins. Utopian, Quixotic, theoretical, illusory, and absurd, are the terms bestowed on much which, if carried out at the time, might have saved France. But safe and lasting reforms are seldom effected in the throes of revolution. It is from evolution in a sound social organism rather than the fever of disease that we may expect progress, and

" Freedom slowly broadening down
From precedent to precedent,"

and may even go beyond precedent to first principles with safety and success; reverencing the past, and careful not to uproot anything that is good, but yet not satisfied to stand still.

It has long seemed to me that on some British colony inheriting the elastic traditions of England, and not bound by a written constitution like America, the radical reform of enfranchising the whole people might be inaugurated. The Australian colonies had early bestowal of democratic institutions;—parties have held together very loosely, and nothing like the strong political organisation of older communities exists there. And the early history of South Australia, the province in which I grew up, gives the first example of QUOTA REPRESENTATION that has come to my knowledge. In the first Municipal Bill for the city of Adelaide, Mr. (afterwards Sir) Rowland Hill, the post-office reformer, who was then secretary to the Colonization Commissioners, inserted a clause by which any twentieth part of the ratepayers, by combining to give all their votes to one man, might bring him in. Of the 18 members of the first town council, two were elected in this way. My father was town-clerk at the time, and explained this unique provision to me.

Thus I had my first glimpse into the correct theory of representation in the year 1840. In the crisis, however, through which the province of South Australia, like all new settlements, had to pass, the municipality was abolished, and after an interval of many years, another was established under a new bill which did not contain the quota clause.

Mr. Thomas Hare, a sound chancery lawyer, with a strong turn for arithmetic, first proposed his plan in 1857, but I did not see anything of it till 1860, and I saw in it at once the most Conservative and the most Democratic reform ever given to the world.

A scheme for an ideally perfect representation of the United Kingdom was proposed, by which supporters of a candidate might combine without the necessity of meeting, and in which by the use of contingent voting, the single vote could be made effective, whatever majority or minority the elector belonged to, was magnificent. This was what would make the democracy I loved real and safe and progressive, and I hoped that South Australia, the land of my adoption, might show the first example of a community where equality was not a fiction, but a fact; where government was really in the hands of the wisest and the best; where the people had provided for the education and elevation of their whole body by calling out everything that was original and special, by such machinery of representation as was equable and self-adjusting, far-sighted and reparatory, by putting a premium on truth and honour instead of lavishing its favour on flattery and dissimulation.

South Australia in 1860 returned 18 members for the Upper House, the whole Province voting as one district, and voting if they pleased for the whole 18. The 18 who had the largest number of votes were returned. This is called in France SCRUTIN DE LISTE, and in America, VOTING AT LARGE, and it gives such power for a party with a slight preponderance to return all the members, that it has discredited large electorates all over the world, as this has been hitherto the only mode of dealing with them. I naturally thought that though the electoral roll, or list of candidates for the United Kingdom, might be somewhat bewildering to the average voter, our Legislative Council list would be the same as before, and the trouble to the voter would be less, for instead of picking out 18, many of whom were unknown to him, if he marked with figures in the order of his preference six or seven whom he liked, he might be sure that his vote was used for the first man on his list who needed his vote, and could use it. If the principle were once adopted for the Council, and found to work well, it would be introduced for the Assembly also. There was absolutely nothing to be said against it, but that it was new and untried, but that was sufficient. The golden opportunity was lost. South Australia has since been divided into four Council electorates, each returning six members, but there are never more than two to be elected at one time as they retire by rotation.

For the Assembly, the Province is divided into 27 electoral districts, each returning two. Each voter can vote for two men, but cannot give two votes to one. Plumping, therefore, is a waste of half of his voting power, in order that he may direct the other half as he wishes. When, as sometimes, a dozen or more candidates offer for the two seats, they may be returned by a third of the votes polled; by plurality, and not by majority.

There is a common confusion of ideas between the function of the majority in the election of representatives, and the function of the majority in the Parliament itself. In a deliberating body of representatives, the majority must rule and ought to rule. There would be no stability in the administration if it did not rest on the votes of the majority. But the word representation means a re-presentment, as in a mirror, of the opinions, the principles, and the aspirations of the whole people and not of a mere section of the people, as is the case under plurality triumphs. When the majority of that plurality make the laws and appoint the ministries, and conduct public affairs inside and outside of Parliament, it is really minority rule. If Parliament is the true mirror of the people, debates will be more interesting than they are at present, personalities and recriminations will be discouraged, and governments will be more stable for administrative work, and more open to reform than they are now.

In order that the governing majority in Parliament which appoints and dismisses cabinets, and deals with the finances and public business, may be entitled to such power, we need effective representation of the whole people. A slight wave of opinion—nay even less—a slight preponderance in activity in the electioneering agents of one party over the other, in watching the rolls and striking off adverse votes and putting on partisans, may reverse the majority in separated districts, change the policy of the country, and give history a new direction. Far more stability would be obtained by equal representation, than by the most scientific mode of ascertaining the absolute majority in uninominal districts, which short-sighted people fancy is democratic.

And what is still more important, politics cannot be moralised by any system of majority representation, because where any material or social advantages are to be gained, there is a strong temptation to capture votes enough to turn the election, by all means, by insincerity, and by bribery direct and indirect. Politics are only to be purified by making the representation equitable. "Seek righteousness," said the Great Teacher, "and all other things shall be added to you." Justice to each, justice to all, is the vital principle on which society should be built, and our political methods have long obscured this truth from our eyes.

If any intelligent inhabitant—say of the planet Mars—were asked how he thought the people of the city of Brussels should be represented by 18 deputies, and that there were 36,000 qualified voters who came to the poll, he would probably reply that if any 2,000 of them could agree as to a man, he should represent them, and not that the half, plus one, should have it in their power to return all 18, leaving the half, minus one, without any. This is what happens, and the government falls into the hands of the Catholic or of the Liberal party according as a narrow fringe of votes turns. In the same way, it depends on a doubtful and often a corrupt fringe of votes in New York State whether the 36 presidential electors vote Republican or Democrat, and this difference of 72 votes generally decides who has power for four years over the people of the United States, far exceeding that of any European monarch.

CHAPTER II.

METHOD OF VOTING AND FORMATION OF THE QUOTA.

In writing on this subject, I do not treat it merely as a student. I have put it to a series of tests among people of all sorts of classes and opinions. I have given public lectures all over the settled districts of South Australia, and I have illustrated the simplicity and certainty of the method by means of voting papers, calling on the audience to vote according to their convictions, and then asking 12 men from among them to act as scrutineers of the votes given for 12 candidates—six being to be returned—by the single transferable vote. I did not not need to explain the method of voting, I simply asked them to do it. I did not need to explain the method of scrutiny. It was all done within their sight and hearing. What seems complicated when described is simplicity itself when reduced to practice.

The voting-papers which I used contained the names of four candidates of each of our two main parties, these parties being Capitalist and Labour, and one candidate for each of four outside parties with considerable following. The Instructions to Voters were printed with the voting-paper, which was perforated, so that these could be torn off and kept. The quota needed for return was found by dividing the votes taken by six, and whether the number was 42 or 154, the principle was the same. By carefully reading over the voting paper and instructions which I annex here, any person of ordinary intelligence can grasp the principle.

INSTRUCTIONS TO VOTERS.

1. There are here twelve Candidates ;
six are required to be elected.

2. Vote by numbering the Candidates
in the order of your choice, that is to say:—
Place **1** against the name of the man
you like best.
Place **2** against the name of the man
you like second best.
Place **3** against the name of the man
you like next best, and so on.

3. Vote for six names, or for fewer.

4. The same number must not be put
against more than one name.

5. The numbers must be placed in the
squares opposite the names.

MEMO.

Your vote will be *used* for *one* Candidate, according to your preference.
If a Candidate you like most, either
(*a*) Does not need your vote
(Has enough votes to elect him without your vote).
Or
(*b*) Cannot use your vote
(Has so few votes that he cannot
possibly be elected).
your vote will be transferred to the man
you like next best (as shown by your numbers), and *used*, not *wasted*.

Outside Parties.		Main Parties.
	☐	Angas, Capital.
	☐	Baker, Capital.
Single Tax.	☐	Birks.
	☐	Buttery, Labour.
	☐	Charleston, Lab.
	☐	Fowler, Capital.
Irish Catholic.	☐	Glynn.
	☐	Guthrie, Labour.
	☐	Harrold, Capital.
Temperance.	☐	Magarey.
	☐	Robinson, Lab.
Woman's Suffrage.	☐	Stirling.

Whatever may be the number of candidates in the field, I think it is advisable to
limit the votes, first and contingent, to the number of members needed. The elector may
vote for fewer names. He ought not to vote for any men he would not like to see in Parliament. In the list of candidates for a large constituency, he cannot but see several whom
he prefers to the rest.

The benefits of the system cannot be secured with less than six to be returned. I
should prefer a larger electorate still, but I was led to adopt six from the City of Adelaide
returning six, two each for three separated districts, east, west, and north. I took Adelaide as my unit, and as there were no conflicting interests, it was accepted as a whole.
In suburban and country districts I presented the same well-known names for that electorate and two adjoining ones, so that if the local men did not please, the voter might find
one standing for another part of the newly or imaginatively formed electorate who did.
There will always be some localism left, though the choice is extended.

The singleness of the vote was the chief novelty to be impressed on the voters. They
were asked to choose six names out of 12, and they naturally thought they voted for all
six. Here I used as an illustration a list sent to a circulating library by a messenger, by
a subscriber who has only a right to one book. The first book on the list which the messenger can obtain, he takes to the subscriber. If he can get the first book he goes no
further; if he fails, he goes down the list till he finds one obtainable. In the same way,
if the man marked " 1 " on the electoral ballot needs the vote, and can use it, it counts for
him, and aids his return, and the contingent votes have no weight whatever.

We might carry the parallel a step further. Tom, Dick, and Harry are three brothers,
living in the same house, and each subscribing to the same library, at a little distance from
where they live. If each of them sent a list of books by a messenger with the same book

7

marked "1," there being only one copy in the library, only one could get it. The first list handed in would secure that book, but if the brothers are friendly, all three will get all they want with it; they will read it. In the same way, a candidate whom we prefer, who is brought in by the votes of our friends, is as serviceable to us as if our own vote had not been taken after his quota was complete. Our own vote is not wasted, but transferred to the next man, as in the book-ballot, it was transferred to the next book.

If there were open voting, and the state of the poll were declared every half hour, people would cease to vote for men already in, or impossible to bring in, and would direct their weight towards men whom they could serve.

The ballot paper puts the voter in the position to transfer his vote in every contingency. The single transferable vote actually gives a certainty of effective representation to every citizen.

The formation of the quota is the most important of the details, and I propose to consider in their order the different methods in which this factor in securing Proportional Representation has been dealt with by various writers and experimenters.

I.—The first and in my opinion the best, is the simple natural quota of Mr. Hare, formed by dividing the number of valid votes polled by the number of representatives needed for the district. All votes above that quota should be allotted according to each elector's second choice, or third if the second did not need it or could not use it, following the series of perference till some man was found to utilise it. After the surplusage, if any, was worked off, the Returning Officer and scrutineers next dealt with the minus votes, beginning with the man who had fewest votes, and who had no chance of making up a quota, and distributing these according to contingent votes in the same way. Then come the votes of the next lowest, and so on working up the minus votes till only the number of representatives needed for the electorate are left standing, when these shall be declared elected, whether they have reached the full quota or not. Towards the end of the scrutiny there are always some votes which cannot be allocated, because they are given for men already in, or impossible to get in, and Mr. Hare allows of an approximate quota for the last man or men who get returned.

Thus in a public scrutiny of 3,824 votes taken by me at various meetings in South Australia, on the ballot paper already shown, the quota required was 637, and though the surplusage had often been large at the small meetings, it had been given so variously that when all were massed together, it had no appreciable influence on the result. The favorite labour candidate being best known, polled 47 more than 637, and owing to the votes of women, the Temperance man had a surplus of 19. The tabulated result will be found in Appendix "A" and it will be seen that the quotas of the other successful candidates were made up in far larger measure by the minus votes.

At the end, there were 144 votes which could not be allocated, but only two were utter failures, because the voters had picked out the six men who could not obtain sufficient for their return? This I think proves the efficiency of Hare's natural quota. As a school-teacher said to me, it was founded on justice, common sense, and arithmetic, a threefold basis absolutely perfect.

II.—Sir John Lubbock seems to object to the natural quota, and proposes instead what he calls a mathematical quota. He divides the votes polled by one more than the representatives needed, and he adds one to the quotient, because if as in the case of these 3,824 votes, six men get 546, the mathematical quota, there will not be so many left for any seventh. By this means it is probable, though not quite certain, that all six successful men would have reached this lesser quota, but it leaves 542 ineffective. By Hare's plan there were only 144. It is true that in neither case are the votes really wasted as they are under majority representation necessarily and in enormous numbers, but after trying both ways, we found the simple quota the best.

III.—The Liste or party ticket system, which is actually carried out in three Cantons of Switzerland —Ticino, Neufchatel, and Geneva, — is an imperfect adaptation of proportional representation. Each party prepares a list and the votes are interchanged within the limits of the list. It certainly has made representation more just, and whereas on the past only Catholics and Liberals were represented, in the last election for Geneva, 33 Democrats, 38 Radical-Liberals, 6 Radical-Nationals, 8 Socialist-Labour and 15 Independent representatives made the 100 deputies. The ticket system lends itself to party organisation beforehand, and limits the choice of the elector.

It is not advisable to limit the number of candidates either by caucus or by the forfeiture of a sum of money if he does not poll a certain percentage of the votes. This often checks the full discussion of new and important things in parliament and by the press, and under what I call effective voting, we need not prevent any man from coming forward. The checks were needed to prevent waste of votes under majority representation, but under an equitable system we may give every candidate and every elector a perfectly free hand.

IV.—The advocates of proportional representation in Belgium and Switzerland, though welcoming the Liste system, confess it is imperfect, and extol the method of D'Hondt as mathematically accurate. This gives each elector a power equal to one vote, but he may either give it all to one, or if he votes for two each counts for a half, if for three for a third, if for four for a fourth, and so on. According to this plan, an earnest minority which cannot make up as large a sum of integers as the larger parties can make, from integers and fractions combined will completely lose their votes. Popular candidates would have too many votes, and the surplusage as well as the minuses would be wasted. It would be majority representation with a difference, and not so educative to the voter as Tuckerman's method, which is the best form of the cumulative vote, as it contains Hare's system of graduated preference.

According to D'Hondt, if a man votes for more than one candidate he ceases to prefer one to another. Now man naturally loves to compare and to decide, and my experience at sixty public meetings with ballots was that people had preferences and expressed them by figures.

V.—Tuckerman's plan would count every first vote on my ballot paper as equal to six, and decrease till the sixth only counts for one. It is much better than the Cumulative vote of Illinois, because it proposes a larger electorate than one to return three, but it is open to party manipulation beforehand, and it wastes many votes in surplus and minus. I have tried my papers by it, and found it inferior. It demands the same enlargement of constituencies, and the same exercise of choice on the part of the voter, and it is not true proportional representation after all.

In my experience with my 3,824 voters, I came to the conclusion that a first vote was better than a second by more than a sixth part of the voter's power, and the same all down the line. The labour men voted fearlessly for Charleston to make him safe, and any surplus would pass according to each voter's wish with undiminished force to his next choice. By this means, large parties get the full advantage of their numbers, which they might not do if the vote diminished in value. Smaller parties either secure an independent representative of their own, which is a positive good, or they can modify to the full extent of their numbers, the members returned by stronger parties.

VI.—The Gove System. In ordinary elections for a six or eight member district, I believe there will be no surplusage at all, but Mr. Hare's original scheme, by which if a man did not like the candidate standing for his own district at Land's End, he might vote for one offering for Caithness or Cork, was open to great accumulations of votes for popular candidates, and this has called out criticism as to allocation. The minus votes are always the more numerous of the two but these can only be dealt with in one way, and that an absolutely just one. The second votes on surplusage may vary in the votes taken for quota, and those distributed as surplus, and people who see every day half the votes cast wasted, say that this uncertainty puts the ingenious scheme out of the pale of practical politics. Mr. John Berry, of Worcester, Mass. who has long advocated electoral reform, says that "Mr. Hare, distributed his surplus votes, by a complicated and perplexing method" which is quite incorrect for the method is clear enough, and suggests instead what he calls the Gove System for the election of the State Senate of Massachusetts. This requires every candidate to announce before the election takes place, to whom his unnecessary votes shall be transferred. Each voter therefore votes for a single man, but with the knowledge how it will go if it is not used by him. This gives to the candidate the power of choice which ought to be the voter's. He might like "A" himself but he might not care about "B" or "C" to whom "A" consigns him.

In this proposed bill there is only allotment of surplusage, and after that is dealt with, those who have a fortieth part of the whole votes cast are returned, and the full number of forty representatives is made up from those who come nearest to that number. It is quite possible that the utilization of minus votes might change the personnel of these last. The Gove system suggests the use of the lot in case of a tie. Under Hare's plan, there is no such thing as a tie. Even in the improbable case of an equal number of votes, they are not of the same value. The votes of lower value are taken first for distribution.

VII.—The Danish electoral law, which was the first to embody the proportional principle in actual working, (M. Andrae and Mr. Hare having made the discovery simultaneously) has some notable defects, and can not be taken as a model. As working peacefully since 1855 for the Upper House, and surviving the change in the constitution of 1867, and actually used in the final election for the Landsthing or Senate, it deserves our acknowledgement. For that Landsthing however, there are twelve members appointed by the King. In the second place, an electoral college is chosen in districts at large, or by SCRUTIN DE LISTE. It is only in the electoral college itself that proportional voting comes in. It is preferential voting, but only as far as surplus is concerned. After all who make up full quotients are returned, the remaining number needed to make up 66, are as in the Gove plan taken from those who come nearest it, but there must be half the quota reached. The Danish law has compulsory voting, at least those who do not vote are fined.

VIII.—It is scarcely worth mentioning the limited vote, so fallacious a method of representing even a very large minority, except to say that when it was first proposed by Mackworth Praed in 1832, it was to give the elector the right to vote for only two out of four candidates. When it was made law for a few constituencies in England, it was reduced to two out of three, while he could not give two to one man. It would need a compact minority of two-fifths to bring in a member, if there was organisation with the majority. The thirteen three-cornered constituencies have been all cut up, and England has only uninominal electorates now. As for the cumulative vote of Illinois, it is fairly just to the two contending parties. As there are only three votes to dispose of, there is some certainty about them, but in electing large bodies like the London school board, the waste of voting power is very great. The adoption of the single transferable vote would have saved all this waste, given a more accurate presentment of the wishes of the elector, and have been simpler for voters and scrutineers. The voter works in the dark, he may give unnecessary votes to make his favorite candidate safe, or he may believe him safe when he is not so, and direct his voting power to an inferior. With the preferential vote, he signifies what is to be done with his vote, in every contingency.

CHAPTER III.

OBJECTIONS ANSWERED.

Every new and untried thing must encounter opposition, both from ignorant prejudice and from intelligent criticism. The first we can afford to despise, however huge and stolid he may be, and as Mrs. Stetson of San Francisco says,

> "Just walk directly through him,
> As if he was not there,"

but intelligent criticism is a thing to be courted, to be weighed, and to be answered.

I. The first objections were that the method was too difficult for the voters, and too complicated for the scrutineers. This in my own case was met by a series of test elections, and by a final scrutiny in public. The number of informal votes was no larger than in ordinary voting, and the time occupied in the final count with the tally kept by all 12 scrutineers, as shown in Appendix "A," was by no means long. After the separation into first votes, it took little more than two hours to allot surplus and minus votes, and at the same time tabulate the results as shown in Appendix "A." The 12 men were inexperienced in the work, with one exception, and he was the slowest because he was hampered by majority traditions.

II.—The most obstinate questioning which the reform has had to encounter has been with regard to the uncertainty in allocating surplus votes, and this could not be satisfactorily answered till all the votes collected at various meetings had been massed together. At the small meetings there was often a surplus, and sometimes a large one, but it fell to different people. On the general average, there were only two inconsiderable surpluses, and these were accounted for by special reasons. In ordinary districts for six or eight members there will be no surplus at all. And as Sir John Lubbock puts it, where the surplus is large it follows a uniform trend, and where it is small it is of no effect on the large number of votes dealt with.

And all this protest about uncertainty is made in the interests of possible candidates ;—every elector has his wishes carried out. If his first vote is effective, he obtains the thing he most desires ;—if his fellows have been beforehand and brought his favorite in, he falls back on his second choice. The 47 spare votes for Charleston were distributed after cutting the pack of votes once, to prevent any chance of manipulation, and fell in the usual order. Magarey's surplus of 19 were mostly gained by Stirling, because Temperance and Woman Suffrage go very much together. This objection was thus answered. In the clause of the draft bill appended to this essay the votes are all mixed together and then taken out one by one, and when the quota is reached the remaining votes are counted as surplus.

III. Uncertainty of result. The difficulty of forecasting how the election will come out makes effective voting distasteful to election agents, party leaders, and party newspapers. And yet results are far from certain now. Every extension of the suffrage, and every step towards secrecy and purity of elections has been feared and opposed on account of the additional uncertainty it introduced into the contest. What a leap in the dark it was when the Conservative party with the noble ambition to "dish the Whigs" outbade them in giving electoral rights to a new and vast body of the people !

It was uncertainty for both of the parties when the secret ballot was given to the people of the United Kingdom, when the voters who had been counted like so many sheep and so many goats were no longer marched to the poll, and open voting no longer warranted the security of the promised vote. The collective conscience of America has forced the Australian Ballot upon most of the States of the Union, and no doubt a good deal of uncertainty has resulted from it.

Parties can, however, accommodate themselves to everything, and as effective voting would have this element of certainty that the people would be really represented, the people may feel their minds easy whatever the wire-pullers may say, and however gloomy the prognostications of those who stand behind them may be.

IV. That it will be impossible to form a strong government under Proportional Representation. It is quite possible for a government to be too strong. Mr. Bryce in his invaluable work, "The American Commonwealth," says that for the term of office, the American President, who is his own prime minister, who exercises a real veto, and can go on ruling in the teeth of an enormous majority in the House of Representatives—the people's chamber—and who is the actual, and not like the Queen of England, the nominal commander of army and navy, has more power than any European sovereign. No Englishman since Oliver Cromwell exercised the power Lincoln did.

Even in times of peace, the president has enormous patronage, and that is supposed to be power, but so much of the time, effort, and thought of able presidents has been occupied in apportioning rewards to supporters *in esse* or *in posse*, which ought to be given to important and necessary work, that "The Spoils System" seems falling to pieces by its own weight, as well as from the collective conscience on the country. Each successive president, beginning with Garfield, makes fewer displacements.

The Cabinet Ministers of the president do not sit in Congress, as they do in England and the colonies ; they keep their places till the next shuffle of the cards at the presidential election decides on the complexion of politics for the next four years.

In England, in Canada, and in Australia, there is continuous antagonism carried on inside and outside the walls of parliament, against the ministry in office. A ministry may be dismissed in consequence of a single night's debate, and a fresh Cabinet formed from the ranks of its enemies. In England, the parties depend largely on class and caste; they have historic roots in the past; they throw out their branches and tendrils towards the future. In spite of all the conservatism of the ancient nation, buttressed by hereditary titles and by the law of primogeniture, England moves steadily towards more and more democratic opinions and institutions. On the other hand, in spite of the successful efforts of reformers carried out in every possible direction, England still stands the most conservative of modern nations. But I question whether party government based on majority representation, is the source of her strength.

In a debate in the Belgium Chamber in May, 1892, M. Beernaert, Minister of Finance, in introducing a new electoral bill, sought to alter a clause in the constitution so as to allow of proportional representation, and when the objection was raised that under that system it would be impossible to form a strong government, he replied in these words: "I, who have the honour of speaking to you to-day in the name of the government, and who have at my back the strongest majority that was ever known in Belgium, I owe it to truth to say that our opinions have not a corresponding preponderance in the country, and I believe that if that majority were always correctly expressed, we should gain in stability what we might lose in apparent strength. Of what use besides are very strong majorities, when we have a fixed resolution to oppress nobody? Gentlemen, in the actual state of affairs, to whom belongs the government of the country? It belongs to some two or three thousand electors, who are certainly neither the best nor the most intelligent.

"I see to the right and to the left, two grand corps-d'armée, Catholics and Liberals, of force almost equal, whom nothing would tempt to desert their standard, and who serve that standard from conviction and with devotion. Well, these grand corps do not count, or scarcely count. On the day of battle, it is as if they did not exist.

"What triumphs, what decides, is another body of electors altogether, a floating body, knowing little what they wish, and too often swayed by their passions, by their grudges, and what is worse still, by their interests. These are our masters, and according as they veer from right to left, the government of the country changes, and its history takes a new direction.

"I ask is it well that it should be so? Is it well that the government should be at the mercy of such contemptible elements as these?"

M. Beernaert is right. It is the party government that is essentially the weak government. It cannot afford to estrange or offend any one who commands votes. It has been said that every prominent member of the English House of Commons is being perpetually tempted and tormented by his friends not to be honest, and perpetually assailed by his enemies in order to be made not to appear honest.

The opposition are ready to trip up the ministry at every step. They exaggerate mistakes, misrepresent motives, combat even measures they believe to be good if brought forward by the other party, they bully in public, they undermine in secret, and count all things fair in political warfare. The opposition is always prepared to step into the shoes of the ministry, and to undergo the same treatment from the defeated foe. And this is the sort of strength which is supposed to be imperilled if the nation were equitably represented in the Legislature!

Colonial parties have not the same sharp lines of demarcation; ministries are frequently brought in and defeated on merely personal grounds, but they are often less scrupulous than English politicians. There must always be "the ins and the outs," and these in Canada and in Australia are more keenly apprehended than the time-honoured parties of order and progress. Perhaps there are fewer great questions to discuss, and local and personal politics preponderate.

Whether the legislative bodies are paid or un-paid, it makes a difference to the locality which he represents, if a man votes with the ministry or against it, or if he is a member of it himself. Nor is it merely the loaves and fishes that make office so desirable. Every citizen is disposed to think he is as clever as his neighbours, and when that citizen is an elected member of parliament, he is inclined to think he is quite fit to administer public affairs. Gratified activity is the greatest pleasure in life, and there is credit as well as profit to be gained. Thus votes of no confidence are brought foward by weak men as well as by strong, and coalitions are formed of the most discordant elements, and you hear men lament there are no strong parties in the colonies to form strong governments. Strength is to be sought in quite another direction.

In the present state of the world, it is of the first importance that public administration should be watched from all sides, and not merely from the point of view of the party which desires to sit on the treasury benches. In order that government should be honest, intelligent, and economical, it needs helpful criticism rather than destructive opposition, and this criticism may be expected from the less compact and more independent ranks of a legislature which truly represents the people.

V.—There would be a difficulty in case of a by-election caused by death or resignation of one member of a large constituency.

It could not be filled up by proportional representation. Where the tenure is for seven years as in England, there is a natural desire to gauge public opinion through a by-election, but for the shorter terms in Canada, America, and Australia, it is not necessary. Let the voting papers used at the last election be preserved, and those which had returned the retiring members be distributed according to contingent votes among the unsuccessful candidates, and added to the number of first votes polled by each, and let the candidate who has the plurality be returned for the remainder of the term. (For example, see Appendix B.)

VI.—If constituencies were fixed now on an equal basis, what should be done in case of growth of population? How shift the boundaries? I should not suggest shifting boundaries at all, for that lends itself to dishonest gerrymandering. At present in the United States, the uninominal districts are gerrymandered in the interests of party. Where the Republicans are the stronger, the changes are made to throw the Democrats into one district, so that several others which lie round may bring in Republicans. Where the Democrats are stronger, the process is reversed. One electoral district may curl like a salamander round another, or may stretch like a long ribbon through the middle of a state. A single county actually belonged to five electoral districts in nine years.

Let no one say that as these tactics are practised by both parties, one injustice rectifies another. Satan cannot cast out Satan! Injustice can rectify nothing! It is always and everywhere an intolerable evil.

The larger electorate will be more stable as to relative population than the uninominal one. But according to our system, there need be no shifting of boundaries at all. After each decennial census, a readjustment might be made, and one member more given to any district which had made an equivalent comparative increase, while one member was taken from any which had comparatively declined.

There are already too many representatives in Canada and in Australia, and I should recommend their decrease. It was a great mistake to fix by the Constitution that Quebec should send always 65 members to the Dominion Parliament, and all the other Provinces in proportion to their population as compared with hers. Where all members of the legislature are paid, such large numbers are a heavy tax on industry and production, and half the present number would do the work better. And besides the Dominion Parliament, there are also the local Provincial Legislatures to be paid, and fitting men to be found. When New Zealand federated she gave up the provincial parliaments, though she retained more local government and better means for it than we on the island continent have evolved for ourselves.

In the larger electorates necessitated by proportional representation, it will be easier to reduce the number of members than it is now, when each little growing locality demands increase of political influence, yet the declining will not consent to reduction. Local interests would be so far shorn of their power that the voice of reason and common-sense might be heard.

Before we are federated in Australia, I hope some limits will be put on the number of legislators. Perhaps the financial crisis through which the colonies are passing may direct public attention to the unnecessary cost of our whole administration, and that the people and the press will demand from the parliament reduction of numbers, if not of pay.

VII.—The objection has been raised that in delocalising politics, or at all events greatly diminishing the local benefits sought from congressman or member of parliament, people would become quite indifferent to politics. I expected to hear at my meetings that the people disliked being merged in a large group, but it was never brought forward except once by a member of parliament, who was in the chair, and he did not give as his own opinion, but as an objection natural to the electors. I suppose I had so thoroughly convinced my hearers that however large the electorate might be, no vote would miss its aim, that they did not object.

I suppose that in South Australia as elsewhere, a voter thinks his member ought to do something for him or for the district, but still he may be able to see that if every member did the same for other voters and other districts, more taxes must be paid by all. Every one can see that log-rolling practised for the advantage of other districts is done at his cost, and it needs little acumen to perceive that ministries would be more stable and more honest, as well as more happy, if their hand was not so often forced by the need of votes which demand local concessions. Party spirit might decline, local and parochial matters might suffer, but real public spirit would be strengthened and purified.

There are three kinds of interests which an honest man should watch, lest they lead him astray. The first is his personal interest. He may have a piece of land to sell to the government or to the municipality, for which he may ask a higher price than he would gladly take from a private individual. The next is his class interest. This leads him to desire laws passed for the benefit of his trade or his business, at the cost of other trades and businesses. The third is his local interest, which seeks an advantage to his town or his county, at the cost of other towns and counties.

Our personal interests are, however, watched by people who have interests in other directions, while our class and local interests are flattered, exaggerated, intensified, by the public opinion which is nearest to us—that of our own class and our own locality, who would also be benefited, and who have the same bias as ourselves. "Tax the squatters (the pastoral lessees) to make our roads," said a South Australian farmer some years ago in my hearing. The squatters did not need the roads. This was both a local and a class bias, but we hear a good many such cries. "Give us some advantage for ourselves, for our class or our district, at the expense of other people, other districts, and other classes." If it needs the chance of local appropriations to induce interest in public matters, the electoral stuff must be poor indeed. It is time public spirit was fed on better food and roused to better purpose.

With regard to the delocalising of politics, people are apt to speak as if because the elector may vote for another man than stands for the segment he lives in, he will always do so. This is contrary to human nature. The great majority of the votes will be given to the local man who best represents the elector's views. There will be local centres in every large district which will compete, but not for local votes only, and therefore they will be anxious to bring forward good men, who might win first and contingent votes to aid his return. Even Mr. Hare expected most of the votes to be polled for the local man candidates, although he allowed free range over the whole United Kingdom. The nomination was to be for the district, though power was given to escape from it.

In the smaller district which I propose, locality will tell more strongly than in Mr. Hare's scheme. It will retain much that is good in local representation, its direct interest in the district doing itself credit, which will be stimulated by healthy emulation with other districts, but it will lose much of its narrowness and selfishness. An elector chosen by a quota of the ninth part of the votes of all Liverpool, would occupy a higher position in public estimation and in his own, than one elected by a bare majority in a ninth part of that great city.

VIII. While some seem to fear that a strong government cannot be maintained under proportional representation, others say that without the strong organised opposition of the "outs" the "ins" cannot be sufficiently checked. Is there really true strength and progress under the perpetual reign of see-saw, with unfair handycapping on alternate sides, than there would be on a stable government built on a true representation of the people? Methods might indeed be varied. Capable men adjust themselves to changes, however great and far-reaching. There would be opposition to what appeared bad, criticism of what was doubtful, support to what appeared to be good, more certain than when the leader of the ministry and the opposition count noses, and the debates which fill the newspapers make no change in the following of either.

At the time of the Reform Bill of 1832, the party of order predicted a cataclysm of destruction, and the party of progress looked for a millennium of liberty and prosperity. Neither expectation was realized. Successive extensions of the suffrage and successive inroads upon privilege have been likewise feared and hailed as if the issues were of life and death. Still in the year of grace 1893 the party of order finds institutions that are worth preserving, and the part of progress demands further and further advance. The standing ground is shifted, that is all.

A noted politician in South Australia, Mr. Thomas Playford, proposed recently in his election address, that ministries should be elected for the session by the parliament, and that during that term the proceedings of government might be watched and criticised, but no attempt should be made to oust them. A great part of each parliamentary session in the Australian colonies is often spent in trying to unseat the cabinet, and when the opposition succeeds, the mover of the "No confidence" vote has the difficult and invidious task of choosing a new team, and offends more men by leaving them out, than he can please by including them. A ministry elected thus, according to Mr. Playford's idea, would be all pretty much of one party, and would all possess the confidence of the majority in parliament to start with, at any rate. If any one forfeited it, he would not be elected for next session.

This suggestion shows how burdensome a practical politician finds the present conditions of office. He would rather have the choice of colleagues taken out of his hands than have to make compromises and concessions in order to strengthen his position. If the parliament were elected on proportional lines, a ministry thus formed would be strong for work, and legislation and administration would go on more quickly and more thoroughly when the ministry were relieved from factious opposition during the session. Next session they might be displaced if the parliament was dissatisfied.

There would not be so many slaughtered innocents, there would not be so many bills passed or rejected by the Upper House without due discussion, if more time was given to work and less to wrangling for place. It may be said that this method would force on the premier a team he does not like, but experience shows that people as unsympathetic are forced on him by the exigencies of party government.

IX.—Another objection made is that the districts would be too large to allow of personal canvassing, but as most honest politicians find it hard to go through this ordeal with a clear conscience, and would be glad to be relieved from it, it is of no moment from their side. The elector might complain perhaps, for it is the personal canvass which flatters him most. At that moment, if at no other, he feels that he is the master of the situation, that he can make and unmake parliaments and governments. But the candidate's public addresses and speeches would be far more candid and courageous, far more enlightening to the constituency, if he appealed to every elector in a large district who thought with him, or who might be induced to think with him, than if he had to deprecate the antagonism of people who might vote against him in a small district. He must make his appearance at one or more centres in the electorate, and submit to searching questioning from all points of view. His speeches and replies as well as his address, would be widely circulated, so that first votes and contingent votes may be won. These would come from unexpected quarters without personal canvassing.

I have already said that I do not think it wise to require a deposit to be paid by every candidate, to be forfeited in case he does not poll a certain percentage of the votes. Open candidature is the right thing for a free and progressive country. The caucus and convention cannot dictate who shall enter the lists under proportional representation, and by means of the contingent votes no man need lose his vote even if his first choice falls on a most unpopular candidate.

X. An objection originally made to Mr. Hare's vast scheme, that it would fill the House of Commons with faddists, is still brought against such a modest modification of it as is advocated here. Crotchetty people are of course completely extinguished by majority election, but it would be only to the extent of its following that it would be represented in Parliament according to proportional representation. And the most valuable and vital of all reforms are at first looked on as mere Utopian crotchets. Mr. Grote's Ballot, Mr. Villiers' Free Trade were crotchets for many years. Woman's Suffrage and Proportional

Representation were crotchets brought forward in Parliament by John Stuart Mill, which prevented his return to the House for a second term. The electors of Westminster tried him once, but he was too unpractical for them. Under proportional voting, England would have retained his services. In the modification here proposed no extreme crotchet could be resented absolutely. Any reform which did not secure the sixth part of the votes given for a six-member, or an eighth part of those for an eight-member constituency, would not be able to return an independent member of its own. But should such minorities lose their power altogether, as is the case with considerable minorities now, when like the Prohibitionists, they conscientiously cast their ballots for the man who truly represents their convictions? No, they should not be extinguished, but should be allowed by means of the contingent votes, to support the most favourable or the least objectionable of the other men standing for the large district. Even if, like George Eliot's old woman, there is but a choice of mislikings in this world, there are some mislikings which by comparison are desirable.

The waste of votes given by conscientious third parties is so much political capital to the main contenders, as it narrows the field, and when we add to these the votes that are angled for by promises of concession, we see that everything plays into their hands. Sinking all minor differences, all third parties ought to unite in the demand for equitable representation, and they would get it, because they would be reinforced by the honest and thoughtful of the main parties themselves.

I have thus endeavoured to answer *seriatim*, the various objections which have been made, or which may be made, against this radical measure of electoral reform, and I hope I have shown that those as to complexity for voter and returning officer are groundless ; that the uncertainty as to surplusage in no way affects the result in such districts as are proposed; and that party leaders will accommodate themselves to the change of methods. I hope I have also proved that governments are likely to be more stable and the opposition more intelligent under the new system, and that the filling up of vacancies and the adjustment of electorates would be easily provided for on equitable principles, and that the best local interests would be preserved, while their mischievous operation would be greatly checked. The process and the results would also be interesting to the electors themselves, as well as to the candidates who offer themselves to the enlarged and truly enfranchised constituencies.

CHAPTER IV.

EFFECTIVE VOTING.

The exclusively majority representation which is organized in most civilized countries, gives rise to party government. It creates the impression that there are only two parties in the state whose views are entitled to consideration. To the ineffective third parties, to the original, to the idealist, these parties say scornfully, "Become a majority and then you will be attended to," but at the same time, they carefully close up the avenues through which converts are made in sufficient numbers for such results. "The truth is great and it will prevail," may be true in the long run, but it has to run the gauntlet of indolence and apathy, of prejudice and opposition, of vested interests and rooted traditions. Meantime all changes in law and administration are made in the real or supposed interests of one of the two parties which happens to be in power at the time, and sufficiently predominant to bear down the organised opposition of the other.

Not only does this party dualism reign supreme in the legislature ;—it dominates the chief instructor of the people, the newspaper press. In proof of this we may instance that although proportional representation by means of the single transferable vote has been brought forward by competent advocates for over thirty years, and treated in books and magazine articles as a real issue of the first importance, for the rectification of parliament and the purification of politics, no ordinary newspaper has taken hold of it, and it still remains with a sort of academic halo about it, quite apart from the bosom and business of ordinary men. Editors of papers will not admit articles or even letters on the subject because they "consider it unwise to open the question of improved electoral

methods, which might divert public attention from more important and practical matters."
I must except the newspaper press of South Australia, which has taken up the subject as a practical matter recently, but this was greatly due to the interest excited in the public mind by the lecturing and the trial ballots used all over the Province.

I have been asked how many members of parliament in my Province are in favour of proportional representation, and have been tempted to reply in the words of scripture, "Have any of the Pharisees or of the Scribes believed in Him?" Until a radical reform like this is brought home to the people so strongly that they demand it, members of parliament do not care to touch it.

When I advocated proportional representation under the title of Effective Voting, I caught hold of an experience that was familiar to all. Every one knew of how many votes were wasted at every election, and many knew instances where more votes were lost than were utilised? The reform goes under many names, preferential voting, equal representation, distributive voting, the single transferable vote, representation of minorities, and it deserves all these titles. It is equal because it is proportional ; it is proportional because it is transferable ; it represents minorities as fairly as majorities, it is worked by distributing surplus and minus votes preferentially, and because it is all these things it is effective. It is no party weapon. It is equally just to all. It has thus the advantage of appealing to all parties alike. But it has the defect of its qualities. Because it does not promise any exclusive advantage to either of the great parties who have in the past exchanged place and power, neither of them are at all eager to take it up. The members of the legislatures who are now there, owe their position to majority or plurality representation. Their success depended on making all votes ineffective except what were polled for themselves. They know the old ropes, and how to pull them. They cannot tell how they would fare under a system of absolute righteousness. This is the uncertainty which makes so-called practical politicians warn theorists against flying from some small evils which we know of, lest we may encounter other evils probably greater.

If the people do not demand it with a very loud voice indeed, the ordinary political candidate will not touch it with the longest pair of tongs, and even men who believe in the principle hold it back, lest they should be stigmatised as theoretical and Utopian. Thus the one thing needful is to arouse public opinion, and that not merely by essays read by the few, but by public lecture, familiar speech and practical illustration.

It is a long time since Thomas Hare and John Stuart Mill delivered this Gospel to me, but all the years since have only emphasised the world's need of it. The course of politics in England, France, America, Canada and Australia, has been a running comment on the original text. When people tell me "You have waited thirty years and more ; the mills of God grind slowly, but they grind exceeding small. In the course of another generation or two, truth may prevail. All will come right in time ;" I can only reply that nothing will come right unless those who feel that they have the truth, speak, and work and strain, as if on them only depended the destinies of the world. In the substitution of the co-operative spirit for the competitive in politics, I believe we may find deliverance from many evils that are eating into the heart of humanity. Therefore I call upon all who see this truth to aid in the spread of it, and not to keep it as a private opinion. Unless our disciples become apostles, our progress will continue to be slow.

It is easier for a good man to gain a quota in a large district than a plurality in a small one, and he is most likely to get it by the best means ; by courage and sincerity, by character and abilities. It is easier for a bad man to get a plurality in a small district than a quota in a large one ; and he may gain it by the worst means ; by trimming and truckling to what he fancies is the popular feeling ; by misrepresenting the views and the motives of his opponents ; by pandering to local and class interests ; by encouraging too many candidates to start, so that votes may be lost, if not by bribery outright.

I was asked at one of my meetings if I really believed that Effective Voting would put a stop to bribery, and I replied that as each vote must count, and no vote extinguished any other, every vote must be bought, and that would be too expensive.

My questioner said that supposing the quota for the district was one thousand, a rich man who wanted very much to get into parliament would be willing to give a thousand pounds for them.

To this I replied that he might indeed be willing, but where in any district of South Australia, could he find a thousand men willing to sell their birth-right for such a poor mess of pottage? There are a few weaklings who may be cajoled, and a few crawlers who may be bought, by means of whom the scale may be turned in a uninominal constituency, but they are an insignificant portion of any quota.

The use of this doubtful fringe has been long known to electioneering agents, and so long as we have plurality representation, the temptation to gain through their means is very great. How to secure a win for our side is the main object, and while it is merely satisfactory to win when we have an undoubted majority, the crowning glory of tactics is to make a victorious plurality with an undoubted minority of the votes. How often the president of the United States is brought in by a minority of the popular vote; in the case of Harrison amounting to a hundred thousand (100,000)! The Liberal-Unionists congratulated themselves on their tactics in Birmingham and the Midland counties, which were so successful that while it took somewhat over four thousand votes to return one candidate for them, it needed eighteen thousand to return a Gladstonian. Elsewhere the process was reversed, and the Gladstonians had the advantage.

The respected deacon of the church who confessed that when election time came round and he acted as an agent, he had always to shut up his conscience in a box, and not take it out till it was over, did not take out the same article he put in. No, you cannot ignore justice and take every advantage, and trample upon every consideration for others, during the weeks or months of canvassing and polling, without grave moral deterioration. "Everything is fair in politics" they say, but unfairness is met by unfairness, and what is gained here is lost there, even by the party itself. The only certain result is that the tone of morality is lowered, and that the best men keep out of politics altogether.

When you hear this phrase so glibly spoken by travelling Americans and Australians, you scarcely appreciate the importance of the fact. It cannot but injure in its most vital points any nation when the best men leave the large issues of national life, and the progress or decline of the land to which they owe a citizen's duty and devotion, to professional wire-pullers and their backers. Meanwhile they immerse themselves in business, or waste themselves in idle pleasure, or at the best, indulge in literary leisure, or cultivate an æsthetic fad, or even a cloistered and academic virtue for their private benefit, and allow a great nation to decline, perhaps to perish for lack of wisdom and courage.

Mr. Bryce, in "The American Commonwealth," looks on this lightly talked of defection of the best men from political life as the most dangerous feature in the United States. He says so much about the party machine and the work it does, that one expected him to suggest some radical cure. But he only diagnoses the disease, and trusts to nature and to time for the remedy. As the intrinsically honest character of the people and their practical common sense has prevented the worst of machinery from doing more than half the mischief that it was likely to work, he believes things will right themselves. The Australian ballot and the diminution of the "Spoils" system are the most hopeful signs in his eyes, but so long as the caucus limits the choice of candidates, the free ballot is of little value.

With the spoils system he considers that the evils of American political and municipal organisations are bound up. Independent of the spoils of office, by which party can directly reward adherents, there are many indirect and secret ways by which wealth in the hands of individuals and corporations can vitiate elections and misrepresent the people.

Mr. Bryce lays his finger on the greatest hindrance to radical reform. This is the essential conservatism of the American people. Probably no statement in the book surprised European readers more, but it is quite true. The parchment constitution under which such gigantic evils have grown up is reverenced—almost worshipped—by the people. Children at school are taught its provisions. It is the citizen's Bible.

The British Constitution has been the slow growth of centuries and therefore venerable, but there is not a single point in it that is not open to criticism; it has been profoundly modified by men now living, and it is threatened with greater changes still. The American constitution was the work of the great men who made the nation. It was the outcome of the best thought of the time, and provided for dangers which the fathers of the state could see, but it could not provide for what they did not dream of. The unification of the States as a single power against a foreign foe, and the free interchange of commodities with each other were indispensable, and to secure these a compromise was made with slavery, which afterwards bore such bitter fruits. The unification of the Republic could only be effected by granting to the sovereign states the largest measure of independence outside those necessary lines, and giving the federal government the greatest strength possible within the limits prescribed. It was a grand idea, but it did not cover all the ground, nor could the framers of the constitution foresee that the checks which seemed to them wise to restrain popular impatience and make presidential and senatorial elections peaceful and dignified, would be over-ridden and undermined by the strength and craft of party. The election of United States Senators by the State Legislatures makes these bodies which ought to deal with domestic matters in a business-like way, chosen by the party on party lines, and has helped towards the invasion of parties into municipal elections also. The electoral college chosen by the citizens for the presidential election are simply mandate-bearers, called out for one purpose. The voting in each state is at large, or by *scrutin de liste*, and a slight wave of public opinion in New York may change 36 Republicans for 36 Democrats, and virtually elect the President.

While the power of the Sovereign of England and of the House of Lords has dwindled during the century, that of the President and the Senate has increased. It is the strongest Sovereignty and the strongest Upper House in the civilised world. The Senate being not only stronger collectively than the Representatives, but fewer in number, lobbying goes on there to a far greater extent than in what is supposed to be the People's House. President Harrison, during the last two years of his term, had three to one against him in the Representatives, but got along with a narrow majority in the Senate. Imagine Mr. Gladstone or Lord Salisbury ruling with three to one against him in the House of Commons !

It is indeed singular how the American seems to enjoy the exercise of the veto by the President, and even by the Governor of a State against the Representatives. He has voted for his Governor and for the presidential electors, and these have been returned by the plurality to whom he is bound to submit, and he admires the pluck of one man against many. In this as in many other respects, America is less democratic than England. The Electoral College dreamed of by the founders of the Republic was a wise deliberative body, and not a lot of message boys. But the thing is so favourable to professional politicians and their employers, and so intrenched by the conservatism of the people, that it stands strong. Great is Diana of the Ephesians ! Great is our glorious American Constitution ! Touch it, and our craft is endangered.

Perhaps there is a third part, or at least a fourth part of the American people who think reform is necessary. They can do no good so long as they only cast hopeless votes to outsiders, or make terms with insiders. If Prohibitionists, Populists, Socialists, Single-taxers, and the great inarticulate Labour party would make common cause, and go on together till they secured honest representation, no party force or fraud could withstand them. So long as each of these voices of discontent is single, the wirepullers, the monopolists, and " the corporations smile." United, they are masters of the situation.

The idea is new to the general public, but the time has come when that which has been whispered in the ear must be proclaimed from the house tops. Let the principle only be grasped by the plain people of Canada, Australia and America, and we shall see a peaceful revolution, founded on peace and good will.

The twenty-three chapters which Mr. Bryce devotes to the Party System and the Party machine were a revelation to the English people, and yet he rather understates the case. He is just to the people, while condemning the system which tyrannises over them. We hear it said that governments are what the people make them, but I do not blame the people. It is the machinery through which they work that is responsible for the faults in American administration. They are not represented in any true sense of the word. It is not even the majority who rule ! It is calculated that 47 per cent. of the votes cast return all the representatives to Congress, and these are only what the caucus brought forward.

What would we think of a mirror that only reproduced what was ugly and common-place, and not the fine expression or the delicate lines of the features ? The electoral net is so coarse that the best elements in the nation escape it, and those who haul in that net desire that it should be so. There are good men everywhere whose colours are not those of the party, and whose weapons are not those of the duel, whom a better system of representation would secure for the country, to work independently or in conjunction with others likeminded, without fear or favour.

Effective Voting does not fear the most searching criticism. It is not a mere theory, not the fad of the professorial chair, or of the mathematical mind, but when shown to average men and women, it commends itself as equitable and practicable. No party can return more representatives that its numbers entitle it to, and need not return fewer under Effective Voting.

Lord Beaconsfield complained that parliaments were in their decadence and that county and parish politics prevailed over large national questions. If this was said of England, what may be said of Canada and of Australia? Government grants and appropriations are the main demands of local constituencies. In Canada the members sent to the Dominion Parliament were all Conservatives, while the Local Parliaments elected by the same votes were of the other side, because under a Conservative Ministry, there was more chance of grants if the locality supported them.

It is in South Australia and in New Zealand that I hope to see the first steps taken towards equitable representation. Both these are more democratic than the other Australian colonies. They have "one man one vote." Both colonies have taken steps towards the taxation of land on the best basis. South Australia, eight years ago, imposed a tax of a halfpenny in the pound on assessed value of every acre of freehold land in the Province, whether it is a rood or a hundred thousand acres, and it is the most cheaply collected and certain of all our sources of revenue. New Zealand has tried several modes of direct taxation, but the last, of exempting from the land tax all improvements up to three thousand pounds, is the best, and other plans to encourage settlement and to stop the selling of Crown lands altogether, are in advance of anything done on the island-continent of Australia.

In New Zealand, in 1888, the Atkinson Ministry brought forward an electoral bill embodying Sir John Lubbock's modification of Hare's system, for districts returning from four to eight members, and taking his mathematical quota. There were some other new points about the bill open to criticism, and any how the Ministry failed to carry it. As allowing of the transferable vote for quota representation, it would have been most valuable, and not misleading to the public like the contingent vote in the new electoral law in Queensland, voted under for the first time this year.

This is meant to secure that there shall be an absolute majority for one man in every uninominal district. It is intended to exclude everywhere and always all minorities, and it was a conservative measure passed by a parliament where the capitalist party had the majority, and designed to prevent earnest and compact minorities from obtaining a member which their numbers did not entitle them to. The Trades and Labour unions including the Shearers' union had scored some triumphs through the divisions of votes among other candidates, so by the use of the contingent vote in case the first choice does not poll sufficient for return, the lost votes are heaped on another, so that he is returned by a majority and not by a mere plurality. The labour party have also difficulties placed in the way of registration, which in the case of a large nomad population of shearers and knock-about hands is of great importance, by requiring identification by a J. P., not always friendly to the labour vote. Thus the contingent vote which under Hare's quota would be the means of their complete enfranchisement, is associated with this obnoxious bill.

No doubt the contingent vote used thus is much better than the second election to secure an absolute majority which is required by French and German law, whereby the two highest at the poll are put up again. The election agents try all they can to secure a first or second place for their candidate, and in the second trial they go to work anew, not only to secure the lost votes, but to change the destination of those previously given to the only remaining competitor. Greville Murray's brilliant novel "The Member for Paris" shows how strangely the result may come out.

But why did this bill pass the Queensland Parliament so easily, while the far more valuable bill was lost in New Zealand? Because the Conservative party saw that it would work in their interests. The great Maritime strike, the Shearers' strike, and the Broken Hill Miners' strike had alarmed capitalists and merchants, pastoralists, sugar-growers and shippers. All the moneyed interests of Queensland were threatened by the claims of labour. And by this apparently just system, they could extinguish the voice of labour in all but two or three electorates in Queensland. There was no such motive for passing the New Zealand bill.

M. Smet de Borman, in the debate in the Belgian Chamber from which I quoted M. Beernaert's remarks, speaks thus on the wisdom and justice of combining a provision for proportional representation, with the extension of the suffrage from its former limit of the payment of direct taxes to the amount of 45 francs :

"For whom then do we ask the right to vote ? Is it for the bourgeoisie, greater or smaller ? No, it is for the toilers. It is their situation which we are told has not been sufficiently studied; it is their grievances which have found no echo in Parliament. These are the malcontents whom we desire in the spirit of patriotic justice to disarm, and what do we propose to give them ?

"I do not hesitate to say that without proportional representation, we give them nothing, while it we give them all to which they can legitimately aspire. Let us admit even manhood suffrage; I assert that in almost every district in Belgium the workers would be excluded from the representation.

"Out of 600 deputies how many working men are in the Parliament of France ? We scarcely count two or three! And France has a paid parliament and manhood suffrage! So we hear the same complaints and the same attacks on parliament by the Labour party in France as we read in the Belgian proleteriat press. Neither in Brussels, nor in Liége, nor in Ghent could the Labour party succeed in sending a deputy to parliament even with manhood suffrage, unless it allies itself with the bourgeoise advanced party. By means of such alliance a representative may be returned who only knows the working man because he applauds him at the meetings, and makes use of him as a stepping-stone, or the labour party flourishing their own standard may be crushed in detail in every electorate in the kingdom." Thus this reform is truly a working man's measure.

If South Australia takes the lead with Effective Voting, I trust she will take a better grasp than was attempted in new Zealand, and not cumber the reform by other doubtful provisions. It can be adapted to the present electoral law, and only requires the change of a few clauses. If Canada takes the lead for the Dominion Parliament, which most needs the reform, it will be a more prominent example than can be furnished by a distant Australian province. But whether an Australian or a Canadian province sets the example, it will be followed.

The fact that simultaneous interest is aroused as to electoral reform in Canada, in Australia, and in America, as well as in Switzerland and Belgium, and that the minds of thoughtful men are turning from tinkering to radical changes, is a presage for good. Some blunders may be made, many reformers are shortsighted and onesided, but the greatest hindrances to progress are the inertia of indifference, and the apathy of despair. Citizens who talk constantly about the evils of the political machine without doing anything to amend them, and as if they were incidental to a free government, intensify these evils, for they create a despair of good.

CHAPTER V.

PALLIATIVES : THE INITIATIVE AND THE REFERENDUM : THE IMPERATIVE MANDATE : DIRECT LEGISLATION.

It is often said that party and party spirit are excellent things, necessary and helpful to right government. Party spirit and a party organisation bring indifferent and reluctant voters to the poll, without fining them as the Danish law does. The lynx eye of the opposition checks the hand of the other ; a strong opposition is as useful as a strong government. Is it then a mistake to suppose that a house divided against itself cannot stand, and is constant see-saw the true condition of progress with stability, which is the ostensible aim of all parties ? All the excesses of party spirit, its malice and uncharitableness, its injustices and deceptions are set down to the occasional abuse of what in itself is a good thing.

These evils are however, inherent in party spirit, and not accidental to it. Gerry-mandering is a party weapon, only to be checked or extirpated by the collective conscience. Thanks to that conscience, political morality makes progress in the world in spite of defective methods and machinery. Bribery has always been a party weapon, and in the days of Fox and Pitt it was no disgrace to bribe, though it was discreditable to be bribed. Going back to Walpole, we see there was no discredit in either paying or receiving money for votes in or out of parliament. Nowadays, both law and public opinion make either giving or accepting bribes disgraceful in England. In America every one knows that bribery goes on, and that in spite of the recently introduced secret ballot, money exercises enormous power at all elections, political and municipal. The actual agent who pays over the money, and the man who receives it are no doubt looked on as contemptible characters, but who finds the money ?

Who provides the election funds for the campaigns conducted for victory or defeat ? Who does not know how a large portion of the money is expended ?

We cannot wash our hands publicly of the matter if our hands privately have furnished the means of corruption. Closing our eyes to the ugly machinery we have set to work does not exonerate us from responsibility. If the evils inherent in party government depend on majority representation, we can only get rid of them by truly democratic representation—that is by the re-presentment of the whole people in the legislature.

Among the palliatives proposed for the acknowledged abuses from which America suffers, the most noteworthy are the Initiative and the Referendum, used in the oldest of federal republics, Switzerland. Those who groan under the tyranny of the caucus and the ticket, hope that by means of the Initiative new and valuable legislation might be forced on a reluctant or apathetic congress, and that by the Referendum, mischievous or interested legislation or administration might be reversed.

Whatever may be the need of such things now in America, it seems paradoxical and absurd first to elect a body of men to do the national business, and then to make a requisition to drive them to attend to it, and to put all their work to the test of a plebiscite as to whether it was done properly. The Initiative might work fairly well in a country like Switzerland, but in America it would be taken up by a caucus, and as for the Referendum, just fancy the whole people of the United States voting en masse on every measure.

If the parliament is justly elected by proportional representation there would be no need of any Initiative to drive the people's representatives to undertake important reforms. The representatives of earnest minorities would be there in the House ; sent there for that very purpose, and they could be trusted to introduce and to advocate those measures which are neglected and ignored under our existing system. Nor would there be any need to refer to any plebiscite any measure which had passed both Houses of Legislature, when the really important House (the people's) really represented the whole people. The decision in doors will correspond with the convictions of the real majority out of doors, and will be argued better in a deliberative assembly than in the harangues and the rhetoric presented to a plebiscite.

It is noteworthy, too, that it is in Switzerland, where the Initiative is in operation, that there has risen an effective demand for proportional representation. When three-fourths of the measures passed by both Houses were reversed by the Referendum, the fact that majority representation did not really represent was made patent. The Canton of Ticino (Italian speaking) and the Canton of Neufchatel (French-speaking) were followed by the more important Canton of Geneva, and the proportional voting by lists, as is explained in my second chapter, has been successfully worked in all three. Two other cantons are agitating for the change, so that the brave little European republic, which was a model for the Transatlantic republic in its inception, goes on still ahead. Those cantons which have adopted proportional representation will soon drop the useless appeals to the people, and it will be amusing if it were not so mischievous if the great United States caught hold of the machinery that Switzerland has outgrown, fancying it to be a real safeguard to liberty.

There is also a demand made in the United States for recourse to the Imperative Mandate, requiring a member of the Legislature to resign his seat on the demand of two-thirds of his constituency. With such a short term of office as the House of Representatives has, one long and one short session, it seems unnecessary to recall a representative during that term. The Imperative would be impossible under proportional representation, for under the secret ballot it is impossible to discover who are any man's constituents. Two-thirds or three-fourths of the qualified voters in the electorate may have voted for others and may desire his recall, but yet he may be the chosen of an earnest minority, and as such I think it is in human nature for him to be true to his principles. It is noteworthy that in Switzerland, which originated the Imperative Mandate, it has fallen into disuse and is never heard of. Switzerland has found out better means. This at last has been outgrown.

One feels glad to hear a demand, even for these Swiss methods, from the American people, as it shows they are willing to change the old bad methods or to supply something in the shape of an antidote. But it is as if when the hounds are in full cry after the fox, a red herring is trailed across the scent, and they are drawn off to something of no value. Tinkering at defective machinery and bolstering up abuses which should be destroyed, only delays radical reform.

Another demand that is made is for direct election of President by the whole people, so that the choice should be made by the popular vote and not by the state vote for electors to elect. This seems reasonable enough. The United States Senate too would be more righteously elected by the people of the States than by the legislatures, and the domestic assembly would be elected on better lines for state business, if there was no *arrière pensée* of choice of United States senators in the mind of the citizens. Probably this restriction to domestic legislation and regulation would lessen greatly party spirit in them, and tend to keep it out of municipal affairs. The reduction of the number of elective officers would purify municipal matters greatly, and save money and heartburnings all round. An American municipal ticket is a fearful and wonderful thing, and it is hard to vote, on the Australian ballot system. Where every office from mayor to coroner, from rate-collector and surveyors to judges and police magistrates is competed for by many candidates, all bracketed according to their politics, it presents a far more bewildering array of names than any modification of Hare's system of voting I have ever seen.

There are far too many elections in America, and the Initiative and especially the Referendum would indefinitely multiply them.

The indirect or distilled election adopted in the American constitution to secure calmness and wise deliberation is pointed out by Mr. Bryce as perhaps the most striking instance in which a written and rigid constitution bends and warps under the actual force of politics, for the caucus—the majority, for the time being, in the local legislatures settle the matter without deliberation, generally before the houses meet. To imitate Pope's lines:

> " Blest paper credit ! last and best supply,
> That lends corruption quicker wings to fly ! "

the machine politician and his backers may sing :

> " Elect electors ! Glorious double means
> For wealth and craft to oil the state machines ! "

CHAPTER VI.

CONCLUSION.

The reform of Mr. Hare was originally known under the name of the Representation of Minorities, and that was somewhat misleading. An idea arose that it was meant to make minorities rule. Under party government, people fancy that majorities always rule, while in point it is only a majority of a plurality elected parliament, a fraction of the people who appoint and dismiss the cabinet, and administer the affairs of the country. Mr. J. M. Berry, of Worcester, Massachusetts, has calculated that less than twenty per cent. of the vote elected the working majority in the Canadian Parliament, and this is not due so much to gerrymanders as to the inherent vices of the system itself. Proportional representation would secure that it is the real majority in the country who have ascendancy in parliament.

I cannot say whether the adoption of this equitable system would be of greater advantage to minorities or to the majority itself.

It is a good thing when there is no dissatisfied, unrepresented class in the community, and it is a very bad thing when political life has no charms for our wealthy citizens, or for

8

our best educated young men. But great as are the advantages to minorities of having their votes freed, and their individual powers of action made available, the advantage to majorities is no less.

In the first place, they can make sure of having honest representatives. Those who differ from them can appeal to other voters in the larger constituency, and go in free; they are not exposed to the temptation of concealing their convictions as the only means of entering parliament at all. We are told that there is no need for the reform, because there are men in our present parliaments of every shade of opinion. But every man whose convictions were different from those of the real or supposed majority in the district for which he sought election, had to submit to a lowering style of canvass and to a cross-questioning, legitimate enough if minorities can be represented, but under the exclusive power of plurality, weakening to the moral sense of the candidate.

The second advantage to the majority would be that they would hear all sides of public questions, and that objections to their party measures would have to be met fully and fairly. Questions would be discussed in parliament, in newspapers, at election meetings and public meetings generally, in a very different way from what takes place now. A minority unrepresented is apt to be a sulky and a useless thing, going about continually with a grievance for which it has no redress, and unable to make its voice heard in parliament, or through the popular press. A minority represented is the sharpener of the wits of the ruling powers, the educator of the people, the animator of the press. It is the only strong and moralising opposition: without it there may be struggles as to who shall be in office or out of it; for as long as there are such things as place and power, those who have them will want to keep them, and those who have them not, will desire to obtain them, but such opposition is too often factious and dangerous—not constitutional and progressive.

It is not only when they are in the right that represented minorities could give such life and vigour to the body politic. Right or wrong, the sincere expression of opinion is always the friend of truth and progress. We never believe anything so firmly, as when an adversary whom we cannot silence, or ignore, or ridicule, has marshalled all the arguments on the other side, and we have proved them fallacious. And if the minority should perchance be in the right, will it be wise to silence them, and lose the truth that is in them? There are many ways of losing truth. One is by persecuting it; another is by not listening to it; a third is by being too stupid to understand it. Persecution has gone out of fashion, except perhaps in Russia, but inattention and stupidity are not yet obsolete.

I hear it said that you cannot make men moral by any electoral system whatever, and France is instanced to show that all sorts of methods have been tried without any real betterment in legislatures or people. France has never tried proportional representation. I should be as unwilling to charge the people of France with the corruption in the legislature recently exposed, as to say that the American party abuses are what the American people choose to make them. It is what the machinery has made it. Improve the machinery in France and in the United States, and then we shall see things mightily changed for the better.

As Mr. Simeon Stetson, of San Francisco, in his trenchant pamphlet "The People's Power: How to wield the Ballot," points out, the difficulty is not really a moral one. When people ask how it is possible that a simple readjustment — an arithmetical device, can purify politics, educate the voter, and raise the character of the legislature, he replies that there is enough of virtue and honour among the people of France and of America, only they are shut out by the party machinery. Change the machinery so as to give equality of opportunity to the higher elements of society, and you will transform the whole political world.

There is no doubt that some methods of representation make men immoral. We have been so long in the habit of excluding reason and fair play from electioneering, that we have almost grown into the belief that such drawbacks as we cannot but see, are inseparable from representative institutions themselves, and a part of the price we must pay for liberty. It would be absurd if we blinded ourselves to the relations between cause and effect in ordinary life. It is not the ascertaining of people's opinions and preferences, but the means we take to ascertain them, whereby one's loss is another man's gain, that creates the injustice and the bitterness.

Just fancy a mother, who wanted a peck of peas shelled, setting all her children old and young to do it, promising to give the one who shelled the most the reward of an apple. Suppose her disregarding all the cries for fair play, when Tom the eldest boy pulls the basket towards him, and does all in his power to prevent his brothers and sisters from obtaining the pods from which to extract the peas. Fancy her thinking that by giving each child a measure stamped by authority, she has done all in her power to equalise their chances of success; and then bestowing the reward on the virtuous Tom, whose stronger nails had more easily opened the pods, and whose vigorous arm had kept possession of the basket. Fancy her saying when the younger children made faces at Tom as he munched his apple, and called him a bully and a cheat, that she did not understand how it was, but they always quarrelled about the peas. She did her best to excite a little wholesome emulation, and never gave the apple but to the child who shelled the most. *She supposed it must be something in the peas!!!*

Politically speaking, I agree with the popular orator, "One man is as good as another." I only object to the commentary or addition of his Irish admirer, "Yes, that he is, and better too." By majority representation, we give the Irish interpretation to the equality. Yet though political equality is desirable, mental and social equality is not desirable, even if it were possible. In Democratic communities, it is of supreme importance that everything individual, original, and even eccentric, should be called out and utilised.

The average man and the average woman have things too much ordered according to their liking for their own advance beyond mediocrity. What John Stuart Mill feared was that originality would dwindle and die under the reign of the common-place. The comfort and convenience, mental as well as material, of the mass of humanity would be too exclusively studied, in their eating and in their drinking, in their education and their amusements, in their politics and their religion. But pure Democracy such as is advocated in these pages, would give scope to individuality. What can a man of genius give to the world of more value than just a bit of himself? All that is wanted is equality of opportunity for expression;—the best will come to the front and keep there. For the benefit of all, for the service of all should the varied gifts of all earnest men and women be used and strengthened by use. Life would be enriched, would be elevated, would be moralised by the free play of the higher elements in society.

Our competitive system has had its day and done its work. It has spurred many individuals to laborious and continuous efforts, and in many directions man has essentially served the community, when he was primarily seeking his own profit or his own fame. But even in the past, the race has not been always to the swift, or the battle to the strong. Nowadays King Capital appropriates, not only a very large amount of the earnings of labour, but also almost monopolises the rewards of invention. Too often only the crumbs from the rich man's table are flung to the creator of wealth who by some happy discovery has cheapened production or transportation by some machinery or appliance which the rich man was incapable of inventing himself. King Capital too, often tempts the artist out of the straight narrow way to which his genius prompts him, into the primrose path which leads to money making and ephemeral applause. No common-placeness of the vulgar taste is more fatal to true art than the conventionalism which the wealthy art-patron loves.

"Art for the people," has in it the true elements of progress. The power of admiration grows when it is fed with worthy objects. Democratic art can scarcely be said to exist, even in democratic countries. Mr. J. Addington Symonds, in his penetrative essay on 'Democratic Art,' says that with the single exception of Walt Whitman, neither poet nor novelist, neither painter nor sculptor, has yet adequately recognised the people.

If it is said in an essay on electoral representation and the rectification of parliament, suggestions as to the rewards of invention and on democratic art are out of place, I beg to submit that they are in place. We hear much about the correlation of forces, and the interchangeableness of much that we used to believe were distinctly separate in the physical world. In the intellectual and moral world, all thinking men and women see the same correlation and interdependence, and they cannot look on anything as isolated and detached. Religion is of no value if kept only for Sunday services and stated seasons, and does not penetrate the whole daily life. Honour and honesty should not be confined to one's personal affairs, and be kept out of corporate matters and political action. Intelligence should not be restricted to the acquisition of knowledge, but should be allied to our religion and to our bread-earning avocation, and to all the duties of a citizen. And the democratic spirit which sees in every man a brother and in every woman a sister, should not be kept for platform orations, but should be felt in the church and in the state, in the factory and in the shop, in the author's study, in the newspaper editor's den, and in the artist's studio.

It is on account of this interdependence, this inextricable complexity of human motives and actions that the exclusively dual character of political representation is so misrepresentative of modern society. In olden times, when the people had to struggle against monarchs and privileged classes, there was a definite dualism in politics, and party organization on one side or the other was a useful, perhaps a necessary, thing. But in that very country which has worked the party system longest, in the United Kingdom, we see every year more and more important questions withdrawn from the limitations of party, and "This is not a party question" is publicly given out; members on both sides of the House are free to speak and vote for or against it; and if it is brought forward by the ministry, the loss of a majority does not compel them to resign.

Under proportional representation there will be more and more liberty given to individual thought in parliament, and this will react on the people outside.

The pocket boroughs of England once represented localities, opinions and people. But when a demand was made for their reform in 1832, they represented nothing but the prestige of rank, the bribes of wealth and the venality of a handful of voters. Great cities like Birmingham and Manchester had no representative at all, while a dozen depopulated hamlets in Cornwall sent two members each to parliament. After they were disfranchised, was there a single voice heard all over the United Kingdom for their re-instatement? No, not one, although before the passing of the Reform Bill, the whole Conservative forces of Great Britain protested against laying unhallowed hands on the sacred ark of the constitution.

Thus it was, and thus it will ever be. The advocates of the radical reform of enfranchising minorities, are confronted with the whole conservative and traditionary forces of the world. Local separation of small districts from their fellows has been the invariable rule in the past; districts whether large or small, have always been carried by the plurality of votes, however small the preponderance may be, and under this hap-hazard system England and her daughter states have managed to jog on. Practical politicians would be put out of their reckoning and embarrassed in their tactics under proportional representation. How often is it necessary to remind the world that national organisations do not exist for the advantage of practical politicians, or merely to suit their convenience, but that politicians exist for the sake of the nation! If plans which are pooh-poohed as doctrinaire and utopian, are shown to the plain people who really direct public affairs, to be just and practicable, the practical politicians must accommodate themselves to the changed conditions.

Every extension of the suffrage was dreaded by the Conservative party as certain to lower the character of the elected representatives. This has not been the case. Although the first change of 1832 has been followed by extensions more sweeping and modifications more subtle, the tone and character of the British House of Commons is higher than it was previous to the first Reform ill. The evils and shortcomings which still exist in it proceed from party government, and this rests on majority representation. This therefore is the radical evil which must be attacked from all sides with arguments as various as individual minds can present.

The demand of the Canadian Institute for contributions towards the solution of this vital question from the whole world is one which is wise and timely, and which ought to give a great impetus to the cause. But if the demand only rests with the reward for the best essays, and their publication, and distribution among coteries of students and thinkers, little will be done towards the realisation of better things. Unless the publication of these essays stirs up active efforts among the people of Canada, the rectification of parliament by electing it on equitable principles may be indefinitely postponed. The Reform Bill was not carried by essays. The ballot was not won by pamphlets. Free trade in corn was not obtained by writing books. The thinker and the writer may furnish arguments, may give facts and figures, but if their disciples do not become apostles and missionaries, and preach this gospel where opportunity offers, or where opportunity may be made, no real practical issue can be expected.

With confidence that men and women may rise to the height of their responsibilities, and of their opportunities and take up this, the greatest political reform of this great political century, and not lay it down till they have embodied it in law. I submit these pages for thoughtful consideration to the Institute of Canada.

SOUTHERN CROSS.

CHAPTER VII.

DRAFT BILL FOR THE PROVINCE OF SOUTH AUSTRALIA.

The condition that along with the essay on electoral representation, there must also be forwarded for consideration a draft bill, applicable to countries with a parliamentary system similar to that of Canada, is somewhat hard on writers who are not legal or parliamentary experts.

The essay may indeed indicate the principles on which an Act of Parliament should be framed, and may describe practical methods, and yet the essayist may lack the legal technicality requisite for details.

In any case, it is unnecessary to construct a complete electoral Act. The qualifications of voters, the methods of registration, the fixing of polling places and the definition of the duties of returning officers, the penalties for bribery, treating, and corrupt influence must be the same under proportional representation as they are under the present majority system. The points necessarily to be provided for are the enlargement of constituencies, the conditions of candidature, the method of voting, the method of counting votes, so as to return each representative by quota, the filling up of vacancies, and the readjustment of the number of candidates to electoral districts according to relative increase or decrease of population.

In some of these points I avail myself of certain clauses in Mr. Hislop's Bill presented to the New Zealand Parliament in 1888, in the time of the Atkinson Ministry, and lost. As however he uses Sir John Lubbock's mathematical quota instead of Hare's simpler one, and as he takes the contingent vote as used in Queensland for uninominal elections to fill up a vacancy, while I fall back on the votes of the retiring candidate to ascertain which of the unsuccessful candidates at the last election makes a plurality over the others, and allot the seat to him without a new election at all, there are several features in these suggested clauses quite distinct from Mr. Hislop's.

Proposed clauses to be introduced into a new Electoral Act for Election of Members of the House of Assembly for the Province of South Australia, in order that the principle of proportional representation by means of the single transferable vote may be carried into practice in the said Province.

PREAMBLE.—Whereas it is expedient that the system of voting in the Province of South Australia shall be altered so as to give equal representation to the whole people: Be it enacted :—

1. That the Province of South Australia shall be divided into nine electoral districts, or divisions, following the natural geographical divisions of the country, and as nearly as possible of equal population ; the 27 present electorates being amalgamated into nine groups to return each six members to the House of Assembly.

II. Any duly registered elector, with his consent, may be nominated as a candidate for any district by not less than ten electors thereof, by a nomination paper in the form and to the effect set forth by regulation, and given to the returning officer, or transmitted to him so as to reach him before the last hour appointed for receiving nomination papers.

III. Any duly registered elector may vote for any candidate who presents himself for the larger electoral district, but he shall record his vote in that division for which he is registered, and at the polling place appointed for such division.

IV. Every duly registered elector shall have one vote only, but may vote in the alternative for as many candidates as he pleases; and his ballot-paper shall be deemed to be given for the candidate opposite whose name is placed the figure 1. But it shall be transferable to the other candidates in succession in the order of priority designated by the figures set opposite their respective names, in the event of its not being required to be used for the return of any prior candidate.

V. The voter having received a ballot-paper, shall retire into one of the inner compartments provided, and shall there, alone and secretly, insert opposite to the names of the candidates for whom he wishes to vote the figures 1, 2, 3, 4, 5, 6, or fewer, in the order of his preference. He shall not strike out from the ballot-paper the names of any candidate.

VI. As soon as all the ballot-papers are received from all the polling-places in the electoral district by the Chief Electoral Officer at the central polling-place of such district, the said Electoral Officer shall open the boxes in the presence of the Resident Magistrate of the district, or of two Justices of the Peace, who shall attend at his request, and taking the said ballot-papers from the several boxes or packets, shall mix them up together and place them in an open box without unfolding any of them.

2. The ballot-papers after being thus mixed, shall be drawn out of the box, and in succession; each paper as it is drawn out being marked with a number in arithmetical series beginning with the number "1," so that no two papers shall have the same number, and the resident magistrate or the two justices of the peace shall sign a document stating the entire number as a whole, of the ballot papers received from the various returning officers, which shall be carefully preserved by the said election officer for production when required by lawful authority.

3. The election officer shall first reject all ballot papers which have not the official mark on the back, and all on which no numbers have been placed by the voter, and all those in which the same number has been placed against more names than one, but he shall not reject any ballot paper whereon the numbers of designation are fewer or in excess of the number of members to be elected.

4. The election officer shall then proceed to ascertain the quota by dividing the aggregate number of all the ballot papers tendered at the election by six, and the quotient, exclusive of fractions, shall be the number required for the return of any candidate.

5. Every candidate who has a number of first votes equal to or in excess of the quota shall be *declared elected*, and so many of the votes as make up the quota shall be set aside as his votes—his constituency—to be of no further use.

6. On each ballot paper beyond the necessary quota, the name of the elected candidate shall be cancelled, and the candidate marked "2" on each paper, shall take the first place and the election officer shall transfer the vote to him.

After the surplus votes, if any, have been transferred according to the contingent choice of the voters, the election officer shall declare the candidate having the fewest first and transferred votes *not elected*, and his votes shall be given to the second choice in each ballot paper, if he is not already elected, when the third is made use of. After this distribution, the ballot papers of the man who now has fewest votes are dealt with in a similar way and given to the first name down the series who has not been declared elected, or who has not been declared not elected. This process shall be applied successively to the lowest on the poll until there are no more candidates left standing than are required for the electoral district, when these shall be declared to be elected, whether they have attained the full quota or have fallen short of it. For example of an actual scrutiny for the return of six representatives out of twelve candidates, see Appendix I.

For Filling up a Vacancy.

VII. All the ballot papers given at each election for each electoral district shall be preserved by the election officer, and the ballots appropriated for the return of each candidate shall be kept together and labelled with his name, and a correct record shall also be **kept of the number of first votes given to each of the unsuccessful candidates which were afterwards transferred.**

VIII. When by death, resignation, or other cause, any seat shall be declared vacant, the election officer, in the presence of the resident magistrate of the district, or of two justices of the peace. shall take the votes which made up the quota for the dead or retiring member, and shall distribute such of these as are not limited to the six successful candidates among the unsuccessful candidates, and add these contingent ballot-papers to the number of first votes originally polled by each man, and the candidate having the greatest number, shall be declared elected for the remainder of the term for which the retiring member was appointed to act as representative.

For an example of how this would work. see Appendix II.

For Readjustment of Electoral Districts.

IX. After every decennial census, a revision of electoral districts shall be undertaken by a parliamentary committee, and whenever an electorate shall have increased proportionately to the aggregate population of the said Province of South Australia by one 54th part, (be the same a little more or less) that district shall return seven members at the next and succeeding elections, and whenever an electorate shall have decreased in population by a 54th part, (be the same a little more or less) that diminished electorate shall return five members at the next and at succeeding elections, but the number of representatives shall remain the same, 54 representatives for the whole Province, and shall not be altered without a vote of a two-thirds majority in both Houses of Parliament.

Legislative Council of South Australia.

For the Upper House, or Legislative Council of South Australia elections, all the change that would be necessary to secure proportional representation would be that in the four electorates returning six members each, all six should retire at once and not two in rotation, and to require the qualified electors to record preference by the single transferable vote as provided for in the preceding clauses for Assemblymen.

It would indeed be better if the Upper House could be elected by the votes of the whole Province, as was originally done, but unfortunately by *scrutin de liste*, or voting at large—the very worst system of majority voting. If it were done by means of the quota ascertained by the single transferable vote, it would be Hare's grand ideal realized in one English-speaking community, at least.

APPENDIX I.

Results of Scrutiny of Voting Papers filled in at various meetings held for Effective Voting, 10th March, 1893.

TOTAL VOTES, 3,824—QUOTA, 637.

PARTIES :—C Capital, L Labour, S T Single Tax, I C Irish Catholic. T Temperance, W S Woman's Suffrage.	FIRST VOTES	ANGAS	Minus distributed. No. 8—342. BAKER	BIRKS	No. 7—290. BUTTERY	Surplus. No. 1—45. CHARLESTON	Minus No. 6—216. FOWLER	GLYNN	Minus. No. 5—187. GUTHRIE	Minus. No. 4—95. HARROLD	Surplus. No. 2—19. MAGAREY	Minus. No. 3—76. ROBINSON	STIRLING	
C Angas ...	419		139		12		44		7	10	2	4		637
C Baker	262				15	1	47		6	10		1		
S T Birks....	361		27		64	11	17		31	2		4		517
L Buttery ..	190					2	11		7	2	2	11		
L Charleston	682													637
C Fowler...	167					1			9	37	1	1		
I C Glynn ...	320		127		88	3	28		32	11		6		615
L Guthrie ..	136					18				2	1	30		
C Harrold..	93					1								
T Magarey .	656													637
L Robinson.	72					4								
W S Stirling ..	466				31	4	63		22	21	13	17		637
	3824		293		210	45	210		179	95	19	75		3650
Ineffective Votes*			49		80	6			8			1		144
														3824

*Having voted for members already returned, or others not possible.

In order to follow the tabulated result it is necessary to observe first the number of first votes given in the vertical column of figures after the names. This shows two candidates who have a surplus.

The larger 45, Charleston's is Count No. 1, and down Charleston's column we see how these went.

Magarey's surplus of 19 is taken in Count 2.

Count 3 begins the minus votes, and Robinson's are eliminated for distribution first, as he has fewest votes.

Count 4 distributes Harrold's.

Count 5 distributes Guthrie's.

Count 6 takes Fowler's.

Count 7 distributes Buttery's, and during that count Stirling makes up his full quota of 637 ;—following the horizontal line we see that the 466 first votes have been swelled by accessions from two surplusages 4, and 13 ; and by 31, 4, 63, 22, 13, and 17 votes given for men who failed to make up a quota.

At this point in the scrutiny there are three men returned with full quotas, and four left in the running ; this is the crisis between the competitors as to who is to be thrown out, on which the uncertainty with regard to allocation of surplus from the top from the bottom or the middle, has been made an objection to the Hare system altogether. In point of fact both Charleston's and Magarey's heap were cut once, and the 47, and the 19 votes taken then from the top. But at this crisis how did Birks the single tax candidate stand in comparison with Baker the second man on the capitalist side? What effect would any change in distribution of surplusage have had on the relative position of the two?

Birks had 361 first votes and 129 contingent votes, 490 in all, while Baker had only 262 first and 80 contingent, 342 votes in all, so there was no question which should go. In two other scrutinies with considerable numbers, one of 1,423 votes for six poets out of twelve at Port Adelaide, South Australia, and another of over 1,100 in the Register (S. A.) newspaper office, called the Ministerial Ballot, there was the same great disparity between the last man to be thrown out and the last man left in.

If we note in the tabulated results of the scrutiny of 10th March, 1893, that 144 votes were apparently ineffective because given to men who had not been able to reach the quota, and men already in, we know that to that extent some men will have short quotas. Glynn was 22 short and Birks 120, and there were 2 votes beyond the required number, a remainder from 3,824 divided by six. In all these 3,824 votes, I found only two really ineffective, because they had voted for six unsuccessful candidates. These might have a chance in case of a vacancy,—treated in Appendix II.

It may be noted that each of the outside parties succeeded in bringing in a representative, but this was owing to the greater interest taken in this subject by third parties. The four capitalist candidates only mustered 941 first votes, and the four labour candidates had 1080. To make up two full quotas required twice 637, or 1274, so neither of them could return two men. The contingent votes for capital helped Stirling who had capitalistic opinions along with his woman's suffrage, and were given to Glynn rather than to Birks. The contingent labour votes assisted Birks and Glynn and Stirling.

In an ordinary election, probably only two of the outside parties would succeed in obtaining a representative, but the contingent votes of the unsuccessful would affect the return of other candidates.

APPENDIX II.

Method of filling up a vacancy by death or resignation of any member of parliament during the term for which he was elected. The voting papers must be kept, and all votes appropriated to the return of each member shall be tied up together. Suppose in this case Stirling retired. The number of first votes given to each unsuccessful candidate has been tabulated, even though their votes have been distributed, and to these original numbers should be added those which may fall to each from Stirling's 637 votes. The list may run thus:—

ORIGINAL FIRST VOTES—STIRLING'S CONTINGENT.

Baker	262	+	65	=	327
Buttery	190	+	59	=	249
Fowler	167	+	185	=	352 Returned.
Guthrie	136	+	79	=	215
Harrold	93	+	100	=	193
Robinson	72	+	42	=	114
Votes confined to the six successful candidates and therefore unused			97		
			637		

Thus the distribution of Stirling's votes brings in Fowler, who makes a larger total than any of the others—and as having the larger share of Stirling's votes, he seems most worthy of stepping into his shoes.

SOUTHERN CROSS.

EQUALITY.

Representative government is a series of mechanical devices which in modern civilised countries performs two functions. First, by means of it the electors of a county, nation, district or city, unable on account of their great numbers, to meet together for purposes of legislation, attempt to delegate the law-making power to a limited number of persons. Second, the persons thus delegated have opportunities for information, deliberation and wise judgment, superior to what the busy people themselves could obtain were they assembled in mass meeting.

Representative government is not an immutable unconscious creature of natural laws, but is an artificial creature of self-governing people. It is not a sacred and moral institution like the family, nor is it a fundamental, organic institution like the State itself, but it is simply a contrivance invented by human beings, improved and remodeled as a result of various experiments, and intended to serve as a set of machinery for expressing and enforcing the popular will. It has never fulfilled its purpose precisely, has always failed and broken at points, but on the whole, has succeeded in solving momentous political difficulties.

Yet as society becomes more complex, and problems more intense, weaknesses of the machine become more and more serious. The stage coach, which in former days served well the needs of rural society and small cities and villages, would poorly support the traffic of a world and the shifting populations of a continent.

Representative government originated without much thought regarding principles of government or political philosophy. It grew out of necessity. It was continued to secure an immediate result. Not until several hundred years after its first introduction did it become a subject of study, and then it had become so firmly established that to many students it was a sort of shock to discover that the system had had a beginning. When the system under new circumstances reveals weaknesses there needs must be a conscious study of its principles—and this is the era which began with the eighteenth century.

The essential idea of representative government consists in the election of a deliberative body of law-makers, whose will stands for that of the community and is obeyed as the voice of the electors themselves. The executive and the judiciary may also be elected, but this is not essential. These are expected to execute the laws, not to make them. They are the agents of the legislature. If they do not obey the law-making body, then representation is a failure. Provisions for their obedience are a necessary part of the machinery of representation. But it is subordinate to the main mechanism.

Representative government is a modern invention. It belongs to those modern nations which we call civilized, i.e., those which have taken their rise in Europe and have spread thence over the new world.

In these nations the idea of representation has achieved an astonishing development. Not only the important interests of government are dependent upon it, but in every phase of private life it finds a useful and necessary place. The stockholders in a private corporation have no immediate direction of their property ; they delegate control into the hands of directors and managers. Religious organizations are controlled by representatives instead of by the body of the communicants, from the local communities which manage the local churches, to the delegated assemblies, conferences, synods and parliaments, which direct the interests of an entire national ecclesiastical body. Educational interests and institutions are managed by committees and trustees. Political parties are not groups and masses of voters, but "machines" composed of those who are supposed to represent the party's voters. All of this delegated power, often so absolute and powerful, would have been incomprehensible to the ancients. Why Greece and Rome never adopted this device of representation is an interesting and pertinent question.

J. S. Mill, in his profound treatise on representative government, in asking how far forms of government are a matter of choice, observes that "political machinery does not act of itself. As it is first made, so it has to be worked by men. It needs, not their simple acquiescence, but their active participation, and must be adjusted to the capacities and qualities of such men as are available. This implies three conditions. The people for whom the form of government is intended must be willing to accept it, or at least, not so unwilling as to oppose an insurmountable obstacle to its establishment. They must be able and willing to do what is necessary to keep it standing. And they must be able and willing to do what it requires of them to enable them to fulfil its purposes."

Exactly these qualities of practical co-operation are above all others required in government by representatives. The people must be obedient to law. They must yield their immediate wishes to the decisions of their deliberative bodies. They must be capable of political co-operation with definite purposes of public policy, else they will cling to some striking personality or magnetic leader, and submit their wills to his. They must be free from the "inveterate spirit of locality." A petty local selfishness which cannot look beyond the interests of the immediate neighborhood can never permit the broad movements of policy which take in nations and subordinate localities. Consequently Mill observes that nowhere does history furnish "any example in which a number of these political atoms have coalesced into a body, and learned to feel themselves one people, except through previous subjection to a central authority common to all." The consolidation of tribes and principalities into kingdoms and nations has been the result of conquest. And representative government has arisen, not as a device for promoting this consolidation, but as a result of it, in order to protect the people against the oppression of a military conqueror and his successors. It was the sufferings they endured from a common oppressor which drew them together in common opposition.

The growth of representative government, then, is the growth of freedom and democracy. It is the institution of the masses. It fulfils its highest functions when it unites distant tribes and peoples into mighty nations, and at the same time assures them freedom and local independence. It is thus the link that unites a powerful, far-reaching central government to patriotic and independent millions of citizens. The question of representative government is therefore a fundamental question of democracy.

It is not to be supposed that the ancients were without any institutions which took the nature of representation. We read of councils of elders among the very earliest records of the Jews, the Greeks and the Romans. But these elders were not elected elders, representing the free choice of the people, but were hereditary chiefs and patriarchs of clans. They represented their followers by divine and inherited right instead of by popular choice.

The history of all races that have achieved distinction has been a history of federation. Back in the dawn of history there are traces of small independent village communities living isolated lives and united by the ties of blood. Each village had its patriarch who was at the same time king, priest and chief. But soon these village clans were drawn together by alliances, at first temporary and afterwards permanent, for purposes of defense and conquest. Now, the chief of one clan became permanent over the others. But his supremacy was not absolute. He could act only with the consent of the other chiefs. In council he was the presiding officer. Thus the king and his council of hereditary elders were the ruling representatives of the people in the time of the judges in Israel, of Homer, and of the kings of Rome.

Every reader of the history of politics is familiar with the universal growth of the power of the people in making laws. From the very first, the king and his elders found it necessary to submit the result of their deliberations to the popular assembly of men in arms for rejection or ratification. But there was no public debate. The warriors simply expressed by their shouts and clashing of arms their assent or dissent.

But not until the principle of election was substituted for that of heredity, did the people themselves gain control of the laws. This principle, however, was of slow growth. The history of Athens in this respect is characteristic of all ancient democracies. First, the king and his council of elders promulgated the laws and sought the assent of the people. The first conflict in this arrangement was not between this council and people, but between the king and the elders. Popular sovereignty has never spread out and downward among the masses of the people by leaps, but has always been preceded by an aristocracy and an oligarchy. The elders in Athens were the first to demand and secure the principle of election. They made the king a limited monarch and acquired the right to choose him, first for life, then for a term of ten years, and finally they elected nine archons or kings for a term of only one year. The elders thus developed into a nobility and an oligarchy, making the kingly office wholly dependent on their own will.

But meanwhile, the people were growing restless and revolutionary. The oligarchy, in usurping the powers of the king had trampled upon the rights of the people and had oppressed them through harsh debtor laws and the monopolization of the land. The next step was to make the aristocracy itself elective. This was the work of Solon. The nine archons were to be chosen for one year by a popular assembly, not from the people at large, but only from the ranks of the nobility and the wealthy. Their duties were executive and judicial.

The popular assembly included all classes except slaves. It elected the magistrates and enacted some of the laws. But it did not originate the laws. This was done by a new body of representatives, the Senate of Four Hundred, chosen for one year by the popular assembly from among the three propertied classes, and presided over by the archons. It was therefore a kind of aristocratic House of Commons. It could enact most laws without reference to the popular assembly. Finally, there was the senate of the Areopagus, the Athenian House of Lords, the remnant of the old council of elders. Membership here was for life. It had no legislative power, but only a kind of general supervisory authority.

Thus Solon endeavored to establish a representative democracy with a conservative balance wheel, and a limited popular referendum. But the people were not yet able to maintain this sort of government. After a short period of anarchy it ended just as the republics of Mexico and Central America and Hayti have ended, in a tyranny under the forms of representation. Peisistratus held autocratic sway for fifty years, supported by the votes of the popular assembly and practically appointing his henchmen to all the elective offices, just as a city "boss" to day in America nominates his candidates, and the voters excite themselves with the show of electing them.

Still, the popular assembly was educating the people. When the sons of Peisistratus abused their power, the people deposed them and chose Clisthenes to draw up a new constitution. This constitution introduced the ripest fruits of Athenian democracy, and under it Athens reached her pinnacle of power. The suffrage was extended and equalised. Every citizen was made eligible to the senate of five hundred, and the senate of the Areopagus was limited in its powers. All magistrates were elected for terms of only one year. The popular assembly engrossed the law-making powers into its hands. An extreme democracy was reached when minor magistrates were chosen by lots. Thus it will be seen that Athens never successfully adopted representative government. She could not trust her representatives. Her citizens took from them the powers of legislation, both in its initiative and final determination. But so large a mass meeting could not enact laws, and therefore they followed their popular leaders, like Peisistratus and Pericles. They simply expressed the decrees, but the laws proper could only be made and altered and harmonised by a smaller body of representatives. Without a proper control over this revising legislature, the Athenian system could never succeed. But compared with modern states and cities, we can see wherein are to be found the elements of success which it actually achieved. Athens, with the whole of Attica, was a small community, covering no larger area than an American township. Its population at no time exceeded 500,000, and four-fifths of these were slaves and had no part in government. Its citizen population numbered only 90,000, of whom 18,000 were eligible voters. They were supported by slaves, and could therefore give their whole time to public affairs. How different from the citizens of the modern city! There are no slaves—all are voters. Not only do the manual workers have a share in controlling the local politics, but the wealthy classes do not look upon business as dishonorable, as did the Athenians, but business is the main vocation of their lives, and politics has a very subordinate place. The Athenians being limited in numbers, with abundant leisure and small distances to travel, could easily assemble in mass meeting. Hence political parties on a national basis with local machinery and strict discipline could not arise. Instead of the party caucus, with its intolerance and ambition for party advantage, opposing orators addressed the assembled nation on the broad issues of the day, and the Athenians were educated in wide views of policy. There were no partisan newspapers, which the party voter read in private, but the public meeting was his press and the street discussion his newspaper. There were no private corporations of great wealth requiring legislation, and therefore no organised and paid lobby. Yet, notwithstanding all these advantages, the Athenian system broke down. The suffrage was extended, new and ignorant voters came into political prominence, and through the privileges of the mass meeting and majority rule they overrode all the better elements of the city. The voters became corrupt and indolent, the easy prey of the demagogue and the briber. And finally, when Athens came under the power of Macedonia, and later of Rome, she lost her right to elect her own magistrates.

Had the hundred independent cities of Greece ever been brought into a united nation, they might have developed a system of federal or state representation. Some progress was made in this direction in the Amphictyonic Council. But it is the famous Achæan league to which we look for the nearest approach to a federal representation. "This league acted through an assembly, which met twice every year, and to which was entrusted, not only the election of all confederate officials but also the supreme direction of every affair which affected the foreign relations of any city in the league, even though it were an affair not of general but only of local interest. The business of the assembly was prepared by a council which was probably permanent. There certainly was here a better frame work than the Greeks had ever known before for concerted national action. Its chief defects lay in the composition and procedure of the assembly. That body was composed in theory, of every free man of the cities of the league who had reached the age of thirty years. In fact, of course it consisted of the whole body of the free men of the town where it met, (usually Aegium, or in later days Corinth) and of such citizens of other towns as had the leisure or the means to attend. The votes of the assembly were taken by towns, not decided by the majority voice of the free men present. The few chance attendants from some distant city within the league spoke authoritatively for their fellow townsmen, the smallest delegation had an equal vote with the largest, and yet there was no fixed plan which would make the vote of one delegation as representative as that of another."*

When we turn to the Roman republic we find far more apparent than in little Greece the need of representation. The progress of democracy was parallel to that of Athens. First the king was displaced by two councils elected by the senate of nobles. A popular assembly did not arise until the plebs, having revolted against the harsh judgments of the patrician magistrates, acquired the right of electing tribunes. The tribune had power to suspend the judgment of any magistrate upon a plebian. They were the representatives of the people. They soon became the leaders of the people. Had the tribunes been elected into a legislative body co-ordinate with the senate, they would have furnished the natural prototype of the popular branches of modern legislatures. But such a device did not occur to the Romans. The tribunes became simply the leaders and orators before the popular assembly—the *comitia tributa*—of the people. This assembly gradually engrossed the greater share in electing magistrates and deciding laws. But the hereditary and wealthy senate was never completely subdued. As the citizenship became more numerous and more degraded, anarchy followed for a long period, and finally the empire restored peace and prosperity.

Especially was the lack of representation oppressive to the wide extended provinces which the Romans had conquered. Provincial governors sent out from the city were wholly irresponsible to the people they governed. The provincials had no redress or appeal except to a corrupt popular assemblage at Rome, and had no voting power that could have compelled attention to their demands. We may quote in conclusion the words of May, who says : † "With the lights of modern experience, we are naturally led to consider how far a system of representation would have brought these conflicting forces into harmony. By such a remedial measure the forces of the people would have become less dangerous, while the senate would have been strengthened by its moral support. The responsibilities of the senate would have been increased, and the political alienation of classes replaced by mutual confidence. The varied forces and interests of society would have been consolidated. The wealthy aristocracy would still have ruled the state, but they would have shared their power with other classes of citizens ; and the policy of the state

* Wilson, The State, page 91-2.
† May, Democracy in Europe, Vol. I, page 223.

would have been determined, not by irregular conflicts but by timely concessions to popular demands. Representation is the only safeguard against anarchy in democratic constitutions. In Rome representation was peculiarly needed, as it offered the only means whereby large bodies of citizens, enjoying the Roman franchise, but living at a distance from the capital could have exercised their political rights. Without it, the citizens of Rome itself, usurped all their powers; and Roman citizenship outside the walls of the capital was but a barren honor."

It is to England that the world looks for the origin of true representative government. The peculiar circumstances and history of the country suggest as naturally the form of representation which we enjoy to-day, as did the circumstances of the Romans suggest the tribune of the plebs. These circumstances were the primitive local government of the Anglo-Saxons, and the centralized imperial government of their Norman conquerors. The combination of these two elements on English insular soil, separated from the conflicts and conquest of the continent, worked out through internal forces the institutions of representation.

The germ of representation is found among the Teutonic conquerors of Britain long before the time of the Norman conquest. These Teutonic conquerors came over in small companies during a period of one hundred and fifty years, and scattered in groups throughout the country. Each group was independent of the others, having its own system of popular government. A process of federation and internal conquest at once began, small kingdoms were built up, and finally the whole of England was united under one king. But the original townships and minor kingdoms retained much of their powers of local legislation. The township is the "unit of the constitutional machinery." The alodial owners, or the tenants of the manorial lord, met in popular assembly, elected their own officers and passed their by-laws. Their chief officer, the constable or *gerefa*, was *ex officio*, the representative of the township in the courts of the hundred and the shire, and with him went the four best men, or selectmen, of the township. They represented the township as a unit in the higher assemblies of the people.

The hundred was a union of townships. With the progress of federation it tended to disappear and to be merged into the shire or county. The shire court was composed of all the freeholders resident in the district, together with the representatives from the townships. Thus it was both a popular assembly and a representative body. "The primitive Teutonic conception of an assembly," says Hannis Taylor,* "whether local or national, rested upon one simple idea, and that was that every freeman resident within a state or district had a right to appear and represent himself in the assembly of such court or district." With such a conception as this there could be no true representation, as we understand it. Our representatives have the exclusive right to stand for their constituencies in the assembly. If individuals could appear in their own right there would be not representation of all, but only of the wealthy and the politicians. This was exactly what occurred in the national assembly of all England after its final consolidation. This assembly was not a folk-moot but a witenagemot, i. e., an assembly of the "wisemen" or the "best men." It was not a great tumultuous assembly composed of the whole body of the people, but a small assembly composed of the great and wise men of the land, who met as councillors of the king. "The only consistent theory upon which this changed condition of things can be explained, is that as the progress of aggregation advanced, the limits of the greater kingdoms so widened as to render a general attendance both irksome and difficult, and for this the mass of the people simply ceased to attend. In this way assemblies purely democratic in theory, without the formal exclusion of any class, shrank up into assemblies purely aristocratic."†

In the hundreds and the counties, however, the idea of representation existed along with the idea of a popular assembly. It is probable that the selectmen from the township were not at first just four in number nor elected formally by the votes of all the tunmoot, but they held simply the individual proxies of the various voters. They were the wealthier members of the township, who happened to be going to the county court on their own account, and their neighbors in an informal way transferred to them their own

---

* Origin of the English Constitution, page 247.

† Taylor, p. 247.

right to go. Gradually this proceeding became more and more formal until the four men were elected by general consent. The mixed character of this county court, being thus partly represented and partly primary, must have given undue influence to the freeman of the township where it happened to meet. It remained for a later day and a new set of political circumstances to develop this primitive unsatisfactory germ of representation into a formal and exclusive principle.

After the Norman Conquest the old idea was continued, which gave to every freeman the right to appear in the national assembly. But for the same reasons as in earlier times only the wealthier land-owners attended. This assembly became known as the Great Council. It was not a representative body, but every member attended in his own primary right. It possessed, with the king, all the law-making authority of England. The king and his council of magnates was the government of England. But there was little legislation to be done.* The customs of the people were adequate for laws. The king was expected to administer these customary laws as they had been handed down to him. He was not dependent upon the legislature for revenues, because, according to the feudal theory, he was expected to meet the public expenditures for peace or for war out of the customary revenues from his own immense private domains. These were the ancient feudal dues, aids and reliefs, paid by his tenants, the amounts of which were determined not by competition, but by immemorial and well-known custom. In the course of time the alienation of portions of his domains, and the growing expenditures of war and administration, compelled the king to seek out sources for other and "extraordinary" revenues. The experience of a couple of centuries showed that this could not be successfully done by arbitrary exactions from his subjects. He must obtain their consent. It was found, too, that their hearty consent and co-operation could not be obtained when they were approached privately and individually. Hence the practice grew up of summoning them collectively in order that the king might lay before them the state of his exchequer and the urgency of his needs for additional funds. These assemblies became in time not merely financial but also political assemblies. The king laid before them the general affairs with reference to which he desired their advice and approval and which he considered them competent to decide. In still later times they claimed the right to present petitions for redress of grievances, and even to withhold grants of supplies until their petitions were allowed.

It is not the ultimate powers of those assemblies, so well known, but the manner of their constitution with which we are concerned. They were far from being assemblies for the whole people or of representatives of the people, as we understand such assemblies in our day. They were merely conventions of different interests and classes of men. The earliest financial assemblies were naturally those of the military tenants of the king. The greater tenants, those holding upwards of six manors, and who had hitherto paid their feudal dues directly to the king, were summoned by name. The lesser tenants, who had hitherto paid their customary dues to the king's lieutenant, the sheriff, were summoned indirectly, through writs issued to the sheriffs directing them to attend the assembly. But they all met together, voted the aid desired, and returned home. The clergy were summoned in like manner, and met in assembly at different times and places from the military tenants. Finally, when incorporated cities began to acquire wealth, they were summoned to send representatives for their own peculiar assembly.

It was Edward I. who first consulted these assemblies regarding interests other than financial. Says Hearn, regarding this important phase of the evolution of parliament,† "It was no part of his design to carry his changes, however beneficial, with a high hand. In words that well became the noble king of a free people, he acknowledged that "what touched all should be approved by all." But these words conveyed a different meaning in the fourteenth century from what they imply in the nineteenth. In those earlier days the cohesion of our national elements was still imperfect. It is only in an advanced state of political development that the social organism exhibits that independence of its various parts which binds them, whether for good or evil, into one national life. Five centuries ago the divisions of society, now so minute and intertwined, were few and

---

*Hearn, Government of England, page 417.

†Government of England, page 423-5.

distinct. There was little in common between the burgher and the knight. There was still less sympathy between these two classes and the cleric. The general interest, therefore, and the general approbation, which were assumed to be inseparable, were the interest and approbation of each great class of the community. Each class was concerned in its own affairs and was neither competent nor desirous to interfere with the affairs of others. Edward accordingly seems to have designed to establish councils of advice for each of the great interests that then existed in the kingdom. While he retained his own authority and the services of the Great Council for legislation, he invited the assistance of all the tenants of the crown, either personally or through their representatives, on all questions relating to estates or tenures; of the clergy in like manner on all questions relating to ecclesiastical affairs; and of the citizens and burgesses, through their representatives, on all matters relating to trade and commerce. It had at all times been the duty of these several classes to meet for the purpose of considering the wants of the king and the propriety of affording him pecuniary assistance. They were now asked under a more complete organisation to perform the additional function of giving to their sovereign information and advice as to their own respective wants and the means of their satisfaction. Thus out of the financial assemblies Edward formed special consultative bodies, each dealing exclusively with its special class of subjects. In legislating upon these several classes of subjects he sought the advice of the appropriate assembly, although the legislation still proceeded from the king and his council. But in matters not directly affecting any of these classes, or when no charge was directly imposed upon any of them, the king in his council was free to legislate as he saw fit."

It will be noticed that these assemblies were both primary and representative. The assembly of military tenants was originally altogether primary. In 1254 we find the first recorded instance of the introduction of representatives. The lesser tenants, who had been hitherto summoned by the sheriffs, were seriously burdened by the expenses incurred on account of their long journeys and the poor roads. In the above year, " Henry III., in contemplation of a campaign in Gascony, and in addition to other preparations, commands each of the sheriffs to send his council two good and discreet knights of his county, whom the men of the county shall have chosen for this purpose, in the stead of each and all of them, to consider along with the knights of other counties, what aid they shall grant the king in such an emergency."*

One year later the lower clergy were first asked to send representatives. Ten years later occurs the first representation of cities and boroughs. These had heretofore been looked upon as little more than despised labor organizations. But their wealth and influence had now greatly increased, and they were destined to play an important part in all financial matters. This innovation was not the work of the king but of Simon de Montfort, the liberal patriot, who summoned both the knights of the counties and the burgesses, because in his revolt against the king he found his natural adherents among the lower orders of the people. He directed the towns to send to his parliament two of their more discreet and worthy citizens or burgesses.

There were, then, at the end of the thirteenth century, four distinct legislative assemblies with recognized functions. The Great Council of Nobles, which with the king was the ultimate law-making body; the assembly of military tenants, including members of the Great Council, and the representative knights from the counties; the clergy, including all the higher clergy and representatives of the lower; the burgesses, including the representatives of the towns. How these assemblies coalesced into the modern bicameral system is an interesting evidence of the growing community of feeling and interests among the middle classes of the English people. The clergy were gradually deprived of their power to legislate even on ecclesiastical affairs. The higher clergy, then, merely retained the place which they had always held in the Great Council, and this became the modern House of Lords. The lower clergy, so far as they had political influence, were merged in the electorate of the counties and the towns. In the year 1333 occurs the first recorded instance of the joint deliberation of the knights and the burgesses, though they had previously submitted to the king and council their joint petitions. And in the latter part of the fourteenth century they appointed a permanent speaker to represent them before the higher authorities. This coalescence of town and county was the origin of the House of

---

*Hearn, page 477.

Commons. It was based on newly discovered common interests and the need of combination against the exactions of the Great Council and the aristocracy. It was the primitive consolidation of the Knights of Labor and the Farmer's Alliance.

When we turn to the colonial history of the United States, we find in each of the colonies a curious repetition in miniature of the evolution of representative assemblies which took place centuries before in the mother country. As truly as the physical child, according to the biologists, repeats in a few months its ancestral history of geological ages, so did these children of English liberty pass in a few years through that development which in medieval England was the slow and painful growth of centuries. In all cases we find the same problems and the devices of representation to meet them. There were no studied theories nor contemplation of general principles, but the development took place in almost that unconscious way which we observe in the natural world. There were immediate pressing exigencies, and the colonists, with determination to maintain their liberties, took the shortest way of meeting them.

In some of the colonies the full record of the development has not been preserved. What it was can only be surmised from the history of those concerning which we have information. It was in Maryland that we see old England most quaintly depicted. The following account is abridged from the scholarly work of Doyle.*

"The constitution, as originally conceived by the proprietor, was to consist of a governor, a council and an assembly. . . An ordinance sent out by Baltimore in 1637 vested all judicial power in the governor and council. . . The original deliberative and legislative body, in the case of Maryland, was a primary assembly at which any freeman of the province might present himself and vote. . . At the outset, while the colony was but a single encampment of log huts, all the freemen might easily meet together for the trifling business of the colony. But as the settlement gradually expanded over a wider area, how could the planter leave his corn to be eaten by deer, his cattle to stray in the woods, his pig to be stolen by the Indians? Every year the assembly would have become more and more a little oligarchy of those living at or near the centre of government.

"One would suppose that the remedy of representation would at once have suggested itself. But before that was adopted a more cumbrous and far less efficient device was tried. In 1638 the assembly met for the second time. Their proceedings, unlike those of the previous session, are recorded. On this occasion, those who could not appear in person were allowed to send proxies. If such a system avoids the evils incident to a primary body, it brings with it other evils of a directly contrary kind. It may be bad that an energetic and ever-present minority should have everything its own way. It is worse that energy and constant attendance should count for nothing, and that the voter who delegates his power to another should have as full a share in legislation as the voter who exerts himself to attend.

"The evils of this system were amply illustrated in the events of the year. The assembly, undeterred by its failure, proceeded to enact a set of laws. . . While the proposals of the assembly, or rather a part of it were under discussion, a rival set of laws was sent out by Baltimore. Apart from the intrinsic merits or demerits of the proposed laws, it was clearly a most serious question whether the initiative in legislation was to belong to the proprietor or the colonists. . . The division which followed illustrated forcibly the evils of the proxy system. The acts sent out by the proprietor were rejected by thirty-seven votes to eighteen. Doubtless there were proxies on both sides, but in the minority twelve of them were in two hands, those of the Governor and Councillor Sawyer. No better illustration could have been found of the danger to the liberties of the colony involved in this anomalous system.

" . . Early in the next year another assembly was called. Its constitution brought the colonists one step nearer to the system of representation. Regular writs were issued to the various hundreds instructing them to return representatives. Yet after the election one person at least came forward and claimed the right of appearing in person, on the ground that he had voted in the minority, and so was not represented. The claim seems to have been allowed, and nothing could illustrate more forcibly the complex and hybrid system on which this assembly had been formed. It showed that the

---

*English Colonies in America. Maryland, Virginia, and the Carolinas.
9

logical result of that principle was that in a constituency of fifty, a majority of four-fifths might have two votes, and a minority of one-fifth, ten.

"This was not the only anomaly in the constitution of the assembly. The proprietor claimed, and it would seem obtained without challenge, the right of summoning members by writ. The claim evidently proceeds from a confusion in the original constitution of the legislature. That an upper chamber should be nominated by the proprietor was only in accordance with the principle of the English constitution. But that arrangement presupposes a division of the legislature into two chambers. To allow it, while the whole body, those summoned by writ and those elected by popular suffrage, sat, voted and deliberated together, was simply to enable the proprietor to swamp the representation of the Commons with his own creatures.

" . . . The incongruous combination of a representative with a primary assembly disappeared three years later. The legislature when it met in 1639 declared by its first act that the assembly should consist of the governor and secretary, those named by special writ, lords of manors, one or two burgesses from every hundred, and all freemen who had not consented to the aforesaid elections. . .

"In the next assembly the right of personal appearance was in at least one instance claimed and refused. Nevertheless in 1642 the governor reverted to the earlier system, and required the freemen of the colony to appear either by themselves or their deputies. Out of 106 persons who obeyed this summons, 72 availed themselves of the right to send proxies. One of the first proceedings of the assembly was to define the constitution of the legislature by limiting the popular representation to the elected deputies, and with this reform the last trace of the earlier system disappears."

I have quoted this scholarly description of the origin of representation in Maryland, because it presents lucidly in miniature the problem of representation as it appeared to al primitive English communities. We have here the aristocratization of the original primary assembly, the device of the proxies, then the election of representatives by districts with the old idea still remaining that every freeman had his own right to appear if the elected delegate did not represent him. But this attempt to do justice to the minority in the districts was abandoned, since it would have enabled the primary voters to swamp the representative element of the assembly. All who were not duly elected were ultimately excluded, and thus the problem of minority representation from the apparent necessities of the case was given up as a hopeless undertaking.

In Virginia representative institutions sprang suddenly into full being without the preliminary transition from a primary assembly. In 1619, according to the oft-quoted expression of the Tory historian, Hutchinson, a "House of Burgesses broke out in Virginia." It was summoned by the governor in obedience to instructions from the Company in England. Every freeman had a vote, and every county and hundred was to send two members. Certain outlying plantations, too, had the right of sending a member.

The colonial Virginia legislature is remarkable mainly for the brilliant men who in later years were returned to its halls. The presence of such men, we may be sure, was due to the oligarchical nature of the county governments which returned them. The richer families became connected by an unbroken chain of close intermarriages. Thus in Virginia a strong sense of caste grew up among the dominant order.* "The Virginia system, concentrating the administration of local affairs in the hands of a few county families, was eminently favorable for developing skillful and vigorous leadership, and, while in the history of Massachusetts during the revolution, we are chiefly impressed with the wonderful degree in which the mass of the people exhibited the kind of political training that nothing in the world except the habit of parliamentary discussion can impart, on the other hand, Virginia at that time gave us—in Washington, Jefferson, Henry, Madison and Marshall, to mention no others—such a group of consummate leaders as the world has seldom seen equalled." †

Representation in the colony of Plymouth went through a process of development like that in Maryland, says Doyle:‡ " A primary assembly was superseded by a system of

* Doyle, p. 395.

† Fiske, Civil Government in the United States, p. 66.

‡ Puritan Colonies, page 71-72.

representation, and there was a period of transition, during which the two were in the same measure combined. But the superior political intelligence and constructive power of the New Englanders is manifest throughout the process. At Plymouth the change was effected easily, indeed almost spontaneously and completely, with none of those compromises which accompanied it in Maryland. . .

"The growth of new townships gave an impulse to the political life of the colony. So long as Plymouth was the only settlement, constitutional machinery of a simple kind sufficed. The power of making laws was vested in the whole assembly of the freemen. The judicial and executive body, called the Court, consisted of the governor and seven assistants elected by the assembly. . . The addition of Scituate and Duxbury made some system of delegation necessary. Complete representative government did not, however, come at once. In 1636 eight deputies met, four from Plymouth, and two from each of the other colonies, and in conjunction with the court revised and codified the laws. . . The selection of deputies was only intended as a temporary measure for a special purpose. But in November 1636, another step was taken in the direction of a representative system. The functions of the General Assembly were divided. The meetings for legislation were to be kept distinct from those for electing the governor and assistants. At the former the whole body of freemen were to attend as before; at the latter, proxies were to be allowed. The need for this change was illustrated by the fact that two years later sixteen freemen were fined for absenting themselves from the assembly.

"In 1638 the system of representation was definitely introduced, and the functions of the legislative assembly of freemen were definitely transferred to deputies. Plymouth returned four, each of the other towns two. . . Apparently the new system did not formally supersede the old. The primary assembly still seems to have remained in theory the supreme legislative body. In practice, the advantages of representation asserted themselves, and the more cumbrous system fell into disuse."

In the colony of Massachusetts Bay we find again similar conditions and a similar outcome. "The growth of fresh settlements brought with it an expansion of the constitutional machinery of the colony. Of all the colonies that have yet come before us, Virginia is the only one where a system of local representation came into existence at once in full working order. In every other case it was reached after a variety of contrivances and compromises. The reason is plain. Every other colony enjoyed a certain amount of independence before it had grown large enough to make a local representation either needful or possible. Only in Virginia had the colony the needful materials for a representative assembly at the time when it first acquired the right of self government. It might be thought that the rapid formation of separate plantations would have made Massachusetts a second exception. But if it be not a paradox to say so, the constitution of Massachusetts was older than the existence of the colony. The legislature of the colony was simply the general court of the company transferred across the Atlantic. At the same time the dispersal of the settlers at once unfitted that body for the work of legislation. The remedy first applied to this difficulty was, not to substitute a representative assembly for a primary one, but to limit the functions of the court. It is clear that there was an oligarchical temper at work among the leading men in Massachusetts. The action of this was plainly shown by the transfer of all legislative rights from the court of freemen to the governor, deputy-governor, and assistants. At the same time the election of the governor was handed over from the freemen to the assistants. . . .

"True to English precedent, Massachusetts found the salvation of her constitutional liberties in a question of taxation. When the governor had intended to change his abode to Newton the assembly resolved to fortify that settlement at public charge. . . . To meet the cost a rate was levied on each town by order of the governor and assistants. Against this the men of Watertown protested. . . . Though the men of Watertown gave way on the main issue their protest seems to have borne fruit. In the next year the powers of the governor were formerly defined by an act. It was also enacted by the General Court in the following May that the whole body of freemen should choose the governor, deputy-governor and assistants. A further step towards self-government was taken in the resolution that every town should appoint two representatives to advise the governor and assistants on the question of taxation. We can hardly err in supposing that this was the direct result of the protest made by the men of Watertown."[*]

---

* Doyle, Puritan Colonies, p. 104-106.

It was in Connecticut that the origin of representative government first appears as a federation of independent towns, rather than a delegation of local representatives to resist a central authority. The three towns which had been settled along the Connecticut river, united in January 1638, and "formally declared themselves a commonwealth with a constitution of their own. . . . A system of representation was adopted at once instead of being slowly worked out through a series of expedients and compromises. The legislature was to consist of a governor, six assistants and deputies. The governor and assistants were to be elected annually by the whole body of freemen, met in a general court for that purpose. The deputies were to be elected by the three existing towns, four from each. As fresh towns were formed their number of representatives was to be fixed by the government."[*]

The other colonies passed through similar experiences. A common form of government was developed in them all. At the time of the revolution very conservative changes were made to suit their newly acquired independence. "First, there was the two-chambered legislature, of which the lower house was the same institution after the revolution that it had been before. The upper house, or council, was retained, but in a somewhat altered form. The Americans had been used to having the acts of their popular assemblies reviewed by a council, and so they retained this revisory body as an upper house. But the fashion of copying names and titles from the ancient Roman republic was then prevalent, and accordingly the upper house was called a senate. There was a higher property qualification for senators than for representatives, and generally their terms of service were longer. . . In most of the states there was a lieutenant-governor, as there had been in the colonial period, to serve in case of the governor's death or incapacity : ordinarily, the lieutenant-governor presided over the senate.

"Thus our state governments came to be repetitions on a small scale of the king, lords and commons of England. The governor answered to the king, with his dignity very much curtailed by election for a short period. The Senate answered to the House of Lords, except in being a representative and not a hereditary body. It was supposed to represent more especially that part of the community which was possessed of most wealth and consideration ; and in several states the senators were apportioned with some reference to the amount of taxes paid by different parts of the state. When New York made its senate a supreme court of appeal, it was in deliberate imitation of the House of Lords. On the other hand, the House of Representatives answered to the House of Commons as it used to be in the days when its power was really limited by that of the upper house and the king."[†]

Little need be said in this place on the origin of the federal legislature. It is well-known to have been a conscious imitation of many features in the different state or colonial constitutions. As the result of a compromise between the large and the small states, the Senate represents the states as corporate bodies, and the House of Representatives represents the people of the states in proportion to their numbers.

The development of representative institutions in Canada was like that in the United States in its ultimate results, but in its origin there was nothing like the primary assembly or local self-government. "The British government, after its experience of the old Thirteen Colonies, decided to guide the affairs of their remaining possessions with the hand of a gentle despotism, and did not permit the formation of institutions which might weaken the allegiance of the people to the Crown."[‡] Especially had the French colony of Quebec been utterly devoid of the semblance of local government. And when in 1791 a representative assembly was established for the colony, to bring it into harmony with English habits, there was found to be no local governments which possessed enough of the organic nature to warrant their recognition as "units of the constitutional machinery." The parishes and townships were simply administrative divisions, ruled over by the appointees of the central government and by the parish priests. The people took no part in government, consequently new arbitrary territorial divisions were created for parliamentary purposes without reference to previous organizations. In the report of Lord Durham to the

* Doyle, The Puritan Colonies, Vol. 1. page 159-160.

† Fiske, Civil Government in the United States, page 164-165.

‡ Bourinot, Local Government in Canada, 67.

English authorities in 1839* are the following words: "If the wise example of those countries in which a free and representative government has alone worked well had been in all respects followed in Lower Canada, care would have been taken that at the same time that a parliamentary system, based on a very extended suffrage, was introduced into the country, the people would have been entrusted with a complete control over their own local affairs, and been trained for taking their part in the concerns of the province by their experience in the management of that local business which was most interesting and most easily intelligible to them. But the inhabitants of Lower Canada were unhappily initiated into self-government at the wrong end, and those who were not entrusted with the management of a parish were enabled by their votes to influence the destinies of a state."

In Upper Canada similar arbitrary divisions were made for the purpose of representation. But the inhabitants here were Englishmen, and they soon developed both a vigorous and local parliamentary system.

It was not until 1840 that parliamentary government was fully established in the province of Canada. At that time the arbitrary irresponsible power of the Crown's appointees was supplanted by the creation of a responsible ministry dependent upon the support of the lower branch of the legislature. In 1867 the British North America Act performed for Canada what the constitution of 1787 performed for the United States, it created a federal government.

With these historical and elementary facts before us, and knowing the present organisation of representative government in the different countries under review, we may profitably draw a comparison between the circumstances and problems which characterised its origin and those of the present day. We shall find that not only are the circumstances and problems to-day radically different, but the very nature of representation itself has changed in company with other social and political changes.

1. In the first place, the original problem of representation was that of nationalization. The government of England was formed by the welding together of independent local communities into a unified central organisation, without wholly destroying the original local organisation. The "inveterate spirit of locality" was yet paramount, because of the lack of highways, traffic and intercommunication. The youthful spirit of nationality was just beginning to breathe. Representation was not the representation of individuals, but of corporations and localities. "The basis of English representation has never been personal, but always organic. . . Our electors have always voted, not because they were men or even because they were Englishmen, but because they were freeholders of a particular county, or because they were citizens or burgesses of a particular city or town. Their right is circumscribed by locality. . . Thus our system of representation is the representation not of interests or opinions or of population, but of population organised. . . It regards men not merely as men, but as neighbors. In one sense it is obviously true that a district cannot have other rights than those of the people who inhabit it. But the rights of a district are those of its organized population. Its inhabitants by virtue of their residence have, as compared with the inhabitants of other places, separate habits and interests and associations, peculiar views on public affairs, and peculiar sympathies and modes of thought. These distinctive habits and feelings produce a distinctive character. The individuality, the independent life of each political body is established, and it acquires and desires to express its special shade of feeling and thought." †

This is the original and primitive idea of representation. But to-day the institution is quite different. The change has come so gradually that it is hardly appreciated. The problem of nationalisation has been fully settled. Not only the kingdom of England but the kingdom of Great Britain has become a single organism. Localities have lost their significance and their adoration. Railways, telegraph, the newspaper press, internal traffic and communication and political representation have brought the people together. Foreign relations, a world-wide system of colonies and dependencies, national armies and navies have exalted a national flag and inspired a national patriotism. The representative to-day is therefore not a mere agent of a close corporation, having general powers, it is true, but speaking and acting only for his constituents. Besides this, says Hearn, "he is a member of the supreme council of the Crown. He is to give the king true and faithful

*Cited by Bourinot, Local Government in Canada, page 24.

† Hearn, Government of England, p. 501-2.

advice to the best of his judgment. . . Thus, although he has been selected by the electors or a portion of the electors of a particular district, he represents not merely those who voted for him, or even the inhabitants of his district, but the whole kingdom."* Mr. Hearn in continuing, holds that this was the ancient conception and usage. However that may be, its significance was not appreciated so long as the great council retained the chief legislative powers. When the representative body became supreme then it could be said in the words of Burke,† "Parliament is not a congress of ambassadors from different and hostile interests, which interest each must maintain as an agent and advocate against the other agents and advocates. But parliament is a deliberative assembly of our nation with one interest, that of the whole, where not local purposes, not local prejudices, ought to guide, but the general good resulting from the general reason of the whole. You may choose a member, indeed, but when he is chosen he is not a member of Bristol, but he is a member of parliament."

In the United States, too, the problem of representative government from the earliest times until the reconstruction period, which followed the war of 1861-65, was that of consolidation and union. It passed through three stages. The first was the union of counties and towns into independent colonies. The second was the confederation of states for military revolt. The third was that of nationality. By the first our state legislatures have arisen. By the third our national Congress. A division of powers between state and national legislatures has recognized a difference between state and national questions. But each in its own sphere stands for a unified people. The representative in the state legislature, no matter from how remote a county, does not represent alone that county. He represents the people of the state. He legislates upon the common interests of all. And so it is with the national Congress. The senators represent in a peculiar sense semi-sovereign states, and partake of the nature of ambassadors, and the representatives come more directly from the people of the states, but both are national and not local officials. They draw their salaries from the national government. They vote upon the common interests of all the states and all the people. The members from California make laws for the people of Florida.

In Canada, the original problem of representative government closed with the British North America Act of 1867. At that time an independent nation was practically consummated.

2. On account of the long-developing organic nature of the whole English nation, many of the questions and policies which were considered in ancient times as local and class questions, and were treated by separate assemblies, are now national questions in which every citizen and every individual has a pressing interest. In the 13th century, export and import duties were the especial interest of the merchants and buyers. It was upon their petition that customs tariffs were imposed, and the other assemblies were not consulted. So too, with mercantile law. Questions relating to the tenure of land were referred only to the assembly of military tenants, and the greatest statutes of English real property were determined without consulting the burgesses or the clergy. The clergy managed their enormous estates without reference to other assemblies. And the great council enacted laws of a political nature, like the government of Ireland and Wales or foreign relations which were supposed to have no concern for clergy, knights and burgesses, without consulting these popular bodies. But all of these questions now affect every Englishman. They are national questions, and the representatives who deliberate and legislate upon them, must do so from the standpoint of the nation, and not from that of their locality or class. More important as a national question than any that have been mentioned, is that of taxation and expenditure. It would be unthinkable to-day to leave these matters to the determination of those sections and classes which were immediately interested.

The same is true of the United States and Canada. The intercommunication of all kinds has so bound together the states and provinces into an organic whole, that national laws are vital to the interests of each. Foreign relations, currency, customs duties, are national questions, and we have seen citizenship and rights of property come under federal

* Hearn, p. 506.
† Quoted by Hearn, p. 507.

protection, and federal control has reached out for the two most influential business interests, banking and railways. Federal interference has grown into marvellous ramifications, and with the consolidation of enormous trusts and syndicates, we may expect to see it still further extended.

3. Growing out of these historical conditions we can perceive the impressive significance of the modern growth of national political parties. Before there were national questions there were no national parties. But even the early development of party divisions was on territorial lines. The Whigs were almost unknown in the counties, and the Tories unknown in the cities. Consequently, there was no important minority in either division which was unrepresented. Cities were unanimous on national questions, and so were the counties, because the only important question they had to meet was the demand of the king for additional subsidies. More or less the distinction between city and county continues to the present day, but district lines have been changed from their original boundaries, villages and counties are thrown together, national parties are often evenly divided in the territorial districts, and a representative of the majority, therefore, does not represent the opinions and wishes of the mass of his constituency. The minority is simply crushed for the time being.

In Canada the character and political influence of political parties are about the same as in England. But in the United States this power has reached a height unattained by those of any other country. This power is the growth of not more than fifty years, and especially has it made its greatest advances since the period of the civil war. The peculiar feature of the development has been the supremacy of that new force in political parties, the "machine." Party organisation is an essential element of party government, but the extent, perfection and detail of this organisation in the United States is something bewildering. It controls both candidates and voters with an iron-like grip, and they glory in their subjection. These parties are not divided on territorial lines. They are divided on national questions.

In colonial times parties were unknown. Or, rather, we might say there was a court party represented by the governor and his council. But the legislatures, the representative bodies, practically stood for a united people. The upper house being appointed by the governor, the lower house was drawn together as a single unit, representing all the people. No matter from what county a representative was returned, he was the ablest man in the couty, for the people were unanimous in their wishes to withstand the party of prerogative. Furthermore, the districts were all alike, being exclusively agricultural, and a representative from one was in harmony with the people of the others. There was no minority in any district to be unrepresented by a delegate chosen by the majority.

But to-day, the legislature, instead of being the organised representatives of those who protested against the government, is itself the government. Within its halls occur the conflicts for the control of the fortunes and destinies of the people. There is no outside enemy whose constant presence enforces harmony and mutual help. But two great parties stand face to face in conflict, and whichever masters the legislature masters the people.

4. Furthermore, from the earliest times suffrage both in England and the United States was narrowly limited. In England this continued until the latter half of the present century. The masses of the people were not considered as citizens or entitled to political consideration. In the counties, serfs, copyholders, and the lesser freemen were excluded from the suffrage. Only the freehold knights were voters. The cities were close corporations, made up of the mayor and aldermen and a few of the leading men of the guilds. Altogether, perhaps not one-fifth of the adult male population were entitled to vote for representatives to parliament. As a result, these classes in their respective districts were practically unanimous on the few questions of national interest for which they were required to select representatives. But in modern times the great political questions are those which grow out of the citizenship of the manual laborers, the former serfs. They have to do directly or remotely with the profound problem of the distribution of wealth and the betterment of the social conditions of the lowest classes. These classes are distributed throughout all districts. They form the great foundation structure of every community, upon which the other classes are built. They form the majority of the voters. They feel that they have not heretofore been represented in the councils of the nation.

They are unaccustomed to political power, and therefore they are the fertile soil for demagogues and partisans. They hold the balance of power. They must be placated and pacified. The party or candidate who presents to them the most specious appeals wins the day. They themselves are not allowed to combine according to their natural divisions and elect their acknowledged leaders to parliament. Could they combine throughout the kingdom, the labor unions scattered as they now are through a hundred districts would unite, and the more intelligent of the laborers would select those who represent them as a body, just as they select their union presidents and secretaries. As it is, they are forced into artificial territorial divisions and are compelled, along with the whole of the electorate, to submit to the dictation of the candidates who appeal to the more ignorant, thoughtless, prejudiced and easily influenced minority. The trial of representative government in England did not really begin until 1867 and 1884 when the laborers were enfranchised.

We have seen how the local governments of the American colonies were close corporations. In the South, it was the aristocratic families, united by ties of blood and marriage. In New England it was the church members, who alone held the suffrage. But in the United States of to-day not only the native Anglo-Saxon is admitted to the suffrage, but also millions from antagonistic races. Especially is this true of the cities. If England is threatened by the widening of the suffrage far more so is the republic of America.

5. Again, legislation in the olden times was very limited both in the number of subjects discussed and the details of the regulations. The people were satisfied to live according to the customs of their ancestors. Government was simply a matter of administration. The king, his council, his officers, and his judges were not called upon to make new laws but to learn what were the customs of the land and then to act accordingly. But to-day, legislation is the most intricate of arts depending upon the profoundest of sciences, and dominating the most vital of human interests.

There are hundreds of pressing problems requiring legislative direction, which the assemblies of Edward I, or even the Parliaments of George III never dreamed of as having a social importance. "Time was," says Wodrow Wilson,* "in the infancy of national representative bodies, when the representatives of the people were called upon simply to give or refuse their assent to laws prepared by a king or by a privileged class in the state, but that time is far passed. The modern representative has to judge every weighty plan, preside over every important reform, provide for every passing need of the state. All the motive power of government rests with him. His task, therefore, is as complex as the task of governing, and the task f governing is as complex as is the play of economic and social forces over which it has to preside. Law-making now moves with a freedom, now sweeps through a field unknown to any ancient legislator ; it no longer provides for the simple needs of small city states, but for the necessities of vast nations, numbering their tens of millions." The modern legislator must therefore, be a well equipped man. He must give the greater part of his time to parliamentary duties, and above all must have a long experience in his particular art. These qualifications, it is true, England secures in her parliamentry leaders better than other countries. But new conditions are fast making short-term men of the majority of the members of parliament. This tendency is checked only by that wise custom which permits the election of non-residents to represent a district. To the American, bound by the three spirits of local pride, local spoils and democratic equality, this custom is incomprehensible. Indeed. it rests on tradition. So important is this principle as a relief from the restrictions of the district system that the following account given by Hearn † of its origin and purpose is in place.

"There is no room for doubt that originally members of parliament were required to be residents in their respective electorates. The early writs invariably commanded the election of two knights *de comitatu tuo*, and in like manner of citizens and burgesses of each city or town in the bailiwick. In the first year of Henry V an act was passed expressly providing that the knights should be resident, at the time of their election, in the counties for which they shall be elected, and that the election for cities and boroughs shall be of citizens resident and enfranchised in the same cities and boroughs, and none

---

* The State, p. 583.

† Government of England, 524-5

others. This statute, which was merely declaratory of the common law, was comfirmed more than once in the following reign. The disposition to infringe upon the old custom which thus called for legislative interference, was perhaps due to the desire of employing the services of professional men. We have seen at least that practising lawyers were excluded. But to whatever circumstance it may have been due, the tendency against the old restriction was too strong to be resisted. Non-residents were constantly elected. . . At least in 1681 Lord Chief Justice Pemberton ruled that " little regard was to be had to that ancient statute (1 Henry V.) forasmuch as the common practice of the kingdom had been ever since to the contrary. . . .''

" This limitation was originally designed to secure a trustworthy statement of the wants and opinions of each electorate. But for its continuance another and different reason prevailed. The old restriction was sometimes useful as a protection against the nomination of the Crown or the neighboring nobles. . . . But even those who on these grounds defended the old law were not insensible to its inconveniences. A compromise was suggested (in the reign of Elizabeth) that one of the members for each borough should be a gentleman resident, if not actually in the town, at least in the neighborhood, and the other should be a man of learning " who could speak ". The principle of residency was indeed inconsistent in two respects with our political developement. While this law was in force and the motives upon which it was founded were influential, no true conception could be formed of our national representation. Further, if it had been enforced, the great popular movement of the 17th century would have wanted its most prominent intellectual leaders. In the time of the Tudors and for some time afterwards, none of the country gentlemen had or could acquire any political skill. Statesmanship was then exclusively confined to the servants of the Crown. The country party was therefore obliged to seek its leaders from the Bar ; and for the most part the leaders thus chosen could not and did not reside in the towns which they represented. Nor was the influence of the lawyers confined to the services, great though they were, which they rendered in their capacity of leaders. It was their professional habits and modes of thought which brought to the contest that strong legal character which it never afterwards lost."

The American people have never suffered by the principle of residency as would the English because political ability has always been more widely diffused. But it is well-known that our ablest and most experienced leaders are often found in districts where their own party is in a minority, or else a hostile legislature especially creates such a district for them. The English system enables a party to keep its great leaders in parliament for a life time. There can always be found a number of districts which have sure majorities for the given party, and in these districts the national leaders of the party can be put in nomination. Thus the English House of Commons is an assemblage of giants, representing not localities but the nation. In the course of decade after decade of honorable service they acquire knowledge, experience, wisdom and national views, so necessary to manage the affairs of a modern empire. This makes possible too, an institution which cannot exist in America, the executive administration of the country by a cabinet chosen from the members of the legislature.

6. There is one feature of modern legislation so extremely important in its influence upon legislative bodies themselves, as to demand special notice. This is the private corporation with its professional lobby. Corporations are as recent as party machines, and both have grown up together like Siamese twins. The professional lobbyists are nearly always the managers of the political machine. They carry in their pockets the political fortunes of the legislators. The "Third House" is really the modern legislature, at least in the United States. Corporations from their very inception, and in their daily activities are creatures of the government. Their life is legislation. They cannot, if they would, dispense with their lobby.

This is an entirely new feature in the constitution of representative assemblies. A legislature that may have sufficed for simple duties in the days of isolated individual industries, is almost sure to wither and rot in the era of private corporations with public functions and fabulous resources.

Municipal Legislatures.

It has appeared from the preceding pages that the origin of representative assemblies in state and national governments depended upon the existence of local governments

separated by wide territorial areas. This necessitated the adoption of what has become
the district system of electing single delegates. Such a system still has its justification in
many respects, and especially in a country like that of the United States, which comprises
millions of square miles, a seven day's journey by fastest rail, dissimiliar sections in
climate, resources, products and peoples. But why this system should survive to the
present day in the election of city legislatures is one of the enigmas of politics, to be
solved only by reference to their traditions and inertia of mankind. In the United States
and new countries there are not even historical reasons for the adoption of this system.
With them the transition from primary assemblies to representative assemblies was made
simply by way of imitation. It was to England that the framers of our municipal constitutions turned their attention when our cities had advanced beyond a size convenient
for the ancient popular assembly. It is therefore in the origin of English cities that we
shall find the explanation for the origin of the district system.

The earliest records seem to indicate that English cities were merely concentrated
hundreds and shires. Says Stubbs*, "The "burh" of the Anglo-Saxon period was simply
a more strictly organized form of the township. It was probably in a more defensible
position ; had a ditch or mound instead of the quickset hedge or " tun " from which the
township took its name ; and as the " tun " was originally the fenced homestead of the
cultivator, the " burh " was the fortified house or courtyard of the mighty man, the king,
the magistrate or the noble. . . In these the idea of the free township was retained ;
municipal authority depended on no different organisation ; the presiding magistrate was
the *gerefa* ; in mercantile places, such as London or Bath, the *port-gerefa* ; in others the
wic-gerefa or the *tun-gerefa* simply. . . The constitution of the larger towns resembled
that of the hundred rather than that of the township ; and in fact, each such town
generally contained several parish churches with a township organisation belonging to
each." In Norman times the larger cities were organised like counties with their sheriff,
their country court, composed of all the freeholders of the county and the conventional
representatives from the townships. Here we have the original councilmen elected from
the minor districts. But the city was not at all an organic body with recognised common
interests. It was a curious mixture of all the different interests which happened to be
thrown together in the neighborhood. For example in primitive London, †" there were
the original military tenants of the crown, with their independent manors and the
agricultural serfs ; there were the parishes governed by the bishop, the chapter and the
monasteries ; and there were the guilds administered by their own officers, and administer-
ing their own property. It was for the most part an aristocratic constitution, and had its
unity not in the municipal principle but in the shire." Over all these jarring interests
the sheriff presided as the representative of the king.

But the circumstances of the times and the needs of defence drew the residents nearer
together in common interests. This appears first in the development of the guilds of
merchants. Through commerce they gained wealth, this brought political power, and
soon the merchant guild absorbed the law-making power of the entire city, its charter
became the city charter, and its *maire* the city mayor. "In the reign of Henry II. there
can be little doubt that the possession of a merchant guild had become the sign and token
of municipal independence ; that it was in fact, if not in theory, the governing body of
the town in which it was allowed to exist."‡

In still later times, when manufactures arose into prominence alongside merchandising,
new guilds were organised representing different trades. There were the weaver, the shoe-
maker, the goldsmith, the butchers and many others. Each of the craft-guilds had its
own *alderman*, or president. They soon demanded a share in the city government, which
was finally granted, and their aldermen were given the right to sit together as a law-
making body, each representing his own guild. In the reign of Edward II., all the citizens
were obliged to be enrolled among the trade-guilds, and in the reign of Edward III. the
election of the city magistrates was transferred from the representatives of the ward-
moots to the trading companies."§ Thus to-day "London, and the municipal system

* Constitutional History of England, Vol. I., p. 92
† Stubbs, Vol. I., p. 407.
‡ Stubbs, Vol. I., page 418.
§ Stubbs, I., 419.

generally, has in the mayor a relic of the communal idea, in the alderman the representative of the guild, and in the councillors of the wards, the successors to the rights of the most ancient township system."*

The question arises, how did it come about that so rational a system as the election of aldermen by the different organised interests of the cities should have been displaced by the arbitrary system of election by territorial districts? The answer is brief. The ancient system itself was practically an election by wards, because the different trades were all grouped together, each in its own district of the city. And when the federation of guilds was abolished and elections thrown open to a widened suffrage, it seemed wholly natural to continue that district system, which was seen to be in vogue elsewhere.

When American cities adopted representative government they adopted the English system. The transition is vividly portrayed in the history of Boston.† Until the year 1822 the government of Boston had been a primary assembly. On the first of May, 1822, the population had grown to 45,000, the qualified voters to 7,000 or 8,000. In that year the general court of Massachusetts drew up a charter entitled "An Act establishing the city of Boston." It was presented to the voters of Boston and accepted by a vote of 2,797 to 1,881. . . "As authorising the first departure from the system of local government which had been in operation nearly two centuries, it was regarded as a measure of the very highest importance. Not a few of the old residents who had fought under the eyes of Samuel Adams in the town meetings, looked upon the act which divided their great folk-mote into twelve separate and silent gatherings, where men delegated their rights to others, as the beginning of the end of Democratic government."‡

Had the people of Boston and of the American cities while copying the English district system, also copied the English custom of free choice of candidates irrespective of residence, the system would not have been so arbitrary in its results, nor so destructive to aldermanic ability.

Little need be said about the difference between the problems of representation in cities in its origin and its present development. The city is above all political organisations a unit in itself. Aldermen and councillors do not represent wards—they represent the city. The ward has no place in city politics except perhaps as an administrative division. It is well recognised that cities present the most aggravated failures of American politics, and so far as the legislative branch is concerned, the following pages will attempt to show that the failure lies mainly in this unnatural partition into petty districts.

CHAPTER II.

THE FAILURE OF LEGISLATIVE ASSEMBLIES.

The American people have succeeded fairly well in the organisation of the executive and judicial departments of their government, but there is a universal feeling that the lawmaking bodies are a painful failure. This applies to all grades of legislatures, municipal, state and federal. The newspapers are supposed to say what is popular, and, judging from their sayings, nothing is more popular than denunciation of aldermen, state representatives and congressmen. These diatribes do not extend to other officers of government, but are heaped upon the legislators. Every winter when Congress is in session, the business interests are reported to be in a gasp of agony until it adjourns. And the cry that goes up towards the latter days of a state legislature's session, is sickening.' A Sacramento daily has just earned the petty spite of the California legislature by printing across its title page in glaring type the words "Thank God the legislature adjourns to day". And the San Francisco Bulletin is quoted as recently saying "It is not possible to speak in measured terms of the thing that goes by the name of legislature in this state (California). It has of late years been the vilest deliberative body in the world. The assemblage has become

---

* Stubbs, I., 424
† See Bigbee, The City Government of Boston, in Johns Hopkins University Studies in History and Political Science, 5th series, page 22.
‡ Bigbee, page 23.

one of bandits inst ad of law-makers. Everything within its prasp for years has been for sale. The commissions to high office which it confers are the outward and visible signs of felony rather than of careful and wise selection." Every state in the Union can furnish examples more or less approaching to this.

These outcries are not made alone in a spirit of partisanship, but respectable party papers denounce unsparingly legislatures whose majorities are of their own political complexion. The people at large join in the attack. They have come thoroughly to distrust their law-makers, charges of corruption and bribery are so abundant as to be taken as a matter of course. The honored historical name of alderman has become a stigma of suspicion and disgrace.

As might be expected this distrust has shown itself in many far-reaching constitutional changes. The powers of state and city legislatures have been clipped and trimmed and shorn until they offer no inducements for ambition. The powers of governors, mayors and administrative boards have been correspondingly increased. The growing popularity of the executive veto is one of the startling facts of the times. Cities have been known to turn out in mass-meetings to illuminate the heavens with bonfires in honor of a mayor's veto which has rescued them from outrages and robberies perpetrated by their own lawfully elected "city fathers." The latest reform in municipal constitutions has been the transfer of many legislative functions and a great deal of the legislative discretion from the city councils to the mayors. This has been done on the plea of concentrating responsibility, and there are many people who would be glad to see municipal legislatures abolished altogether and their duties handed over to the mayor and his cabinet.

The recent constitutions of the new states of North Dakota, South Dakota, Montana and Washington, may be taken as a consensus of the American people at the present time regarding the character and functions of State legislatures. Says an observing writer,* " The work of the four conventions brings into sharp relief the essential difference between the tendency and the character of political changes in England and in the United States. In England every reform in government for a thousand years has had for its immediate purpose the limitation of the powers of the executive ; in the United States since 1776 the opinion has steadily grown that it is safer to limit the powers of the legislature and to increase the powers of the executive. Englishmen distrust the Crown and grant almost unlimited powers to Parliament ; Americans distrust the legislature, especially the state legislatures, and give great powers to their president and their governors. . . The articles in the new state constitutions on the "legislative Department" are long and detailed. They seem to be composed by the framers in order to declare what the respective legisl tures cannot be permitted to do. . . The perusal of these new constitutions suggests that the people have lost confidence in their state legislatures, and that the conventions, responsive to this feeling, have sought to anticipate great evils by limiting the powers of the legislature, or by substantially limiting them in declaring by what procedure the legislature shall act, on what it shall not act, and to what extent it may act. The chief limitations on the legislature are with respect to special or private legislation, corporations, political corruption among members, taxation, and power to use the credit of the state. . .

" Among administrative officers (all of them filled by popular election) are several of economic significance, as those of insurance, railroad, agriculture, and labour, prison and public land commissions. The first state constitutions knew nothing of such offices...... When are considered the demands upon the modern legislature, and the character of that legislature, according to the confessions of the American people in their state constitutions, the tendency to short legislative sessions once in two years is expressive of a hope of escape from both " over-legislation," which is merely the activity of zealous, but as is sometimes the case, incompetent men, and inadequate legislation which is the confession of mere politicians. It may be that the creation of bureaus in the modern state government is practically the solution of the problem how to escape the danger of a session of the legislation."

The judiciary, too, has gained materially at the expense of the legislatures, both in the express provisions of constitutions and in the popular approval. Conscious of the feelings of the people, judges have steadily encroached upon the very fields of legislative discretion, and, reluctantly it may be, have more and more assumed the right to set aside legislative

* F. N. Thorpe in Annals of American Academy of Political and Social Science, September 1891.

enactments. This has become boldly apparent in numerous recent decisions overthrowing such peculiarly political statutes as those which redistrict a state for the election of legislative representatives. This interference of the judiciary, however justifiable the reasons, can only be fraught with danger to itself. It is thereby forced into the political arena, where are the heated questions of political expediency, at the expense of its integrity in the field where administration and justice alone are its sphere. Nevertheless, the judiciary is forced by the people to take this step, as a further limitation upon their discredited legislatures. This whole movement is portrayed by Mr. Horace Davis, in the following words: * "The executive, all powerful at the beginning (of colonial history) was reduced to a mere shadow of its former glory, and in these later days is regaining some of its lost power. The legislature, at first weak, afterwards absorbed the powers of the other departments, but is now much reduced again. Throughout all these changes the dignity and power of the judges have steadily increased. . . Their greatest power, most amazing to Europeans, is the authority to set aside a statute which they hold to be in conflict with the written constitution. No other courts in the world possess this unique power. . . The scope of this power to declare a law unconstitutional, is much broadened by the modern tendency to limit legislation. The early constitutions were very brief, containing little more than a bill of rights and a skeleton of the government, leaving all details to the descretion of the legislature. Now all this is changed, the bounds of the different departments are carefully defined, and the power of the legislature is jealously curbed, particularly in the domain of special legislation. It will be seen at a glance that this enlarges the relative power of the courts. It limits the legislature, and widens the field of the judiciary at one stroke."

These tendencies to restrict the legislature which are showing themselves so unmistakably, and this demoralization of legislative bodies, must be viewed as the most alarming features of American politics. Just as the duties of legislation are increasing as never before, in order to meet the growing vital wants of a bewilderingly complex civilization, the essential organs for performing those duties are felt to be in a state of collapse. The legislature controls the purse, the very life-blood of the city, the state, the nation. It can block every other department. It ought to stand nearest to the lives, the wishes, the wisdom of the people. It is their necessary organ for constituting, guiding, watching and supporting all the departments of government. Above them all, then, it ought to be eminently *representative*. But it is the least representative of all. Surely, then, for the American people above all others, and in a high degree, too, for all nations who depend upon representative institutions, it is pertinent to inquire carefully into the fundamental nature of these institutions, the causes of their failures and the means if any can be found, which will adapt them to the exigencies of modern times. It will likely be found that there is no simple reform that will revive them. Many different reforms must cooperate in so complex and momentous a problem. But there is at least one feature that reaches the fundamental nature of these institutions, with which all the others are intimately related and out of which they grow. This feature is the system of electing each representative by a single district established on territorial lines. As has been shown, this is an inheritance from the past, when representation was in its infancy and when its problems were very different from those of the present. It was adopted without any political philosophising, and has been inherited, like complexion and hair and real estate, without any questioning. To-day is the time to test it and see whether it suits new conditions, and if it is found wanting to devise a system which shall be based on solid foundations adapted to modern needs.

CHAPTER III.

THE SINGLE MEMBERED DISTRICT.

The position of the modern voter who essays to independence of choice is well known to be an unenviable one. When he comes to the polls to cast his vote he finds that there

---

* American Constitutions—Johns Hopkins University studies in History and Political Science, 3rd series, pages 55, 59.

is just one candidate to be chosen for any given office. He finds that through the machinery of the political party with which he has been accustomed to vote, there is one candidate offered to him. There are practically but two candidates in the field—those of the two great parties. It is known to every one that one of these two will be elected. If the voter is dissatisfied for any reason with the nominee of his own party there are three courses open to him: to vote for the opposing candidate, to vote for a third candidate, or to stay at home. It is likely that his dissatisfaction with the opposing candidate is far more extreme than for his own party's. Only in periods of exceptional unrest or as a protest against an exceptionally corrupt candidate do large numbers of voters make so radical a revolt as to go entirely over to the enemy. The great majority of the dissatisfied simply stay at home. This is their only comfortable way of condemning their party's nominee. But should they be intensely exasperated, or should they be of an uncompromising turn of mind, they may go to the extreme of nominating and voting for a third candidate. In this case their offence is even worse than if they vote for the principal opposing candidate. They indeed give him a half vote, just as they do when they stay at home, but they gain the opprobrium of a "crank" and the scorn of having "thrown their votes away." More bitter than the hatred towards rivals, says Bryce,* is the hatred of Boss and Ring towards those members of the party who do not desire and are not to be appeased by a share of the spoils, but who agitate for what they call reform. They are natural and permanent enemies; nothing but the extinction of the Boss himself and of bossdom altogether will satisfy them. They are, moreover, the common enemies of both parties. Hence in ring-governed cities professionals of both parties will sometimes unite against the reformers, or will rather let their opponents secure a place than win it for themselves by the help of the "independent vote." Devotion to "party government," as they understand it, can hardly go further."

In this way the party machine is the master of the situation. It alone can name the candidate, the only check upon it is the fear of the bolt on the part of the voters. This fear is reduced to a minimum. Though there may be loud protests and a vigorous show of independence it is well known that most of the protesters will fall into line on election day rather than see the other party win.

Add to the foregoing the fact that districts are bounded more or less arbitrarily, so as to include heterogeneous elements of population, and that boundaries are frequently changed, and we have an additional reason for the supremacy of the party organization. The voters have very few interests in common. They see little of each other; they have few o those general and social relations that would accustom them to join and work together. They do not meet in mass meetings as in the old New England town meeting, where individuals of all parties come together and discuss in public the affairs of their district, and the qualifications of candidates before the candidates are nominated. They must therefore look to their party organization for the dictation of a policy and the designation of a candidate. It is in the party that they find their common meeting place.

The party organization is a more or less close corporation composed of a series of practically self-perpetuating committees, the committees corresponding to the different election areas. The party primary of the smallest division - the township or the ward—is the foundation of the system. But the primary is in the hands of its standing committee. A very small percentage of the party voters, for some reason or another, attend the primaries. The majority of the party voters are too busily employed in private callings, or they find the work of primaries and conventions distasteful, or they are systematically barred out. In cities the percentage ranges from two to ten. In the townships from ten to forty. A majority of the voters in these primaries, then, elect delegates to the nominating conventions or nominate local candidates. This is the case with both the ruling parties. These candidates are the only ones between whom the voters can choose at the elections. The nominating convention is therefore practically the electing convention. If this be so, we are faced with the fact that our public officials instead of being elected by a majority of the voters, as is fondly supposed, are elected by a minority of a minority of a majority. And in case the election is determined by a plurality vote or a sufficiently large number of voters have absented themselves from the polls, the candidate is elected by a minority of a minority of a minority.

---

* Amer. Com. vol. II, page 3.

I do not mean that the minority who have this power can use it autocratically. They must keep before themselves constantly the qualities of their candidate which would promote or mar his popularity. They must nominate a man who, as they say, is "available." But within this limit, unless the popular interest has been aroused by some unusual emergency, they have a wide field of autocracy.

Such a system results inevitably in the selection of weak and inefficient officers and representatives. They are not necessarily corrupt, and taking the country as a whole, they are very rarely corrupt. But they are tools and figure-heads. Confining ourselves to the case of representatives and councilmen, let us notice more fully the reasons why inefficient men are chosen. In the first place, the area of choice is arbitrarily limited. It is a universal principle in elective constituencies, that the larger the area over which an election district extends the more distinguished and capable are the candidates of all parties. In all districts representatives must be chosen from the ranks of the party which happens to be in the majority in the given district. It is wholly improbable that the able men of a party will be distributed about one by one in the small districts where the party has its majorities. But even were they so benevolently disposed, the chances are against their being nominated by their party conventions. The political managers must have men who will do their bidding. At the same time, the election of candidates is subject to the dictation of cliques. Especially in close districts and wards, a compact faction bent on its own aggrandisement, can often name a candidate, or at least prevent the nomination of an outspoken and capable candidate. The influence of the saloon element in city and state politics is well known to depend on the power which their close organization and their unscrupulous selfishness give them over the party leaders in the nomination of candidates.

Besides factions within the party lines, there is in the closer districts always to be found a number of voters who hold the balance of power between parties. Hence candidates must placate them. Now it is the characteristic of the greatest of party leaders that they raise up about themselves a body of strong admirers and a body of equally vigorous haters. Consequently we seldom find in American politics that a great party leader can be elected in a close district. This principle comes out distinctly in the election of the President of the United States. Those men who have achieved the highest honors in the leadership of their party, in the halls of congress and in political battles, are seldom elected to that high office. They are not often even nominated, and if nominated they are almost sure of defeat. Unknown and obscure men are hunted out and given the place that in the affections and admiration of the party voters belonged to others. The real leaders must be content with appointive positions. The same principle operates far more inexorably the further down we go to the lesser and lesser districts, until when we come to ward politics we reach the very lowest extreme of political ability and the very highest power of greedy factions.

It is well known that when a party leader has achieved prominence either in the state legislature or congress, the entire resources of the opposite party throughout the state or nation are thrown into his limited district to compass his defeat. And these extraordinary exertions are usually successful, if the district be in any way a close one. Many an eminent leader in Congress, after serving a few terms and acquiring familiarity with the rules, and then becoming the recognized leader of his party, has been defeated in his district. In this way the Democrats lost the able services of their great tariff leader, Wm. R. Morrison, and the Republicans lost also their brilliant tariff leader, Wm. McKinley, Jr. Only in the case of a man like Blaine or Garfield who happened to live in an overwhelming Republican district, could the leaders be kept in the public stations where their services could redound to their party and their country.

This is the main reason why our legislative bodies are composed of inexperienced men. A careful analysis of state legislatures in the United States will likely show that in every election at least one-half the representatives are new men, with no legislative experience. An actual count of the Indiana legislature of 1893 shows that in a house of 100 representatives there are sixty-three men who are there for the first time, sixteen men who are serving their second term, twelve men their third term, one man his fourth term, and one man his fifth term. It is well known that the American House of Representatives is becoming more and more a body of one and two term men. In the fifty-third Congress, out of a membership of 353, there were 133 new men, seventy-eight men serving their second term, and only 142—*i.e.* 40%—who were serving their third term and upwards. Throughout the country it may be asserted, in all legislative bodies, the laws of the people are made by a majority who have never had any previous experience in law-making.

This is the explanation of two most significant facts in American legislative government, the power of the Speaker of the House, and the power of the lobby.

The American Speaker, unlike the English and Canadian, is a man of dictatorial power. In the national government he is ranked next to the President. He appoints the committees, lays down the rules and controls legislation. The reason for this is the same as that which explains the power of a tribal chieftain or an imperial Caesar :—the ignorance, incapacity, and faction of his subjects. Now, leadership is essential wherever a body of men are compelled to act in concert. But there are two kinds of leadership. One is that of ability, merit and enthusiasm, where the followers have confidence in their chief and accept his leadership and act in concert with him voluntarily. This is the leadership of Gladstone in the House of Commons. The other is that of necessity and circumstance, where followers distrust the ability of any leader they may choose, where they distrust their own ability to follow, and therefore they consent to the abdication of self-government and the elevation of a tyrant. This is the leadership of the American party speaker. Perhaps the main reason for the supremacy of the speaker is the lack of acquaintance which exists among the members of the legislative bodies. This is due to the short terms, and the fact already shown, that one-half to two-thirds of the membership of the lower house are new men. They come together for the first time in their lives. They have never met before and perhaps have never heard of one another. They know nothing of the qualifications of each. If they should keep the control of affairs in their own hands there would be nothing but wrangling and wire-pulling over the appointments of committees, and then factions and mutiny on account of the final appointments. The only escape from this evil is in the power of the speaker.

If our representative bodies were composed of able men, if their terms of service were longer, and their legislative experience and acquaintance wider, if the natural party leaders were not excluded from their midst by a petty district system of election, then the representatives would claim for themselves the powers which they bestow upon their autocrat. They would appoint their own committees, control their own rules, make their own laws, and the speaker would be simply a moderator instead of a dictator.

Though the speaker has a unique dominion, there is another power in American Legislatures and the American Congress still more ominous—the lobby. It is the lobby which controls legislatures to-day. If any law which is demanded by the people at large or even by a majority of the legislature, is defeated or emasculated, its fate can be traced to the dominating influence of the lobby.

The lobby is a new feature of representative government. It is coincident with the very recent growth of large private corporations. It is organised in their interests. These corporations have such immense interests at stake on the turn of legislation that the lobby with their unlimited resources at its disposal is practically irresistible.

But the lobby could not have acquired its powerful influence were it not for certain qualities, or lack of qualities, in the legislative bodies which place them at its mercy. It is a mistake to suppose that there is a large amount of corruption. Legislators fall into the nets of lobbyists mainly because of inexperience and incapacity. The lobbyists themselves are the shrewdest, brightest and most influential men of the state or nation. They often control the party spoils, and an ambitious legislator cannot afford to antagonise them. The lobby is organised far better than the legislature itself. It has its great chiefs who band together. All of the corporations interested in legislation practically combine as a unit. Then these able and honorable chiefs employ their resources of argument and suggestion with individual legislators and before committees. They fully size up every individual who is in their way. But if their honorable methods are inadequate they turn the legislator in question over to the petty lobbyist who carries the pocket-book. Their own hands are clean.

The power of the lobby is found mainly in the fact of the party machine. The lobbyists are usually the managers of the machine. They control state and national party spoils and offices. They have the political future of individuals in their hands. They are the actual leaders in party politics. There must be leadership somewhere. The only question is, shall the leaders be elected to the legislature by the people or shall they control the legislature from outside as mere irresponsible private citizens? As long as the people are prevented from electing the leaders they wish to positions of responsibility, there will surely arise these self-constituted leaders whose shrewdness gives them control over the weaklings and hirelings who are actually elected.

The lack of leadership on the floor of the legislative bodies is shown also in the fruitless bickerings and factious combinations which so often prevent a legislature from accomplishing any results. A party in the majority needs to be held together through confidence in some leader or leaders. But their forces are often scattered and legislation is blocked. It is needless to say that this is the prime opportunity for the lobby.

The district system too, exalts local interests above the general interests of the state or nation. Legislation is too often a mere exchange of favours between localities.

Perhaps the most glaring weakness and injustice of the district system is the opportunity it gives a majority party to wholly crush out and disfranchise the minority. This is seen flagrantly in the "Gerrymander." But even where the system is employed with the fairest of intentions, it is almost wholly a matter of chance whether the opinions of the people shall be justly expressed or not. This danger was not imminent under the earlier conditions of representation, as has already been shown, when electoral districts were natural units and the problem of representation was the federation of local communities. But now that party lines are drawn through the midst of every community, it nearly always happens that one party gains in the elections an unjust proportion of representatives at the expense of others. From the theory of the matter it may be shown to be possible to exclude minority parties altogether and to give the entire legislature bodies to the minority. Suppose a legislative body to be composed of forty members elected from forty districts, and that the popular vote at large of the two political parties stands respectively 120,000 and 100,000. If the districts are so arranged as to have 5,500 voters each and the parties happen to be divided in the districts in the same proportion as they are divided at large, we should have in each district a vote respectively of 3,000 and 2,500. All of the forty candidates of the majority would be elected, and the minority wholly excluded. An extreme result of this kind though it seldom occurs, is not unknown.

Again it may happen, and often does, that a minority of the popular vote obtains a majority of the representatives. In the case assumed, parties may have been divided in the several districts as follows :—

Party A.

Narrow majority in twenty-five districts,	$2,800 \times 25 =$	70,400 votes.
Minority in fifteen districts, average....	$1,973\frac{1}{3} \times 15 =$	29,600 "
Total........		100,000 votes.

Party B.

Minority in twenty-five districts........	$2,700 \times 25 =$	67,500 votes.
Large majority in fifteen districts......	$3,500 \times 15 =$	52,500 "
Total........		120,000 votes.

Where a system offers in theory such fruitful opportunities it is too much to expect party managers from using it. As a result, the district system, in conjunction with party politics, has resulted in the universal spread of the gerrymander. It is difficult to

10

express the opprobrium which ought to be heaped upon so iniquitous a practice as the gerrymander, but its enormity is not appreciated, much for the same reason that a brutal prize fight is not reprobated, provided it be fought according to the rules. Both political parties practise it, and neither can condemn the other. They simply do what is natural, make the most of their opportunities as far as permitted by the constitution and the system under which both are working. The gerrymander is not the iniquity of parties, it is the outcome of the district system. If representatives are elected by districts, there must be some public authority for outlining the districts. And who shall be the judge to say where the line shall be drawn? Exact equality is impossible, and who shall set the limits beyond which inequality shall not be pressed? Every distribution act that has been passed in this or any other country has involved inequality, and it would be absurd to ask a political party to pass such an act and give the advantage of the inequality to the opposite party. Consequently every distribution act involves more or less of the features of the gerrymander.

The gerrymander consists simply in constructing districts in such a manner as to economise the votes of one's own party by giving them small majorities in a large number of districts, and cooping up the opposition party with overwhelming majorities in a small number of districts. This may involve a very distortionate and uncomely shaping of districts, and the joining together of distant and unrelated localities into a single district. Such was the case in the famous original distribution act of Governor Gerry of Massachusetts, whence the practice obtained its amphibian name.

But it is not always necessary that districts be cut up into distortionate shapes in order to accomplish the unjust results of the Gerrymander. A map of all the congressional and legislative districts of the United States would by no means indicate the location of all the outrageous gerrymanders. In fact many of the worst ones have been so well designed that they come close within all constitutional requirements. They are made of compact and contiguous territory and have each a population as nearly equally divided as could be expected. The truth is, that the district system itself is so vicious that constitutional restrictions cannot keep it within just bounds. The national congress has attempted to do so by requiring that districts for congressional representatives must be compact and of contiguous territory and of nearly equal population. But the law is everywhere disregarded. Parties are compelled to disregard it, for a gerrymander in a democratic state can be nullified only by a gerrymander in a republican state.

As a result of the district system the House of Representatives in congress can scarcely be entitled to the honor of a representative body. It has never had a representation in proportion to the popular vote of political parties throughout the country, and at some elections a minority of the people have returned a majority of the representatives. This was most strikingly true of the noted Fifty-first congress in which a republican majority of three enacted the famous prohibitory tariff. That this tariff was opposed by a majority of the people is evidenced by the popular revulsion which at the next election returned a majority of 119 over all and a majority of 128 over the republicans. Such a political avalanche must have had deep causes, and these causes are well shown by the following table taken from an article by Mr. Stoughton Cooley in Belford's Magazine for December, 1891, wherein it appears that the acts of that congress were the work of a minority of the people.

FIFTY-FIRST CONGRESS, 1889-1891.

	ACTUAL.		PROPORTIONAL.			
	R.	D.	R.	D.	P.	U.L.
Alabama		8	3	5		
Arkansas		5	2	3		
California	4	2	3	3		
Colorado	1		1		•	
Connecticut	3	1	2	2		
Delaware		1		1		
Florida		2	1	1		
Georgia		10	3	7		
Illinois	13	7	10	9	1	
Indiana	3	10	7	6		
Iowa	10	1	6	5		
Kansas	7		4	2		1
Kentucky	2	9	5	6		
Louisiana	1	5	2	4		
Maine	4		2	2		
Maryland	2	4	3	3		
Massachusetts	10	2	7	5		
Michigan	9	2	5	5	1	
Minnesota	5		3	2		
Mississippi		7	2	5		
Missouri	4	10	6	7		1
Nebraska	3		2	1		
Nevada	1		1			
N. Hampshire	2		1	1		
N. Jersey	4	3	3	4		
N. York	19	15	17	16	1	
North Carolina	3	6	4	5		
Ohio	16	5	10	10	1	
Oregon	1		1			
Pennsylvania	21	7	15	12	1	
Rhode Island	2		1	1		
S. Carolina		7	1	6		
Tennessee	3	7	5	5		
Texas		11	3	7		1
Vermont	2		1	1		
Virginia	2	8	5	5		
West Virginia		4	2	2		
Wisconsin	7	2	5	4		
	164	161	154	163	5	3

This estimate is made upon the basis of the presidential vote for 1888 which stood Democrats 5,536,242, Republicans 5,440,708, giving, when allowance is made for minor parties, the Democrats 48·63% and the Republicans 47·83% of the total vote. Instead, therefore, of a Republican majority of three, and no representatives of the People's party or the Union Labor party, there should have been seven representatives of the latter two parties and a Democratic majority of two over all.

The unparalleled revolution which took place in the composition of the next congress, giving the Democrats a majority of 128 over the Republicans, likewise displays the fortuitous consequences of the district system. The Democratic minority of 49·6 . of the membership of the House was changed to a Democratic majority of 69·8%, but in the popular vote the democratic proportion of 48·63% of the total was changed only to a proportion of 55·3% of the total. In this fifty-second congress there were ninety-nine Republicans, 227 Democrats and nine Independent and Farmer's Alliance men, giving the Democrats a majority of 119 over all. If the popular strength had been truly represented the Republicans would have had 141 members, and the Democratic majority would have been only thirty-nine. As it was, 168 Democratic votes, giving a majority, were elected by fifteen southern states and the gerrymandered states of New York, New Jersey, Ohio and Indiana, where representation was a follows:—In New York, 500,395 Democrats sent twenty-three representatives, and 421,403 Republicans sent eleven representatives. In New Jersey, 128,417 Democrats sent five representatives and 114,808 Republicans only two. In Ohio a minority of 350,528 Democrats sent fourteen representatives, and a majority of 360,624 Republicans sent only half as many, while Indiana with a congressional vote of 239,858 Democrats and 216,766 Republicans sent eleven Democrats and only two Republicans. Consequently in this state one Democratic vote at the polls was equal to five Republicans. If representation had been proportional, New York would have sent eighteen Democrats and sixteen Republicans, New Jersey four Democrats and three Republicans, Ohio ten Democrats and eleven Republicans, and Indiana seven Democrats and six Republicans.

Mr. John M. Berry has pointed out in an interesting way that in the Fifty-second Congress "less than half who voted at the North secured 202 of the 211 representatives from that portion of the country," and that "3,172,999 citizens elected 167 representatives, a majority of the 332 in Congress from all the states, both North and South, while 3,304,692 who voted in 167 northern districts failed to elect any. . . One half the northern representatives were elected by less than a quarter of the northern voters, and more than twice as many who voted in the same states did not elect even one. . . In the northern states 2,703,976 votes elected 167 representatives, a majority of Congress from the North and South, while 3,420,246 in the north voting at the same time could not elect even one."

In the Fifty-third Congress, 1893–95, if we take the presidential vote as a basis of comparison, we get the following results:—

TICKET.	PRES. VOTE.	REPRESENTATIVES.	
		ACTUAL.	PROPORT'NAL.
Democrat	5,556,562	216	164†
Republican	5,162,874	129	152†
People's Party	1,055,424	8	31
Prohibition	264,066	0	8
Scattering	11,348	0	0
	12,150,274	353*	355

The Democrats, with 45·7 % of the votes, secured 61 % of the representatives, and a majority of 79 over all, whereas they should have lacked 28 of a majority. The Republicans, with 42·5 % of the votes, get only 33 % of the representatives; the People's Party, with 8·3 % of the votes, have only 2·2 % of the representatives, and the Prohibitionists, with 2 % of the votes, get no representatives, though entitled to eight.

The injustice of the district system is seen strikingly when we observe its effects on new parties or minority parties. Such parties suffer for two reasons. In the case of the dominant parties there is a rough equality, because a Democratic gerrymander in one state is likely to be balanced in another by a Republican gerrymander. But a new party cannot establish a gerrymander to suit itself, until it gets control of a state government. Also

* Two vacancies.
† The share of the "scattering" vote is assigned to the Democrats and Republicans.

a new party is usually scattered throughout a large number of districts and states, and the district system prevents them from combining to elect their fair share of representatives. For example, in the Fifty-first Congress the Prohibitionists should have had five representatives and the Union Labor party should have had three, whereas they received none, and in the Fifty-third Congress the People's party should have received thirty-one instead of only eight, and the Prohibitionists should have received eight instead of none.

Endless examples might be given from individual states to show the unrepresentative character of Congressional Representatives. Those states which are close in their political majorities, and whose legislatures alternate frequently, show an endless see-saw of gerrymanders. Ohio has perhaps had more of these partisan displays than any other state. It was during the war that the first Republican legislature overthrew a long standing Democratic districting act, the results of which were brought out forcibly by Mr. Garfield in a speech in Congress in 1870. He said :— " When I was first elected to Congress in the fall of 1862, the state of Ohio had a clear Republican majority of about 25,000, but by the adjustment and distribution of political power in the state there were fourteen Democratic representatives upon this floor and only five Republicans. The State that cast a majority of nearly 25,000 Republican votes was represented in the proportion of five representatives and fourteen Democrats. In the next Congress there was no great political change in the popular vote of Ohio—a change of only 20,000—but the result was that seventeen Republican members were sent here from Ohio and only two Democrats. We find that only so small a change as 20,000, changed their representatives in Congress from fourteen Democrats and five Republcians to seventeen Republicans and two Democrats.

" Now, no man, whatever his politics, can justly defend a system that may in theory, and frequently does in practice, produce such results as these."

The Republicans retained power in the Ohio legislature until 1876 with a consequent unfair advantage in the distribution of Congressional seats. In the latter year a Democratic legislature passed a new re-districting act. Since that time there have been eight re-districting acts, the results of which upon the fortunes of the two parties are depicted by the following statistical analysis :—

REPRESENTATION OF THE STATE OF OHIO IN CONGRESS.

	Congressional Vote.		Representatives. Actual. Proportional.				Acc. to Actual Representation.		
	Rep.	Dem.	R.	D.	R.	D.			
46th Cong. 1879-81..	277,875	264,737	9	11	10	10	1 D. vote=1¼	R. vote.
47th Cong. 1881-83..	405,042	340,572	15	5	11	9	1 R. " " 2⅔	D. "
48th Cong. 1883-85..	306,674	268,785	8	13	11	10	1 D. " " 2	R. "
49th Cong. 1885 87..	395,596	380,934	10	11	11	10	1 D. " " 1¼	R. "
50th Cong. 1887-89..	336,063	325,629	15	6	11	10	1 R. " " 2¼	D. "
51st Cong. 1889-91..	412,520	395,639	16	5	11	10	1 R. " " 3	D. "
52nd Cong. 1891-93..	362,624	350,528	7	14	11	10	1 D. " " 2¼	R. "
53rd Cong. 1893-95..	397,320	407,1.0	9	12	10	10*	1 D. " " 1⅓	R. "

* Prohibitionists get 1.

Representatives to the Fifty-third Congress were elected under a Republican act, and had it not been for a wholly unexpected increase of Democratic votes in several close districts there would have been a Republican advantage similar to those in the 47th, 50th, and 51st Congresses. It will be seen that the Democrats have been in a minority at every Congressional election except the last, yet in four out of the eight elections they have been able to return a majority of the representatives.

The following from a writer in the *Atlantic Monthly*, April 1892, brings out pointedly some of the inequalities of the present system.

The apportionment of 1880 gave to " Kansas seven representatives, which is at the rate of one for 14·3 voters in each hundred. In 1882, the Democrats of that State polled 32·2 votes of every hundred cast for Congressmen, but failed to elect one ; in 1884, they mustered 37·2 votes of every hundred cast, but it availed them nothing ; in 1886, they rolled up 40·3 votes of every hundred polled without breaking the solid Republican delegation ; and in 1888, they polled 31·9 out of every hundred votes cast, with the same result. Not since Kansas was admitted to the Union have the Democrats of that State had a representative in Congress, though they have polled at the different elections from thirty to forty of every hundred votes cast. Minnesota tells the same story. There being five representatives from that State, twenty votes in each hundred should have one ; but the Democrats, in 1882, cast 31·9 in every hundred, and in 1884, 40·9 in every hundred, without effect ; in 1886, owing to the curious make-up of these same districts, they elected two representatives, with a vote of 38·8 in the hundred ; in 1888, a vote of 41·2 in the hundred availed them nothing.

" That this result is not due to climate, altitude, or the innate depravity of the Republicans, Kentucky or any other Democratic State can testify. In 1876, the Republicans of Kentucky polled 34·9 votes of every hundred cast for Congressmen, but failed to elect one of the ten Congressmen, though ten votes in the hundred should have been sufficient to elect one. The same party, in 1878, cast 28·7 votes of every hundred, without effect. Since that time the Republican vote has ranged from thirty-two to forty in the hundred, securing them sometimes two, but more often one representative. In 1890, the Republicans of Missouri polled 39·8 per cent. of the total vote, but failed to elect one of the fourteen representatives from that State ; almost forty out of every hundred men voting cast their ballots for Republican candidates, and the whole was thrown away, though a trifle over seven in the hundred should have been sufficient to elect one. The Republicans of Indiana, in 1890, cast 45·8 votes in every hundred and elected two of the thirteen Congressmen ; 45·8 per cent. of the vote secured them 7·6 per cent. of the representation. In 1888, the same party in Michigan, with fifty per cent. of the vote, had eighty-two per cent. of the Congressmen ; in 1890, it cast forty-five per cent. of the votes, and got but twenty-seven per cent. of the representation ; with a loss of five per cent. of the vote, the party lost fifty-five per cent. of the representation."

In Missouri the Democrats elected the entire contingent of fourteen representatives, though the popular vote stood : Dem., 253,736 ; Rep., 184,337 ; Union Labour, 23,492.

In Indiana, in 1892, the Democrats cast for Congressmen 259,190 votes and elected eleven Congressmen ; the Republicans cast only 5,522 less votes, namely, 253,668, but elected only two Congressmen. It required 126,834 Republican votes to elect one Congressman against only 23,565 Democrat votes, in other words, one Dem. vote was worth 5·4 Rep. votes. The Democrats casting $47\frac{1}{2}$ of the total vote secured, $81\frac{4}{13}\%$ of the representatives, and the Republicans, with $46\frac{1}{2}\%$ of the vote, secured only $15\frac{4}{13}$ of the representatives. The smallest majority received by any Dem. candidate was forty-two, the largest was 3,081, whereas the smallest majority received by a Rep. candidate was 4,125, and the largest was 8,724.

The inequalities of the district system are not at all confined to the United States, though it is doubtful whether in any other country there have been such wide opportunities for the manipulation of the system. The following table, kindly furnished by the Statistician of the Dominion of Canada, through the request of Mr. Sandford Fleming, will show that the relative popular weight of parties is not represented in the Dominion House of Commons :—

CANADIAN GENERAL ELECTIONS, 1891 AND 1887.

1891.	Total Votes on Electoral Lists.	Increase over 1887.	Per Cent. Increase over 1887.	Total Votes Polled.	Vote for Government.	Vote for Opposition.	Majority for Government.	Majority for Opposition.
Canada....	1,132,201	138,287	13·9	730,457	378,355	352,102	27,692 +27,153	539
1887.								
Canada....	993,914	*190,327	23·62	725,056	370,342	354,714	‡15,628	....

No. of Members Elected.			Average Majorities.		No. of Members Elected with Majorities under 100.		No. of Elections by Acclamation.	
Total.	Gov't.	Oppos.	Gov't.	Oppos.	Gov't.	Oppos.	Gov't.	Oppos.
215	123	92	476	230	28	22	5	2
215	125	90	307	351	34	25	4	4

* Increase over 1882. † Net 1891. ‡ Net 1887.

It will be seen that in 1887 51·7% of the voters elected 57·2% of the representatives, and that the government majority of 31 should have been reduced to a majority of 9, the proportionate representation being 112 to 103. In the election of 1891, the government majority of 35 should have been only five, since the true proportion with reference to the popular vote was 110 to 104. In this election 51% of the voters elected 58·6% of the representatives.

Says Dr. Sandford Fleming regarding these two elections;* "The government had on this occasion (after the election of 1887) the largest support given to any administration since Canada became a Dominion; and yet, including every vote polled for government candidates who were defeated at the elections the supporters of the administration represented only 39% of the whole body of electors. The opposition members represented 37% of the whole, counting also the votes polled for the defeated candidates on their side. Thus it becomes perfectly obvious that a large majority of the people, whatever party may rule, has no part whatever through representatives, in the administration of public affairs. In the case referred to 61% of the whole body of electors had no share in the government of the country. The administration was supported by the representatives of 39% and it

* Address at Queen's University, 1891.

was opposed by those of 37% in every measure carried in the house by a party vote : leaving as a net balance the representatives of only 2% of the electors to determine legislation, to settle the policy of the government, and to speak and act for the nation, with the whole weight and supreme authority of parliament.   I have presented no extreme case.   If we take the results of the recent general elections (1891) it will be found that the number of votes cast for government candidates was only 33% of the electors, and the government net majority in the House represents but $1\frac{1}{2}$% of the total number of voters on the list."

Some interesting results for England are given by Sir John Lubbock in his excellent little book, Rrepresentation.*   In the parliamentary elections of 1886, there were contested 460 seats.   "The total number of votes given were 2,756,900 of which 423,500 were for Unionist, 1,333,400 for Home Rule candidates, or a majority of 90,000 voters for maintaining the Union.   According to the votes polled the number of members returned without a contest, viz : 111 Unionists and ninety-nine Home Rulers, would have given 349 Unionists, and 320 Home Rulers, or a majority of twenty-nine.   The actual numbers, however, were 394 Unionists and 275 Home Rulers.   The Unionists, therefore obtained forty-five seats more and the Home Rulers forty-five fewer seats than they were entitled to from the votes polled, making, of course, ninety on a division.   Thus, then, in 1874 the Conservatives obtained thirty-eight seats more than their votes entitled them to, counting seventy-six on a division ; in 1880, on the contrary, the Liberals had forty-four too many, counting eighty-eight on a division.   . . Thus whatever side has the majority, we are confronted with a violent contrast between the voting strength in the constituencies and the voting strength in the House of Commons.†

"In my own County of Kent," continues Sir John Lubbock, "the Liberals polled in the three divisions, at the last election, over 13,000 votes, against 16,000 given to their opponents, and yet the latter had all the six seats.   Taking all the contested seats in the county, the Liberals polled 32,000 votes against 36,000, and yet the Conservatives carried sixteen members and the liberals only two.‡

"At the general election in Ireland in 1880, eighty-six seats were contested.   Of these the Home Rulers secured fifty-two, the Liberals and conservatives together only thirty-four.   Yet the Home Rule electors were only 48,000, while the Liberals and Conservatives together were no less than 105,000.   . . If the uncontested seats were estimated for the results would remain the same." ‖

In the Italian elections of 1884, the popular vote stood in the proportion of 1·85 for the government to 1 for the opposition, but the representatives in the Chamber of Deputies was 5·19 for the government to one for the opposition.

These election results are enough to show that in all countries the people are not actually represented in their legislative assemblies.   This is true whether the gerrymander is employed or not.   Perhaps, taking a nation as a whole, the gerrymanders of the United States do not affect the average result, since, as already shown, both parties practise it, and the work of one is offset by that of another.   The inequality lies in the very nature of the district system of election.

State legislatures show even greater inequalities in the constitution of their legislative bodies than do national legislatures.

Mr. Berry summarizes the vote in Massachusetts as follows :   At the state election of 1892, 162,028 votes elected thirty-five out of forty senators, while 166,776 votes were cast for defeated candidates and 89,391 votes (less than one-fourth of those cast) elected twenty-one senators, a majority of the forty.   116,708 Republican voters elected twenty-five Republican senators while 119,045 Democratic votes failed to elect the Democratic candidates for whom they were cast.

The Democratic vote was 165,606, and ten Democratic senators were elected.   Thus an average of 16,560 votes were required to elect a Democratic senator.   The Republican vote was 185,479, and thirty Republican senators were elected.   Thus an average of only 6,182 votes was required to elect a Republican senator.   A Republican vote was therefore

---

* The Imperial Parliament Series, London, Swan Sonnenschein & Co. 1890.
† Preface.
‡ Page 17.
‖ Page 19.

worth more than $2\frac{2}{3}$ times as much as a Democratic vote. " A change of less than $1\frac{1}{2}$ of the vote in twenty-one districts from the candidate elected to the next higher candidate would have elected the latter, and a majority of the senate would then be made up from the opponents of the candidates actually elected. A similar change of $6\frac{1}{4}\%$ in all the districts would have defeated every senator elected, and made his opponent a senator."

Municipal elections give results equally disproportionate with state and national. The Chicago elections for aldermen in 1891 were as follows:

	Total Vote.	Elected.	Proportional.
Democratic	67,024	21	15
Republican	63,721	11	14
Socialist	3,114	0	1
Independent ..	4,495	0	1
U. C.	1,308	0	0
C. D.	14,022	1	3

In the actual results of the election, it required 3,191 Democrats to elect one alderman, 5,793 Republicans, and 7,011 C.D., while Socialists and Independents were wholly deprived of their rightful share of representation.

All these statistics go to prove conclusively the excessive inequality and minority domination of the present system wherever applied. But we have not yet reached the end of the story of minority rule under this system. We must enter the legislative halls in order to see the final chapter. To say nothing further of the rule by the speaker of the house and by the legislative committees by which power is taken out of the hands of the assembly itself, there is on all party questions the *imperium in imperio* of the party caucus. If one party in a legislature has sixty representatives out of 100, the policy of the legislature is not dictated by an open conference of the sixty with the forty, but, the majority party withdraws, and in secret conclave determines by a majority vote what shall be its united action. Thus thirty-five members—a majority of the sixty—may determine the policy of the legislature and enact the laws of the people.

This is no fanciful sketch. The power of the party caucus is well known. A man who " bolts " the caucus can have no influence whatever in legislation. He is sure to have several measures of his own which he is anxious to have enacted into laws. There may be appropriations of money for improvements or for state or national institutions in his own district. They may be good measures or they may be bad. But he knows that in order to carry them he cannot afford to stand out against the wishes of his fellow partisans on other measures. Thus every representative is in the complete power of his party caucus. He cannot stay out of the caucus, and when he enters he must agree to abide by its decisions. To say that legislatures are deliberative assemblies under such circumstances is the keenest of irony. They are rather war-camps. Deliberation involves consultation between opposing interests and opinions and the development of a compromise policy which will be modified more or less by all who have a voice. But the caucus rule, dominated in the interests of the party rather than of the people, begets intolerance and the overriding of minorities. The party emerges from its caucus like an army from its fortress, runs upon the enemy, listens to no cry for quarter or compromise, beheads its own deserters, and then carouses over its own victory.

CHAPTER IV.

THE GENERAL TICKET.

Enough has been said to show the army of evils which spring from the single district system. These evils have not escaped observation, and various attempts have been made to modify them. Especially in France have very interesting experiments been made by the substitution of " *Scrutin de Liste* " or the " general ticket." Under this method each constituency elects several members, each elector has as many votes as there are members to be elected, and those candidates are declared elected whose votes stand at the head of the list. In this way the majority party gets the entire list and the minority is wholly unrepresented.

There are two applications in this system which lead to important differences in the final results. The first is that adopted in several instances in the United States in the election of Boards of county commissioners and Boards of Education, where the entire legislative assembly is elected on a single ticket. With such a system the question of equal representation plays no part whatever. The minority parties are without a single representative. But the system usually results in the election of abler men than the district system. This would naturally be expected from what has already been said on this point. A party in making nominations for a large area cannot afford to nominate obscure men. For example, the city of Cleveland, Ohio, recently introduced, by the sanction of the state legislature, a far reaching reform in the system of public schools, one feature of which was the abandonment of the district system of electing the school board and the adoption of the general ticket. In the elections which have followed, it is acknowledged on all sides that far abler men were nominated by all parties, and the new boards have been remarkably superior in quality to the old. But the results have been as follows : figures being given for the election of the year 1892 :—

REPUBLICAN.		DEMOCRATIC.	
Bass	15,714	Dodge	13,661
Boutelle	15,595	Goulder	13,551
Backus	15,385	Pollner	13,306
House	15,860	Ryan	12,851
Daykin	16,198	Burke	12,814
McMillan	15,690	Hoffman	12,777
Ford	16,036	Plent	12,804
Total	110,518	Total	91,764

It will be seen that the Republicans obtained the entire board, but had there been a change of only 1,000 to 2,000 votes from Republicans to Democrats the Democrats would have carried their entire list.

The Cook County (Ill.) Commissioners are elected on a general ticket with the result that in 1892, the Democrats with a vote of 133,000 elected their entire list, and the Republicans with 100,000 voters were unrepresented.

The second application of the general ticket is a combination of the district and the general ticket. Districts are made larger and a solid delegation of from five to twenty representatives is sent to the legislature, representing of course only the majority or plurality party of their district. For example, the County of Cuyahoga (including the city of Cleveland) sends repeatedly a solid delegation of six Republicans to the Ohio state legislature, and not one Democrat. The county of Hamilton (including the city of Cincinnati) sends a solid delegation of nine Democrats.

Representatives to Congress in the first half century of our constitutional history were elected by this system. Each state sent to Congress a solid delegation of one party or another, elected either by the state legislatures or by popular vote. So unjust did it prove to be that gradually the single district system was substituted by individual state action, and finally in 1842 Congress made the latter obligatory on all the states.

Presidential electors are still elected by this system, though the state of Michigan made in the election of 1892 a notable departure by substituting the single district system. The legislature of 1893, however, controlled by the opposing party, has repealed the law and returned to the general ticket.

It will, of course, be observed, that a legislative body elected upon this basis will not wholly exclude a minority party. Indeed, the experience of France seems to show that as far as equality of representation is concerned, the general ticket—*scrutin de liste*—is as good as the single district ticket—*scrutin d'arrondissement*. In the election of members to the Chamber of Deputies in 1885, conducted on *scrutin de liste* the Republicans with 4,300,000 votes obtained 366 seats, whereas their numbers entitled them to only 311.

while the conservative-monarchists with 3,550,000 votes obtained 202 seats against their rightful proportion of 257. The general ticket was abandoned in 1889, after the trial of only this one election, and the French method at present is the same as that of other countries.

But the general ticket is wholly erratic and vicious. Sir John Lubbock gives the following account of the Belgian election in 1884 based on this method. He says ; * "The Chamber is elected in sections, and in June, 1884, fifty-two seats were contested with the following result :—

RESULTS OF THE BELGIAN ELECTIONS OF JUNE, 1884.

	ANTI-MINISTERIALISTS.			MINISTERIALISTS.	
	Voters.	Elected.		Voters.	Elected.
Bruxelles....	9,311	.. 16	....	7,924	.. 0
Louvain.....	2,340	.. 5	....	1,211	. 0
Nivelles	1,655	... 4	....	1,568	.. 0
Bruges	1,658	.. 3	....	1,024	.. 0
Ostende.....	572	. 1	....	556	.. 0
Ypres.......	1,182	.. 3	....	690	.. 0
Arlon.......	240	.. 0	....	334	.. 1
Harche	282	.. 1	....	229	.. 0
Neufchâteau .	331	.. 1	....	286	.. 0
Virtors......	293	.. 0	....	300	.. 1
Dinant	818	.. 2	....	502	.. 0
Namur......	1,825	.. 4	....	1,522	.. 0
Phillippeville.	605	.. 2	....	536	.. 0
Anvers	6,818	.. 8	....	5,405	.. 0
Total.....	27,930	50	Total.....	22,117	2

According to their just proportion, the Anti-Ministerialists ought to have carried 30 seats out of the 52, but they actually secured all but two.

This election took place in June. In the following month the same constituencies had to elect representatives in the Senate. Warned by their recent defeat, the Ministerialists exerted themselves to the utmost, and polled 6,000 more votes. This increase, small as it was, turned the scale, and this time they secured 19 seats out of 31.

RESULTS OF THE BELGIAN ELECTIONS OF JULY, 1884.

	ANTI-MINISTERIALISTS.			MINISTERIALISTS.	
	Voters.	Members.		Voters.	Elected.
Bruxelles....	8,969	.. 0	....	9,517	.. 8
Nivelles	1,552	.. 0	....	1,650	.. 2
Gand.......	3,926	.. 4	....	3,547	.. 0
Ostende.....	569	.. 1	....	548	.. 0
Soignies	1,365	.. 2	....	1,246	.. 0
Charleroi....	2,728	.. 0	....	2,855	.. 3
Ath........	895	.. 1	....	875	.. 0
Liège.......	2,477	.. 0	....	3,800	.. 4
Huy	596	.. 0	....	658	.. 1
Verviers	1,803	.. 2	....	1,620	.. 0
Namur......	1,746	.. 2	....	1,558	.. 0
Arlon.......	560	.. 0	....	593	.. 1
Total.....	27,186	12	Total.....	28,467	19

* Representation, pp. 29-31.

Thus the city of Brussels in June sent all its 16 members to oppose the Government in the Chamber ; while in July it sent its eight senators to support them ; so that it is now represented by 16 Conservatives in the Chamber and eight Liberals in the Senate.

Nor are results of this character at all unprecedented ; for instance, in the elections of June, 1882, 29,142 Liberals secured 39 seats, while 28,052 Conservatives only carried 11.

CHAPTER V.

PROPORTIONAL REPRESENTATION.

The general ticket thus shows itself to be crude and barbarous. But it offers an opportunity to introduce with the very slightest of amendments what is destined to prove the most important reform in government since the invention of representation itself. It is an amendment which naturally suggests itself to any one who examines the results of an election on the general ticket. This reform is simply the apportionment of representatives among the different parties on a general ticket in exact proportion to their popular vote. Take, for example, the election already cited, for members of the Cleveland school board.* There are seven members to be elected. Each party nominates seven candidates. Why should it not naturally occur to distribute the successful candidates between the two parties in such a way that the Republicans with 110,518 votes would obtain four members, and the Democrats with 91,764 votes would obtain three members ? This would give each party its fair share of representatives. The total number of votes is 202,286. This divided by seven gives 28,898 as the number required to elect a single candidate. The shares of each party would be determined by dividing in turn their total votes by this quotient, with the following results :

Republican Vote.	110,518÷28,898	3	remainder of	23,824
Democratic "	91,764÷28,898	3	" "	5,070
Total		6		

There being seven to elect and the Republicans having the largest remainder above the three full quotas are entitled to the remaining candidate, giving them four members and the democrats three. The individual candidates elected would be discovered by taking those on each ticket whose vote stands the highest, namely, Republicans, Daykin, Ford, House, and Buss, Democrats, Dodge, Goulder and Pollner.

Could anything be fairer or more natural than this ? Nothing whatever is left to chance. Equality is assured as exact as mathematics can make it. Each party elected its own most popular candidates. The transition from the *form* of the present system is scarcely noticeable, but the transition from its *essence* is profound and far-reaching.

But it must be confessed that a scheme so simple and just as proportional representation requires a multitude of minds and a depth of thought for its perfection. The simplest things in politics as in mechanics are the last to be thought of. Besides there are many details in the election machinery which must be carefully worked out in order to give the greatest freedom to the voters and obviate every possible blunder. In the proposed bill which follows is incorporated the points which seem best and simplest for attaining the desired object, borrowing them from whatever source they may be found. The bill is given here in full, and comment upon its several features is reserved until the reader has surveyed it as a whole. But it may be well first to designate the sources from which its distinctive features have been derived. The machinery of nomination and election and the common official ballot are drawn from the secret ballot law of the state of Indiana, probably the best law of its kind in the United States. Many of the proportional features correspond with the admirable law for the election of deputies to the Grand Council which went into effect on the 3rd of September, 1892 in the canton of Geneva. The

* Page 154.

157

provision for cumulation of votes is borrowed from a bill drawn up by Dr. L. B Tucker-man and Mr. Webster, of Cleveland, Ohio, and introduced by Hon. Tom Johnson in the House of Representatives in June, 1892. A similar device has also been proposed by Mr. Westlake, of the English Proportional Representation Society. The details for the application of the cumulative vote, the plan for the exclusion of a minority party having less than 85% of a full quota of votes and many other details are the work of the present writer.

The bill is made applicable to the election of representatives for the lower branch of the American Congress. In this respect it will correspond exactly (with the proper modifications as to officials, etc.) to the election of the representatives to the House of Commons of the Dominion of Canada. Both these governments being federal governments, it is believed that there should be retained a proper recognition of state and provincial boundaries. Hence a general ticket is not provided for the nation at large, but as many tickets as there are states and provinces. The application of the principle to state and municipal legislatures will require minor modifications, which will be noticed later.

A BILL

For the Election of Congressional Representatives by Proportional Representation.

Sec. 1. Be it enacted by the Senate and House of Rrepresentatives of the United States of America in Congress assembled. That members of the House of Represent-atives shall be voted for at large on general lists of candidates for their respective states, and that representatives shall be apportioned to different lists in proportion to the votes cast for each list.

Sec. 2. There shall be created in each State a State Board of Election Commissioners, to be composed of the Governor of the State and two qualified electors by him appointed, one from each of the two political parties that cast the largest number of votes in the State at the last preceding general election. Such appointments shall be made at least thirty days prior to the general election for Congressional Representatives, and if prior to that time the chairman of the State Central Committee of either of such parties shall nominate in writing a member of his own party for such appointment the governor of the State shall appoint such nominee. In case of death or inability of any such appointee, the Governor of the State shall notify the chairman of the said Central Committee of such appointee's political party, and such chairman may, within three days thereafter, recom-mend a successor who shall thereupon be appointed. *Provided* that if such chairman shall fail to make recommendations of appointment within the time specified, the Governor of the State shall make such appointment of his own selection from such political party. It shall be the duty of said Board to prepare and distribute ballots and stamps for the election of all Congressmen for whom all the electors of the State are entitled to vote, in compliance with the provisions of this election law. The members of such board shall serve without compensation.

Sec. 3. That lists of candidates to be known in this bill as "tickets," may be nomi-nated by State conventions or by petitions as hereinafter provided, and any number of candidates, not to exceed the number of seats to which such State is entitled in the House of Representatives, may be included in a single ticket.

Sec. 4. The said Board of Election Commissioners for each State shall cause to be printed on a single sheet of paper of appropriate size, to be known in this Act as the "ballot," tickets nominated by the State conventions of any party that cast one per cent. of the total vote of the State at the last preceding general election, the said ticket to be certified as heinafter specified to the said Board by the presiding officer and secretary of such convention; and also the list of names of candidates when petitioned so to do by electors qualified to vote for such candidates, providing the number of said electors signing such petition amounts to fifty petitioners for each representative to which the State is entitled. The signatures to such petition need not be appended to one paper, but no petitioner shall be counted, except his residence and post office address be designated. No petitioner can subscribe his name to more than one list of candidates. Each petition must designate one of the petitioners who shall act as attorney for the others. Such petition shall state the name and residence of each of such candidates, that he is legally qualified to hold such office ; that the subscribers desire and are legally qualified to vote for such candidates, and may designate a brief name or title of the party or principle which said candidates represent, together with any simple figure or device by which they shall be designated on the ballots.

The certificate of nomination by a convention shall be in writing, and shall contain the name of each person nominated and his residence, and shall designate a title for the party or principle which convention represents, together with any simple figure or device by which its ticket may be designated on the ballots ; said certificates shall be signed by the presiding officer and secretary of such convention, who shall add to their signatures their respective places of residence, and acknowledge the same before an officer duly authorized to take acknowledgment of deeds. A certificate of such acknowledgment shall be appended to such instrument.

In case of the death, resignation, or removal of any candidate subsequent to nomination, unless a supplemental certificate or petition of nomination be filed, the chairman of the State committee or the attorney of the group of petitioners shall fill such vacancy.

In case of a division in any party, and claim by two or more factions to the same party name, or title, or figure, or device, the Board of Election Commissioners shall give the preference of name to the convention held at the time and place designated in the call of the regularly constituted party authorities, and if the other faction shall present no other party name, title or device, the Board of Election Commissioners shall select a name or title and place the same at the head of the ticket of said faction on the ballot and select some suitable device to designate its candidates. If two or more conventions be called by authorities claimed to be the rightful authorities of the party, the Board of Election Commissioners shall select some suitable devices to distinguish one faction from the other, and print the ballots accordingly—*Provided, however,* that if any political party entitled to nominate by convention shall in any case fail to do so, the names of all nominees by petition who shall be designated in their petitions as members of and candidates of such party, shall be printed under the device and title of such party on the ballots, as if nominated by convention.

Certificates and petitions of nomination of candidates shall be filed with the governor of the State at least thirty days before the election.

The tickets which shall be presented as above provided for, shall be printed by the Board of Election Commissioners on a single ballot, each ticket being assigned a separate column, and the names of candidates on each ticket shall be printed in the order in which they are assigned by the respective conventions or groups of petitioners.

In all respects otherwise than as provided for in this Act the elections of representatives in the several States shall be conducted in accordance with the State laws enacted and provided for the election of representatives to Congress. But no election shall be valid in which the provision of this Act shall not be fully complied with.*

Sec. 5. If the name of any candidate appears on more than one ticket, he shall select the ticket to which he wishes his votes to be accredited. In case he makes no selection, the governor shall notify the chairman of the committees or the attorneys of the petitioners on whose tickets his name appears, and they shall make a choice. In default of such a choice. the governor shall select by lot one of the tickets in which his name appears, and the said name shall be struck off from the other tickets.

Sec. 6. Not less than eighteen days before the election for representatives, the Governor of the State shall certify to the County Clerk of each County the name and place of residence of each person nominated for representative, as specified in the petitions and certificates of nominations filed with the Governor of the State, and shall designate therein the device under which the ticket or list of candidates of each party will be printed, and the order in which they will be arranged. Not less than ten days before the election, the

---

* In case of Canada, the elections shall be conducted in accordance with "The Dominion Elections Act," except as amended in harmony with the present Act.

county clerks shall make public notice in all election precincts, by bulletin, giving in full the lists of candidates, their residence, and the titles and devices prefixed to each ticket as certified to them by the governor.

SEC. 7. The State Board of Election Commissioners shall furnish, at least ten days before the election, to each County Clerk to be distributed by him to the inspectors of the several election precincts, ten ballots for every five voters or fraction thereof in each precinct of his County at the last presidential election. And no ballots shall be received by the judges and inspectors of elections from electors except official ballots as herein provided.

SEC. 7. Every legal elector shall be entitled to cast one ballot, but he shall be entitled to as many votes upon his ballot as there are representatives to be elected from the State whereof he is a resident. This number shall be known in this Act as his "lawful number of votes." All votes in excess of this number shall be discarded.

Every elector shall be entitled to two kinds of votes, namely: votes for tickets, known in this Act as "ticket votes" and votes for individual candidates, known in this Act as "candidate votes." The elector shall be entitled to a number of ticket votes equal to his lawful number of votes and also to a number of candidate votes equal to his lawful number of votes, and he may divide his votes between tickets and individual candidates as hereinafter specified.

SEC. 8. In order to give his total lawful number of votes to a single ticket the elector shall affix a mark or stamp immediately to the left of the title and device belonging to the ticket for which he wishes to vote. This shall be known as a "general ticket vote." In the case of a general ticket vote the total lawful number of votes shall be accredited to the ticket, unless the elector shall have voted also for individual candidates on the said ticket or on other tickets as hereinafter provided, in which case, there shall be deducted from the total lawful number of his general ticket votes all such votes for individual candidates.

SEC. 9. Each elector is entitled to vote for individual candidates, either on the same ticket as that for which he has given his general ticket vote or for candidates on other tickets, and he may distribute his votes or cumulate his votes among the candidates of all the tickets in such manner as he chooses.

To vote for individual candidates he shall affix a mark or stamp immediately to the left of the name of the candidate for whom he wishes to vote. To cumulate on one or more candidates he shall write immediately to the left of the name of each candidate for whom he cumulates, a numerical figure expressing the number of votes which he wishes to have accredited to the particular candidate.

SEC. 10. All votes for individual candidates up to the lawful number of votes shall be counted also as ticket votes, and each ticket shall be accredited, in addition to the general ticket votes herein provided for, also with a number of votes equal to the sum of the candidate votes given to its individual candidates.

Should the sum of elector's votes for individual candidates, as expressed by a mark, stamp or numerical figure, be less than his lawful number of votes, additional votes enough to make a sum equal to his lawful number of votes shall be accredited as general ticket votes to that ticket to which he has given a general ticket vote as provided in Section 8, or, in case he has not given a general ticket vote, to that ticket for whose candidate he has given the largest number of votes. Should his votes for candidates on different tickets be equal in number, provided he has not given a general ticket vote, then his remaining ticket votes shall be equally divided between the tickets for which he voted, and any odd votes shall be accredited to one of the said tickets by lot.

SEC. 11. Should the sum of the votes which the elector allots to individual candidates exceed the total number of his lawful votes, only the highest number shall be counted where the elector has cumulated his votes, until a sum is reached equal to his lawful votes.

Where the elector has given single votes to candidates in excess of his lawful votes, only those votes shall be counted up to the number of lawful votes which are found allotted to candidates on those tickets to which the elector has given the largest number of votes.

SEC. 12. The following ballots are void :—

        1. Ballots having no mark or stamp or numerical figure against the titles of tickets or the names of candidates.

        2. Ballots other than those furnished by the State Board of Election Commissioners.

  SEC. 13. At the close of the polls, the judges of elections in the precincts shall determine the following points and make report to the county clerk, who shall transmit the reports of all the precincts in his county to the Secretary of State of each State, and the said Secretary of State shall thereupon canvass the votes and determine for the entire State, the same points as were determined for the several precincts by the precinct judges, to-wit :—

      1. The number of valid ballots having a mark, stamp, or numerical figure.

      2. The number of void ballots.

      3. The total number of valid votes which should be expressed, obtained by multiplying the number of valid ballots which have been voted by the total number of representatives to be elected.

      4. The number of tickets and the number of candidates on each ticket.

      5. The number of votes given by name to individual candidates.

      6. The number of general ticket votes given to the respective tickets, as provided in sections 7, 8, 10, and 12.

In the final addition of votes, the votes given by names to individual candidates, and the votes given to the tickets in general should correspond exactly to the total number of valid votes which should be expressed.

The Secretary of State of each State shall thereupon as provided by law in each State, for general elections, proceed to determine the number of representatives to be accredited to each ticket and the individual candidates who have been elected, as provided in the following sections of this Act.

SEC. 14. The total number of valid ballots which have been cast throughout the State shall be known as the " first quota of representation."

No ticket shall be entitled to representation, the sum of whose votes is less than 85% of the first quota of representation. If there are any such tickets, the votes which have been given to them shall be deducted from the total number of votes which have been given to all the tickets, and the quotient obtained by dividing this remainder by the number of representatives to be elected, will give a quotient which shall be known as the " second quota of representation." In case any lists are excluded from representation as herein provided, the total number of votes obtained severally by the remaining tickets shall each be divided by the second quota of representation, and the units of the quotients thus obtained will show the number of representatives to which the respective tickets are entitled.

Where there have been no tickets excluded as herein provided, the first quota of representation shall be used as a divisor instead of the second quota, and the number of representatives to be allotted to each ticket shall be determined by dividing the total number of votes obtained by the several tickets by the first quota of representation and the units of the quotients thus obtained will show the number of representatives to which the respective tickets are entitled.

If the sum of such quotients be less than the number of seats to be filled, the ticket having the largest remainder after the division of its total ticket votes by the quota of representation as herein specified, shall be entitled to the first vacancy, the ticket having the next largest remainder, the next vacancy, and so on until all the vacancies are filled, providing that no representative be allotted a ticket whose total vote is less than 85% of the first quota of representation, as herein provided.

SEC. 15. When the number of representatives to be accredited to each ticket is determined as specified in Section 14, the individual candidates of each of the said tickets who have received the largest number of votes shall receive from the Governor of the State certificates of election in the order of the vote received, the candidate receiving the highest number of votes the first certificate, and so on, until the total number of representatives to be accredited to the several tickets has been selected.

If there is a tie between two or more candidates on the same ticket, the older candidate shall receive the certificate of election.

Sec. 16. If a ticket shall have elected more representatives than the number of candidates which it presents, the number of representatives in excess shall be apportioned to other tickets on the same proportional plan as herein specified.

Sec. 17. The names of the candidates not elected on each ticket shall be filed on record by the Secretary of State together with the figures indicating the respective numbers of their votes.

Whenever a vacancy occurs between the elections for Congressional representatives, either through non-acceptance, resignation, incapacity, removal or decease, the candidate who received at the general election the largest number of votes after the last one elected on the ticket in which the vacancy occurs, shall be chosen to fill the vacancy, and shall receive from the Governor of the State a certificate of election for the said unexpired term.

Example.—It is believed that the terms of the bill are sufficiently clear to obviate any detailed explanation of its provisions. But it is quite necessary that the reader be furnished with a practical display of the way in which it would operate if carried into effect. Hence I have subjoined the following sample ballot and a supposed election based upon the same, in a State which is entitled to fifteen Congressmen :—

Sample Ballot 1:—

Vote for a list, or give fifteen votes to individual candidates.

	Dem.	Rep.	Prohi.	People's	Ind. Rep.
I.	Adams	1 Clark	Madison	Fuller	5 Gray
II.	Allen	Butler	Montgomory	Pendleton	McDowell
III.	Williams	1 Carroll	Stark	Wilson	
IV.	Putman	Meigs		Patterson	
V.	Ross	Mercer		Enloe	
VI.	Monroe	Knox			
VII.	Lawrence	Jackson			
VIII.	Logan	1 Holmes			
IX.	Hancock	3 Fairchild			
X	Hardin				

This ballot gives twelve votes for individual candidates, five being cumulated on Gray and three on Fairchild. It gives also five votes for the Independant Republican ticket, and ten votes for the Republican ticket, being seven votes for Republican candidates and three ticket votes for the Republican ticket.

Sample Ballot 2 :—

TOTAL VOTES FOR CANDIDATES AND TICKETS.

	DEM.	REP.	PROHI.	PEOPLE'S.	IND. REP.
I.	382,346	203,414	46,213	250,005	444,671
II.	126,071	112,623	10,711	90,674	2,234
III.	211,321	93,788	8,342	......	......
IV.	89,077	56,712	......	104,399	......
V.	97,240	55,830	......	21,312	......
VI.	101,134	61,221	......	......	......
VII.	56,731	75,631	......	......	......
VIII.	571,000	173,211	......	......	......
IX.	134,203	75,398	. ....	......	......
X.	106,703	......	... ..	......	......
General Ticket Votes.	913,315	1,361,425	269,434	311,820	2,731
Total......	2,889,240	2,402,720	334,700	800,431	449,636

FINAL ADDITION OF VOTES.

Democrat	2,889,240
Republican	2,402,720
Prohibition	334,700
People's	800,431
Independent Republican	449.636
Total	6,776,730
Valid ballots	451,782
1st or full quota of Representation	451,782

Prohibition vote being less than 384,014—85% of the full quota—is deducted from the total vote, leaving a remainder of 6,442,030. This divided by 15 gives the 2nd quota of Representation 429,468.

SAMPLE BALLOT 3 :—

Dem. list having	2,889,240÷429,468	obtains	6+	remainder	312,232	votes.
Rep. "	2,402,720÷429,468	"	5+	"	254,980	"
Peo. "	800,431÷429,468	"	1+	"	370,963	"
Ind. R. "	449,636÷429,468	"	1+	"	20,168	"

Total 13

There are but thirteen full quotas, and the remaining two seats are accredited in order to the People's and the Democratic list, giving a final result :

Democratic	7	Representatives.
Republican	5	"
People's	2	"
Independent R.	1	"
Total	15	

The individual candidates elected in the order of their votes on the respective lists are :

> Democrat—Logan, Adams, Williams, Hancock, Allen, Hardin, Monroe.
> Republican—Clark, Holmes, Butler, Carroll, Jackson.
> People's—Fuller, Patterson.
> Independent Rep.—Gray.

Vacancies before the next election would be filled as follows :—

> Democrat, Ross.
> Republican, Jackson.
> People's, Pendleton.
> Independent Rep., McDowell.

Before entering upon the consideration of the advantages offered by the legal adoption of a bill like the foregoing, there are one or two details which should be cleared up. If proportional representation is advanced as a means of securing justice to all political parties, why should a minority party be excluded when its total vote is less than 85% of a full quota? This is not a feature of the Swiss method nor of the Johnson bill, though a complicated plan for effecting the same result has been proposed by the Belgian writer, M. V. D'Hondt and has been approved by *L'Association réformiste belge pour la representation proportionelle*. I have given in an appendix* the substance of M. V. D'Hondt's plan, and shall pause here a moment to justify the device which I have proposed.

---

* See page 183.

In the first place, exact justice is impossible. A representative is non-fungible. He cannot be devided up like a bushel of wheat and distributed in exact proportions among all his rightful claimants. We must be satisfied with a combination of justice and expediency. The claims of justice are absolutely secured by that portion of the scheme which gives representatives to all groups of electors in proportion to the full quotas which they can muster. That portion of votes which does not come up to a full quota must be satisfied by a division based mainly on expediency. And it seems that the highest efficiency of government would be secured by preventing too excessive influence to petty minorities.

Moreover, it is not clear that the rule given works any injustice. The comparison is not properly to be made between a party, on the one hand, whose total vote is less than the full quota and those remainders of other parties, on the other hand, which are less than a full quota.* The just comparison is between the said minority party and the *average number of votes required to elect a candidate* in the other parties. If a party having less than a full quota is able to elect a candidate by means of a number of votes less than the average number required in other parties there would be injustice. It is believed that on the whole a minimum of 85% would prevent such inequalities.

The present district system works serious injustice to all new and diminutive parties, but that is not a good reason for going to the other extreme and giving these parties an influence excessive beyond their numbers. If once they reach the dimensions of a full quota their claim is indefeasible. Before they reach that figure they should live by sufferance.

But the question is one of degree. The line should be drawn somewhere. 85% may seem too high, and it might be placed even lower, say 75%. In the example given this would still exclude the Prohibition list, since 75% of the first quota is 338,836, whereas if the limit were not imposed at all, they would gain one representative. In the same election given herewith, the apportionment would have been different if the first quota had been employed as in the Swiss laws instead of the second, as shown by the following. the divisor being 451,782 :—

Democratic list obtains	6+	remainder	178,558
Republican list obtains	5+	"	143,810
Prohibitionist list obtains	0+	"	334,700
People's list obtains	1+	"	348,649
Ind. Republican list obtains	0+	"	449,636
Total	12		

The additional three representatives would be apportioned so that the result would stand :

Democrat	6	representatives
Republican	5	"
Prohibitionist	1	"
People's	2	"
Ind. Republican	1	"
Total	15	

If, now, we weigh the influence of the voters of the different parties on the final result according to the Swiss method, we get the following :—

To elect one Democrat requires	481,540	votes
" Republican requires	480,544	"
" Prohibitionist requires	334,700	"
" People's requires	100,215½	"
" Ind. Republican requires	449,636	"

* See page 164 below.

Is this result more just than the one obtained by the method herein proposed, where

To elect one Democrat requires .... 412,748½ votes
"   Republican requires .... 480,544 "
"   People's requires .... 400,215½ "
"   Ind. Republican requires .... 419,636 "

The matter may be stated in another way. Since each elector casts fifteen votes, the actual number of electors who voted for each ticket was as follows :—

Democrats 192,616
Republicans. 160,181
Prohibitionists............................. 22,313
People's 53,362
Ind. Republicans........................... 29,975

According to the Swiss method 22,313 Prohibitionists would have been entitled to one representative. If so, then 133,878 Democrats ought to be entitled to six representatives. But there were 192,616 Democrats. Consequently, 58,738 Democrats would be without their proportionate share of representatives, compared with the Prohibitionists.

But it may be said that in depriving the Prohibitionists of a representative and giving the Democrats an additional one the equality between Democrats and Republicans is disturbed to the disadvantage of the Republicans. This is true, but not to so great an extent as would have been the inequality of Republicans compared with Prohibitionists, had the latter received a representative. It requires 32,036 Republicans to elect a single representative and the Prohibitionists could have elected one with 22,313 electors, whereas under the plan here proposed it requires 26,849 Democrats to equal 32,036 Republicans, a difference in favor of this plan on the score of justice of 21%.

The ground for the whole distinction consists in the fact that a remainder in the case of a large party, is averaged with several full quotas, so that the average constituency of a representative is but little short of the full quota itself, whereas in the case of a party whose total vote is less than a full quota the total vote itself becomes the "average" constituency, and this, not being averaged with any full quotas, may fall considerably below the averages for other parties. To obviate such inequality the 85% exclusion is eminently fair.

Another feature of the bill as distinguished from the Swiss system is the provision made to prevent an elector from losing on any account any one of his full number of lawful votes. So long as his ballot is declared lawful and he is entitled to vote at all, he should be entitled to his full number of votes, and any oversight or misunderstanding on his part should not operate to deprive him of them. It is believed that the rules laid down are sufficiently reasonable to interpret what would have been the wishes of the average elector should he happen to make actual use of only a part of his lawful votes. It is this feature of the bill, as will be readily seen, which results in the identity between the total number of ballots cast and the first quota of representation.

The bill as herein given has been adapted to the National Congress, but it is easy to translate it into terms of State legislatures and city councils For American State legislatures it would prove desirable to adapt the plan to the bicameral system and to make as marked a distinction as possible between the upper and the lower house. State senates could be elected on a general ticket for the State at large, in exactly the same way that the Congressional delegation would be elected. This could very easily be done, as the membership in the senates now varies in number in the different States, from thirty-two in New York to fifty in Pennsylvania, Indiana and Iowa. Perhaps a senate of thirty-five would prove the most convenient. This would give the voters of the two great parties fifteen to twenty senators to choose.

The lower house should be elected by a combination of the district system and the general ticket, like the national house. The State could be divided into such a number of districts that each district would return from seven to eleven representatives. The larger the number returned from each district, the smaller, of course, would be any unrepresented remainder. The lower houses in the State legislatures vary widely in membership, ranging from thirty-five in Wyoming, to 359 in New Hampshire. The latter State might properly be divided into twenty districts.

With this two-fold application of the plan of proportional representation the senate would stand distinctively for State questions at large, while the house would retain a fair share of local flavor. For municipal councils and boards of aldermen the election should be general, like that for the State senates.

CHAPTER VI.

ADVANTAGES OF PROPORTIONAL REPRESENTATION.

In stating the advantages of proportional representation there are two lines of discussion which are necessarily involved, a general and a special. The general principle of proportional representation involves merely the goal towards which electoral reform should be directed, and the results to be obtained thereby. To reach this goal innumerable plans have been proposed, all having more or less merit. The special questions involved are those connected with the formulation and choice of a specific plan. This is a question of method, a mechanical problem. But methods are as important in representative democracy as measures.

The two lines of discussion need not be separated. If a practicable and effective method cannot be devised the general principle is a mere dream. I have proposed a method which seems to me to embody the best in all other methods that have been put forward, and in presenting its advantages I shall necessarily both compare it with other plans and shall expound the general principles to be attained.

1. In the first place, proportional representation recognises the nature of modern political problems. Government is made up of interests and political parties rather than federated localities. Representation is national and not local. This may appear as one of the principal objections to the plan. But a slight thought will show that it has no force. In another place I have called attention to the fact that the gerrymander has taken nearly all the virtue out of a district that it may ever have possessed. There are few Congressional districts that have a unity of any kind, either economical, political, topographical, geographical or historical. The county of Huron, in Ohio, has been in five different combinations during the past twelve years, and now it is in the western part of a district one hundred and twenty miles long and twenty wide; its Congressional representative lives sixty miles away, and had, previous to the gerrymander of 1890, very little knowledge of or interest in the county. In this, and hundreds of other cases, the candidates in some districts at the other end of the State are better known to the voters of the district than are the candidates in their own district. On the other hand, the State is a historical and political unit. Its great men belong to no one district. At present only two of them can go to the United States Senate, and others are shelved as governors, or are compelled to seek some Presidential appointment. Under proportional representation those who are unavailable for Senators would lead their party delegations in the House.

The same is true regarding State legislatures and provincial parliaments. The State or the Province is a unit in itself. But here it may be plausibly urged that the county should be the unit of representation, that the county retains a political unity which in no way belongs to a Congressional district composed of several counties. However, this cannot be realized without serious inequalities. Some counties have a population ten and twenty times larger than others in the same State. Small counties must be grouped and large ones must be divided. Here is all the opportunity needed for the gerrymander, as is well shown by the constitution of any legislative apportionment in the union.

Yet as far as the Lower House is concerned, it seems desirable to compromise between the State and the County System and to provide for a number of districts each electing some odd number of representatives.

For State senates there seems to be no question that a general State ticket is the best. At present no one can tell just what our State senates do represent. Only nine out of the fifty-two Indiana senators represent counties, and two of these are from one county. The others represent the most arbitrary combinations of two, three, and four counties each. In other States the senators are elected on a similar basis. May not the senates be given a distinctive place and character, elected on the broad basis of the State, representing the whole people, and thereby attracting to their halls the recognised leaders of thought and action throughout the commonwealth?

At the same time it would be impossible to do away altogether with local interests in the selection of representatives. A political party with a modicum of sagacity would distribute its nominees either for Congress or for a State senate, as widely as possible over the State. Only in this way could it appeal to the votes of all classes and interests. Even now we can see how this is done in the nomination of tickets for State officers, from the Governor down to the chief of statistics. This tendency in the election of representatives would be wholesome. Localities woulk gain in the long run. But State and national interests would not be subordinated to the deplorable log-rolling and local prejudices which now control legislation.

2. The bill proposed is as simple as any that have been offered for effecting a result of this kind. In fact, there is no complexity whatever so far as the duties of the voters are concerned. There is no loophole left for him to make a mistake. Probably the great majority of voters would choose to vote a straight ticket. In that case they need only to place a mark against the party name of their ticket, or they may place the mark against the name of any candidate on their ticket. This is as simple as any existing plan of election.

Equally simple are the provisions for cumulating and distributing votes among candidates.

If there is any complexity in the scheme it is to be found in the duties of returning officers. But it is the duty of these officers to make themselves thoroughly acquainted with any election law, and their duties here are scarcely more than those connected with the deservedly popular "Australian" secret ballot. They are to keep just two sets of accounts, one for tickets and the other for candidates. The instructions on these points are full and explicit. There is no room for discretion. The only burden imposed upon them will be found in those cases where voters have scattered their votes and have voted either more or less than their lawful number of votes. In other words, the only complexity for returning officers is that involved in the effort to mend the negligence of electors, and to secure to them their full number of votes. This is reduced to a minimum. And the directions cover all possible contingencies, so that there seems to be no occasion for any mistake on the part of electors or officers.

3. Proportional representation it will be quickly observed is eminently elastic in its adaptation to changes in population. There are no district lines which must be changep after every census, but representation adapts itself immediately to every change in population.

4. It is needless to call attention further to the justice and equality of the measure. Frst. every political party is accurately represented in proportion to its popular strength, as exactly as a mathematical calculation can figure it out. Instead of the flagrantly distorted assemblies which by way of rhetoric and rose-water we call representative, we should have true mirrors of the people. We should accomplish what has never been accomplished, and in the eloquent and oft-repeated words of Mirabeau it could for the first time be said "that a representative body is to the nation what a chart is for the physical configuration of its soil ; in all its parts and as a whole, the representative body should at all times present a reduced picture of the people, their opinions, aspirations, and wishes—and that presentation should bear the relative proportion to the original precisely as a map brings before us mountains and dales, rivers and lakes, forests and plains, cities and towns. The finer should not be crushed out by the more massive substance, and the latter not be excluded ; the value of each element is dependent upon its importance to the whole and for the whole. The proportions are organic, the scale is national."

Secondly, every individual elector is represented, providing he votes for a ticket which polls 85% of a full quota.

There are two ways of looking upon this matter of individual or personal representation. It is held by most advocates of proportional representation that a voter is not represented unless the candidate is elected for whom he actually cast his vote. For example, says Sir John Lubbock,[*] "To tell the Liberals of Kent and Surrey that they are represented by the Liberal members for Scotland and Wales is just the old and exploded argument which used to maintain that the people of Birmingham were virtually represented by the members for some other borough. The Liberals of Kent are glad, no doubt, that Scotland and Wales send such admirable representatives. It is some consolation, but it is not the same thing to them as if they were directly represented. Perhaps the one thing about which Kentish farmers care most is the subject of extraordinary tithes. . . . But the farmers of Kent cannot expect the Liberal members from Scotland to help them as regards extraordinary tithes. It is possible that they do not even know what extraordinary tithes are."

Are the Negroes and Republicans of the Southern States represented by the Republicans from the North? Stated in this way the answer must be that they are not. Their votes were thrown away. So it is with all who have voted for defeated candidates. And this may include more than one-half the population. But they are not wholly unrepresented as they are in the case of a presidential election. More than one-half the electors voted against Mr. Cleveland for president. They are not represented in the policy of the administration. But in Congress they are partially represented. Congressmen do not represent simply their localities. They represent the nation. Mr. McKinley stood for more than the 20,000 Republicans in Ohio who voted for him. He stood for every advocate of protection in the nation. Could they all have done so, they would have voted for him, or at least, for a ticket containing his name.

At the same time voters for defeated candidates have no voice in the selection of the standard-bearers of their own party. In this important sense they are unrepresented. And this is the sense, too, which gives the party machine its control over nominations and elections, as will be shown later. Candidates are not chosen on one issue alone, but on several. It is this tempering and modulation of the representative body so as to correspond to all the phases of opinion and policy throughout the country which proportional representation guarantees.

It is to be observed that there are certain constitutional restrictions on equality of representation which do not properly come within the view of this essay. In the bicameral system the upper house is usually constituted for a very different purpose from that of equal representation. In the United States senate the State of Nevada with a population of 45,000 has as much numerical weight as the State of New York with a population of 6,000,000. We are not now quarreling with this practice. There is much to be said for it in virtue of the wide area and divergent sectional interests of the United States. Yet it does not seem that the senate should have the same weight in legislation as the house. It ought to sink to the level of a revisory board like the House of Lords and the Upper Chamber of Canada and the Provinces. This would tend more and more to become its status if the house really represented the people and possessed the ability which would be attracted to such a branch. As it is, the senate shines not by virtue, but by comparison. For the present, proportional representation has practical significance only in its application to that branch of the legislature which assumes to be truly representative.

Another matter with which we are not directly concerned is the basis of suffrage. We are not enquiring whether it shall be wide or narrow, male or female, old or young, white or black, intimidated or fearless. We take the suffrage for granted, and inquire only whether, such as it is, it is effective ; whether with the show of representation there is essential disfranchisement.

5. Proportional representation promises above all, the independence of the voters and freedom from the rule of the party machine. It will not do away with parties. Indeed, parties are inevitable and essential to a free government. At least, it is doubtful whether any one can show how a free government can be possible without them. In the first place there is a fundamental difference existing in the nature of a progressive society which must divide individuals into two groups or sets of groups, the one based on order or conservatism, the other on progress or liberalism. Human interests and temperament determine to which group individuals shall ally themselves. There must be a large class whose interests are in the maintenance of the existing order. Their fortunes, their position,

---

[*] Representation, page 18.

their influence has come about as a result of the social arrangements which the past has evolved. Another class, equally large, are dissatisfied with their lot. They see inconsistency or injustice in social arrangements. They desire change, reform. Society makes progress through the ebb and flow of these two fundamental groups.

But this natural grouping of free individuals is far different from the iron-bound classification imposed by the modern highly-developed party machine. Individuals, if left to themselves, will be continually forming new groupings as new political questions arise. But the machine having control of nominations, as has already been shown, maintains itself in power against the natural regroupings of the voters. Freedom for the machine, then, means, first, power on the part of the voters to control the nominations of their party; and, second, power to defeat obnoxious candidates of their own party without endangering the success of the party. Both of these advantages are provided for in the proposed bill—first, by the provision for cumulation of votes, and, second, by the provisions for independent tickets.

In the first place, let us suppose the nominations have all been made and voters have come to the polls ready to cast their ballots. Suppose there are fifteen candidates to be elected, and that tickets have been nominated as in the sample ballot given on page 161. It is known beforehand very nearly how many candidates each party will elect. The Democrats, for example, are certain to elect not less than six, and perhaps not more than eight. They have accordingly nominated ten candidates. The provision for cumulation now enables any voter to cast his entire fifteen votes for the party of his choice, but at the same time to select among the ten candidates that one who best represents him and to "plump" his fifteen votes for him. The party convention is powerless in the matter. It is compelled to put up nine or ten candidates instead of one. The voter may be so disgusted with some of the nominations that he would willingly stay at home or vote the opposing ticket if there were no further choice for him. This is what he is forced to do in the single-membered district. But with ten candidates there will likely be one or two at least with whom he is satisfied. For them he can give his entire strength. And if there are a sufficient number of voters like-minded with himself, they can elect those candidates who are least subjected to the machine rule.

I believe that herein will be found a very decided advantage over the Swiss method of proportional election. The Swiss ticket is prepared in exactly the same way as the one here proposed, and voting is conducted in exactly the same way, with the exception of this one feature of cumulation. The Swiss voter is not allowed to cumulate. If he votes a party ticket, it must be a straight ticket. He can give but one vote to each candidate. He is therefore constrained by the party machine, not as much as under the district system, but more than seems necessary.

According to the true theory of proportional representation one representative should be elected by every group of voters whose number is equal to the quotient obtained by dividing the total number of votes by the number of representatives to be elected. If 200 voters elect ten representatives, any group of twenty voters should be able to elect one, $i.e.$, each elector should have $\frac{1}{200}$ part of the total influence. But the Swiss method by giving electors as many votes as there are representatives, reduce the influence of the elector in his vote for any individual candidate in exactly the inverse ratio. That is to say if 200 electors have ten votes each the total votes will be 2,000 and it will require 200 instead of 20 to elect. If the elector can give only one of his ten votes to any one candidate he has $\frac{1}{2000}$ part of the total ifluence, $i.e.$, only $\frac{1}{10}$ the influence he rightly should have.

The simplest plan of cumulative voting is now employed in England in the election of members of the school boards. It is also in operation in Illinois in the election of members of the Lower House of the State Legislature. There have been more or less valid objections raised to those schemes for cumulative voting which have been heretofore proposed, namely (1) that they lead to a loss of voting power, (2) that they increase the power of political machines, and (3) that they give too much power to the minority. The present plan differs from all others in such a way that I believe these objections will not hold.

Sir John Lubbock presents conclusively the first objection to this system in the example he gives of the Marylebone election for members of the school board. (November, 1870.)*

---

* Representation, page 52.

There were seven members to elect and the votes were as follows :—

Successful Candidates.		Unsuccessful Candidates.	
Garrett	47,858	Mills	7,927
Huxley	13,494	Powell	7,852
Thorold	12,186	Whelpton	5,759
Angus	11,472	Waterlow	4,994
Hutchins	9,253	Garvey	4,933
Dixon	9,031	Marshall	4,668
Watson	8,355	Guedella	4,635
		Cremer	4,402
		Edmunds	3,973
		Verey	2,130
		Stanford	1,486
		Wyld	334
		Dunn	258
		Brewer	103
		Beare	62
		Total	165,165

"·It will be seen that Miss Garrett received no less than 47,858 votes, while under the circumstances 8,000 would have elected her. Nearly 40,000 votes out of the 48,000 were therefore wasted, and it is obvious that if Miss Garrett's supporters had known their strength, they would have desired to vote so as to secure the return of other candidates sharing their opinions. The Marylebone election was certainly an extreme case, but there have been many others in which the same phenomenon has been repeated."

Out of this fact grows the second objection. If there is danger of wasting votes the only way in which votes can be properly economised is for the voters to know their strength before election. This they can do only through the party organisation. The machine therefore will designate the candidates to be voted for and those of the party voters who do not follow the instructions of the machine will throw their votes away.

These objections seem valid against the simple plan of cumulation. But it will be readily seen that the bill proposed in this essay does away with these objections by reason of its double provision for ticket votes and candidate votes. The elector cannot possibly throw his votes away, because if too many votes have been cumulated on one candidate, as in the case of Miss Garrett in the Marylebone election, the surplus votes as well as the necessary votes for the candidate go to swell the aggregate of votes for the ticket, and thus help to elect other candidates on the same ticket. In this way, too, as is already shown, the power of the machine is greatly minimised instead of increased. ,

But suppose the elector finds that his party ticket has been put forward wholly in the interests of the machine. that there is no candidate offered to him whom he deems worthy of election. Under the district system, as has been shown, he must vote for the party nominee or else stay at home or cast his vote in such a way as to benefit the opposite party. Proportional representation enables him to "bolt" the party ticket and not bolt the party.

Of course, in order to do this, he must join with other protestants against the machine and nominate a new candidate, and a new ticket. The bill provides readily for a movement of this kind by a petition signed by fifty names for every candidate to be elected from the given State. This would be about fifty signatures for every 30,000 voters in the State. In the case of the simple ballot on page 161 the petition would require 750 signatures.

The bill now provides that all tickets shall be printed on a single ballot. This is the well recognised principle of the official ballot, introduced into this country from Australia, and now adopted by States representing ⅔ of the population of the country. The bill provides that this ballot shall be extended into all States in so far as congressional elections are concerned. Indeed, the highest success of proportional representation could not be obtained were it not for the admirable features of the Australian ballot. It gives the voter complete independence of choice, enables him to scatter his votes among different tickets, and to easily pick out from a large number of candidates an individual for whom he may wish to cumulate. The system could readily be applied to the voting machine which has just been introduced into elections in New York State and which possesses many features superior even to those of the Australian ballot.

The independent voter has therefore before him the ticket nominated by his party organization and another ticket of the same party nominated by petitioners outside the machine. Suppose he votes for the independent ticket. He does not endanger the success of his party ticket as a whole, but only of one candidate out of the entire ticket. And he is not running the risk of throwing his vote away, providing only a single quota of the voters of the State cast their ballot for the independent. Under the district system his vote would be wasted unless the voters for the independent were a majority or a plurality of all the voters in the district

Returning to the sample ballot on page 161, the Republicans have nominated nine candidates, expecting to elect six or seven. The Independent Republicans have nominated two, expecting to elect one. From the final result it will be seen that the Republicans could under no circumstances have elected more than six candidates, because the Democrats have elected seven and the People's two, out of the fifteen. But the straight Republicans and the Independent Republicans together have elected the six candidates to which the Republicans were entitled. The Independents have in no way endangered the success of their party, but they have succeeded in putting in a Republican who, standing for the party, nevertheless opposed the machine. The party as a whole gains its share of representatives, but the independent wing of the party has also secured its just share. Had the election been conducted under the district system, the Independent Republicans in order to be elected would have required a majority or plurality of the votes in his district. And in the effort to reach this result, the Democrats would probably have elected their candidate. But in proportional representation the independent is elected if he polls an average of one-fifteenth of the votes in all the districts, and the Democrats do not gain an iota through the disaffection of the Republicans. The present system, in other words, pens up a minority of independent voters in narrow districts under the whip of their party machine, but proportional representation tears down the fences and enables them to combine throughout the State, without risking the success of the opposing party's machine.

That this feature of proportional representation strikes at the radical evil of present politics, is evidenced by the current literature on all hands The evil of absenteeism on the part of the intelligent and business classes is everywhere alarming. It can not be too loudly deplored. In an article favoring compulsory voting Mr. F. W. Holls says : * "The extent to which this duty is shirked is easily ascertained, at least approximately. The interest which centers in a presidential contest is generally sufficient to bring out the fullest vote obtainable without compulsion, and a comparison of the total vote in a presidential year with that in an "off" year, shows almost the entire number of shirks. In the state of New York 300,375 persons who voted in 1880 remained away from the polls in 1889, and 286,278 did so in 1890 In the last mayoralty election in New York city over 35,000 men who had even registered abstained from voting, with the result that the city was once more turned over to an organised gang of plunderers. A more deliberate and extensive betrayal of trust would be difficult to find. In Massachusetts the total vote of 328,588 in 1888 fell to 260,798 in 1890, a difference of 67,790. In Chicago the figures are even more startling. In the spring election of 1887 less than 72,000 votes out of a possible 138,000 were cast—66,000 citizens failing in their duty—while in June o f the same year, at the judiciary election for the choice of judges for a city of almost ¼ million of souls, the total vote was 44,074, less than one-third of the number of qualifie voters."

Prof. A. B. Hart † asserts in a careful review of election statistics that the voting population is one-fourth of the total population, and that in presidential elections five sixths of this voting strength is cast. In New York, in 1880, the vote was 1,104,605, being 23 per cent. of the total population and 95 per cent. of the voters, but in 1891 it was only 259,425. In New York city, in 1888, the vote was eighteen per cent. of the population ; in 1890 it was 11·6 per cent. and in 1891 it was 13·2 per cent.

---

* Annals of Amer. Acad. Pol. and Soc. Sci., April, 1891.
† Political Science Quarterly, vol. vii., page 307.

The *New York Nation* of April 13, 1893, says, pertinently :—

"The Government of Russia has been described as 'despotism tempered by assassination.' In like manner the government of large cities in America may be termed 'bummer government tempered by uprisings.' Nevertheless, we believe that both in Chicago and New York the better element is really in a majority, and could, if it chose, retain the government of the municipality permanently in its hands. This is certainly true of New York, for the bummer element here has never yet polled a majority of the registered vote. Take, by way of illustration, the important election of 1888, at which Tammany got possession of the city. Tammany polled in that year 114,000 out of a total registered vote of 286,000. In 1890 it polled 116,000, or only 2,000 more, which may be called the natural increase of the Bummer Element. We think it is quite fair to set down as Better Element all voters of every description who do not vote the Tammany ticket. This Better Element, then, in 1888, registered 172,000 votes; in 1890, after two years' experience of Bummer rule, 129,000 votes. If the full registered vote in either of these two years had been cast against Tammany, Tammany would have been defeated and the Better Element would now be in possession of the city. But, in 1890, after a full trial of the kind of government the new Bummer régime was prepared to furnish, 30,000 of the Better Element stayed away from the polls and allowed Tammany to retain the city. Why did they stay away? Any one who could answer this question would explain the failure of popular government in American cities. . . .

Now, if it were possible to go around among these 30,000 and ask them severally why, having registered, they failed to vote, we should in all probability get a perfectly intelligent answer from nine out of every ten of them. Not one would say that he did not vote because he was not "organized;" that if anybody wanted him to vote, he must "organize" him. Nor probably would any of them say that they preferred Bummer Government to Citizens' Government. Some would have said, doubtless, that they did not think the election of Scott would be enough of an improvement on Grant to make it worth their while to go to the polls to bring it about; others, that Scott was "Grace's man," and they hated Grace; others, that they would never, under any circumstances, vote for a Democrat; others, that they hated Mugwumps, and that Scott was a Mugwump invention; others, that Scott's nomination was a contrivance for breaking up the Republican party in this city; others, that they wanted to keep Tammany in power as an example of Democratic rule."

But appeals to the voters to go to the polls are of little consequence. What can they accomplish by going? Says a recent writer:[*] "It is only the fear of wasting their votes on good men who have no chance of winning, which deters the people from voting against bad candidates who are forced upon them by the regular machine." Neither would compulsory voting meet the real difficulty. To quote the words of Prof. Hart, in the article already referred to, "To compel men to vote against their will is to tighten the control of party managers. . . Honest voters are indifferent or refuse to vote because they feel their impotence to affect their own party management. Yet they support their party management because experience shows that the men who fight it must make great exertions and sacrifices or be set out of politics; and further because permanent political results can be brought about only through strong and persisting parties. Compulsory voting supplies no new motives, and would not alter those political habits of the American people which are the real evil. Compulsory voting cannot create interest in local affairs, or break up the practice of adhesion to unfit leaders."

Compulsory voting would not stimulate independence. It is but natural that a well known machine Governor of New York should have recommended it to the legislature in one of his annual messages. Professor Giddings has shown[†] that the fringe of mobile voters who change from one party to another, is seldom more than 5% of the maximum total vote in a presidential year, and "the number of voters liable to be decisively influenced by mere opinion, apart from personal, class or sectional interests, is not more than $2\frac{1}{2}$ or 3% of the whole." Compulsory voting might possibly change this proportion slightly, but there is little reason to hope for the good results which its advocates claim for it.

---

[*] Charles Richardson in American Academy of Political and Social Science, March, 1892, page 86

[†] Political Science Quarterly, Vol. VII., page 116, 124.

That proportional representation would bring out a full vote at every election is not to be asserted. There is no experience from which to draw conclusions. The system has been in practice in Switzerland for only one year. But it certainly removes one of the most potent reasons for staying at home. In this respect the election of representatives offers advantages over the election of executives, judges, and other single officers, where, of course, there is no question of proportion. These advantages consist, as already shown, in the fact that there are several candidates to be elected on one ballot, and a small number of voters does not hold the balance of power. If the party vote is reduced even so much as a full quota,—i. e. 15 to 20%—the party loses only one candidate out of a possible five, ten, or fifteen, and this one candidate is not gained by the opposing party but by the independents of their own party. A similar defection in the district system would usually throw the majority to the other party, since, as is well known, the two great parties are closely divided in the majority of districts. A change of 1½% in twenty-one districts is estimated by Mr. Barry as sufficient to give the control of the Massachusetts senate to the opposite party.

As a result of the freedom which would be given by proportional representation to the rank and file of the party voters, the machine would usually be compelled to consult their wishes in nominating its candidates. At present it knows that, whatever their threats, they will not bolt and thus elect the common enemy. But if they can bolt without committing such direful treason, they will be inclined to do so, and the machine must listen. Candidates will be of larger caliber and better reputation and more in harmony with the opinions of the voters.

Numerous writers have called attention to the importance of the primaries, and have emphasised the duty of citizens to attend their party primaries and conventions. In the view here presented of the probable workings of proportional representation, the primary loses much of its significance. A party nominates candidates to win. Though voters do not attend the caucus, yet the machine has the probable action of these voters in mind when it nominates its candidates. The significance of the primary to-day is due to the impossibility of acting independently of machine dictation.

Besides, politics is a business. It requires time and strength. The politician does the very least part of his work in the primary. The real work is done beforehand. America has no leisure class who can afford to give themselves to this work. They must leave it to the professionals. The latter are tacit attorneys. They sound their clients, learn their wishes, and act accordingly. If proportional representation should bring forward an abler and purer class of politicians, more in harmony with the best wishes of the people, the latter could leave the primaries to them.

At the same time, primaries and conventions are the sources of power. They must be recognized as such. They must be brought under legal regulation. Perhaps the most serious evil of primaries and conventions and the one which gives the machine entire control is the practice of exclusive majority rule. It is the almost universal rule to elect committees and delegates by a majority vote on the principle of the general ticket, or else to authorize the chairman to appoint them. The true purpose of a primary, as representing all sections of a party is thereby defeated. It is proper that the majority should elect the chairman or nominate single candidates for offices, but why should the majority be alone represented on committees and delegations? Plainly here is the need for a further application of the proportional rule. A plan is required which will be simple and quickly worked. Such a plan has been proposed by Dr. L. B Tuckerman, and is described in the *Review of Reviews* for November, 1891, as follows :—

The Tuckerman plan provides for *weighing the choices* of each elector. If there are five offices to be filled the elector writes on his ballot the names of five candidates in the order of his preference. Then the tellers, in counting the ballots, allot to each name on the ballot a weight of choice corresponding to the position held by that name on the ballot. Thus if the candidates A, B, C, D, E, are written on a single ballot in the order given, candidate A will have five units credited to him, candidate B will have four units, C three units, D two units, and E one unit. After all the ballots are counted the units opposite the names of the candidates are added up, and the five having the highest number of units are declared elected. Thus only one ballot is required to elect the five officers. Continuing the example given, suppose the candidates A, B, C, D, E, are voted for in the order named by each of the fifty-five delegates. The weight of choice would be as follows :—

CHOICE.	UNITS.		ELECTORS.	TOTAL UNITS.
A.	5	×	55	275
B.	4	×	55	220
C.	3	×	55	165
D.	2	×	55	110
E.	1	×	55	55

" But candidates F, G, H, I, K, receive the support of the minority of forty-five electors. The preponderance of choice will run : "—

CANDIDATES.	UNITS.		ELECTORS.	TOTAL UNITS.
F.	5	×	45	225
G.	4	×	45	180
H.	3	×	45	135
I.	2	×	45	90
K.	1	×	45	45

" Consequently the successful candidates are A, B, C, F, and G. The majority faction has three representatives, and the minority has two—their first and second choice. According to the current method they would have been unrepresented ; but with this plan they can in no possible way be excluded so long as they number one-fifth of the total electors. In such cases their first choice would receive one hundred units, bringing him in ahead of the fifth choice of the majority."

This plan is remarkably simple and effective, and can be applied readily to mass-meetings and conventions. It could be introduced into the bill proposed in these pages by providing that conventions making nominations of Congressional candidates should be required to adopt the plan, and that the presidents and secretaries of such conventions in presenting their tickets to the Board of Election Commissioners should certify that the nominations had been made in accordance with the law. They should certify, too, that primaries and other conventions sending delegates to the nominating convention had also complied with the law.

With a rule of this kind governing primaries and conventions we should accomplish the same results within party lines as would be accomplished by the proposed bill between parties. All classes within a party would be represented, " packed " conventions would be unknown, the party machine would be shorn of much of its undeserved power, tickets would be nominated containing candidates acceptable to all ranks of the party, the necessity for independent tickets would be largely obviated, and citizens would be more inclined to attend their party primaries, knowing that their wishes would be respected.

6. Proportional representation would bring into legislative assemblies able and experienced men, the true leaders and representatives of their parties, and the people. The district system excludes such men.

Social and legal institutions possess a certain capacity of natural selection. They furnish the environment in which individuals grow up and develop. As in the physical universe, those individuals survive and prosper who are best fitted to their environment. This does not mean that the fittest are the best morally. They are the best physically. In society, those individuals come forward and acquire power whose natural qualities adapt them best to utilize the passions, customs and legal regulations of their fellow men.

But society, unlike the physical universe, can change its customs and laws within certain bounds and thereby can change the environment of individuals. New and different qualities now are necessary for survival and power. And this is the essence of human activity controlled by human wisdom, to modify the environment and so to develop those qualities and powers which it deems desirable. This is the rule all the way from raising chickens to organizing governments. If the people desire certain qualities in their law-makers they can modify their institutions in such a way as will secure them. The present breed will then wither and sink away. If they wish to bring forward in their legislatures intelligence, experience, ability, probity and sympathy with popular wishes, they should first develop those forms of government and those technical devices which will ensure adequate support, dignity and security to such qualities.

It is claimed that proportional representation would be an improvement of this kind. In the first place, it would secure all the advantages of the English and Canadian practice of non-residency. Representatives could be selected from an entire State without reference to district lines. The area of choice is widened. A party leader need no longer be excluded from Congress because he happens to live in a district where his party is in the minority. Gerrymanders could not be constructed to exclude him as soon as he has become known. All the money and influence of a wealthy opposing party would effect nothing when thrown into his district. If his party were in a minority in the State, they certainly would be able to command a quota and he would be their choice. Nothing could exclude him except the dissatisfaction of his own followers. This is true of all parties and groups which can command a quota of the votes.

Organized party minorities and factions could not defeat the nomination and election of such men, because they no longer hold the balance of power. In the district system a change of 1 to 5 per cent. of the votes to the opposite party will nearly always defeat a candidate. But 50 per cent. might bolt under proportional representation and the remaining 50 per cent.—if they equalled a quota—could still elect the party leader.

Mr. Albert Stickney, has found in frequent elections and short terms the root of corrupt politics and machine rule.* Indeed he is right. A representative must give his time to carrying elections. He must placate and harmonise factions. He must properly distribute the spoils. He cannot afford to break with the machine and the spoilsmen.

But with proportional representation frequent elections would be combined with life-long service, provided the representative retained the confidence of a single quota of the voters. He would not be called upon for a day's thought on the mere matter of carrying the elections. He would succeed himself as naturally as the season return. His only thought would be to know that in his legislative duties he truly represented his supporters. If the machine repudiated him he would but have earned added strength with his people. No faction could defeat him. Only a wide-spread revolt against his leadership could threaten his service. As long as the mass of the voters had confidence in him they would return him.

Frequent elections, on the other hand, would give the people power quietly to drop the representative who was weak or who had ceased to represent them. They would simply cumulate their votes on their true leaders. Frequent elections under the district system are dangerous to both the good and the bad. Under proportional representation they would endanger only the bad.

The State of Ohio presents a national example of the suicidal crudity of the district system—a State where republicans and democrats have world-famous leaders but cannot send them continuously to Congress where their services are needed. McKinley, Foster, Foraker, are the first choice of the republicans of that State. But they have been gerrymandered into democratic districts, or else local republican factions have made them unavailable in their limited districts. With proportional representation these men would lead their delegation in the House. Republicanism in Ohio, and the nation would be immeasurably the gainers. Every other State has like examples. Many able men, too, now unknown to politics, would be encouraged to look to such a career were the tenure certain and the service free from machine dictation.

The importance of this feature of proportional representation cannot be overestimated. Every interest or class in the State would not only be fairly represented in numbers, but would be represented by its ablest advocates. Every representative of ability would be continued in the legislature until he had acquired experience adequate to his duties. In this way many of the reforms advocated for legislatures would mend themselves. The representatives would be leaders in reforms of this kind, knowing well by experience the evils to be met and being most interested in curing them. The Speaker of the House would no more be called upon to appoint committees, because the delegates, having a long acquaintance with each other and a national reputation, and knowing their mutual qualifications, could easily elect their own committees. They would naturally do this on some proportional plan, somewhat as the committees of the United States Senate are now appointed, or else by adopting a plan like that already suggested for the use of party

---

* See " A True Republic " and other writings.

primaries and conventions. The power of the lobby would be immeasurably reduced. The sinister influence of the party machine would be banished, since the leaders of the parties hold seats in the legislative branches and would be responsible to their constituencies instead of to the spoilsmen and lobbyists. Hasty and ill-considered legislation would be cleared from the statute books. Legislation would be simplified and harmonized.

It may be well to emphasise again the way in which this bill would secure the responsibility of legislators directly to the people. The objections will doubtless arise that it would do away with "party responsibility;" that it will reduce the votes of both the leading parties so close that no party will have a majority and therefore no party can go before the people with a party record to be approved or rejected. But this is an intangible and indiscriminate responsibility. It is like all kinds of multiple or corporate responsibility. There is no particular individual whom the people can select and fasten responsibility upon. And a party, like a corporation, can be held responsible only as its agents are responsible. The growing popularity in the United States of city government by mayors, and the recent transfer of legislative and administrative functions to mayors, are based upon the well-grounded opinion that the responsibility of one man is safer for the purity of city government than the responsibility of boards and councils. When a party is defeated at the polls, both the good and the bad are defeated together. Why should a representative rise above party expediency and create a good reputation for himself individually when he knows that the evil deeds of the other members of his party will drag him down with them?

But there are two features of proportional representation which permit the voters to discriminate directly between individuals, and to hold them instead of parties, responsible. The first is the fact that parties would not be defeated as a whole but would lose only a very small proportion of their representatives. So close are the votes of parties in most States, that a State returning say fifteen representatives, would return only eight of the majority party and seven of the minority. If the majority party should be defeated, so slight is the change of votes—not more than 1 to $5°/_o$ of the total votes—that usually the party would lose only one of its eight representatives, and the other party would gain one, reversing, of course, the majorities. Under the district system, as has been shown, a reversal of the popular vote of $2°/_o$ may give catastrophic results, and an entire party— the good and the bad - may go down together. A very moderate change of popular opinion is exaggerated into an avalanche.

Thus the idea is unduly prominent that the people have become radically opposed to the party as a whole, and the fiction is fostered of "party responsibility." But under proportional representation only a very few of the party candidates would be defeated.

Now, if the voters have power to select these candidates who are to be defeated and to continue the others, shall we not have the essence of individual responsibility? The second feature of proportional representation gives them this power. Not only do electors give their votes for "tickets," but they may scatter their votes as they please among the individual candidates, and they may even cumulate all on one. Thus bad candidates cannot ride into power on a wave of party prosperity, nor can good candidates be swamped in the ebb of party adversity. Each individual stands on his own merits. It is his own record which can be brought directly before him, and by it he can be summarily judged. And whichever way he is judged, his party is but slightly affected. It always secures its rightful quota.

The argument seems conclusive. The wisdom, ingenuity and directness of the plan are fully demonstrated. Parties are held responsible, not as corporations, but through their agents. The people have the widest of freedom in selecting their agents. If the people can be trusted there is nothing to hinder their choice of the best. And they certainly can be trusted better than can the machines which at present do all the choosing. Proportional representation means far more than equality, it means freedom. It means confidence in the people. It means distrust of oligarchies and professionals.

Democratic government in cities is said by many to be a failure. Pleas have been made for a more limited suffrage. Representative institutions, it is said, are not on trial but they have been condemned.

But has true representation been given even a trial? We have a sham representation. It gives a show of fairness. But it is crude and essentially unfair. It is still in re-primitive stages. It is like the steam engine in the time of Fulton. It needs mechanical adjustments and technical improvements. It does not represent the people. It represents the politicians. With true representation democratic institutions will begin a new era. Able, disinterested and patriotic men will come to the front. The people will be free to grant them their confidence and continued support. And they can be trusted to do it.

7. It may seem startling, and yet it is indisputable, to affirm that proportional representation would purify elections by removing the most potent of inducements for bribery and corruption. It is to the district system that must be charged the alarming growth of corruption in elections. The system is a powerful temptation to bribery. The secret ballot has no doubt made the crime more difficult and dangerous but it has not at all touched the inducements to commit the crime. These inducements consist in the exaggerated influence of the purchasable vote in turning the scale. The great majority of the districts are close. Elections turn on very narrow margins. Mr. Berry says that a change of $1\frac{1}{2}\%$ of the vote in twenty-one districts of Massachusetts would have turned the State senate over to the opposite party. The results of elections in general may be said to turn on the balance of power held by 2 or 3% of the voters. Any cause that can influence so small a percentage may be adequate to control elections. I have mentioned already the power held by small and compact factions, like the saloons, and the office seekers. The purchasable vote makes up another similarly factional group. The venal voters are amply sufficient in numbers to turn the scale. Prof. J. J. McCook has care fully investigated the proportion of these votes in twenty-one towns of Connecticut, and he very justly entitles his article, "The Alarming Proportion of Venal Voters."* He finds that the number ranges from 3 to 50% of the total voters of the towns in question, and the average for the twenty-one towns is $15\cdot9\%$. The average for city and county is about $12\frac{1}{2}\%$.

With such a large percentage, it is plain that under the district system elections offer the greatest inducements for bribery. The entire result can be changed by changing a few votes, and considerably more than these few votes are bribable.

But with proportional representation there is no faction nor group which holds the balance of power. A change of 12 per cent. of the votes affects only 12 per cent. of the results. And as the changes of this kind would usually be no more than 1 to 3%, it can be seen how diminutive is the influence of the briber. Successful bribery would endanger only one candidate out of a party's entire delegation. The unbribable voters would not have their just influence in the least reduced by the disaffection of the floaters. No-body would care therefore to bribe the latter. Their occupation would be gone. While the secret ballot makes bribery difficult, proportional representation makes it fruitless.

8. With all parties fairly represented, with able men, with bribery ineffective, legislatures would become deliberative assemblies instead of arenas for party strife. The objection against proportional representation has already been noted that it would do away with party responsibility. Closely connected with this is the other objection that it would give a small minority the balance of power and enable them to dictate legislation. These objections are of apparently great weight. We have frequently noticed the very close popular vote between the parties. Third parties, if given their due weight in legislatures, would often hold the balance.

These objections overlook, in the first place, the questions of fairness and individual responsibility. It may prove here, as elsewhere, that justice is the wisest expediency. But waiving for the moment this reply let us look a little more deeply into the nature of, government itself and see whether we should expect a gain from the more equal division of power in legislative assemblies.

Professor Ernest Naville, the earliest advocate and ablest defender of proportional representation in Switzerland, very wisely observes that outside the ranks of party are always to be found groups of independents who care little for the personelle of candidates and party success, but more for principles and measures In society at large they naturally hold the largest place. They hold the balance of power. If people could meet together in mass-meeting their influence would be felt. But they are not organized. They are not practical politicians. Hence they put forward no candidates of their own, and by force of

* See Forum, September, 1892.

necessity are compelled to vote for party candidates or to stay away from the polls. They consequently make up the large stay-at-home vote. But if they had their own peculiar representatives they would necessarily bring partisans to terms, would force them to put measures above spoils and would be a balance-wheel of legislation, preventing one party from crushing the minority, and thereby making legislation an ideal compromise conserving the interests of all.

As a matter of fact it will be found that very few of the questions of legislation are party questions. A great many are settled on lines of combination running across parties. The only strictly party questions are those concerned with the spoils and with suffrage legislation, such as "force bills" and gerrymanders, which threaten to deprive one party of its votes. If the capture of spoils were ruled out, and United States senators were elected outside of legislatures there would seldom be deadlocks, no matter how narrow the majorities or how obstinate those holding the balance. The points of agreement among parties on other questions are far more numerous than those of disagreement. Parties differ only on the fringe of policies. Their battles are mock battles. When the *outs* get in they do not radically reverse the policy of their predecessors, not even to such an extent as a president of one party often reverses that of his predecessor of the same party. At any given time the masses of the people will not permit radical far-reaching changes. A new party in power must in the main accept what its predecessor has done, and may modify it only in minor points. Take all the important questions of national politics and it will be seen that they are not settled on party lines. The two great parties do not differ more than 20 per cent. on the tariff question. It is simply a question of a very high tariff or one not quite so high. The country would not endure a return to no-tariff, and the Democratic party will not allow itself to be called a free-trade party. So with the silver question. Both parties are split in two on this question. The bill against dealing in futures and options was fought entirely independent of party lines. The voting of pensions brings emulous majorities from both parties. River and harbour bills are settled by individual log-rolling, and exchange of favours. On so many of the vital questions do the representatives in Congress disregard party lines that one is forced to suspect that the fight over the tariff—the only question where party lines are drawn—is only for show to keep the voters in line. Behind the scenes the voter imagines his lately antagonistic Congressmen chuckling together, rubbing their hands and laughing up their sleeves over the success of their "war scare."

The fundamental nature of politics is not party strife or partisan victory, but compromise. There is a blindly accepted aphorism of Bentham's to the effect that the criterion of legislation is the greatest good to the greatest number. Strictly defined this is false. The true goal is the greatest good to *all*. Bentham's dictum is the war-cry of party. The just criterion harmonises and promotes every interest. It is simply and solely compromise.

This was the essential idea in Calhoun's distinction between the constitutional and the numerical majority. But with him compromise was to be enforced in a way that was anarchical—nullification. The true solution is to have it solved within the councils of the sovereign body itself—and then the unity of the sovereign can be maintained along with the promotion of all individual and private interests. The fear of Calhoun would be groundless if legislative bodies were accurately representative. The people themselves differ so little that there is no danger of an intolerant and oppressive majority, providing all are equally represented. Calhoun and all who dread the power of majority are influenced by the exaggerated and distorted constitution of existing legislative assemblies, and the unjust power which the majority thereby usually obtains.

Compromise is expediency. Expediency is nothing more nor less than general principles in process of evolution. The doctrine of compromise rests on the fact of growth. Society is developing out of a primitive barbaric state where human rights were unknown, towards an era where the happiness, honor and dignity of man as such shall be recognised and obtained for every individual. Abstract principles are the goal towards which we are aiming. One by one the *impedimenta* of the past are being thrown off in the steady march towards the goal. And this is expediency—compromise. Fanatics and enthusiasts appeal to the "higher law" and demand that all obstructions be overthrown at once. But this is impossible. The *impedimenta* of social progress are not like coats of mail and trunks and baggage, carried on the shoulder or in a waggon. They are human beliefs, feelings, passions, necessities. They exist in the very souls of men, and are conditioned by their material resources and opportunities. They can be overthrown only as one generation dies and is succeeded by another with new beliefs and feelings, and with larger resources and a greater command over nature. Compromise is that vital principle of organic unity which connects the past and the future. It is simply life itself—the very essence of growth. No more can the human body separate itself from its past development through childhood, and suddenly leap over the period of youth into that of mature and ripened manhood, than can the social body break from its past.

But the social body makes its growth through modifications of social institutions. It does this both consciously and unconsciously. It lops off here an undesirable growth or an obsolete appendage, and there it starts a new line of movement and growth. The institution of private property, for example, has passed through manifold changes, no one of them appearing to contemporary men as radical or far-reaching, yet in three generations the old institution is radically changed. The family, too, the State, the church, all change and grow. But they are growing towards some higher abstract ideal. They are being gradually modified so as to give wider opportunities for individual upbuilding and to bring out more and more the best and happiest that is in man.

But it must be admitted that compromise involves compounding with evil. This is only because evil is deeply rooted in the past of society and in human nature. Yet there are two kinds of compromise. There is another kind which contemplates the perpetuation of evil. This is base. It gives the evil a deeper root in society and makes its future dislodgement harder. It is the doctrine of quiescence. It is not true expediency, but dalliance, pusillanimity. True expediency contemplates the ultimate extinction of hoary evil. It sets the forces to work which in time gather strength and gradually but surely undermine and sap the evil that now is compounded. True expediency is true statesmanship. It is courage, wisdom and a firm grasp upon ennobling truths.

But does it follow, even, that compromise in its better sense will yield the greatest good to all?

First, it should be remembered that not all progress is good or wise. Legislation is experiment. Each new project must be tried. Only experience will establish it if good, and experience is needed to revise it if bad. Hence to adopt a new thing in its entirety would be as bad as to cling obstinately to all that is old.

Again, in society at large, as has already been said, there are nearly always to be found two general groupings of individuals partaking more or less of the nature of parties, namely the party of order and the party of progress. The one rejoices in and is satisfied with the honorable achievements of the past, the other is anxious for change. The one is composed of those whose prosperity depends upon maintaining things as they are, whose interests are "vested interests," whose minds and temperament are conservative. The other is composed of unprivileged classes, restless, experimenting, pioneering, minds. But the lines are not fast drawn. On particular questions there will be slight shiftings and regroupings.

These different classes and interests come together in legislative halls. The circumstances of the times compel change of some kind. The Radicals demand extreme measures. The Conservatives are for doing nothing. Neither has a majority. There is a number who hold a medium view. The measures proposed must be examined, debated, amended, until they reach a shape which will commend a majority of the votes. And there is no measure in politics which cannot be thus modified. Even the question of slavery could have been compounded. There are a hundred intermediate measures between immediate emancipation and permanent slavery. Had a law been enacted in the fifties providing for gradual emancipation, even upon the basis proposed by Abraham Lincoln of a hundred years, the civil war might have been avoided. But the district system of representation had excluded the moderate men from a share in the councils of Congress. Especially is it affirmed by the senate committee which investigated this matter in 1867, and it is well known to students of history, that the South was not fairly represented in Congress. A very large minority of the people were in favor of the Union, and doubtless they could have been brought to gradual emancipation without rebellion. But this minority was excluded from its State legislatures and from the halls of Congress. The machine politician precipitated the South into rebellion. When once the die was cast the whole people were forced to follow. Would not compromise have been better than so deadly a war? Would not the slave himself have been as well off or better to-day with gradual emancipation? Would not the Union have rested on as secure foundation?

If a question presenting such clear moral issues could have compromised with benefit to all classes and individuals, surely the thousand minor questions of politics could find a similarly happy solution. When representatives abandon party lines this is the direction they take. We have seen in America two very ingenious compromises on the silver question—a question which certainly has aroused bitter conflicts and which seemed clear-cut and incapable of compromise. Party divisions were disregarded, and representatives set about to find a common ground of agreement. With able financiers in Congress and a spirit of compromise no doubt a permanent settlement of this question would be found which would bring the greatest good to every one.

If the proper conditions were provided and the people were equally represented in legislatures and Congress, doubtless every other question could be settled in the same way. Party lines would continue but not those artificial party lines perpetuated by party machines.

The legislature of Nebraska has just adjourned with the record of having done the best work of any State legislature for many a year. Yet in that legislature there were three parties about equally divided. The legislature spent six weeks out of twelve in a deadlock over a question of spoils—the election of a United States senator. That is a matter which cannot well be compromised, except by electing an unknown man. This the legislature did, and then set about its legitimate business. It passed fairly able laws on important matters, among them a railroad law which was neither confiscatory nor reactionary, but just to all concerned. This was the character of the other laws. There were no deadlocks on legislation, but every measure was a fair compromise. With proportional representation legislation would take on more of this character, since it would be under the guidance of far abler and more experienced legislators.

If compromise seems tame and devoid of the picturesqueness of party struggles, it should be borne in mind that radical reforms are not permanent. There must follow a reaction. Those noble anti-slavery agitators who saw in the proclamation of emancipation the glorious fruition of their work, and were ready then to pass to other questions, and those extremists who gave the new-fledged freeman the liberty of the ballot, may well to-day look back with chagrin on those exultant measures. The slave is not yet free. He was not ready for the ballot. And the south is a land of smothered anarchy. Surely gradual emancipation and deliberate enfranchisemet would not have been slower in final results than have been these spectacular reforms. "If the process seems intolerably slow," says John Morley,* "we may correct our impatience by looking back upon the past. People seldom realise the enormous period of time which each change in men's ideas requires for its full accomplishment. We speak of these changes with a peremptory kind of definiteness, as if they had covered no more than a space of a few years. Thus we talk of the time of the Reformation, as we might talk of the Reform Bill or the Repeal of the Corn Duties. Yet the Reformation is the name for a movement of the mind of northern Europe which went on for three centuries. Then if we turn to that still more momentous set of events, the rise and establishment of Christianity, one might suppose from current speech that we could fix that within a space of half a century or so. Yet it was at least four hundred years before all the foundations of that great superstructure of doctrine and organisation were completely laid. . . The conditions of speech make it indispensable for us to use definite and compendious names for movements that were both tardy and complex. We are forced to name a long series of events as if they were a single event. But we lose the reality of history, we fail to recognise one of the most striking aspects of human affairs, and above all we miss that most invaluable practical lesson, the lesson of patience, unless we remember that the great changes of history took up long periods of time which, when measured by the little life of a man, are almost colossal, like the vast changes of geology. We know how long it takes before a species of plant or animal disappears in face of a better adapted species. Ideas and customs, beliefs and institutions, have always lingered just as long in the face of their successors, and the competition is not less keen or less prolonged, because it is for one or other inevitably destined to be hopeless."

---

* On Compromise page 233-5.

But it must not be supposed, since proportional representation would compel recourse to compromises, that it would stand in the way of reform. Indeed, it would bring forward the time of genuine reform. And this, not by erratic jumps, but like the steady processes of nature. Reform movements would get a hearing while yet in their beginnings. Legislation would then anticipate and prepare the way for them. The minds of men would get ready for them. They would not come with that suddenness which districts counsel and demoralizes business and all other interests. Under the present system there is a false ignorance of these movements. They are choked and blanketed. They have no spokesman in places of authority until they have become the majority party in various districts. By this time their pent-up fire is raging. A sense of injustice is urging them on. They accumulate wrath, and all the conservative interests of the country are trembling. With a change of party on the tariff question business is almost at a standstill for a year or more. There is a dread of extreme change. Legislation ought to proceed so quietly and advance so naturally that the community would scarcely notice it. It would do so were these new and progressive interests early represented.

Reforms would shew themselves inside the party lines. At present parties tend to build about themselves a crust of tradition. New parties spring suddenly forth and take the place of the old. This is because our party machinery is not elastic. It does not respond to the growing body within. There is a false feeling of security on the part of the managers. In France this is the cause of armed revolution. The party in power sees its large majority in the Chamber of Deputies and goes its way. But the people are ready to burst the shell. There follow catastrophe, disaster, partisanship, reaction.

Proportional representation was defended twenty years ago in the interests of the minority. It was thought to be a promising corrective of popular suffrage. It would protect the rich against confiscation by the mob. This was the idea of John Stuart Mill in his classical work on Representation. But to-day it is plain that proportional representation is in the interests of the masses. John Stuart Mill knew nothing of the lobby. One man of wealth has the influence of ten thousand day laborers. But the lobby is a dangerous machine for legislation. It protects the rich for a while, but stirs those vindictive passions that demand finally indiscriminate spoliation. Much better for one and all would be fair and open compromise, looking far into the future and working in harmony with social forces. If legislatures were deliberative assemblies they would bring together year by year all these forces and promote continually the greatest good of all.

Among the many projects for legislative reform which have been brought out by the recognised failure of representative assemblies perhaps none is more extreme than the demand for so-called direct legislation. This is nothing more nor less than an attempt to return to the primitive town meeting on a large scale and to reduce the legislatures to a perfunctory board. The above discussion of the nature of a deliberative assembly will enable us to pass a fair judgment upon the possibilities of direct legislation. To quote the words of an American advocate of this plan of legislation :

"The great trouble with our legislative bodies is that they have ceased to be the representatives of the body of the people and their acts are not exponents of the will of the majority of the people. The remedy, if there is any practical remedy, is in taking from our legislative assemblies the absolute power of making laws. The people should be the only makers of the laws that are to control them, and they should only delegate to their representatives the duty of consideration and advice. No important principle in government should become active in specific law until it has been referred to the people, and has been approved by a majority vote. This is the position taken by the advocates of the reform called the "Initiative and Referendum." In a political sense "Initiative" has a special meaning and a double function. It signifies the proposal of law by those who have the legal right to do so to the body which may accept or reject the law. In the first exercise of this function the individual or collective citizen may propose a law, and this proposal will start it on the regular course of enactment. This method would have many and obvious advantages. The sovereign rights and duties of the people would be in exercise. The people would originate the laws, would know them and expressly sanction them. Ignorance of the law could no longer be pleaded as an excuse. Inability to secure relief and redress would not be a justification for bloody revolution. The right of initiative with the people would not prevent the same to be exercised by the representative body originating such propositions as their judgment might suggest. The broad proposition covered by the "initiative" is that proposed law shall originate in the aroused and concentrated desires of the body of people. The function of the legislature would consist in digesting and assimilating the crude movements of the popular will for deliberation and final action. This final action is the purpose of the "Referendum." It is to refer all important laws passed by the legislature to a vote of all the people. In effect it holds in suspense before the scrutiny of the public all measures of public welfare long enough to discover and discuss their purpose and adaptation."

Direct legislation is not without a long trial. It has been adopted by all the Cantons of Switzerland, and by the Swiss Federal Republic. Its results in that country under the most favorable conditions would hardly furnish a criterion for America or other great nations where legislation is infinitely complex and public interests both delicate and massive. It is therefore significant that after a long trial the Swiss Cantons are making a rapid espousal of proportional representation. Two Cantons have already done so, and the question is a live one in others and in the Federal Government. The people in their primary capacity are incapable of giving the necessary deliberation to public measures. They decide questions not on their merits but on entirely different considerations, the principal one being the question of confidence in the Congress which submitted the bill. A vote against a given bill is not to be taken as a disapproval of the bill, but as a general lack of confidence in the legislature. The Swiss people have rejected through the Referendum more bills than they have ratified, and then in a few years later have turned about and ratified bills which they had previously rejected. The Referendum has undoubtedly prevented bad legislation, but it has also prevented the good. But the people cannot judge upon such matters. They lack the information and the opportunities of counsel and compromise. They can only express confidence or distrust in individuals. What they need is wise and experienced legislators in whom they can confide, and then to leave the decision to them. Says Albert Teckney* "Do we really wish that our legislators should give us only such legislation as we ourselves think best? Do men wish their shoemakers to make such shoes as they themselves would make, or their lawyer to try their cases as they themselves would try them, or their physician to give them such drugs as they themselves may fancy? What we wish from our public servants is, not such work as we ourselves should do, or as we may think the best, but better work than we know anything about. On any proper theory of government we select our very best men, to use their own brains, and not ours, in our service. We choose them, or should choose them, because they will be leagues in advance of anything we dream of."

However much the powers of legislators may be reduced by the referendum, it nevertheless is necessary to leave great discretion to them. An act of legislation is a growth. It takes days and months, conferences and committees, reports and debates, arguments and amendments, to complete it ready for enactment. Here is where skilled workmanship tells. Here is the opportunity for the lobby. The people are helpless: They must treat the statute as a whole. They can only answer the categorical yes or no. But legislation is far more than this. Its essence is in the details, the working, the harmonising with other statutes.

The same reasons which substituted representation for the primary assembly must hold good, though in less degree, against direct legislation. "Representation," says Hearn,† "is not a makeshift, it is a substantive institution. It is essentially distinct from the government of the Agora or the Forum; and as a political instrument is far superior to that polity. . . The primary principle on which its value rests is the same principle which regulates the exercise of the royal will. The people require checks and limitations and enlightment no less than the king. An aggregate assemblage of individuals must be restrained and informed no less than each individual unit of that aggregate. If a monarchic absolutism be liable to infirmities, democratic absolutism is liable to other and no less dangerous infirmities. For the sovereign Many, therefore, as well as for the sovereign One, the law assigns a specific and exclusive form of expression. The object of this form is the same in both cases. It is designed to secure the well-weighed and deliberate

---

* A True Republic, page 240.
† Government of England, page 496.

opinion of the utterer. . . For popular utterances a suitable organ is found by the aid of the principle of trusteeship. The application of this principle produces several important results. By its means the size of the deliberative body is reduced to reasonable limits. An orderly and comparatively unexcited assembly is substituted for the tumultuous crowds of the market. The selection, too of a few persons to act on behalf of many others never fails even in circumstances of great excitement to produce a sobering effect. The responsibility is in such cases less divided and is consequently more acutely felt. The representative feels too, that a reason will be required for whatever course he adopts, and that he must give his reason subject to criticism. Both in their acts and in their forbearance, therefore, a representative assembly is more careful than a larger and less responsible body would be. Nor is it the least merit of representation that the representative is generally above the average of his constituents. From the very nature of the case, he is selected on account of some superior aptitude, real or supposed. Thus, although the representative reflects and ought to reflect the character of the electors, he reflects that character in its most favorable and not in its less favorable aspects."

I do not hold that there is no place for the referendum. Some kinds of bills can well be put to popular vote. American States and cities practise this method of legislation successfully in matters of constitutional law, taxation and indebtedness. Here the principle has undoubted merits. It might perhaps be extended to other measures. But however far it is extended, legislation must also be carried out by a delegate body of some sort. The referendum gains its strongest claim in the frailties of legislatures. If proportional representation should improve these bodies and make them able, representative, and popular, the people would be glad to entrust to them their dearest interests.

CHAPTER VII.

CONCLUSION.

Professor Emil de Laveleye has said that the remedies for partisan abuses in representative government are : Representation of minorities, secret ballots, civil service reform.

These three reforms are to-day well under headway. The secret ballot is now well-nigh universal in parliamentary countries. Intelligent people are wide awake to the evils of the spoils system. Proportional representation has been adopted in two cantons of Switzerland. In America it has as yet not been fully comprehended. But it fills out the measure of these other great reforms. The three are co-ordinate and complementary. The secret ballot prepares the way for a simple application of proportional representation. It enables the voter to have before him when he comes to the polls several lists of candidates, representing all parties and interests, it protects him from outside influences, it gives him the widest possible freedom of choice. The secret official ballot therefore, gives the movement an advantage which it by no means possessed in the period of reconstruction of the Southern States, when it was widely but unsuccessfully advocated.

Again, proportional representation is impossible in the presence of a spoils system. It would result in constant deadlocks. Legislation would be at a standstill. No measure would so powerfully impress upon the people the need of civil service reform. Legislatures in their own defence would take the initiative in this reform instead of waiting to be driven by public opinion.

With these three reforms co-operating, there need be no fear of popular government. They are not makeshifts or palliatives. They reach the sources of power. A reformed legislature would be the mightiest of engines for handling every other reform. It rightly holds the purse, the very life of government. It controls all other departments. It is nearest the people. It should include the best wisdom, integrity, enterprise of the people. It should represent the opinions and wishes of the people in the same proportions in which they exist at large. It should be the people themselves in conference. It should be a deliberative body in the highest sense, and not a side-show of puppets worked by the party machine and the lobby. It should harmonise all social interests. It should give power to the majority, a hearing to the minority, each in the persons of their ablest advocates.

APPENDIX.—Page 162.

The Distribution of Seats.

M. Victor de Hondt, of Brussels, Belgium, has devised an ingenious and accurate plan for the assignment of representatives to parties. The plan has been officially adopted by the Belgian Proportional Representation Society, and has received wide approval among continental reformers. The rule adopted is simple enough in its operation, but the reasons for it are so difficult of explanation that it is questionable whether it can be successfully advocated at this stage of the movement. Having adopted the free ticket as advocated in these pages, M. D'Hondt determines the number of seats to be assigned to each party by dividing the respective electoral votes by such a common divisor as will give quotients whose number is equal to the numbers of seats to be filled. This common divisor is obtained by dividing the electoral vote of the parties by 1, 2, 3, 4, etc., and taking that quotient which holds in the order of importance the rank corresponding to the number of seats to be filled.*

M. D'Hondt gives the following example :—

Example.

There are seven deputies to be elected.

```
Total vote of the Liberal ticket.................... 8,145
   "      "      Catholic ticket ................... 5,680
   "      "      Independent ticket............ ..... 3,725
```

The common divisor is 2,038.

```
This is contained 4 times in .................... 8,145
   "      "      2   "      .................... 5,680
   "      "      1   "      .........  .......... 3,725
```

Giving the Liberals four members, the Catholics two, and the Independents one.

The divisor is discovered by dividing the votes of the parties successively by 1, 2, 3, 4, 5, 6, 7, 8, as follows :—

```
Divided by 1............ 8,145    5,680    3,725
   "       2............ 4,027    2,840    1,862
   "       3............ 2,715    1,893    1,862
   "       4............ 2,038
   "       5.. ......... 1,629
```

Ranking now these quotients in the order of their importance—

```
1st .................... 8,145
2nd .................. .          5,680
3rd .................... 4,072
4th ..... . ..........                    3,725
5th ....................          2,848
6th .................... 2,715
7th .................... 2,038
8th ........ ..........           1,893
```

There being seven seats to fill, the number 2,038 is the seventh in the order of importance, and is taken for the common divisor. If there were eight seats the number would be 1,893 and so on for any number of seats.

* The complete statement of M. D'Hondt's plan is found in La Representation Proportionelle. Vol. IV, page 360-374 Brussels, 1885.

The plan of M. D'Hondt is mathematically accurate, and is superior in some respects to the simple rule of three which has been adopted in the Swiss legislation, and is advocated in the foregoing pages of this essay. There are contingencies also where the results would be different from those of the simpler operation, especially that it is more likely to exclude small parties from representation. This is certainly an advantage, in the opinion of the present writer, and one that ought to be incorporated in legislation of this kind. Eventually we may hope that it may be done. But at the present stage of the movement it is above all things necessary to ensure simplicity in any proposed legislation. The Hare system foundered on the rock of complexity, and reformers must take warning from its fate. Absolute equality is impossible, under any system. The simpler rule is only slightly less accurate than the rule of D'Hondt. Both are infinitely better than single membered districts. The present problem is to substitute in the mind of the public the principle of proportional for that of majority representation. When once the principle has been accepted and adopted in legislation, its evident fairness will prevent a return to the old system, but will prepare the way for minor amendments to secure the highest possible accuracy and justice.

EQUALITY.

www.ingramcontent.com/pod-product-compliance
Lightning Source LLC
Chambersburg PA
CBHW030841270326
41928CB00007B/1166